CONSCIOUSNESS
Transformed

1963/1964 Hawaii Hotel Talks

Other Writings of Joel S. Goldsmith

CONSCIOUSNESS
Transformed
1963/1964 Hawaii Hotel Talks

Joel S. Goldsmith

I-Level
Acropolis Books, Publisher

Lakewood, CO   Austell, GA

CONSCIOUSNESS TRANSFORMED
1963/1964 HAWAII HOTEL TALKS
© 1998 Acropolis Books, Inc.

For information contact:
Acropolis Books, Inc.
Lakewood, Colorado

http://www.acropolisbooks.com

LIBRARY OF CONGRESS CATALOGING-IN-PUBLICATION DATA

Goldsmith, Joel S. , 1892–1964.
    Consciousness transformed: 1963/1964 Hawaii hotel talks/ Joel
S. Goldsmith. – 1st Acropolis books ed.
        p.   cm.
    "The inspired lessons in this book were originally called 'Hotel
Talks' " – Foreword.
    Includes bibliographical references.
    ISBN 1-889051-07-1 (hc : alk. paper)
    1. Consciousness--Miscellanea. 2. Metaphysics--Miscellanea.
3. Spiritual life.   I. Title.
BP610.G64155   1998
299'.93--dc21   97–42769
                                                             CIP

THIS BOOK IS PRINTED ON ACID FREE PAPER THAT MEETS
STANDARD Z 39.48 OF THE AMERICAN NATIONAL STANDARDS INSTITUTE

Except the Lord build the house,
they labour in vain that build it.

–Psalm 127

"Illumination dissolves all material ties and binds
men together with the golden chains of spiritual
understanding; it acknowledges only the leadership of the Christ; it has no ritual or rule but the
divine, impersonal universal Love; no other
worship than the inner Flame that is ever lit at the
shrine of Spirit. This union is the free state of
spiritual brotherhood. The only restraint is the
discipline of Soul; therefore, we know liberty
without license; we are a united universe without
physical limits, a divine service to God without
ceremony or creed. The illumined walk without
fear–by Grace."

–The Infinite Way by Joel S. Goldsmith

TABLE OF CONTENTS

TABLE OF CONTENTS

TABLE OF CONTENTS

TABLE OF CONTENTS

FOREWORD

The inspired lessons in this book were originally called "Hotel Talks." Earnest students from around the world joined with others in Honolulu, Hawaii, to listen to Joel Goldsmith speak on mystical living. These talks were then sent to practitioners, teachers and Infinite Way Study Centers to be copied and passed on to the student body. This steady flow of fresh manna fed those who hungered and thirsted for spiritual food and refreshment.

In chapter one of his book, *Realization of Oneness,* Joel writes in the section "Across the Desk":

> This year, 1963, the word came to me to take our students from metaphysics to mysticism. . . . To live in the two worlds has always been difficult for me, but it has been necessary as there must be the metaphysical consciousness on earth before the mystical can be attained.
>
> In 1959, I was instructed to give a full year of classes on the basic principles of The Infinite Way and then begin raising up the Son of God in man. Finally this year the word came to lift our students out of the metaphysical into the mystical, and this mission was immediately undertaken.

Joel wrote to many of us that until we assimilated what was given in the lessons of July 14–September 30, he could not take us further into mystical awareness. The lesson of July 28 reveals two great principles that, if practiced silently and sacredly, will release this world from the domination of superstitions that have acted in human consciousness as law.

It was my privilege to attend many of Joel's classes, some of these talks, and to study privately with him in Hawaii. I can truly say, "I knew a man who had his being in Christ," who brought through the Christ message for the 21st Century, introducing the language of Spirit.

Every hour of the day, somewhere around the world, dedicated students of this message are in silent prayer–the prayer of reconciliation: reconciling man to God, thereby realizing the omnipresence of the Christ activity that sets man free of material sense and reveals God's government of grace and truth.

In gratitude,

Virginia Stephenson

THE INDIVIDUAL UNDER GOD

January 20, 1963
The Halekulani Hotel
Honolulu, Hawaii

LAST WEEK WE SPOKE about the sin of mediocrity. But that can be misconstrued; in fact, the whole subject of individuality can be misconstrued. Everything good has been accomplished through an individual, but so has everything evil been accomplished through an individual. In other words, if we are left to ourselves regardless of talents, they can turn into either good or evil. Even knowledge can be turned into good or bad. In the days of the Black and White Brotherhoods, though their education was the same, the White Brotherhood used knowledge for good, the Black Brotherhood used knowledge for evil. Only when an individual is under God does everything he does serve a purpose of God.

No greater issue is before the world today than the individual—*the individual under God. Not* under God, you have destruction. The cliché that in union there is strength is a fallacy. There was no greater union than England and its empire. Certainly, there was no stronger union than Holland and its colonies. But not being under God, it has been broken. In Russia today the people have as much respect for the individual as we have. Individuals, not the masses, create nuclear power: astronauts, scientists, executives—but individuals not

1

under God. For us there must be a definite knowledge that nothing exists greater than individual capacity and individual integrity, but the individual under God. Only then do we have a government under God and a government working for the common good. An individual can only develop spiritually when he comes to know God aright.

When we see a statement like, "I depend not on God nor devil but on my own power," unless it strikes up against a consciousness of truth, that statement can go out and control the world because the world has not understood the non-power of temporal power. Truth always destroys temporal power, but it is the knowing of the truth. Always remember that evil can operate in the universe until it strikes up against a realized consciousness of truth. Nothing in the orthodox mind can stop evil; the power of evil can only be met by an individual under God.

Successful practitioners are the practitioners who have discerned the nature of temporal power as non-power, and the further they go in that realization, the greater is their individual capacity. Just the vision of Jesus, Mrs. Eddy, and the Fillmores changed the course of the world—the realization of an individual of the non-power of temporal power.

There is no such thing as good or bad power—it is only as the individuals use it. There is no danger in any time or space out there, but in the individual. There is neither good nor evil in missiles, but in the individual use of them. And so we must come back again to the individual, but the individual under God.

Each of us has consciousness and each of us has God, but God-power is manifested only in one way—by our realization of non-power. Error could hit up against the consciousness of a Jesus and it would dissolve. The heights to which we rise is dependent upon our realization of the non-power of temporal power.

There are no dangerous intersections on the highways; there is no power out there. See how harmless they are until a careless driver comes along. All danger is in proportion to our acceptance of two powers, so someone must step forth with the realization, "Thou couldest have no power over me unless it came from God."[1] This determines how big or how small we are or how much we can contribute to the world—but only under God.

Every one of us has Christhood in our consciousness and the ability to overcome the world, but it is all a matter of individual unfoldment. Spiritual power lies in the realization of the non-power of temporal power. God is not in the whirlwind, God is not in warfare, fire, or dictators; God is in the still small voice and all who attune themselves to the still small voice attune themselves to spiritual power. There is no evil that can last when it hits up against a consciousness that can look right at evil and know the non-power of the carnal mind. One person imbued with it would break it down over a period of a hundred years. Withdraw from power and let the still small voice come through—that's the trick. In proportion as we can be still and let it come through, are we showing forth individual harmony and being an influence throughout the world. So it is there is only one source and we are all drawing on it.

No, the power isn't external. We must listen for the still small voice—that alone is spiritual power. The still small voice doesn't do anything to evil, it just reveals the non-power of all evil.

You can't be still if you think you are going to generate a God-power. You can only generate God-power by saying "I can of my own self do nothing,"[2] by being still, by waiting. Until that still small voice comes through, the treatment or prayer will not be effective. There is a transcendental presence within me, but if I am expecting it to do something to evil, it will not come through.

Just let me become acquainted with the still small voice, for "where the spirit of the Lord is, there is liberty,"[3] not in order to do anything to anything, but just to know thee aright. It does its own work—we just release it. "I must know thee aright; I am listening for thy voice. Speak Lord, thy servant heareth."[4] That's the attitude. Whatever power is flowing from the still small voice is under God.

There is only one way to know if you are meditating aright. When you look to God for something for yourself or for someone else, the moment you want to personalize it to help me or you, it is no longer effective. Your spiritual light thinks only in terms of God-realization.

PURE CONSCIOUSNESS

January 27, 1963
The Halekulani Hotel
Honolulu, Hawaii

LET US TALK A LITTLE BIT TODAY about *consciousness*. Consciousness is the most important word in the entire Infinite Way vocabulary. Nothing you can think of can ever take the place of the word consciousness. In our human existence we are states and stages of consciousness or degrees of consciousness. In its pure state consciousness is God, and in its pure state it constitutes our being. The moment we are conceived humanly, the consciousness we are begins to receive conditioning. The worst thing happens from the moment we are born, for we are then conditioned by all that parents think. What fears parents entertain and what hopes they entertain are transferred to the child. Then the child gets into school and is conditioned by school teachers, schoolmates, parents of schoolmates—picking up more conditioning. By the time the child gets out into the world it is convinced of ninety percent of things that are untrue. Then, out in the world, it adds to its own conditioning.

From the moment we touch a metaphysical teaching, we begin to condition ourselves along other lines. Suppose it registered in our consciousness when we read, "Call no man your father on the earth: for there is but one, the Father in heaven."[1] If you pondered it and the principle ever registered, you would look around you and say, "Oh, then there is only one Creator and we are all children of that One. Then we are all equal in the sight of God." That alone would wipe out of an individual his prejudices and early conditioning. On this point you have a new consciousness. You have died to the state of consciousness which had biases and prejudices and have become one with your fellow man universally. On this one point you have become a new man.

Eventually you would come to another extension of that same idea and could say, "If this is true, we derive our qualities, our inheritances, from that One." Let me give you a quotation from Emerson: "There is but one universal Mind and all men are inlets to and outlets from that One." If that One is God or Consciousness, then we are inlets to and outlets for its qualities. Once we begin to perceive that we are inlets to and outlets from the Father, we perceive that we are inlets to a divine intelligence and not limited as we thought. Now we are not dependent on what our human parents were, but we are dependent on our source. No longer are we limited once we acknowledge, "There is one Father, there is one mind and we are an inlet and an outlet for it." It might take months of pondering, but eventually it would sink in and we could then say, "Whereas I was blind, now I see."[2] You begin to draw on this infinity just by this one truth. You are in a new consciousness in which two things have happened; you have lost your bias and your bigotry and you have thrown off some of the handicaps and limitations of your ancestors. It is no longer true that "the sins of the fathers shall be visited on the children unto the third and fourth generation."[3] Once you have taken that one principle and worked with it you are a freer state of consciousness; you have thrown off the dependency on anyone and have learned to go within to the source. In the moment of realization of this one truth, you are not the same person—and that is with just one spiritual truth.

Every one of us from childhood has been told to fear the external, whether in the form of germs, infection, contagion, weather. We have been taught to fear external powers. Now supposing you were to catch a glimpse of the metaphysical principle contained in "Pilate, you could have no power over me.[4] I and my Father are one."[5] God gave me dominion. Since God has given me dominion there can be no power in the external world. The acceptance of this principle sets us free from seventy to eighty percent of the world's fears. We are no longer fearing the power of anything external to ourselves, and again on this one point we are a different state of consciousness. We have died to our fears.

We haven't died to our main fear: our fear of death. It is this fear that makes our illnesses appear so fearful. If there is such a thing as becoming immune to the fear of death, then we would have demonstrated living eternally—not, however, staying on earth forever. We would still have to make a transition. When we have served our purpose on earth, it is a nice time for the transition and while we look forward to the transition, we no longer have to look forward to death. The act of losing the fear of death sets us free from most of the diseases of this world. When there is even a partial movement into that state, you are not the same person you were before. No longer are you fearing outer conditions and circumstances. You have moved into still another degree of consciousness.

By this time in our spiritual life we are an entirely different state of consciousness than we were the day we found ourselves on the spiritual path. We are no longer giving power to the external, we have fewer superstitious beliefs, we have lost some of our ignorances. The progress we have made up to this moment is only as we take one principle after another until they ring a bell and register within. Consciousness is what we are in our pure state–God-given life and immortality. As consciousness is purified, as we get rid of conditioning, more and more are we approaching the pure consciousness. "Father, give me the pure consciousness I had with thee before the world began."

The principle that is magnified so much in The Infinite Way is the principle that there is neither good nor evil but thinking makes it so. A realization of this gives you the purest consciousness you can hope to attain. There is neither good nor evil. We look neither to the external good nor fear the external evil. There just *is*. The grass *is*, the weather *is*, the water *is*. The only power there *is*, is Being. The closer you can live to the consciousness that all this is Being–God-created–God-endowed–the more you would find yourself attuned to the love of God and grace of God.

Just realize that nothing has been empowered with evil. God has given us his own spirit, his own consciousness. The degree of our failure is the degree to which we have picked up man's consciousness. Each one of us has within us our own degree of realization of that mind which was also in Christ Jesus. When you consciously know the truth that we are attaining that mind in proportion as you are giving no power to the external, you will understand that eventually the lamb will lie down with the lion. You will find that, as you adopt this principle in your life, you are affected less and less by the external. The closer you come to the principle, the closer you come to a consciousness of good. This becomes more and more true as your consciousness can accept the revelation that there is neither good nor evil—only the universal sense makes it so.

Then this changes my consciousness, doesn't it? Yes, a life free of some of the old fears is a whole new consciousness; and as through our meditations we receive inner impartations, in that degree are we freed from the early outside conditioning. Every time we receive an inner impartation, it knocks out some external fear. If you look back ten years and try to identify yourself you would say, "Why, I am not that person."

The reason consciousness becomes our most important word is this: we know the goal of our work is changing our consciousness. In accomplishing this we have to leave the world alone—the change has to come within our own consciousness. What is our reaction to persons, weather patterns, theories? What is our reaction to death? We ourselves do not know what particular conditioning, in mind, is our particular barrier, and it is because we do not know what is limiting us that we need these meditations. Eventually we come into an awareness that our consciousness determines the nature of our life. It is only as we accept a change of consciousness that the change comes. No teacher or practitioner makes a change in a student; they were only the instrument through which the student made the change. Whatever degree of changed consciousness comes to us depends upon our devotion to that end. The teacher or practitioner is only the means to the end. They have the power to bring out what is in you and no more—and then only in proportion to your humility and willingness to pitch in.

There is something inside of us that is pushing us toward attaining a pure consciousness. Somewhere along the line in your past incarnation or the present one, something happened to spark your spiritual center. You get closer to the pure state of consciousness as each one of these specific principles becomes illumined in you. As we make each of the principles our own, we have one step less of human bondage—we are tied to one less of human limitations.

When we come to the place where we realize there is neither good nor evil, we come to the top. In proportion to our ability to grasp that, we become more and more pure consciousness. Pure consciousness is that of which we are composed, and the states of consciousness are superimposed by the beliefs of the world. It is a process of dying daily. Every time you drop a theory, every time you drop an anxiety or a superstition, you have died to this world to that extent. When the Master said he had overcome the world, he had overcome these temptations. When he had overcome death, he had really overcome the world. Personally I don't think he overcame the world until he was in the Garden of Gethsemane. There he faced death—he left his human sense of life there. No one fully dies until he faces death—then he is in the fourth dimension, and alive not in the human sense but in the spiritual sense.

As Ye Sow

February 3, 1963
The Halekulani Hotel
Honolulu, Hawaii

A QUESTION COMES TO MY MIND this week which is, "How many of our students are reading or studying the writings objectively?" How many still read them with a measure of emotion or sentiment? A letter came to me this week from one of our students. It describes a nice and respectable family that engages in orthodox religious worship, but very good. A terrible tragedy has struck that family and the question is asked, "How can such a thing happen to such a nice family?"

Is there any one of our students who does not know what the answer is? If you are in any doubt as to the answer to that question then you are not studying objectively because there isn't a book or a tape or a *Letter* that does not have the answer to it. If there is anything we know and know that we know, it is the reason for error. That we know. If we don't know anything else, we do know that—and if there are any in doubt on that subject, they are not seriously studying the message. They are reading it but not reading it objectively.

Even the most casual reading reveals the "natural" man is not under the law of God and indeed cannot be. As long as he remains the creature—the natural man—he is neither under the law of God nor protected by God

11

nor maintained or sustained by God. This really is the entire history of the human race and accounts for some becoming dictators while others become the lambs led to the slaughter. As you read in history of the rise to power of Mussolini or Hitler, you will soon see there was no God on earth to protect the people on earth—no God to intercede for them. In the same way, if you read the earlier history of the United States and the coming to power of some of our so-called big corporations, robbing, cheating, defrauding, you would soon ask, "Where was God in all this?"

So if we have given you nothing else, we have certainly given you the reason why iniquities and injustices exist on earth. We have also provided a way for the overcoming of these, but at this particular time it remains with the individual. An individual can free himself of all these powers and influences by a clear-cut understanding and application of the principles of The Infinite Way. With enough understanding, that individual can even help to free others; but it is only when this practice is far more widespread than it is now that this consciousness can change the world. At the present time we are operating on the level of individual consciousness, but we cannot enter the consciousness of this world and force people to be free—they must first be open to it. Those who are not open to spiritual help do not often receive it; some do because inwardly they are crying out even when outwardly they are resisting and fighting.

Every problem that comes to you or me represents some degree of our inability to be children of God, to be under the law of God. This is not said nor is it meant to be taken as criticism, judgement, or condemnation, because whatever degree of humanness is still in us is not because of our wish but because of our inability. On the other hand, we ourselves must recognize this truth, that every problem is an opportunity. What would be the use of getting rid of a disease, what would be the use of getting rid of lack or limitation without an understanding of the principle involved? Sooner or later everything of a physical or material, human nature which we are expressing we must lose. If we continue on with material abundance alone, or health alone, some day it will be stripped from us. We must be reborn into spiritual awareness.

Now let us understand that every problem facing us can be solved, but it is up to us. Even if we ask a practitioner for help, it does not relieve us of the necessity of coming to an understanding of the truth. Unless there is a change of consciousness, there will be a reoccurrence of discord. No, we ourselves must attain the consciousness of truth.

Let us see this. It has to do first of all with two points, and we call the first of these two points knowing the nature of God. This really means knowing that regardless of what your concept of God has been or even perhaps still is, it is wrong. This is a faith in an unknown god whom you ignorantly worship. No matter how high the concept, it is still a concept. Eventually you have to reach the consciousness that *God is*, and then leave that subject alone. With your mind you are never going to know what God is.

Now let me briefly tell you about the problems we meet in our experience. They are all based on a law of cause and effect. Every problem is based on a law of cause and effect. "As ye sow, so shall ye reap."[1] If you accept the world's belief that there is power in person, place, or thing, you are sowing to corruption. As long as you are giving power to form, you are sowing to the flesh. Anything in the outer picture on which you place your reliance is sowing to the flesh, and anything you can be made to fear is sowing to the flesh, because anything in the external world of form, whether thought or thing, is not God. We overcome the law of cause and effect in proportion to our realization of this point. Can you not see that this is leading us back to the point that the kingdom of God, the kingdom of power, is "within me."[2] If it is within me I need have no fear of anything or anyone.

Now just think of the mistake you make if any form of orthodoxy clings to you, because every orthodox church in the world clings to cause and effect. They pray that the law of cause and effect be set aside and it can't be. There is no God that can change the law of cause and effect. There is no God who can set aside the law of stupidity. The issue is within ourselves. The Master put it right in our laps: "Ye shall know the truth and the truth shall make you free."[3] Now the truth is that "God is in his heaven and all is well." In order to experience harmony we must enter that kingdom. We don't change the law—we change ourselves. That is why the lamb will even lie down with the lion.

There are many old sayings to the effect that when you stop chasing something it will come to you. They are based on an absolute truth. People chasing money never have an abundance. This is a law, a law of cause and effect, and the moment you can leave off chasing money it has a way of chasing you. Also, the very thing we fear and are trying to get away from, finds us. This is all based on cause and effect. If you do not put love, hate, or fear into a thing, you are free of it.

All former concepts of God sent us to God for something and that is the barrier to our getting it. Some of our tapes are based on the principle of realizing God. Let God go. All you will do is set up a barrier. God is running this universe, but not by our influencing God to come to us or to go to our neighbor. We can influence ourselves or our neighbor to go to God. We are the only ones who can break the law of cause and effect, and we begin to do it the moment we recognize that God has nothing to do with our good or our evil, when we release God and realize that the overcoming of our problems is the overcoming of the law of cause and effect. The responsibility is squarely on our shoulders, then the problem is an opportunity. We might as well face the problem or it will continue. The reason the law of cause and effect continues to operate in our consciousness is because we give power to this law. Eventually we must come back to "No, God has given me dominion and there is no power outside of me." This breaks the law of cause and effect. This has to be the basis of our work. "Ye shall know the truth and the truth shall make you free."

We want to stay as we are and yet have the law of God do something for us—but the only way we benefit by the law of God is by changing our nature. Are we loving or hating or fearing something in the external? Nothing that I am saying must interfere with the love we feel towards each other, or even the love we feel toward our enemy. The love I'm talking about is the love that places our dependency or hope on someone. In other words, we must get back within ourselves. "God gave me dominion. I and my Father are one." I have only to recognize its presence and it goes to work. We recognize spiritual power and let it function. We don't use the power of the sun—we just let it shine. We don't search around for ways to use spiritual power—we let it use us. *Let it.* "The kingdom of God is within me." Rest in that word. Then it performs its function.

If our students understood *The Thunder of Silence* there wouldn't be a need for a class. My hope for you is that you reach a point where you have nothing to stand on but nothingness: not a thing, not a thought. *God is;* God is functioning, and whatever of God is not in manifestation is our fault. We have not sufficiently cleared ourselves of a dependency and we have not seen that the law of cause and effect will continue to operate because we have not realized its non-power. Nothing is power, but thinking makes it so. The moment we realize our God-given heritage of dominion, the moment we let it, in that degree do we become free of the law of cause and effect.

Of course the greatest sin that was ever perpetuated on earth is the sin of praying to God. It had its origin in paganism when the peoples of the world looked around for a supernatural power. That has been perpetuated in the forms of prayer. Now the great truth is that we don't need what we seem to need. We need the realization of God and that is all we need. In attaining the presence of God, the sin, the lack, the disease is revealed as non-presence. "Where the spirit of the Lord is, there is freedom."[4] Where God is, there is already liberty. God realized is the attainment of the light in the presence of which there is no darkness, in the presence of which there is liberty, abundance, fulfillment. "Thy grace is my sufficiency in all things."[5] Not money or investments or health, just thy grace.

So orthodox religion continues its belief in a God to whom to pray for things, and this externalizes in lack. No, our prayer must be for the realization of a presence already within us. "I and my Father are one."[6] We are already one. Now, for a realization of this oneness.

I hope you will all take up *The Thunder of Silence* again and see what is hidden in those pages. It is a radical book. It will blow sky-high our concepts of God built up over the centuries.

Then it must be clear to us that our problems are in proportion to our inability to come to a realization of these things. We may know them, but not clearly. So let us begin to face our problems without a desire to get rid of them, without a fear of them. I'm going to acknowledge there is an error and I'm looking at it, but there is a solution. With some realization of truth, we are finding error doesn't exist. See the problems as an opportunity. The problem must be licked through understanding. "Don't let these problems go until I have the truth behind them."

Everybody deserves everything that comes to them, not because of bad behavior, but because of ignorance. No, we get through our problems through understanding. *God is.* So let God run his universe and let us turn our attention back to ourselves. Let us realize that our problems are brought about by a law of cause and effect, "As ye sow, so shall ye reap," then realize the non-power of karmic law. It is the universal belief in two powers. There is only one power and that power is incorporated in my consciousness, so I can go to sleep and wake up well. Consciousness never sleeps, so we can sleep in the realization that consciousness is the only power and nothing operating outside of consciousness can affect us.

The belief in two powers is the universal one. The overcoming of that belief is an individual one, an individual experience. No one can do it for us.

Someone wrote me this week that I should give him a word of encouragement to keep him on the path. No, unless something pushes you, don't stay on the path, for it is straight and narrow. Only then can we stand fast when the temptations come. The further we go on this path the more temptations we meet tomorrow. No one avoids them. It is for that reason that the drive within us must be greater than the human inertia. A problem isn't as deep as it seems because a problem in and of itself has no power. The only power is the universal belief. So every problem we meet through understanding makes each successive one a lesser one. The more problems we meet the less power each succeeding problem has until eventually we must come to that place where a problem is only an appearance and doesn't get a rise out of us.

Now you know why there are problems: because of our ignorance of truth. Everyone who is looking to God is perpetuating the problem because God is not a power we use. The power is our realization of the powerlessness of the appearance.

BESIDE GOD THERE IS NO OTHER

February 10, 1963
The Halekulani Hotel
Honolulu, Hawaii

ARE THERE ANY QUESTIONS from the tape that you heard this morning? Are there any points that need clarifying? I know it was a very important tape. (1960 Denver Closed Class: Advanced Spiritual Healing Class: *Protective Work.*)

Question: *I am interested in what you said about the Christian attitude towards business. You said that John Wanamaker of Philadelphia started pricing at a set price and that this was a Christian way of doing business. Can you explain?*

Answer: There isn't anyone in the world who is not affected by business. When we speak of the right way of doing business, we speak of business on the basis of the Golden Rule, on the Christian–conducted basis.

Before Wanamaker, no store ever had a set price. Everything was bargaining ability, so at first he nearly went bankrupt. People saw the price tags and then started to bargain. At first, when they were told there was to be no bargaining, they walked out.

The closer you get to a spiritual way of conducting business, the more just and equitable a type of business

19

would be conducted. In this present era, business is about as un–Christian as it could be; we have reverted to cutthroat business. Once you start humanly manipulating prices, you will find a hundred ways of manipulating them. Very few people are paying a fair price for the merchandise they buy; they are either paying too much or too little. The same thing is true in the stock market where some stocks are too high or too low.

It all comes to this: that individually we may attempt to live our lives in accord with a principle but not be permitted to while we are in an era like this where prices are determined by outside factors. If it is the law, then we have to conform to it. That is unfortunate for those who would like to live by principles. However, it would not prevent an individual's spiritual development. Everything takes place in consciousness, not what you do externally.

A person on the spiritual path has no right to be in military service. But if he refuses he commits a worse crime, for in so doing he is asking someone else to do it for him. That is the point that is overlooked. A conscientious objector, by his very attitude, is harming two people—himself and the person who has to replace him. *The Bhagavad Gita* has a good passage on that: "He who shall say, 'Lo! I have slain a man!' He who shall think, 'Lo, I am slain,' those both know nought. Life cannot slay. Life is not slain."

So it is that in our business lives very often we have to do things outwardly which are the custom, things which in our inner hearts we do not agree to. We are judged not by what we may have to do outwardly, but what we feel in our hearts. In our business life just as in our home life, we are always facing the situation of doing that which comes nearest right, and that would certainly not include shifting the burdens to the shoulders of others. We are having the same situation in international relationships. A certain attitude would be the Christian one, but we cannot take that course. However, anything done externally is the "suffer it to be so now." In fact, most of our home conduct is on the basis of "suffer it to be so now."[1] But the important question is, how do we take it inwardly? We cannot judge by what is right or wrong, but by our attitude.

If you heard this morning's tape aright, it must have been indelibly impressing itself upon you that whatever value there is in the message of The Infinite Way, whatever power is in it, is in this point: that there is only One—that you are never using one power over another, nor are you protecting yourself from a power. Your protection is the realization of your Self as the only power. However, there are points in that that could fool the select. We make the statement that God is the only power, and that could fool us unless we realize that the God we are talking about is the *I* of our own being. There is no such thing as a God protecting us. The *I* of us is the power and there is nothing to be protected from. That is why I go back so often to the *1955 Letters*, Chapter 3. It is very important.

There is no God protecting us because there is nothing to be protected from. If you want to be free, you have to leave this world and get into God's kingdom. Only in proportion as you can recognize the impersonal, universal nature of error and then realize it as a non-power, only then are you protected and only then actually can you do healing work. There is no God and a disease. There is only God, and everything that happens to us as sin, disease, lack, or limitation represents an appearance, and the recognition destroys the appearance. "Ye shall know the truth and the truth shall make you free." In the presence of God there is liberty. In the presence of light there is no darkness. Darkness is merely the absence of light. There is no entity called darkness. In the same way there is no entity called disease or sin. So it is you don't heal sin or disease or false appetite–they are illusory concepts. The illusory concept is always in mind; there is no such thing as an externalized illusion. When you know the truth, the illusory concept is gone, but nothing is really gone with it. Sin or lack don't go anywhere, you have merely proven they were not there.

It is on this point that many metaphysicians go off the beam, that God is a power they are going to use over error. God-power in an individual is in direct proportion to the individual's realization that God constitutes individual being and that it is always functioning and never has to be used, never has to be sent to Mrs. Brown or Mrs. Smith. The truth always has to be *is*-ness, *I*-ness, divine being as individual being, and all else is an illusion of sense. The moment we start to do battle with it we lose the case. "Not by might nor by power but by the truth.[2] Resist not evil."[3] This statement alone would be enough to transform your life.

The Master must have discerned that evil had no power, that nothing is good or bad but thinking makes it so. It is not your thinking, however. The wrong thinking is the universal belief, but you have the power individually to correct it. It is individually met. The moment you accuse your patient of wrong thinking, you are a malpractitioner. In spite of appearances, the individual is constituted of God and whatever inharmony is evident is due to the belief in two powers. This is the "knowing of the truth." It is necessary to realize, "The place whereon I stand is holy ground,"[4] and this is in spite of appearances, because God constitutes my being. This is the truth that constitutes the light, and in the light there is no darkness.

When facing each new day we should realize that we are facing the universal beliefs of the world and nullify them in the realization that "God constitutes individual being. Beside God there is no other, and any belief in a power apart from God is a mental illusion. The place whereon I stand is holy ground."

In ancient days humanity had God and devil, and as you know, that never saved anybody. Then the philosophers, refusing to accept God and devil, impersonalized it and then the people had good and evil. Even when the metaphysicians came up with mortal and immortal, they still had God and devil, just substituting names. There is only God, and what appears as satan or devil is the illusory sense. When you know this, you are grounded on a rock. See devil or evil or mortal as terms denoting nothingness, as Mrs. Eddy called them, then drop it. If you keep on arguing with the appearance, you are involved in it.

Not only is one power of major importance, but that power must not be something external to you. That power must be the Self of you, the identity of you. Otherwise you again have duality: God and you. No, we have God appearing as you, God manifesting himself as you, God expressing himself as you, not you expressing yourself as God. This is always universal in spite of any appearances to the contrary.

The same thing is true if you have a duality based on spirit and matter. When you see that spirit is the substance of all being, then you do not have one power acting on another, you have spirit appearing as what the world calls matter. Matter is indestructible; even if you burn it up you have the same amount of matter as you had before. Nothing is indestructible but God. Therefore, all that constitutes matter is indestructible and indivisible.

If you catch this point, you will realize why health is not in the body or of the body. Health is in spirit manifested as body. The body is a form and there is no health in it. The health of the body is the health of spirit. So until we look to spirit for health, harmony, intelligence, we are looking amiss. Intelligence is omnipresence, so is health omnipresence because intelligence and health are qualities or activities of spirit. The spirit is the creative principle of man and his body.

Many of the Eastern teachings miss the mark because they all look on the body as matter and themselves as spirit. Once you separate spirit from body in your mind, it is like separating yourself from God. God must function in every avenue of life. "Acknowledge him in all thy ways."[5] If we leave God out of any one of our ways, we separate ourselves in belief from God and then this belief governs us. The body may be matter as a name, but body is not worthless because it had its origin in God. The body is not an illusion; the mortal concept of body is the illusion. The body itself is "the temple of the living God."

You see how it is that the word *consciousness* sums up everything in our work. It is what you are conscious of that operates in your experience as a law. "Ye shall know the truth," and then the truth functions as a law. Come out and be separate—give up ignorance and superstitions. "I and my Father are one," but I am taking my body right along with me. Whatever my body is, and remember I cannot see my body, I want to take it with me wherever I go. Never permit yourself to become separated from God in any way. Have God as omnipresence. Realize, "God constitutes my being and my body. God constitutes my business for I and my Father are one. The body of God is the body of me, for there is but one body."

The law of God that governs the universe must govern our business and our bodies, or there would be something outside the jurisdiction of God's law. As long as we hold to the consciousness that the law of God is the law of my business, whatever is erroneous will be corrected. This same principle applies to the body and health, but if we do not consciously bring the body and business under the law of God, so it will be unto us. Everything must be consciously realized. You must consciously know that the law of God is the law of your business, intelligence, health, and household. What you take into your consciousness becomes the law unto your experience. Salvation is individual. To get free of universal law you must embrace truth and this means dying daily. Every day we have to make truth a part of our consciousness.

This path is not a lazy man's work because we are continually faced with the appearances of universal belief, and every day we are called upon to reject them as illusion and replace them with: "Spirit is the law unto me and in spirit I find completeness. I find my wholeness in spirit and the wholeness of spirit constitutes the wholeness of my body and business."

Humanly we are the man of earth, made up of all the universal beliefs; but from the moment of our first metaphysical experience, we are making a transition from the man of earth to being "that man who has his being in Christ." In my Sonship I find my abundance. In my Sonship I am heir of God. But the transition has to be a conscious experience. "Consciously I know that I and my Father are one, that the quantities and qualities of God constitute my individual being. Consciously I know that I have my good in Christ."

You see, there are these major points in The Infinite Way and their importance is not in the fact that they are in a book, but that they may become active and alive in you. The degree to which you embody these truths in your consciousness makes you free. "Ye shall know the truth," and the truth you do not know is not going to make you free.

God Constitutes My Consciousness

February 17, 1963
The Halekulani Hotel
Honolulu, Hawaii

LET US MAKE A MOVE that separates us from most of the metaphysical world. As humans we have our supply in money, or the representation of money, and we find health in the body. If the heart beats so many times, if the assimilation acts according to this rule, if the elimination acts according to that rule, then we have health. We associate intelligence with the brain and we find our life in breathing. Take away our breathing and we have no life, or we find our life in the functioning of the heart.

When you come to our work, what you are really doing is making a transition, so that your healing work is never in correcting what is wrong in the body or the mind or the pocketbook. I think it is in *The Infinite Way* that you will find, "You cannot meet a problem on the level of the problem." So, if you are faced with a problem, if you try to do something to that problem, you would not succeed. You first have to move outside the realm of the problem in order to find harmony.

We find our harmony in spirit, and you might call this the point of demarcation or separation. We find our harmony in spirit, in consciousness. Since God is consciousness, and since God is supply, we find our supply in God or in consciousness. In the same way, since God is health, we find our health in God or in consciousness. Even the Bible knew this, that "God is the health of your countenance."[1] Yes, health must be found not in the body but in consciousness–then the body expresses health. Likewise with supply.

You must leave the realm of the mental and material and find yourself elevated to consciousness. We have to find our health, we have to find our supply, we have to find our intelligence in consciousness; even our longevity we must find in consciousness. If we try to perpetuate ourselves by patching up the body, the results would be temporary. Medically it is possible to change sickness to health and, if that is all the person is seeking, he can find it there. There are not many incurable diseases in materia medica. If we are seeking a principle of life whereby we wish to find our immortality in the fullness of our being, then we have to leave the realm of mind and body and find our good in consciousness. Since the realm of consciousness is invisible, you can be given no proof in advance that this is true. No signs shall be given in advance.

So, we start at some particular time in our spiritual journey; it could be today for some, next year for others. One day we have to make a transition from looking for our supply in our bank accounts, looking to our body for our health or to human beings for our happiness, and realize that wholeness and completeness in every department of our lives is embodied in the God-consciousness which is our individual consciousness.

For awhile this leaves you hanging nowhere; you are in space, as it were. Scripture says, "He hangeth the world upon nothing,"[2] so in this particular transition we have nothing to cling to because we are no longer looking to the body or the pocketbook or the brain, and we cannot see, hear, taste, touch, or smell consciousness. We do not even know what consciousness is, yet we are putting our complete reliance, our complete dependency on it.

God constitutes my individual consciousness, therefore my consciousness embodies the fullness of the Godhead. Therefore, my consciousness is the law unto my health and my supply. My consciousness embodies every activity of intelligence, guidance, and direction.

At this point you can know the truth but still find yourself hanging in space, because you do not know what is to come next. All right, I am transferring my faith to consciousness, but I have no way of knowing what consciousness is. All I can do is continue to hang in space until consciousness comes through with a demonstration which convinces me beyond all doubt that "I am on holy ground." Remember:

God constitutes my consciousness and in the beginning God gave me dominion—all of the supply necessary, all of the health necessary—and God planted it in my consciousness. Therefore, all that the Father has is mine because God constitutes my consciousness. My consciousness embodies the infinity of being.

There are *no* limitations. You see, we limit ourselves. There is no real limitation anywhere in the world except the limitation we place on ourselves. Everyone on the face of the globe could have the allness of God, because we are talking about indivisible consciousness. So it is that any individual can have an infinity of supply and yet have enough left over so everyone else can have an infinity of supply. God constitutes our consciousness and God is infinite being.

When you make this transition, your whole state of consciousness undergoes a change because now, instead of looking to the body for health, your vision is up in consciousness. "Know the truth, and it will make you free," and the truth is, "My life is not in man or in matter, but in God. God constitutes my life. Therefore, my life is eternal." The more you live with that, the less you look to the body and the less fears you have of those aches. "God is the health of my countenance," and remember, God is omnipresence. So you are really never separated from your health or your supply, or your happiness, completeness, and perfection.

Enjoy human relationships, certainly, but do not be so dependent on them that their absence breaks your heart. Once individuals make this transition, even in a small measure to where they say, "Yes, I find my completeness in my consciousness," the whole nature of life changes. There are no vacancies or losses in consciousness—there is only the going and coming of the human scene as the fulfillment of the activity of our consciousness. When your whole experience is the activity of consciousness unfolding, you will find a complete continuity of harmony.

Until you are ready for it, this is a difficult thing, this matter of transition, where you find your allness in consciousness rather than in man or body or purse. To some it must be a matter of daily and hourly practice to remember continuously: "I have my good in my conscious- ness. I find the harmony of being in my consciousness, and it is the harmony of my body and my human relationships. My supply is God, or consciousness. God constitutes my consciousness, and all that the Father has is mine." This must be a matter of hourly practice until that moment of transition when you can say, "Whereas I was blind, now I see."[3]

The reason that you cannot get more specific than this, is that consciousness is not embodied in your body, because your consciousness is actually omnipresence. Your consciousness is not confined to time or space (and always remember why), because "I and the Father are one, not two, and all that is true of the Father is true of me. God is the Selfhood of my being, but this is universally true." Therefore, the moment you are called upon for help in any part of the world and you close your eyes to realize omnipresence, you can be certain that your patient anywhere in the world will receive your treatment. There is but one being, and God is that being. To be able to close the eyes and shut out all persons and to say that, "In consciousness is my good, my companionship, my experiences of life," would mean that, on opening the eyes, you would find yourself in the presence of those necessary to your experience—but first the human experience must be blotted out. "You cannot meet the problem on the level of the problem."

To find our good in the consciousness which I am, is to bring such a change in consciousness that, bit by bit over a period of time, you would see your whole life transformed and on higher ground. You find yourself in a whole new consciousness. "I am an individual, one with God. All that God is, I am. All that God has is mine, for I and the Father are one." That realization of oneness is your assurance of completeness and perfection.

All of this universe is embodied in my consciousness, the skies above, the earth beneath, the waters and all that is in them is embodied in my consciousness, because God constitutes my consciousness.

This brings to you the statement of the Master, "I am in the Father and the Father is in me."[4] This is oneness. "This universe is embodied in my consciousness. Because God constitutes my consciousness, I have infinity. The infinite allness of God is mine." This acts to break the human ties of dependency on person, place, or thing. "God constitutes my consciousness. Therefore, all that the Father has is mine because of oneness. In my oneness with God, I am all."

In one experience after another you will transfer your allegiance or faith from effect back to cause. You will break your dependency on "man whose breath is in his nostrils,"[5] in the realization of your self. "I and my Father are one and that oneness constitutes my infinite allness. I am hid with consciousness in God. I live and move and have my being in and of God." This shuts out "man whose breath is in his nostrils" and the things of this world.

Since God constitutes my consciousness, and God constitutes your consciousness and the consciousness of every individual on the face of the earth, I am one with everybody.

With every appearance of discord, lift your thoughts immediately: "I find my oneness in consciousness which is cause, not in matter or effect. I look to cause for my peace, my wholeness, my satisfaction, my joy," and all of it becomes manifest in what we call tangible form.

Remember that this is an activity of transition which must happen at a specific moment of your life. At some moment you must say, "I shall live in consciousness. I shall find my health and my supply in consciousness." Then drop it, and let it rest. Sometime later in the day you will again remember, "I am seeking my good in consciousness, omnipresent." As you persist in that, you bring the day closer when the transition does take place. Then there are no more statements or declarations— there is just the living of it.

You understand, of course, that you cannot explain this to anyone, and you have no right to. This is an experience to be lived but never talked about. The human mind could never understand what you meant by *transition* or *consciousness*.

Self-surrender

February 24, 1963
Halekulani Hotel

SOMETIMES WE WONDER how it is that the message of the Master was lost. When we stop to think of the fact that he spoke to people who could not read or write for the most part, then we do not wonder any more. The miracle is that anyone remembered what is in the four Gospels, because they were written thirty years after the crucifixion. In other words, someone had to remember for thirty years in order to give us even the little that we have. I believe this is the reason we have so little of the Master's teachings. We today are in a different position. When anyone speaks today, their words can be preserved in writing, in recordings, and in so many different forms, that a message that proves good today should never become lost.

For the past two weeks we have been on a subject, a principle of life really, that should change the nature of our lives—not because we have heard the message but because, in addition to hearing it, we have it on paper and this paper will serve as a reminder.

The principle with which we were concerned last week is probably the most important principle in all mystical literature on mystical living. To hear it once is good but, unless it actually registers within us, it does not do too much for us. Therefore, the responsibility rests upon us to practice it, to work with it, and to meditate upon the principle until we are able to demonstrate it. Now let us go back to last week for just a moment. Remember that the principle revealed was the fact that spiritually we live in God, we are supported by God, we are sustained by God. I have an illustration. Some of you remember the hymn, "When All Material Streams Are Dry, Thy Fullness Is the Same." Many of us have experienced this. Through a deadly disease, or a period of lack or some circumstance of human relationships, we come to a place in our lives where there is no material help. Our back is against the wall. There is no human means of help available, there are no human resources to draw upon, there is no human way out of our dilemma and we rest back and say, "God, you will have to take over."

Just think what you are doing when, just in blind faith, you say, "God if you do not rescue me, I am lost." Actually, with this there is a sense of surrender, a complete realization that "I of my own self can do nothing." There is nobody else to turn to in the particular situation, and you give up. It has often been discovered that, when this happens, something or someone takes over. Sometimes a spiritual healing takes place, and in this way we have discovered that God really is available. Self-surrender is when we give up in order that God may take over. There is really no need for us to come to a desperate situation for God to take over, but the conditions are the same—self-surrender. There has to be a particular moment when we consciously agree that humanly we are not doing too well with our lives, humanly we are not attaining our ultimate goal, humanly we are not finding that "peace that passeth understanding." We do not have to wait for a point of desperation to arrive in our lives. At any moment we can agree that I of myself am not making too much of a success of my life. We can come to a point of self-surrender in the realization that God *is,* but above all that God is omnipresence, that there is a spirit in man, *the* spirit, really. "He that is within me is greater than he that is in the world."[1] Through contemplation, or meditation, or contemplative meditation, we can bring ourselves to that place where we realize, "Whatever the nature of God is, the God that maintains the universe in its orbit, whatever the nature of this law or being or power is, it is spirit."

That brings us to last week's lesson where we realize that health is in God, supply is in God, happiness is in God, peace is in God. Remember, "My peace give *I* unto you, not as the world giveth."[2] What is *my* peace? It is spiritual–it is the kind of peace that only God can give, and God can give it whether or not we have health or whether or not we have supply. When we receive *my* peace, we have health and we have supply and we have happiness, because God is infinite being.

You have had a whole week with this lesson, and now you will have the paper with last week's lesson. Begin to work with it, so that every time you think of health, whether for yourself or for someone else, you realize, "health is in spirit, not in the body." Then drop it. Do the same with supply. When faced with any discord, whether your own or someone else's, realize that the answer to it is in spirit. Spirit is something real and tangible. Spirit is not an unknown God. Spirit is absolutely tangible, "closer than breathing, nearer than hands and feet." In fact you live in it and it lives in you, and it governs all that is necessary to your experience, not only through this lifetime but through many lifetimes to come.

The source of our good is this invisible Spirit, which in reality *I am.* Therefore, it is always "closer than breathing." Even on the battlefield your life is in spirit, governed and controlled by spirit.

There is the universal belief that life is dependent on the body, but your transition reveals to you that your life is in divine sonship, not in a piece of matter. Yes, your life is in the fact that you are the divine son; but, if you do not consciously know this truth, this truth cannot make you free because of universal beliefs. Consciously we have to make the transition. You must know the truth, and the knowing must be a concrete act. The truth is, "My life is in and of God, hid in spiritual worship. My life is eternal because I am the offspring of God, made of the same substance as God, spirit. My life is not at the mercy of matter in any form. My life is spirit and it lives in spirit. My life is under spiritual law." It may not be a problem of health or life. If it is a problem of supply, you have the same principle. "My supply is not in money, but in the spirit which I am. All the supply I will ever need unto eternity is in spirit, in my sonship with God."

As a human being I am cast off and cast out, I am a "branch that is cut off, that withers and dies." Recognize your sonship with the Father, recognize that your supply rests in your relationship to God. We can take any situation in our experience and find the same thing. We find our justice in spirit, in consciousness, in the life which I am. Justice is embodied and incorporated in my being. No one can either give or take away justice. I find my justice in my spiritual sonship with God. The very fact that all men are spiritually sons of God assures me of justice. I must myself consciously acknowledge that all men are children of God. When we live from this basis, that "I find my allness, completeness, perfection in spirit," we come eventually to a place where all responsibility falls off our shoulders and we say, "God is living my life." We come to a place of resting and relaxing and letting thoughts come to us, instead of trying to create thoughts. Think how wonderful it is when we relax and receive the thoughts that emanate from infinite intelligence. "My thoughts are not your thoughts, neither are your ways my ways."[3] Then surrender your thoughts and your ways, and listen for the still small voice. "I live in spirit and spirit lives in me, and spiritual law alone governs and controls me." Therefore, take no thought about material or mental laws, and realize the infinite nature of spiritual law.

God has never cast us off; through ignorance we have taken ourselves out of God's government. It has been discerned that we can return to the Father's house—that we can "turn ye and live," that it is an act of our own consciousness. When the prodigal son is in dire straits and he consciously turns his steps back to his father's house, quickly he finds that the father is rushing out to greet him with the royal robe and the royal ring of sonship.

Always in our moments of self-surrender we will find the Master because the Master was never crucified, was never buried and never raised. The Master is consciousness, the Son of God, which is our real identity, which every one of us incorporates within ourselves.

So the moment we surrender in the realization of our nothingness, in that moment the Master is omnipresent to take over our experience. None of us has any idea how the Christ will function in our experience. Self-surrender means a total surrender so God can work his miracles in our experience. There can be no outlining in our thoughts. We cannot function in the human way of thinking. We are consistent with our surrender. "Thy will be done, not mine."[4] No, I must have no outline. I must be the beholder and watch how the spirit "goes before me to make the crooked places straight."[5]

We attune ourselves to this: "Life is not a matter of body but of spirit. Life is not lived in or through body, but in and through the spirit. I live and move and have my being in spirit, not in body or a bank account. Then I find all things added unto me. Spiritual law governs my life, mind, body, being. Every facet of my life is governed by spirit. I have to take no thought for my life. I can only be a beholder watching God at work."

You can see that this is a transition, but you must consciously make the transition by the realization of this. "My life is in and of spirit. My supply is in and of spirit. My companionships are in and of spirit. My relationships are in and of spirit—not in medical laws or legal laws or economic laws." We are taking our life out of material sense and placing it where it belongs, in spiritual awareness. The issues of life are in spirit, not in matter. This is a way of life. Some people are living their lives as if they had to consult food or weather or climate or germs. Most people live their lives as if their supply had to do with whether we have boom times or depression times. But the spiritual child of God is not human but spiritual, and depends only upon spiritual law, spiritual government, spiritual substance.

As you work with this principle, you will discover eventually that you have made a complete transition to

where you are living in and of spirit, and spirit is living
in and of you because of oneness. "I and my Father are
one. I am in the Father and the Father is in me." So, by
placing all the issues of life in spirit, you find an adjustment taking place in your life which will lead to fruition.

I must caution you here. At first glance it would
appear that, when we reach that goal, we would just lean
back and sort of float around with the human equivalent
of wings or a harp, but this is not true. Since the goal is
immortality and eternality and infinity, the real joy is in
attaining. As long as we tabernacle on earth, there will
be higher attainments ahead. There will always be a new
horizon, a new step, and this is the joy of life—always
higher attainments. As a matter of fact, the ego can take
very little pleasure in this form of life, because it is never
your understanding that brings about the demonstration
of peace and harmony. It is God's understanding. The
further we go, the less and less our humanhood becomes. The height of our attainment is nothingness, in
order that spirit may come alive in us.

Let us see how much further we can carry ourselves
into this transition. It is by conscious and specific work.
You already have the notes of last week, and soon you
will have the notes of this week. Work with them,
understanding that you yourself must make the transition. The teacher can lift you in consciousness only. You
have the same infinite intelligence, the same amount of
divine love, only you must use it. The function of the
teacher is, "I, if *I* be lifted up, will draw all men unto
me,"[6] but the teacher cannot carry the student unto
heaven. That is what the Master meant when he said, "If
I go not away, the Comforter will not come to you."[7] So
it will be with us if we do not let the teacher lift us up to

the point where we can say, "Let the Father do the works through me and as me."

All that it leads up to is the Master's statement, "Take no thought for your life."[8] As we take no thought "out here," we receive divine protection, divine grace. This means the ability to surrender the self so that it may receive the wisdom and the activity within. Then you find it makes us very active in the outer world. It gives us plenty to do.

DIVINE SONSHIP

March 3, 1963
The Halekulani Hotel
Honolulu, Hawaii

BY NOW YOU HAVE DISCOVERED how difficult it is to make the transition from finding your health in the body to finding your health in divine sonship, or to making the transition from finding your supply in currency and investments to finding your supply in your spiritual sonship, in your relationship to God. You know now how difficult it is to make the transition from finding your good in the world to finding your good in God–in your divine sonship. In fact it is so difficult that the Master said that, "The way is straight and narrow, and few there be that enter."[1]

We were born into mortal or human consciousness. When we were conceived, our parents had nothing in mind but human conception, and, after we were born, they expected us to respond to material laws. We are now in the process of dying out of that consciousness and being reborn into another consciousness. In this new birth or new consciousness, we find ourselves equal, and that means equal in the sight of God, equal in the sight of each other. There is no black or no white, there is no high or no low, there is no large or no small, there is no young or no old, there is no rich or no poor. We are all equally spiritual offspring, and we are all equal in our joint sonship to all of the heavenly riches. "Son, thou art ever with me, and all that I have is thine."[2] We do not earn our money by might or by power. There is no such thing as earning our supply or being worthy of it. We inherit it; it is ours by divine right of our sonship.

In this new birth we have to overcome the belief that God rewards goodness and that God punishes our natural mistakes. This is difficult. For years people have carried burdens of guilt and this makes it difficult to accept the fact that our good is dependent only on our relationship to God, and that this relationship exists whether we have been good or bad. No crime on the calendar could break that relationship, because the relationship is *oneness*. There are not two—there is only one. "I and my Father are one.[3] Son, thou art ever with me and all that *I* have is thine." This does not mean if, and, or but. It means straight out that our relationship to God is oneness. "All that the Father is I am. All that the Father hath is mine."

We have now established in our consciousness our true relationship to God. Then, as a claim arises, whether it is one of disease, false appetite, sin or lack, your answer is, "My harmony is dependent only on my relationship to my source—God. The harmony of my body, the harmony of my purse, the harmony of my good is dependent on my relationship to God, and therefore it is mine by grace." This is the truth which, if you know it, will make you free; but you must actually know it to the point of conviction that your good in an amount up to infinity is yours because of your relationship to God. Now you can say, "Ah, no. This sickness is a superstition, it is a state of mind. Why? Because my health and harmony is found not in my body but in

God. I of myself am nothing. Because of my oneness with the Father, all that the Father is I am, and all that the Father hath is mine by right of relationship."

So it is that, regardless of what temptation comes to you, you can answer back: "No, I find my good in my relationship to God, in my divine sonship. My health is not in my body but in my sonship. My intelligence is not in my brain but in my sonship. My companionship is not in men and women but in my divine sonship." In fact you are companioning with everyone around the world who is recognizing his sonship. "I find my companionship in God by virtue of my relationship to God. No matter how much alone I seem to be, this fills me with companionship. I am inwardly companioned. That is why I cannot feel a loss or a void, because it is not there. I and my Father are one.

This will change your whole metaphysical approach to living your life. You will not be living your life by right thinking or by treatment. You will be enjoying the harmony of your being by the right of divine sonship, and you will approach every claim from that standpoint, "I do not have to do anything after I have recognized my divine sonship. I take no thought for externalized living. I now allow the hidden manna to come into expression." Think how many times the words *hidden manna* are in the writings and recordings. What does hidden manna mean? It means the infinity of good which I cannot hear, see, taste, touch or smell, but which is stored up in me and which I know is there because of my divine sonship.

Because of the world's mesmerism, I may seem to be lacking something. That can happen to anyone as a temptation; but never blame a temporary sense of lack of demonstration on God, or on your neighbor, or on someone in the external world. Whatever we are, we are because of our present state of consciousness, and when a lack of something manifests, it is up to us not to place the blame out in the world. Get within and realize our own inability to grasp that "the whole world is mine by virtue of my sonship." World mesmerism would bring these claims to us, and so instead of going back to some old metaphysical way to get out of them, stop believing in two powers and recognize, "The earth is the Lord's and the fullness thereof.[4] Son, thou art ever with me and all that I have is thine by virtue, not of my own worthiness, but of divine sonship." To claim that some are better than others is foolishness. The truth is that we are equal, equally children of God. God is no respecter of persons. In the consciousness of God, the good is equal to the bad, the rich is equal to the poor, the old is equal to the young.

No fault ever lies with God, but in the human teachings that do not allow us to hold to a single principle of, "I and my Father are one, and all that the Father hath is mine." Actually Israel, or God's anointed, are all those who know the truth. Israel means the children of God, and the children of God can be of any race or religion when they come to the realization of, "I and my Father are one." Then we are all brethren.

To claim your good without the understanding that your good is your good only because of a divine relationship, would be feeding the ego and the ego must not be fed. By virtue of the fact that "God is spirit and I am spirit, then the perfection of God is the perfection of my individual being. Therefore, I find my good in my spiritual relationship to God, or I find my good in my divine sonship." Then, when anything tempts me, I can withdraw my gaze from this world and say, "No, in here closer than breathing, is my contact with infinity, with eternality, with immortality. I am as young as God, but I am also as old as God. All the qualities and all the quantities of God are mine by right of sonship, by the divine right of heir." We are all equally offspring of God and we do not divide up the heavenly good among us. We all inherit all that the Father hath. God is spirit and cannot be divided or cut up into pieces.

The allness of God is omnipresence. Never forget that the allness of God is omnipresence. "Where I am, thou art. Where thou art, I am." There must be an inner spiritual intuition that says to you, "The place whereon I stand is holy ground because I and my Father are one, not two." This is omnipresence carried to the degree of infinity. Just think what this does to you in the nature of your human relationships. No longer can you look to man whose breath is in his nostrils. No longer can you blame man whose breath is in his nostrils. "I shall not fear what mortal man can do to me. When dare I make a statement like that? When I am standing in my rightful relationship to God—and only then—can I make this statement, that "None of the weapons that are formed against me shall prosper."[5] Why? Because of my divine sonship. Only then can I say, "I shall not fear what mortal man can do to me, for I find my good in my heirship, in my sonship."

You see then how this permits you to take your gaze from the world and live more in the within-ness, to live more periods of your life in inner meditation or contemplation because, as the world's problems touch you, you need to remember, "No man in the world gives to me;

no man in the world takes from me, because of sonship. I am living only in my relationship to God. I am not living in or for the world. I am in God, and God is in me, for we are one. This is my relationship to God, and all because of sonship. *Son, thou art ever with me."*

Remember that the son is never somebody separate and apart from God. The son is always one with the Father and includes all that the Father has. There is no process of God giving or God withholding. "All that God is I am," in oneness.

Why should you take no thought for your life? Why should you take no thought for what you shall eat, what you shall drink, or how you shall be clothed? There is only one reason, because of your relationship to God, your relationship of sonship. I am heir to all of the heavenly riches. Or: "Because of my Christhood, all of the heavenly riches are mine." You will notice in healing work that, regardless of all the truths you may know, you are not going to do any healing work unless you can come to the point where you can stop voicing truth and start to listen for truth. Then you realize exactly what I am speaking of. Yes, when it comes to the healing work, Joel has to be quiet and let it have its way. Then this Christhood, which is "closer than breathing," does the same work that the Christ did two thousand years ago. It heals, it feeds, it raises.

Know this, that the world is always tempting you to a belief in the absence of something. There is always something absent from us, but remember that the antidote is shutting out that appearance, and realizing that nothing is absent from your consciousness because of your relationship with God. "I and my Father are one." "Thou seeth me thou seeth the Father that sent me." [6] I was never born and I will never die. How do I know this? The son of God is an eternal relationship, "Call no man on earth your Father."[7] You have never been born. The period of birth was really only when you became visible on this plane. Likewise, the period of death is only when we become invisible on this plane. This point of sonship, rightly understood, makes you completely free of the world because all is yours by right of sonship. Living in this consciousness is what produces harmony—and it means *living* in it. "The government is on his shoulders."[8] My part is to know this truth. We have been cheated for two-thousand years, but now it is restored to us. If, at this moment, there is a claim of lack or limitation in any form, realize right here today in this instant: it is impossible. That which appears to be absent is really mine here and now because of sonship. All that the Father hath is mine.

Work with this during the coming weeks, going back over the Sunday notes and see how this has gradually been evolving up to the unfoldment of today. And remember that you have to make a practice of living this. "My good is mine because of divine sonship. I find my health and my supply and my harmony and my opportunities in divine sonship, and all because of my relationship with the one source. The earth is the Lord's and the fullness thereof, and all that the Father hath is mine." This is a transition from the man of earth to that man who has his being in Christ, who finds his good in his Christhood as heir of God. This will also show you the necessity of not living in the past and not living in the future, because living in either the past or the future is living in humanhood. Recognize that, "Here and now I find my good in my Christhood." The human mind cannot grasp this. It is something that must be revealed to you through intuition. There is an intuitive process. Then you will understand why, in so much of our work, you find me bringing to light that "I will never leave you nor forsake you—*I,* this divine Christhood." In other words, my relationship to God was established in the beginning and it is mine by divine right.

Then what about punishment? Punishment is the very moment when you leave the relationship of divine sonship. The moment you leave divine sonship, you have me and mine, you and yours. Try to think of living in this atmosphere, in the relationship of your Christhood. No matter how you try to live in this relationship, temptations will come; they can come at any period of your spiritual progress. When they come, we must be alert and be able to say, "Get thee behind me, Satan.[9] This is an appearance, not a fact. My good is in my sonship."

Again I must caution you. This truth must be held as something secret as well as something sacred, because if you voice it, you spill it. The only time you are ever called upon to voice it is when you find someone far enough along on the path. Then you can share it, but only then can you share it. Do not forget that spiritual truth should not be placed before the human mind. Keep it secret, keep it sacred, and voice it only when you are with someone whom you know will receive it in the same secretness and sacredness.

Relationship of Oneness 1

March 9, 1963

I WAS JUST TRYING TO SEE if I could find any spiritual reason for celebrating a birthday or an anniversary. Emma and I have been celebrating ours with a little family group every year just as a matter of human enjoyment, but I have been trying to think if there would be any spiritual significance in a birthday or anniversary. For one thing, it does serve as an excuse for a group of people to get together, for it is a wonderful thing for people who are like-minded to be together in this way. Still the question is, is there a spiritual significance? The only answer that would come is for the sake of giving us an opportunity, just because we use numbers, to look back for a few minutes to see how we have developed spiritually in the last few years. What manner of unfoldment has taken place in that time, what sense of togetherness? It would serve a good purpose to see if the past years are unfolding in some beautiful way.

I think the only purpose really, that I can see at this moment, is that you can ask yourself, if it is a birthday, "What use am I making of my years?" Yes, this just comes up in my thought: "Lay not up for yourselves treasures upon the earth, where moth and rust consume, and where thieves break through and steal; but lay up for yourselves treasures in heaven, where neither moth nor rust doth consume, and where thieves do not break

51

through nor steal: for where thy treasure is, there will thy heart be also."[1]

From a spiritual standpoint it would make no difference in the passing of years, if we were using our time to lay up spiritual treasures. You can't take money with you, you can't take bank accounts with you and you can't take university degrees with you. It doesn't even matter if you have been president two or three times. The only thing we can carry with us is whatever measure of spiritual truth or spiritual consciousness we have attained.

The same purpose is true on celebrating an anniversary. We would have to look at it not from the standpoint of how many years we had been together, but to what extent is each year increasing our desire to be together; in other words, what spiritual attainment are we reaching? The passing years should bring a deeper and a riper relationship between a couple because their togetherness is founded on spiritual qualities rather than human attractions. I can see that both with the birthday and the anniversary celebrations we can use them and benefit by them because we can look back and see whether or not we are laying up spiritual treasures with the passing years so that we have a great spiritual treasure laid up for us when we cross the river. Younger people (those for whom there is no thought of what confronts those in later years) also have the opportunity of looking back on every birthday or anniversary day to see whether or not they are bringing as much spiritual unfoldment into their lives as they can.

Some weeks ago we talked about mediocrity as one of the major sins. Of course, an element enters into that subject which must be allowed. Mediocrity in a person who does not have the capacity for anything can be excused. If they have no soul capacity, if they have no mental capacity, nothing can come forth from them. Most people do have a greater capacity to do things than they are doing; most people have a greater capacity to make use of their souls and minds than they are yet using. Here is where mediocrity is a great sin.

To have a consciousness that can be developed and not to use it is just wasting God's gift. It was said in my home, and probably in some of yours, "Waste not, want not." Just think how horrible it is if we have a mental storehouse and a spiritual storehouse and deliberately waste it–if we let ourselves be mediocre in our attainment when we have the innate capacities to really achieve something. Regardless of what anyone says in this world, or mystics who "talk down" on it, attainment is God-given and it must be a sin to waste any of it. We ought to be using all of our capacity for development of Soul consciousness, spiritual consciousness.

We should be using all we know to improve our human relationships. It is probably easier to have good relationships outside of the home than in the home, but it doesn't mean we should not increase our relationship at home. It takes two to make a bargain, but if our intentions are not met with that same response, then regardless of what the other one is doing, we can say, "I am going to do it myself." The greater degree of harmony we can prove in our relationship inside the home partnership, the greater the treasure we have laid up and the greater is our spiritual capacity to rise. On the occasion of a birthday if we look back a year, two, three, five or ten and find that we haven't left that "old" man one hundred years behind, look up and say, "Before the

next birthday rolls around there is going to be a greater
development of my spiritual capacities." Note if our
spiritual relationship in the home is progressing, because
if it isn't it can easily be remedied. It only means one or
the other, or both, are neglecting the opportunity to
develop more.

Most of the discords or inharmonies in the home can
be met through meditations where a couple meditate
together, and even where they meditate separately, but
more especially when they meditate together. I think this
has been my experience; it is impossible for me to be
unjust with a person with whom I have meditated to any
great extent. To me it seems a bond is created between
myself and those with whom I meditate. (Strangely
enough this bond never has been broken. In my thirty-
two years of meditating with people, never once has a
sense of sensuality developed. In these meditations in
which we meet the Soul within us, we are left with a finer
and a nobler feeling than we had before. It just seems that
if people have ever meditated together they become one
and you don't come down and lose your high estate.
Meditating together makes our interests one.)

So you see, an anniversary would give us the opportunity to see how our relationship is coming along. Is it
sweeter and riper? Probably this is the only legitimate
use we can make of the past. We are living so much in
the present, the past doesn't exist, but we can look back
just to be sure we are making spiritual progress and that
we are developing spiritually. Aside from that you have
seen in our Saturday and Sunday groups what a wonderful bond exists between all of us. We are all individuals
that belong to nothing regarding each other, and yet see
how beautiful this relationship is.

Those who have seen us in England, Holland, etc., know the relationship is just the same. In London, when the class is over, a group of us go out to have tea together. It is always arranged to spend the final Tuesday night at Hope House in London, and Sunday with Mary Salt and a group of students—you would think we were one little family. I could tell you that the same thing happens wherever we travel.

When I arrived at Johannesburg, over fifty people there came to meet me and they had arranged for a tea at the airport in the V.I.P. Room. I can look back on all of my trips and see how this relationship has grown. You have seen it when the Spencers and Beth Huntington were here from England. Yes, I can look back on these last twelve years of international travel and see a progressive relationship unfolding with all students all over the world, and this is one thing I will carry with me into heaven. I will carry it with me wherever I go. This is some of the spiritual consciousness I have stored up.

I want my family life to be the same. I want my family to know me and love me after I am invisible. All those human honors will be nothing in the next world. The only thing that will count will be the love I have stored in the hearts of those I have known and their love for me. So I can see a legitimate purpose to celebrating birthdays—just to see whether we are fulfilling ourselves spiritually and whether we are fulfilling ourselves in relationships with others, for those are the treasures we are going to carry with us. Well, I guess that is enough on birthdays and anniversaries!

The present unfoldment is all aimed in the direction of spiritual sonship. No one should be looking for health, supply, or companionship in this world. They should be realizing to a greater degree their only health, wealth, or companionship is in their spiritual sonship. By constantly abiding in that, they must attain some measure of that spiritual identity. The only thing to which I can lay claim is that which I have in my relationship to God. That stands out so clearly in our current work. Whatever is mine is only mine in my spiritual relationship to God. My health is due not to a condition of body, but to immortality. My supply must come only in my relationship to Deity—then I have sufficiency, my needs are met. I can never again be concerned if I know that my supply is mine by reason of my relationship to God.

The students will have difficulty because they have to break down the belief that they are getting what they earned, or deserve. My supply is infinite because of my relationship to God. "Son, thou art ever with me and all that I have is thine," not because of work I am doing, or study—just because of my relationship to God. I am no longer working for money, I am working for *Self* expression.

We are taught health is in the body, that some part of health is due to heredity, that some part is due to the fact that we shouldn't overwork, overeat, or worry too much. With the revelation we have been having these last weeks, health is one of the things I have inherited from my Father. "Know ye not that ye are the temple of the living God?"[2] Health is mine by divine right, given to me by inheritance, given to me by my Father. We can know peace, safety, and security. This is mine by a divine right. I know that I am protected—why? Because I am in God, and God is in me and we are one. This relationship is my safety and security. I can't get outside of my good.

Those students hearing it should be attaining the consciousness, "Yes, I really have this by right of divine relationship." The children of Rockefeller and Ford are millionaires because of their relationship to their fathers. We are healthy, wealthy, and wise because of our relationship to "our Father," and in our case it is a greater Father than any human Rockefeller or Ford, for it is a divine relationship.

God doesn't divide between his children. He gives his good to every child. If only that one term stays in our head—*by right of relationship*—that one term should take care of our healings for us. This is mine by right of relationship. We can forget it then and let it manifest in its own way. I can't be one with God and lack anything. If in any department of my life there is lack, it is some degree of mesmerism and I will throw it off; I will have harmony in my life because of my relationship to God. I am heir: "All that the Father hath is mine."[3] It ought to be well impressed on your consciousness and set you apart from the rest of the world.

You are separate from the rest of the world and you are free of most of its lacks and limitations in the realization of my oneness with God constitutes my infinite abundance, harmony, purity of mind, and Soul. By virtue of my relationship to God, I am heir to all the heavenly riches. It is all mine by inheritance—it isn't whether I deserve it. Remember the one who came last got just as much pay as the rest? This may not seem fair, but it isn't unjust on the spiritual scale. There is just as much available to the one who has just become awakened, because in God, all is equality.

Relationship of Oneness 2

March 10, 1963
Halekulani Hotel

First of all, of course, is to find some way to express gratefulness for these two days of celebration we have had, two days of feast together. It is difficult to find words to express gratitude for the spiritual feast that underlies the external feast.

In The Infinite Way we have watched experiences like this, in beautiful expressions of gratitude and love, shown not only to us but to those who have come here from the mainland, England, Australia. When we have been in London and the continent of Europe, we have witnessed the same gratitude, not only to us, but to the students who have traveled to England and the Continent. Therefore, what I am trying to say or to express is that not only is the gratitude expressed to us, but this same gratitude and love is shown to anyone, anywhere, who comes into The Infinite Way atmosphere. Just what you are expressing to us and to these visitors from overseas, The Infinite Way students overseas express to us and to those who come from far places.

Behind these outer expressions of love and gratitude and sharing is the relationship that exists between us as Infinite Way students. The relationship that exists between us—this is the heart and the core. There are no human ties between us. We belong to nothing and we belong to no one. In The Infinite Way nobody is greater than anyone else, because everyone in this work has problems at times. No one of us has risen to become a God. Therefore, there is no one of us who could set ourselves above others, for none of us have fully attained. However, whatever our level of spiritual attainment is, it has for its basis our relationship with each other. What is the basis of our relationship? The answer is, our relationship with God. Our conscious oneness with God makes us one with each other.

As I have told you before, for about fifteen years I was the only Infinite Way student in the world. Now what has drawn to me on a worldwide basis such groups as you are? There is only one answer: my living and moving and having my being in the consciousness that "I and the Father are one, and that my oneness with God constitutes my oneness with all spiritual being and idea." Also, because of the truth that you who were seeking spiritual light were drawn into the atmosphere of The Infinite Way. I never could have reached many students worldwide, humanly, because for years I never moved out of California, and later, Hawaii. Nevertheless, The Infinite Way drew unto itself students from all over this globe. This could only be accomplished either by a go-getting organization that went out beating the bushes, or else by staying at home and abiding in the consciousness of my oneness with God, and by the realization that The Infinite Way was not mine. It was God expressing itself to this age. If I ever claim The Infinite Way as mine, not only would I lose it, but it might be that even the world would lose it in this generation. No, it is not mine. It was God expressing itself in the language necessary to this age, and I was fortunate enough to be the instrument that voiced it. There are reasons for that which have to do with past lives, and there are reasons which have to do with this life. I had no religious training—I was neither Jew nor Gentile, and I was born in New York and went to a public school where there was neither black nor white.

The message of The Infinite Way can never be received by those who continue to have biases, bigotries, and prejudices. A pure message of Godliness, of the fatherhood of God and the brotherhood of man, can only be received in the consciousness of those who acknowledge, "Call no man on earth your Father. There is but one Father, who is the creative Principle."

The world has divided itself up into Jews, Catholics, Protestants, white, black, and yellow—but in the kingdom of God there are no more differences than we find in our gardens. With our violets, roses, papayas, and bananas, we do not hold one as being better than another. No, each is just a different form of God appearing. So, for persons to be not merely instruments for The Infinite Way, but to be able to live by the principles of The Infinite Way, they must be equally free of prejudice, bigotry and bias so they can look out at this entire world and realize that we are brothers. Only in this way will the "backward" people, people who have been made backward by a society who thinks of them in this way, be given the opportunity of equality and social and economic freedom. There are backward people, but remember it was the "enlightened" people who kept them that way, just as in this age it is the enlightened people who are giving them the opportunity to become free.

You can see that the relationship between all Infinite Way students is due only to the fact that in some degree we recognize our oneness with God. We are not foolish enough to believe that it is a personal relationship that belongs to you or to me, but that it must be a universal relationship. "God is no respecter of persons or religions."[1] When we read that Israel is the chosen people of God, remember that by Israel we mean "enlightened consciousness," whether it is Jew or Gentile, White or Black. The very moment that consciousness is illumined, it is Israel—or one with God. Now carry this a step forward and you will discover that, through your life in The Infinite Way, good comes into your experience, not only in one form but usually in many forms, whether better health, or supply, or improved relationships in the home, or greater opportunities for freedom, and certainly more peace. As you rehearse in your mind the blessings that have come to you, remember that they have come to you because you have awakened to your relationship to God, to the source of all good.

Look out at this world from any point and see what God's grace has given to this world in the way of oceans, rivers, streams, land and all that has been planted and placed there—the birds in the air, the fish in the sea, the cattle on a thousand hills, the diamonds and rubies and pearls. Look at all this that is on earth through God's grace, and realize that it can only become yours by virtue of your relationship with God. If you fail to establish in your consciousness your relationship of oneness with God, you have no right to the blessings that are in this world, because these are God's given blessings to the children of God. They are only yours by right of your relationship to your source, your conscious oneness with God. If you follow this message, you will find yourself healthier, but from whence comes this health? It is only yours by virtue of your oneness with God. "God is the health of my countenance. God is my bread, meat, wine, and water. God is my abiding place—*home.*" Do you see why you cannot claim any of this humanly? Do you see why so many people have to earn their living by the sweat of their brow? Only because of their ignorance of their relationship to God. God has not demanded any price or effort for that which he has put into this earth. It is all there by grace.

There is a story to the effect that the reason for the many coconut trees on these islands is that a coconut drifted here from the South Seas and planted itself on the water's edge, took root and grew. No man planted the first tree on this island. In this work you must occasionally look out and see the God-given beauties that surround us. You must give thought occasionally to the fact that man did not create mathematics—he discovered it. Everything is here by God's grace, and can only be ours by virtue of our relationship with God. But you must see that our relationship with God constitutes a relationship with each other, because if I am the offspring of God and you are the offspring of God, then we must be brothers and sisters.

Can you not see why there is trouble in the world? The world does not treat each other as brothers and sisters. Do the people who have been negotiating in the newspaper strikes in New York and Cleveland, or the sugar negotiations here, see each other as brothers and sisters? No, they are not viewing themselves as one with God, or each other as one with God.

"Take no thought for your life, what ye shall eat, what ye shall drink or wherewithal ye shall be clothed."[2] You find that passage in every one of my writings. Sometimes

I wonder if you do not get tired of my repetition of it, but it reveals a great truth. Why do you need take no thought? Because of your relationship to God. God has done all the thought-taking and his thoughts are not your thoughts, his ways are not your ways. His way is the way of grace, and you cannot come into that grace except by conscious realization of your oneness with your source. You have to *consciously* live and move and have your being in God.

There is one more thing you have to do. When you realize your relationship to God, and that you do not have to take anxious or fearful thought, and you have attained a consciousness of peace—you have to consciously bestow that peace on all who come into the range of your consciousness. In other words, while walking on the street or driving a car, there must also be the conscious realization that the peace which you have found will envelop those who surround you, whether in the home or in business or on the highways. If you are not sharing the consciousness you have found, it remains locked up inside of you and cannot function. You can only get in proportion to your giving. You must "open out a way for the imprisoned splendor to escape." Therefore, when you consciously realize your relationship to God, look around you several times a day and remember that this is the truth about your neighbor. The fact that he does not know it makes no difference. You must spread the aroma of the atmosphere in which you live. You must forgive by remembering that you are not forgiving but that, through you, God is forgiving.

You do not have to struggle for your life, or your livelihood or for health, if you are abiding in the realization of your relationship to your source. Often I speak of hidden manna. I think you all know that, to me, the term *hidden manna* is a very alive *something*. In fact, hidden manna is probably one of the most important and vital realizations in my life. What does it mean? The hidden manna is the truth I know, the truth of my relationship with my source. That is my hidden manna. I can not display it, I cannot tell it to the unillumined, but I can live it. I can live in the constant realization that my good emanates from the truth I know about my relationship to God. "The earth is the Lord's and the fullness thereof.[3] Son, thou art ever with me and all that *I* have is thine."[4] That is my hidden manna.

It is that which enables me not to look to any person for my good, not to expect it from this person or that person, but to abide in the realization of, "God's grace is my sufficiency in all things."[5] I do not have to expect anything from anyone, but I must expect a great deal from myself. I must live up to my highest sense of right. I must recognize that I must meet all the demands made upon me, but I must expect nothing of anyone else. Why? Because I have overcome that part of the world, which is the belief that any man owes me anything for any reason. Their relationship to me makes no difference. Why? Because I have the grace of God. On the other hand, I owe everybody an obligation by virtue of having this hidden manna. I have to share everything that is given me of God. No man owes me anything because "I and the Father are one[6] and all that the Father hath is mine."[7] There are no powers in heaven, or on earth, or in hell that can operate against God's grace. This is universal, and everyone in the world could experience an infinity of supply, and infinity of health, an infinity of youth, and infinity of vitality if they knew that it is theirs by right of their relationship to God. "Ye shall know the truth, and the truth will make you free."[8] Without the truth that is your hidden manna, you will not be free. The world cannot see why you are so happy, so healthy, so prosperous, because it cannot see your hidden manna; but those of spiritual discernment will see your hidden manna, and it will come to be their hidden manna.

Do you see why you cannot share this with your friends or relatives until they have come far enough along the path to be able to grasp it? None of this raises a question in your thought because you have the inner feeling, "This is truth. This is what I must live by." That would not be true if we went to an auditorium and told it to several thousand people. That is the reason I prefer to talk to these small groups, rather than talk to hundreds who could not hear. I love my smaller classes.

There must be a preparedness to receive truth. You cannot receive truth with your mind because, if you could go back five or ten years and sit here and listen to this, it would sound like a wild man's tale. Yet, to every one of you, this rings true—but that is because of your preparation and previous dedication. At some time you were touched by the spirit of God for a hunger for truth. Remember that in proportion as you demonstrate that your good is yours only because of your conscious oneness with God, in that degree are you attracting to you those who sooner or later will be prepared to hear about your hidden manna, your hidden source of supply.

Just think of being heir of God. That is not merely poetry—that is a true relationship. The child is always heir to all the parents have. How did you come into existence if God did not have something to do with it?

Could humans produce this body? "Your body is the temple of God. God fashioned your body." If we are not showing it forth in its beauty and youthfulness, it is because we have taken it away from God and considered our bodies as being human. Our bodies will change in proportion to our understanding of our relationship to God. So will the body of our supply improve. "Not by might nor by power does your good come to you, but through the grace of God, by virtue of your relationship to God. Take no thought, but seek ye the kingdom of God." Seek more of an understanding of your divine relationship.

Once you catch a glimpse of your relationship to God, you find you cannot withhold. You have to be pouring, sharing, cooperating, and yet–because of the understanding of the nature of your hidden manna–you do not look for any return. As others come into this atmosphere of God, they also become pourers of good. "I and my Father are one. Thou seeth me thou seeth the Father that sent me, and it is in this oneness that I receive God's allness. Only in this conscious oneness do I receive the grace of God. Son, all that *I* have is thine." The more you believe that others owe you an obligation, the less you are realizing your own hidden manna, your own infinity by virtue of your relationship to a supreme Source. You can really say, "I have overcome the world,"[9] when you can set every human being free.

Suppose something arises tomorrow, indicating that you have a lack of something, something of health, or supply, or companionship or home. The first thought that must come to us is, "I already have it because of my relationship to God," and this sets us free from desire. You have read in the writings that desire, even right desire, is sin. Why? Because it is based on the belief that it is not already yours. And so you abide in this, "All that I have is thine." Fear drops away, and in its time it will make its appearance, sometimes in the most astonishing ways.

You see how this enables you to stop struggling for health and realize that "health is mine because of my relationship to God." Then stand. Abide in that Word. Eventually this idea that the world is yours, by reason of relationship, will make itself so real to you that from that moment on you will be living in a new universe. You will be living in a whole new atmosphere and altitude of life. It seems to cut you off from everything and everyone out here, from the standpoint of dependency, but it seems to establish a warm bond with everyone. You do not voice it, but by silently knowing, you prepare the way for others to know. Abide with it silently, secretly, sacredly. Let it demonstrate itself, and then all those who are ready for the spiritual revelation will be drawn to you and you can share it.

You will discover that the kingdom of God is already come upon earth for you as you abide in this hidden manna, this particular secret that "the allness of God is mine by right of my relationship to God."

Can you not picture Jesus looking up and down the Holy Land, knowing this truth, and why he could say to Pilate, "Thou couldest[10] have no power over me," and why he could say, "My words will never pass away."[11] Can you not see him standing up and looking at Jerusalem and saying, "Oh Jerusalem, Oh Jerusalem, I would put my arms around you, but you would not."[12] He could be rejoiced and he could be saddened.

THE TREE OF LIFE

March 17, 1963
Halekulani Hotel

YOU MAY HAVE NOTICED that it takes several years after you receive a spiritual idea or principle before it is yours, and before you can demonstrate it. This is normal, this is natural, and it would be folly to expect anything different. It has been so with every one of us. We hear a spiritual principle and we read it. In fact we read it over and over again, and we hear it on tapes or in lectures or classes, and therefore we think that we know it and wonder why we cannot demonstrate it. Remember that this is normal and natural and true of each of us.

Even principles that have come through my own lips have really not become mine until several years later. Even though they come through my own consciousness, they did not register at the time in a demonstrable degree. It was years later before I could say, "Whereas I was blind, now I see. Whereas before I could voice it, now it is an incorporated part of me. Now I can live it."

One of these principles is one that you heard this morning and one that you will find in most of my writings, and that is the *tree of life*. Usually I have used this example: Imagine a tree in the middle of this room, and then visualize each one of us attached to that tree as a branch. Then you will notice that we are all being fed from the same source. The sap that comes up through the trunk of the tree, the life that is flowing up through the trunk, this feeds and sustains and nourishes us and each of us draws from the same source. Now the meaning of this is that there is actually an invisible tree in this room. There is actually an invisible thread connecting us to the trunk of that tree. That tree is the spiritual tree of life and each one of us, by an invisible thread or bond is united to this tree of life. We are maintained, sustained, guided, directed, illumined from the same source, the life or sap that flows up through the roots into the trunk and out into each branch.

Now, if you were to use this as the subject of a meditation, you would note first of all that this life is not in the tree or the roots. It flows first from the surrounding soil, and actually it is the sunshine and the rain and the snow and the winds that pour into and over the earth; it is that which forms the sap that runs up and out through the branches. And so it is this invisible tree, through its roots, draws from God the substance of God, the laws of God, the life of God. All this flows through the roots of this invisible tree, up through the branches, and out into you and me.

As you continue your meditation, you will say, "What about my employment? What about my parents? What about my husband? What about my inheritance? Am I not drawing from them?" No, they are branches on the same tree, and one branch does not draw from another branch. Every branch is drawing through the trunk, through the roots, from God. It does not take too many such meditations to give you a clear picture of this relationship to God by virtue of being a branch of the tree, and it takes only a little while longer to realize our relationship to each other, because of our relationship to the tree.

The disappointing thing is that, even after you realize it and live with it for awhile, you do not seem to demonstrate it. That is normal and that is natural. There is another step and that is called realization. That is when this illustration strikes you so forcibly, usually at some time when you are not thinking about it, that it registers in your spiritual center and from then on you begin to live it. You can observe now the forms of good that are coming to you from other sources—new activities and new talents.

I have told the experience of a mother and daughter who attended my work in a city and who, after I left town, began to write songs. One wrote the words and the other wrote the music, and before the year was over, they had four songs being played on radio throughout the nation. This was the fruitage of their becoming consciously one with their source. The talent they had and knew nothing about, came alive. Aside from being a new activity, it also proved to be a source of income.

When we have the realization of this relationship to God and to each other, we find that there are people beginning to play parts in our lives who not only never had before, but probably there was no human reason for them to do so. Humanly we may have no relationship with each other, but spiritually there is this bond. When you see it in this way, you never receive anything from anyone without heartfelt thanks to them as an instrument, but neither do you forget to look further and see that it came to you by virtue of the spiritual bond.

Your individual contact with God makes me an instrument of bringing truth to you. It is not my will—I have only received instruction to speak or write it—but do you know who hears it? Those who have a longing to know God, those who have a longing to know truth, those who even unconsciously have made some contact with their source. They are then drawn to me and I am but the instrument or transparency. You must know this, that it is coming to you only because of your oneness with your source.

One of the greatest causes of unhappiness in the human world is that we have human obligations and usually those who receive from us, and I am speaking humanly, begin to resent it. Sometimes, because of an obligation, those who are doing the giving also begin to resent it. That is natural for the human race.

All of this changes when you realize that you are no longer the giver or the receiver, and that whatever you are pouring forth is really coming forth from the Father and you are only the transfer agent or transparency. This brings about the greatest release in the entire human experience. The moment we release everybody, including our family, from obligations and realize, "You owe me nothing but love, for I and my Father are one," then we come to a realization in which we never give for human reason. We give only for the joy of sharing. In turn the other receives, not because of an obligation, but because of their awareness that it is a mutual flow and not the result of a human obligation. It is literally true that we are to owe no man anything but love, nor are we to hold anyone in obligation to us except through love—freewill shared.

Now all of this is dependent on your ability to realize the nature of the Tree of Life, and your oneness with it. Therefore, since you know this with your mind at least meditate on it as often as may be necessary for you. Make it the subject of a conscious meditation until the light breaks and you can say, "Ah, before I heard it with my ears, but now I know it in my Soul. Now I can live it." You see, this example of the tree of life and our oneness with it has undoubtedly been a part of my consciousness for a longer time than I can remember, but it was only in 1947 or 1948 when the word came out of my consciousness, "My conscious oneness with God constitutes my oneness with all spiritual being and idea." Only then did it actually register, because then I saw that the only tie I have to anyone, and the only bond there is between me and anyone else, is the bond that has arisen because all of us are one with the source. It makes no difference whether the relationship is man and wife, parent and child, next door neighbor or neighbor in its universal sense, every one of us has a spiritual bond with each other. Therefore, we owe it to each other to share with each other such as we have. With some our sharing will be silver and gold, with some our sharing will be other kindnesses, bestowings, coopera-tion; but with every one with whom we come in contact in life, and those we never meet, we have a spiritual bond.

Since each of us is individual in our expression of God, I draw unto me men and women throughout the world who are also interested in the spiritual path. Some are beginners on the path and some are already masters, but they come within my orbit, because that is my particular way of showing forth God. Another may be a musician, and he will draw unto himself whatever is necessary for his musical welfare, whether it be teachers or students or opportunities. Regardless of what your particular nature may be, lawyer, doctor, teacher, architect, designer, the realization of your oneness with your source and the realization that, thereby, you are one with all spiritual being and idea, will draw unto you everyone and everything necessary to your particular unfoldment.

In the human way, people go about demonstrating this differently. They advertise, or they go around looking up this person or that person, this thing or that thing. There is always effort and struggle, but in the spiritual way, harmony is accomplished without might and without power–just by *knowing* this truth.

There are, in The Infinite Way writings, many, many principles of life. No one of us can demonstrate all of them, but if we live with them and take them into meditation, those necessary for our experience will reveal themselves to us. If you should wonder why time is an element, let me show you this. Suppose you had been brought up in some church and taught that if you were good, God would reward you, and if you were not good according to some particular standard of the church, you would be punished. Then you open an Infinite Way book, and you read that "God is too pure to behold iniquity." Do you think for a moment that this would mean anything to you? No. No, it would take years and years of study before the realization would dawn that God does not reward or punish. That is why time is an element. How many years we read metaphysical literature and still reach out to God to do something for us or for someone else, as if God were not the all knowing mind and we had to direct God where to carry his blessings. No, it takes years of reading Infinite Way books before that image would get out of your mind and you could accept the higher concept.

You have seen how many years it has taken before you could pray without words and without thoughts. Why? Because it has been grounded in you that you had to have words and thoughts in order to go to God. Nothing could be further from the truth, and everyone must eventually learn this. Otherwise, you are not "knowing God aright."

Perhaps you have noticed in The Infinite Way literature how many times we repeat *omniscience, omnipotence, omnipresence.* Probably by now, when you see those words, you hurry past them because you think you know them—but of course, you really do not know them at all—you know only the words without the inner meaning. When the meaning dawns, then you can close your eyes because, by the time you know those three words, you have become a receptivity or transparency for God, and you then play no more a part in prayer than a pane of glass plays in letting sunshine into the room. In its nothingness, the pane of glass is a clear transparency.

Suppose there was a threat of danger to us here and now from any direction—an epidemic, a threatened war or any threatened danger, and we were to select someone to lead the prayer for us. Would that someone know what we needed or how God could save us? Of course not. No one could possibly know in what way God would answer our prayer to be saved. Therefore, do you not see that the effective prayer would be to close the eyes, open the ears, and just "let God in." Then God, in his mysterious way, would provide the cloud by day, or light by night, or open the Red Sea, or throw an invisible concrete shelter over this room. Do you see that prayer in its highest sense is not possible to a person who does not know the nature of God and the nature of man's relationship to God. Do you see that effective prayer can only be if I know that "Where God is I am," and it makes no difference if it is on a battlefield or in the midst of disease? I am one with God and therefore, by opening consciousness, God can come through. In the Master's revelation, he speaks of God as "the Father" and as "the Father within." The reason is that Hebrew scripture looked on God as Father, and evidently Jesus knew what this meant. None of us in this modern world knows what Jesus meant in speaking of God as Father. None of us has any idea what Father means because Father means nothing like a human father. And so we merely pay lip service when we speak of God as Father.

In the Orient, more especially in India, God is thought of as the Self of us, and always with a capital "S." And, since there is only one Self, that Self is the Self of each of us. It is very difficult to understand that, because the moment we say *self,* we think of our human identity and Self has no relationship to that. It is for this reason that it would be well if we would take into meditation the word *God,* and see if we do not receive a revelation of what God is. Not all of us will arrive at the same meaning, but we will all arrive at the same identity of nature. When Jesus received his higher revelation, it was shared only with his disciples, not with his followers. He spoke of God as "*I*" or "*I Am,*" and he said "I am the way,"[1] meaning God is the way, "I am the bread,"[2] meaning God is the bread. Many people have decided they were God and have written books to this effect. But Jesus did not mean this. He meant that *I* am God, and this is quite different.

It can be that you may receive a revelation within yourself that would absolutely clarify the "Self" or "The

Father within" or the "*I Am.*" If not, you would receive another revelation. You might not be able to reveal it, but you would have had the experience yourself, and you would then *know*.

The point of all this is this: Never forget that God *is*, and meditate and meditate on some relative subject until you discern your relationship to God, and thereby, your relationship to everybody and everything of a spiritual nature. This must be the basis for your spiritual development, because without this, the subject of prayer and the livingness of spiritual principles cannot be made plain to you.

It is only now that some people in the world are beginning to agree that the life revealed by Christ Jesus is the most practical way of living. Once a minister wrote a series of sermons on living according to the principles revealed by the Master. Perhaps you all know the book, *In His Steps* by The Reverend Sheldon. Possibly more copies of that book have been sold outside of Shakespeare or the Bible, but it has never been tried. People love to read it, but say that it is so impractical. We are beginning to see how practical it is if the intellectual reading or knowledge is followed by realization.

Yes, we must have the spiritual revelation or realization of oneness with God and all spiritual being and idea, but it cannot be made demonstrable by those who merely know it with their mind. Yet it becomes the most practical thing in the world when the truth of it has been spiritually discerned. Once you have an actual revelation or realization that "I and the Father are one. All that the Father hath is mine, and by reason of my oneness with God, I am one with everybody who is one with God," at that moment of realization you never again have an anxious thought about the future. Then you are actually living such passages as "Man shall not live by bread alone, but by every word that proceedeth out of the mouth of God."[3] From then on the only thought you take is to hear the next word of God, and then the next word of God, and then the next word of God, because every word of God is the bread and the meat and the wine and the water of life.

Do you not see that having faith in God will not do it for you? No, no, no. It has to be a realization or revelation within you. One such revelation opens up the whole Bible to you, opens up all spiritual truth to you, and then you find one truth after another coming into consciousness. Therefore, do not get impatient with yourself if you read or hear statements of spiritual truth and cannot demonstrate them. That is natural. It takes time for them to register in our consciousness, and it takes time to wipe out the past images of God and prayer with which we were brought up.

Be sure that at least one of your daily meditations will have something to do with the nature of God and the nature of prayer. Or take the passage "Man shall not live by bread alone but by every word that proceedeth out of the mouth of God." In your meditation you will ask your inner Self, "What does it mean—*bread?*" You will soon perceive that it means you do not live by any effect, you do not live by any outer things. No, they are the added things when once you hear the still small voice, the word of God. Then you will discover, and this is the great secret the world does not know, that it is literally a fact that when you begin to receive the Word of God within you, that it becomes the substance of every outer experience. It is a literal fact that every individual who comes to where the still small voice is heard, where the Word of God comes in, from then on you live by *that*–not by the outer forms. It is the still small voice, or the Word of God, that produces all these nice outer experiences. Intellectually you can agree that we live by the Word of God or by the still small voice, but you cannot demonstrate it intellectually. No, it takes you to that point where there is an inner response that says, "This is it," or it makes you feel that, "This is it."

Just remember that both the Christian faith and the Buddhist faith have for their foundation the loving of God and the loving of your neighbor as your self, and remember that one-half of the world believes this. Now look around the world and see how little it is lived. The reason is that the intellectual acceptance is not the answer. There must be this inner experience, this inner click or light or something that lets you feel that you have made the contact. From then on you cannot violate any brotherly edict or relationship. It would be impossible, because the spirit has taken over and is determining your life. There must be spiritual realization. Once you have made contact with this inner being which is our real being, it governs our conduct and our relationships in the outer world.

Someday you will go higher in realization than what we have brought out today. Someday, through your meditations, you will realize the true meaning of *I*. Then you will know yourself as *I*, and another new life will open to you. Jesus reserved that revelation for his disciples and none of them ever grasped it. Therefore, none of them ever lived it. Only John later received it in full, and then revealed it in full. Yes, we must realize our relationship to God and our relationship to each other.

THE INNER LIFE

March 24, 1963
The Halekulani Hotel
Honolulu, Hawaii

THE MASTER SPEAKS ABOUT PRAYING in secret, of
going into the inner sanctuary, not to be seen of men.
He speaks also about giving our benevolences in secret,
not to attract attention to ourselves as though we needed
the praise of men. Both these principles are especially
important in The Infinite Way. Outwardly we must not
seem to be more righteous, we must not seem to be
different from our next door neighbor, and yet in our
inner life we must be so different that you would think
we are people of two different worlds. Unlike this world,
we can no longer indulge in prejudice, bias, bigotry,
revenge, or the ambitions. Why? Because these are
barriers to spiritual progress, and the main barrier to
spiritual progress lies in the personal sense of the word
I. Whenever we say "I am healthy, I am wealthy, I am
grateful, I am loving, I am forgiving," we are indulging
in personal sense which is the barrier to our reaching
our ultimate goal.

Everyone on the spiritual path—and the path may be
of any name or nature—has the same goal: to reach the
place described by Paul, "I live yet not I, Christ liveth
my life," and ultimately to reach the high point of
realization announced by the Master, "Thou seeth me,

81

thou seeth the Father that sent me."[1] Let us forget the second revelation for now and let us go back to the first one, "I live yet not I, Christ liveth my life."[2] Do you not see that Christ is not "living my life" if I live by personal sense, by jealousies, bigotries, hatreds, revenge, animosities? No, all those human qualities leave no place for the Christ to live.

Suppose we have a human ambition of any name or nature, what chance would Christ have to live our lives? What chance would Christ have to live our lives if we look out at this world with personal sense, with judgement or criticism as to religion, race or color, or if in any way we try to make others subservient to us? No, this is the meaning of dying daily; more especially it is the meaning of dying to the personal sense of self. It means we can have no personal wishes, no personal desires—even good ones. This is the barrier. You are not dying to the personal sense of self, the personal sense of I if you have any good desires. No, your only desire must be to let consciousness live your life as your individual experience. Then, without these personal desires, we can really begin to act out that which is coming through us.

Last night I was very much interested in listening to Ed Sherman's television interview with Marlon Brando, because I have had the feeling that Marlon Brando had something the world was not seeing—and indeed I was right. He used forty-five minutes of that interview to show that his success has not been worthwhile and to say that it never can be, that it can only lose him his life and his Soul. Why? Because with that type of success there comes the world's adulation. When your success is purely in the realm of the material, you have nothing to offer the world and the only thing the world can want from you is to fulfill its own selfish interests. When you subdue that personal self to the degree that you are not indulging in personal feelings, those who are attracted to you for personal reasons would drift away and you would be left with those who are "like minded."

Marlon Brando said last night that he is completely lonely because people are interested only in the public figure. So it is with us. If we are presenting to the world an image purely of humanhood, we come up against the two opposites—good and evil. In other words, the world has an image of you based on what they think you are. So it is that the outer image we show forth should be no different than our neighbors. Then, what we have *inwardly* takes over and lives our lives. The world will never behold the Christ, but those spiritually drawn into our orbit will behold it. Then, instead of worldly success, you will find yourself not needing to isolate yourself like Greta Garbo and live away from the whole world. You will be able to be "in the world but not of it," and have good friends—sharing friends. Then life becomes a most beautiful and meaningful experience.

I had a letter this week from Mrs. Pinks, telling of her great joy in spending time with our students. You could see that wherever she went she found friends, human companionship—but at her level of consciousness—and it made for a very happy and joyous experience. All of our students have found the same thing.

What is the consciousness of the person who needs companionship? You will find that it is a consciousness of personal sense. There has been a desire to get, but not a desire to give and to share. There has been a desire to get attention, to pull rank as it were, and of course in the end that always ends up by a lack of companionship.

Enjoy the outer certainly, and its beauties, but always be able to go beyond and see what produces the outer effect. Then you find yourself with the companionship of those who have found the "inner life," not always on the same level, but remember that musicians and artists also make wonderful companions in the spiritual life. No one should ever be so ingrown that they are always thinking in terms of religion. In fact if we really want to be free souls, we must love not only the arts and the cultures but we must love industry. In other words, there is just as much fascination in Tolstoy as in Walt Whitman.

The main thing is that, whatever our life is, we do not live it to be seen of man because that is immediately putting on a false face and setting that up to be admired and acclaimed. Whatever our life is, it should be an internal one and, above all, it should be lived in the realization that whatever the outer form, it must be the product of an inner grace—an inner contact with the spirit—an inner communion.

The word *persona* itself means a mask—the mask of personality. If you look at a personality, you cannot see the person. No, we are looking for individuality. We are looking to consciousness to live our lives, not in a personal way but in an individual way, and show forth its qualities. You would be surprised how different you are from the mask you wanted the world to believe was you.

Now all of this has a bearing on the entire message that has been coming through during these many weeks, because it all relates to the one word *relationship*. If I know that whatever I am, I am because of my relationship to God, that I am heir of God to all of its character and qualities, then I am not building up my personal ego but I am deflating it.

You see ultimately we all want to be free of disease, lack and limitation, sin or sinful desires, but remember that we are not free yet except in a measure. We have not achieved it, but we can achieve it by realizing that our qualities are derived from our source, and then give them the opportunity to be expressed.

In the same way we all want to be free of material law. This is one of the reasons we are on the spiritual path; once we reach sixty-five humanly, we are on the downward path. We have seen enough to know that there is a way in which we can avoid suffering from every material claim that comes along; however, we cannot do it by ourselves. No, it can only be accomplished by making the transition to where we realize, "Consciousness lives my life." The only chance we have for immortality or eternality, or even for living out a perfectly normal span in good health and with healthy faculties, is if we can make the transition to where we are living not by bread alone but by every word of God that permeates our consciousness—when we can say, "I live not by bread alone but by the grace of God. Consciousness is my spiritual bread, my spiritual meat, my spiritual wine, my spiritual water, the Word of God. This is the ultimate of the spiritual life. If you can make the transition to where consciousness is living your life, it is then no longer subject to disease or sin or lack or limitation. You are now paying more attention to "storing up treasures in heaven," rather than to this world.

Business, politics, and government are really Christ-like activities if they can be lived by the Golden Rule. Some day this will be so. Do not make the mistake of believing that you can have the ambition to live this life through and in consciousness, and at the same time keep indulging that word "I" in its human sense. The two are contradictory to each other. The only form of dying daily is watching that word *I*. There was a woman who for years and years and years had a claim that would not yield, who had tried everything known to metaphysics and who said to me, "Isn't there some way?" I said, "I think so. Let us go until Monday without thinking of the word *I*." Immediately she responded with, "Oh, that is easy," but by Monday she called and said, "I am looking for you with a gun!" Surely, surely.

There is a whole series of quotations which can serve a good purpose as reminders. Whenever there seems to be a need of any kind, it will always appear as something external to us. If we can remember, "Man does not live by bread alone (effect), but by every word of God (truth),"[3] this breaks desire and we can say, "Oh, I do not need it. I am living by the word of God which is stored up in my consciousness." In the same way, when anything touches our lives which involves this personal sense of I, if we can be quick enough to remember, "I live yet not I, Christ liveth my life," this helps to break personal sense.

Do you know how the mistaken idea came about of sacrifice, self-abnegation and torture–the sack cloth and ashes of the Hebrews of old? The basis was a teaching originally revealed in Egypt, that of denying self. They thought that, by denying themselves of food and other necessities, this was sacrificing self. It was really self-righteousness and building up the self, and so you have people today who do not properly enjoy the things of life. They are only glorifying the ego; the more pain they endure, the greater the ego. The answer is to live completely in the realization that "I live yet not I, Christ liveth my life." Then any erroneous thing will disappear. When consciousness takes over, it eliminates any erroneous trait or desire that we may have, and it does it in its own way and in its own time. If we try to eliminate them ourselves, we are only being self-righteous. Normalcy, normalcy—whatever we are today in consciousness, that is where we are and that is where we live. Otherwise, we are indulging self. It is much more important than you know.

Because Christian Science, the Unity people and some of the New Thought people have been able to show forth healing in the last century, the whole world is becoming interested. What is not yet realized is that first their natures must change—there must be a purification or change of consciousness. Those who are now coming to spiritual healing in the orthodox churches are not going to have their healings until they have a change of consciousness. So many "selves" must first be given up. Consciousness must change, but no one in the external world can do it.

More and more the world is going to look to us, and so we must show forth that which we are proclaiming. If we disappoint the churches, they have no one else to turn to. There has to come into this world a remnant of people who are not quite living the human life, who are a bit above it, yet who are appearing in the world in the dress of the world and the life of the world. We have to be a body of people who worship nobody, who respect and honor and show gratitude to every pioneer on every spiritual path, former or present. If you cannot see the integrity that animated Mrs. Eddy, the Fillmores, and Ernest Holmes, then you cannot see the spiritual vision at all. If you cannot see and honor them *all,* you cannot honor the universal nature of the Christ. We are not seeing the universal nature of the Christ. If we do see it, we will have at least overcome the mistake of the church which says, "We had the *only* living example."

Potentially every one on the face of the globe is the Son of God. If they are not showing it forth, do not be too harsh or too critical. Remember that "The way is straight and narrow, and few there be that enter."[4] Yes, be glad and rejoice in the experience of those of the past or the present who are in some measure showing forth "Christ liveth my life." I say to you, if you cannot behold the Christ as a potentiality in every individual, then you are missing the way. You are personalizing when you say, consciously or otherwise, "No, the Christ only functions in *us.*"

Eventually for us as individuals, if we want to get beyond the state of responding to every claim that is in the wind, we must begin to live less with that word "I" and more with the idea that "Christ liveth my life." The remembrance of it will bring about a change in your life. You will not bring about a change, never forget that, but the remembrance will. It is not what you read or hear or study that is the miracle; it is your developed state of consciousness that is the miracle. By letting the Word of God occupy more and more of your attention, there will be a miracle, a transition. The old man dies and the new man is born. You cannot heal the old man or patch it up. Of course not, but by living with the truth you let the personal sense of I die, and then the new man or con-sciousness is reborn in you. The old has died and the new is born.

My Consciousness

March 31, 1963
Halekulani Hotel
Honolulu, Hawaii

I WAS VERY MUCH SURPRISED when I came in today and saw so many of you greeting me as if you knew me, because I am not the same fellow I was yesterday. Appearances must be very deceitful because the Joel of yesterday is gone. So this may not be a talk but a soliloquy. Up to yesterday I had been saying in my correspondence with some who know me very well that all of the inner unrest in me is because my song has not yet been sung—but my song now *has* been sung. Last night I sat up reading the chapters of the new book and it is all there, so from now on I am a retired gentleman of leisure! As you again go over the tapes and the writings of the past fifteen years, you too will find that it is all there. You just have to separate the metaphysics from the mysticism, and you will find that it is all there on both subjects.

To begin with, you note in the writings and in the recordings that attention is called over and over again to the statement that our principal task is to know the nature of God, "whom to know aright is life eternal." You cannot possibly realize how true this is until you catch the first glimpse of the nature of God, not intellectually but in your heart. Then you will be able to look up and out at this world and say, "No wonder you have had such horrible troubles all of these centuries because you have never known God."

No one would ever pray to God if they knew God or knew the nature of God, and I mean pray in the way in which orthodox people have been taught to pray and the way in which metaphysicians have been taught to treat. What makes it so difficult is that regardless of what our religious background has been or has not been, we still think of God consciously or subconsciously or unconsciously as if there were a God separate and apart from our own being. It is only when you realize, "God is my own consciousness" that all of a sudden the shoulders relax and you breathe a deep sigh and say, "Oh! There is no reason to take thought any more. My consciousness knows all about me and all about my needs."

Yes, consciousness knows about your needs, even on the physical level. What is it that is digesting your food, assimilating it, eliminating it? What is it? Certainly it is nothing separate and apart from you. Regardless of what you may be consciously thinking or doing, your body under normal circumstances keeps functioning and you are taking no conscious thought about it. What is doing it? You might say "It is God or nature." Yes, but these are really only words. It is your *consciousness* that is at work. As soon as you ate your lunch your consciousness went to work to digest it, assimilate it, and eventually eliminate it, and it uses many activities to accomplish this.

Do you realize that there is a part of you that is awake when you go to sleep, and awake before you awaken in the morning? This too is your consciousness. It operates to give you your sleep, your rest and then to awaken you. Do you know that the more effort you make to try to go to sleep, the more awake you would be? Yes, it is only when you "let go" and *let* whatever it is take over, that you go to sleep peacefully. You cannot go to sleep when your mind is working, but all this is merely on the physical level.

Consciousness operates to a far greater extent than that. Before you were born your consciousness was operating to bring you to earth or you could not have arrived here. Seeds did not bring you here; your consciousness produced the seeds which were used as a channel to bring you here. Consciousness functioned in pre-existence to see to it that you were born. Consciousness is intelligent; therefore, it did it for a reason. Since your parents did not know the reason for your birth, and you were too young to know it, it is rare indeed that any individual ever fulfills the purpose for which he or she came to earth. The fact that one has a destiny means nothing because the individual does not know it and neither do the parents.

So it is that consciousness is constantly struggling with us. Consciousness is knocking at the door of our temple and we are looking out at this world for fame or riches or healings. Why? There is only one reason: because we do not realize that consciousness is the secret word, not only consciousness but *My* consciousness. Why should I consult you as to what I should do–you–any you? Why not go within and consult *My* consciousness and then follow its leading and let it "feed me and clothe me and house me and go before me to make the crooked places straight." The answer is that we really do not know that *My* consciousness brought me to earth and gave me my particular qualities and talents and activities, and that *My* consciousness contains all of the elements necessary to my ultimate and complete fulfillment. What else could the Master have meant when he said, "The kingdom of God is within you?"[1]

At the height of mystical experience, we find that "I myself am that very consciousness," but in our present estate we may think of ourselves as Joel, Bill, or Mary. Ultimately we recognize that "*My* consciousness is omnipresence, omnipotence, omniscience." As long as there is a sense of Joel as a separate self, he may look to his consciousness. The great secret is that God is that consciousness, but it does not change the fact that it is *My* consciousness.

Certainly it is permissible to say *my* God. My God is very personal to me, but that does not change the truth that this same God is very personal to you. In the same way half a dozen children can say *my* mother, yet mother is personal to each of those six children. Yes, mother is personal to each of us, but we have no exclusive to *mother*. However, we do enjoy thinking of *my* mother or *my* father, and so we can think of *my* God, and so we can think of *my* consciousness. "God is *my* consciousness and *my* consciousness is *my* God." Therefore, I close *my* eyes to shut out the world and turn within and am receptive and responsive to *my* consciousness. "Because God is *my* consciousness, *my* consciousness is infinite. It is *that* consciousness that is responsible for my being here, and it is *that* consciousness that will accompany me when I leave this plane, going before me to prepare the way." If I have not seen that this is *my* consciousness, I will go out of this plane looking for a God somewhere. No, no, *my* consciousness is all there is to me. Then can you not see why "to know God aright is life eternal," is to know you have the secret of life? You would know then why Paul could say, "Neither life nor death can separate me from the love of God,"[2] and that love of God or life of God is the same thing. Life is love and love is life. Even on the human level this is so. Whatever degree of love there was between our parents was responsible for our being here. Love is the cause of life and the factor of life, so I will never be separated from love or life.

My work on earth could never be complete until that is so clearly revealed that those who find the message of The Infinite Way will find their God. I am so sure that in this new book it is so stated, I could even understand it myself. Likewise, my work could never be complete until it is made clear that God is not a power to be sought or used or needed, but rather that those things the world has sought to gain from God are omnipresent as activities of our own consciousness. The evils of the world that the world wants a God to destroy are not evils, because they are not power and they need no God to destroy them.

Even though you have not been one-hundred percent successful with this, and no one of us has been, you have had enough spiritual healings to know that the conditions of which you have been healed spiritually did not require a God or a doctor or a medicine. The times in which we have failed in this realization just means we have to go higher in consciousness until we attain such a consciousness of omnipotent omnipresence as the very nature of our own consciousness, that we will stop trying to be healed either by God, a doctor, or by medicine or by metaphysical treatments. Instead, we will *let* "nothingness become nothingness."

You see, these are the two major functions of The Infinite Way. The one under the heading of "the nature of error" is its metaphysics and the other, a revelation of "God as your consciousness" is the mysticism. It is the highest realm of mysticism when you realize, "*I* and consciousness are one and the same. . . . Thou seest *Me,* thou seest the consciousness that *I* am."

Only when you use our little exercise of examining yourself from your toenails up to the topmost hair of your head and discover that you are not in there, will you have the realization of your incorporeality. Yes, that is what makes you Melchizedek, that is the part of you that was never born and will never die. You realize it when you catch that glimpse of your incorporeality and realize that you are just using this body for your instrument just as you use your automobile to travel around in. Just as you get another automobile when you weary of your present one, so one day when this body has served its full purpose for you, you will throw it away and take a new one. Up until puberty your body had a purpose and you used it for that purpose. Afterward your body had the function of parenthood, and as long as that was necessary, it functioned as such. Your body in time outgrows that function, and then you will discover another use for the body. Now, each one of these bodies were different bodies, developing different organs; and so it is that your next body will have its functions, and if organs are required, it will develop them because your consciousness will fit your body to its needs, visibly or invisibly.

You know, I have been trying for thirty years to "sing this song." I think it is sung and stated so clearly and so simply that anyone ready for it will find it there. That does not mean that we have any right to expect the world to accept it tomorrow or next week, because you are already discovering that you cannot make even those near and dear to you accept it. This you must respect, and not try to make otherwise, because we are states and stages of consciousness. No, there is no use trying to thrust on us that for which we are not ready or that which we have outgrown.

I for one am of an unfortunate breed who tried to force education on youngsters and I do not seem to learn from my own failures. It seems I want every child to have an education. This is really stupid because Thomas Edison did not have an education, nor did Henry Ford nor Mrs. Eddy, and all got along fine. Perhaps education is not as important as we sometimes think it is, for if there is one thing we do know, it is that all the troubles in the world today were brought on by educated people. Yes, they all had degrees. Certainly education is all right, but for those whose natures are in that direction. We make such effort trying to live other people's lives because we judge them by our own standards. This we will not do when we realize that the consciousness of every individual is God, and then trust that consciousness to lead them in their individual pathways.

We are going to learn through this message that *consciousness* constitutes individual consciousness, and then we are going to let our shoulders drop, relax, and say, "Thank God!" Think of knowing that God is your own individual consciousness. Just think how you can now rest and relax and stop taking thought. Think how possible it is not to take anxious thought for tomorrow when we will have the same consciousness tomorrow that we have today. For those who know that God is their consciousness, there will be no age, decrepitude or wearing down of the mind and the intellect. No, the recognition of their own incorporeality will save them from it.

To know that I can turn within to my consciousness at any moment and find a message to give our classes is to acknowledge "God constitutes my consciousness"; and in turning to my consciousness, I am turning within to God for infinity. Then to know that *all* evil appearances are not power, sets me free.

When you look at television and your particular hero is in a very tight spot, just remember that he has a thirty-week contract and he has to be there for the next performance, and you will be so relieved! Yes, we do that all the time. As soon as our "hero" gets in trouble, we can say, "He has a contract." We need not worry or be concerned. Think, if you could look out at your problems and say, "I have a God here within me." Would it be possible to take anxious thought again? Certainly not, certainly not. Remember that, as long as you think of any form of evil as something needing a power to either eliminate it or overcome it, you will be in orthodoxy no matter what you claim for yourself.

Now, this leads to probably one of the highest Infinite Way revelations of mysticism: The revelation came to me first through the Master when he said, "Do not pray to be seen of men. . . do not do your alms to be seen of men."[3] If this secret ever reveals itself to you, you will understand that as long as you are in obedience to the spiritual law which is *love*, you will never have to depend on man whose breath is in his nostrils, nor will you ever have to advertise who you are or what you are because he says, "The Father that seeth in secret will reward you openly."[4] This we translate as, *"My* consciousness is the law and the activity of my being, and I need look to nothing else."

No, I do not have to appear before you with a title or a robe. Emerson puts it in our modern language: "What you are shrieks so loudly, I cannot hear what you are saying." What I am within myself is so apparent that if I tried to fool you with words, or if I tried to appear as somebody else, you would not believe it. What I *am,* not what I claim to be, I cannot hide from you. If I wear a mask, sooner or later you will see behind it. Therefore, I do not have to concern myself with praying before men—it will not fool them for long. What I *am*—that is what eventually comes forth into expression. Therefore, be still. Say nothing, claim nothing, but develop your Soul capacity by studying and meditating and let *it* speak for you. Rest assured you will be heard down in Africa, the Orient and in Europe, and you do not have to do anything about it yourself. Sit at home and let the world come to you, that part of the world which you can bless, and let the rest of the world go by. You do not need it. What I am trying to say is, "Go and tell no man."[5]

You have an inner consciousness that knows you, that *is* you. If your thoughts and actions are not in accord with your consciousness, you will have what the world calls punishment. If your thoughts and actions are in accord with your consciousness, you will have what the world calls reward. What it means is this: My system is geared to fresh, clear water, and it is not geared to dirty water. What I am talking about when using the term clear water is the word *love,* for love is what our consciousness is geared to and it is revealed by the Master in passages such as: "Do unto others as you would have others do unto you.[6] Love thy neighbor as thyself and God supremely."[7]

Yes, *love* is the word, and you can always tell whether you are dealing with clear water or dirty water by what manner of love you are expressing. If you are expressing impersonal and universal love, if you are holding no man in condemnation, if you are not dividing up black and yellow and brown, if your attitude toward God and man is one of love, if you are helping your fellow man, if impersonal love is motivating you, you are taking in clear water. Every act of yours which is an injustice is like taking poison into your system. Do not be surprised if it injures you.

Just as *consciousness* is your key word because God is your consciousness, so *love* is the next word. You are only in tune with the infinite, you are only one with God, when love is the animating principle of your existence: non-judgment, non-violence, no revenge, no punishing anyone—disciplining, yes, but not punishing. Truth is simpler than you believe. What made it seem so difficult is that the world brought you up in mythology and told you it was truth. That is why the Master said, "A child could receive it."[8]

I do not feel I want to teach any more! "The song has been sung," and those who are ready for it will have to learn the words and the music for themselves. I may teach, because I never learned to play games as a pastime. I cannot even travel because I have been there.

There remains just one thing: You cannot enter into this spiritual life until you have forgiven yourself your past. You have to just close your eyes, look back on the years and say, "Yes, they were just full of insults to God and to my fellow man. They were just full of sins, but now at last I know it and I know they were wrong. It may be that I can never right the particular wrongs to the particular people involved, but at least I can recognize the nature of my sins and be done with it. I have control over this minute and even succeeding minutes, and I can close my eyes now and be at peace because I am doing no injustice to anyone. I know now that I am my neighbor and my neighbor is me; I know now that we are one, and as long as I am one with my neighbor in this way, I am loving my neighbor and *thereby* I am loving God supremely."

Now it is easy to close the eyes and be at peace, because we are in tune with the infinite. Nothing is flowing through us but love, and love is life so nothing is flowing through us but life. When you are attuned to yourself, when you are no longer violating yourself, you are in tune with the infinite, you are one with God and with the spiritual identity of everyone on earth. Be at peace with your consciousness and you will be at peace with everyone and everything in the world. Be at peace with everyone and everything in the world by withdrawing malpractice, and you will be at one with the infinite.

Do you know what contribution we could make to the world if we could just reveal by our own living, that we are at peace with the world and thereby at peace with God and with every man? In that you have every remedy for every ill there is in the world; but, just as it can only function as you can accept and live it through a recognition of oneness, so must the world first accept it before they can begin to live it.

HEALING: TO KNOW GOD ARIGHT

April 7, 1963
Halekulani Hotel
Honolulu, Hawaii

RELIGION IS A THING of the heart, and yet without some specific knowledge that is an activity of the mind, it is impossible to complete the religious life. The religious life has nothing to do with the church. Sometimes it may be found in a church, but a church is not necessary for religion because there are religious people in places where there are no churches. Religion is of the heart, and no one is religious except as the heart moves them toward it. That is why it is impossible to give anyone religion or a religious instinct. This is something that takes place within an individual at a certain period of his or her "ripeness." Sometimes in the Orient people use that very word "ripeness," or they speak of an individual being ripe or not ripe, and always it means the same thing—ready for the spiritual experience.

Some can have this religious instinct and pursue it and yet not fulfill themselves, unless somewhere along the line certain aspects of the religious life are revealed in one way or another, which make it possible to attain illumination, attain fulfillment, attain that "peace that passeth understanding." One of these principles or facets you will quickly recognize. It is impossible to attain inner peace as long as you think of God as something

101

separate and apart from yourself. Even if you have God "close to you" or "near you" or "caring for you," you still have missed the mark because God is the Self of you, your very own inner being, your very consciousness. Until you come into that awareness, there will always be an uncertainty or doubt, an incomplete relaxing in God. In the same way, you can never attain God realization while God remains a power, while you are looking to God to do something to someone or something. No, you cannot then be in God and at-one with God because there is no such God. That false image of God would always be a barrier.

In The Infinite Way you will find that any word you have in mind or thought which describes God is just an image in your mind, a God that either you yourself have created or a God that someone else may have created for you. Never is this God. No, there is no such thing as any idea you can have of God being God, because always there remains a creation—not a creator. Then can you not see that until you have erased from your thought every image of God that you have ever entertained, every thought, every concept, you cannot come into an awareness of the one true God, "whom to know aright is life eternal"? You would just be going from image to image, concept to concept, never reaching God. Paul spoke of the "unknown God whom you ignorantly worship."[1] He was talking to the Hebrews who had received their concept of God as a great power, a mighty warrior. Paul knew this image was false because he had received his own awareness of God in a blinding flash within himself. God does reveal himself to man when man has that in his heart which drives him to religion, to the search for God, to the search for truth. God does

reveal himself when man learns to be still enough to let
God reveal himself as he did to Moses and others of the
Hebrew prophets–Jesus, John, Paul, and quite a few
others.

Then, to "know God aright" really means that you
must not go to man whose breath is in his nostrils for an
understanding of God. Even a man you revere can only
tell you of that which he has received within, and this is
of but relative value to you. So, in the end we must all be
"taught of God." In the end the only relationship will be
man's relationship with his Creator, the relationship of
oneness, the relationship of *attunement.*

We start with this: "Religion is of the heart," and cannot
be given to anyone except in proportion to their own
devotion and dedication to the search. On the other hand,
we will not complete our religious journey until in some
way or other two major revelations reach our consciousness. We in our work speak of the "nature of God," but I
notice that the Bishop of Woolwich says in his book, which
is causing such a furor in England, that as long as you have
a God "out there," you cannot arrive. He says that as long
as you have a God separate from yourself, you have no
God and you will have empty churches.

So, eventually, in order to attain "that mind which
was also in Christ Jesus" or at least some measure of it,
it becomes necessary to drop all images and concepts of
God and settle down until the kingdom of God within
yourself reveals itself and you come through experience–not reading or hearsay–to know beyond any
doubt that God is the divine being of you, your very life,
your very Soul, the Self of you.

Secondly, you cannot fully attain, not even in a
measure, until in some way *it* reveals itself to you that

God is not a power we can use—God is not a power that will destroy our enemies—God is not a power that will obey our will or heal our diseases or our sins. Of course not. How can you come into at-one-ment with a God whom you so little understand? You can watch this in your experience, or the experience of those who come to you, and note how long we postpone our own God experience. This is either because of ignorance or because we have been so conditioned that we cannot release God in the understanding that God is omniscience and knows all there is to be known, God is omnipotence and is not fighting with any other powers, and God is omnipresence and therefore does not have to be sent for. To be able to believe this enables the seeker to come into an atmosphere of receptivity.

You remember how many times it has been brought out in our work that prayer is an attitude and an altitude. Prayer is an attitude in the sense that if our attitude on the subject of prayer and God is not correct, we shut out the experience of God. Our attitude, of course you know: that we must accept a God of omnipotence, omniscience, omnipresence, and then be willing to be still and listen for the voice of God. Yes, let the voice of God utter itself, if you want to see the earth of error melt. This is an attitude, but it is also an altitude, because you are already in a high consciousness when you can mentally relinquish the hope and the belief that God is going to do something and be still enough to let the presence and the power of God flow. God is a power in this sense, that God maintains and sustains its spiritual kingdom, and the moment we drop our thought, the kingdom of God becomes our experience on earth. The kingdom of God comes to earth at any time that an individual can relinquish and release God in the full conviction and assurance, "God sent me forth into expression and I am God's responsibility, not mine." In that assurance I can rest and in that moment, in some measure, the kingdom of God comes to earth for me.

Oh! "A thousand may fall at my left, ten thousand may fall at my right, but they cannot come near my consciousness, or dwelling place, as long as I abide in the secret place of the most high.[2] Nothing can touch my inner being as long as I live, not by might or by power, not by taking thought for my life, not by battling evil or hoping God will destroy my enemies, but by God's grace. I rest in quietness and in confidence in the assurance that God is the creator, the maintainer and sustainer of all that is."

Since God's thoughts are not my thoughts, and since God's ways are not my ways, in what way could I possibly be qualified in giving my thoughts to God or believing that my thoughts have any weight with God? I doubt very much that any individual who has ever lived, is living now or will ever live, knows the thoughts of God or the ways of God. Therefore, the attitude and the altitude of prayer demands complete humility. "Nevertheless, not my will or desires or hopes or ambitions, but thine be done in me." Then listen. "Speak, Lord, thy servant heareth,"[3] so that God's thoughts may be revealed to us in action, in effect.

This subject is of vital importance at this moment. Many years ago a minister or priest of the Church of England, or the Episcopal Church of the United States, became so interested in the subject of spiritual healing that he determined to bring it into the churches; and, after great opposition and hard work, he did succeed in establishing spiritual healing in some of the churches. However, in those churches where it has been accepted, perhaps not more than ten percent of the congregations have accepted it. Since that time, evangelical healers have made somewhat of a start and have aroused an interest in spiritual healing, and now we find a greater interest in that subject in many of the protestant churches. In fact, there is a movement, even in the Hebrew church, of mental healing. It is for this reason that this subject becomes important at this time.

All of these people who are engaged in an activity of spiritual healing, the very sincere ones, the dedicated ones, are discovering that they have reached a point where they can go no further. The reason is, that they do not know the basic principle of spiritual healing, and until someone reveals it to them they are not going to find out. Most of the effort at spiritual healing is still done under the belief that it is God who heals disease, and of course you see the fallacy of this. If God could heal disease there would not be a person in the world with a disease, because God is no respecter of persons. In fact, in our work we have learned that it is often easier to heal someone in prison than the very righteous person. Certainly. Why? Because of their humility and their very lack of self-righteousness.

When you understand the cause of disease or the cause of sin, you have the answer to spiritual healing. God does not visit disease on anyone, and this you know. God does not cause anyone to be a sinner, nor does he at any time or for any reason cause death. No, no. The secret of sin and disease was revealed as far back as Adam and Eve. The world has refused to accept it, but we do.

When you accept the belief in two powers, the power of good and the power of evil, you are subject to this belief. Certainly the universal mind of man has accepted two powers, and it has tried to use God to destroy the evil powers—but of course, we know it has not worked and it cannot work. In proportion as you can accept within yourself, and only then by divine grace, that the omnipotence of God makes evil an impossibility, as you can look out at any condition of an erroneous nature and know that it is not of God and therefore has no power, then what happens? The images in the universal mind, of two powers, evaporate. To illustrate this, I have told you the story of the two men who were sitting in a bar and drinking heavily. One finally looked up at the other and said, "You have got to stop drinking. Your face is getting blurred." Certainly. But remember that even beauty is in the eye of the beholder, not in any person or thing.

You know from all you have witnessed, that spiritual healings take place in proportion as your practitioner or minister can say, "Thank God this is not ordained of God. It is but the arm of flesh or nothingness. It exists only because the universal mind of man is made up of two powers." There really are not two powers, and when the kingdom of God comes to your individual experience, you discover that the things or persons you feared as being so powerful have lost their power. Then you are at that state of consciousness where "the lamb will lie down with the lion."[4] One with God is a majority.

God's consciousness cannot be antagonistic to itself in any form, but are you sufficiently aware of this truth? Certainly God constitutes your consciousness, but God also constitutes the consciousness of the enemy, the animal, the beast. There can only be one consciousness out of which this universe has evolved. "In the beginning, God."[5] There was nothing else. Therefore, everything there is has evolved out of God-consciousness and *is* God-consciousness at various states or levels. Yes, God is the universal consciousness out of which the world has evolved. What causes difficulty is that you think that you are different than I am. All human experience is based on one law—self-preservation is the first law of nature—and this law is universally recognized. You see that none of this could happen if it were accepted that God is the consciousness or Soul of this world; and therefore, the consciousness which is mine is the consciousness which is yours. Then we could say with the Master: "Inasmuch as ye have done it unto the least of these my brethren, ye have done it unto me. Inasmuch as ye have not done it unto the least of these my brethren, ye have not done it unto me."[6] Why? Because you *are* me, and I *am* you. There is only one.

Why is it that love is the greatest factor in the religious life? Because *love* is God and God is *love*. Not human love—no, no. Human love enables you to give your child an education and ignore the child next door. No, the love which is God breaks down the barrier which is "me and thee" and says, "What I do unto you I do unto me, because the self of me is the self of you." Do you see how, in that consciousness, we can accept the Master's teaching of "forgive seventy times seven"[7] and "pray for your enemies."[8] Humans cannot do this. It is very difficult, but it is not difficult for any individual who has been touched by God, by the religious life, because he or she can then see that wrongs are committed through ignorance. Then he or she can say, "Forgive them, Father, they know not what they do."[9]

When faced by any form of sin, sickness, lack, or limitation, your first reaction must be, "This is an appearance and I know it–but it is not of God, and I know that too." In this inner assurance you can release yourself and you can settle back into an inner peace. You are learning to "judge not after appearances," and literally you find yourself as "the lamb who is lying down beside the lion." Humanly we are trained and we are conditioned to react to appearances, to fear some appearances. So it is that even when we have come to this way of life and believe we are on the path, we still have tremblings when faced by appearances. Even the Master was a rabbi and a spiritual light when he had the experience of the three temptations.

From the human standpoint it is natural to react to appearances, and no one has fully outgrown this. When temptations come to you to fear appearances, do not try to affirm yourself out of it. Instead, look straight at it and then acknowledge to yourself that you are being tempted by an appearance out of the carnal mind. God has never had an enemy, not at any time. We may fear we have enemies, we may fear the pictures out of the carnal mind, but remember that God is absolute omnipotence, omnipresence, omniscience, beside which there is nothing.

It is for this reason that as you approach healing work, it is important to remember that God is the consciousness out of which this entire universe is formed. Therefore, this consciousness of God which is "too pure to behold iniquity" contains nothing destructive to the consciousness which is God. Then you will know that it contains nothing destructive to man because man is the emanation of the consciousness of God. If

you live and move and have your being in the realization of God as consciousness, the *divine* consciousness,
you will be living in heaven, and then heaven will be
your Earth—the laws of heaven will function as your
laws of Earth. Only remember that if you ever accept
good and evil, if you believe for a moment that God has
any chosen people, you have lost it all. You must see
that behind this world of form, there is an invisible
consciousness from which all that exists is formed.
Think—think. Can you go so far as to accept God as the
consciousness of poison ivy? God is the universal, divine
consciousness and there can be no exceptions.

Now, one last point. You can lose the gift of spiritual
healing if you believe that spiritual healing is dependent
on what an individual does or does not do. The truth of
God is not dependent on what man does; it is dependent
on man's awareness. "Ye shall know the truth, and the
truth shall make you free."[10] Therefore, the moment you
see any human condition as being either punishable by
God, or not subject to God for any reason, you lose it.
You must be able to bring the saint and the sinner, the
enlightened or the ignorant, into the truth.

The greater the ability to relax in the assurance that
God really is omnipotence, omnipresence, omniscience,
the greater will be your healing capacity because the
attitude and the altitude of consciousness that relin-
quishes the belief in two powers is the activity that
restores harmony.

RESTING IN CONSCIOUSNESS

April 21, 1963
Halekulani Hotel
Honolulu, Hawaii

I THINK I AM GOING to make a suggestion. Mentally relax, and take the attitude that you are not going to try to understand what I will say. Instead, let my words be like seeds dropped into your consciousness and then let them mature. Get away from any mental efforts to understand, because I am going to try to say something that will not lend itself to being understood.

Since this is just another in the long series that we have had, every one of these Sunday talks has been leading up to this, so that it will be a cumulative effect. It is not as if each one of these Sunday talks were separate and by itself, but they form a continuity and this makes a cumulative effect. Today should be a logical follow up and, since what has gone before has formed the consciousness with which you hear today, it will be better if you relax, let my words fall on your ears, and then let happen whatever may. You will not lose anything by it even if you do not remember, because when the seeds break open and take root, the message will reveal itself to you as if you had never heard it before. It is like a student who just wrote me that, after studying for ten years, he had had the most wonderful revelation that there is no power in effect. To him it was as though it was an original revelation and that is good, because it came from within and established itself.

During all of these weeks, the nature of the message has been to reveal God as your individual consciousness. To be able to realize that enables you to sit back as comfortably, as joyously and confidently as a baby sitting on its mother's lap. You know the baby is in heaven because it has its only God right there. Its mother is that; mother is protection, food, clothing, housing, and she is love in every form. And so it is, to glimpse God as your consciousness enables you to relax and rest, and "live and move and have your being" in him. All the responsibility is upon him, and your only function is to rest, relax, enjoy, be. Keep the picture of that child in your thought and notice that it does not have to ask its mother for anything, nor does it need to tell its mother of its needs. It just relaxes, rests, and accepts. When you are resting in your consciousness, it is this same attitude and this same altitude. It's both an attitude and it is an altitude of consciousness that enables you to relax in your own consciousness, knowing that God is this consciousness and there is no other.

In this attitude and altitude you eventually hear your own consciousness saying to you, "*I* am your bread, *I* am your meat, *I* am your wine and your water. Fear not, *I* am with you. Be not afraid, it is *I*. *I* will never leave you nor forsake you," and you actually have the awareness that "As *I* was with Moses, moving out of Egypt and through the forty years of wilderness, so *I* am with you." Because we have so much temporary help from our practitioners and teachers we are rather impatient and feel that, because through their consciousness we can receive immediate help in many directions, we should also be lifted into heaven—preferably the day before yesterday. Please remember those forty years of Moses, and the long period in the wilderness of Elijah, and the three year ministry of the Master. Remember these, because the temporary help which you receive may make you more comfortable, may even help to hold you to the path, but it is the transition of your own consciousness that brings you inevitably "home in the Father's bosom."

The material sense into which you were born, and in which you lived for many, many years, is not going to yield itself, or give itself up or die quickly. Perhaps the biggest devil that you meet on your entire spiritual journey is the religious teaching you have had all your life that made you believe there was a God somewhere waiting to do something for you if only you could meet his terms. Yes, religious teachings are your biggest drawbacks and your biggest temptation because they have anchored your faith in a non-existent God and it is difficult to shake it.

Not only is it new to read in our literature that "God is not to be found in holy temples or in holy mountains, nor yet in Jerusalem," but you are beginning to hear now from many churches that the true God must be understood. You will not understand the true God until the day when, with no words and no thought, you can rest back as if upon a cloud, rest in your own consciousness, knowing this is why God is closer than breathing. This attainment makes it possible to cease looking to "man whose breath is in his nostrils" for anything; it makes it possible to cease looking to princes, or to powers, even to Gods. Rest back in your own consciousness and "take no thought for what ye shall eat, what ye shall drink or wherewithal ye shall be clothed."[1] Take no thought for the morrow. Forget about the past and live in the luxury of this *now*.

You cannot analyze what consciousness is, so there is no use letting your thought go to "What is consciousness?" No, because the only time you have it is when you are not thinking of it. Not only can consciousness not be seen, heard, tasted, touched, or smelled, but it cannot be understood through thought and the reasoning mind. This was the original meaning of the word *faith*, but the word faith became perverted when it became faith in something or someone, even God. That would place our faith in an external, a person or thing, an idea or concept, and that kind of faith is but the opposite end of the stick of fear of bombs, germs, or weather. There must be no faith in anything or anybody, just as there must be no fear of anything or anybody. Then you can rest back in the assurance of *is*.

The moment we have faith in a thing or a thought, an idea or concept, we have built a graven image and then we must bow down and worship it, whereas we must really have a great big nothingness. When we say faith, just remember that it must not be faith *in*. When we in The Infinite Way speak of freedom, we do not really mean freedom from anything, for this is the opposite of having faith in something or fear of something. Therefore, when we speak of freedom we mean freedom in spirit, freedom in being.

When you say I AM, you do not need any faith because I AM maintains itself. The minute you need a faith, you will want a faith to maintain I AM and I AM does not need any help. So you must understand the word *faith*, and you will understand it if you withdraw the word *in*. There can be no faith *in* anybody or anything, any concept or any idea, and this is the only real faith there is—the faith that trusts God to run his universe without help from man.

At first this type of faith calls for a degree of courage, because it means that as long as there are any negative or evil appearances, you must learn not to fear them and not to want help for them. Yes, even when you request help, the help you are asking for should be the help to attain faith and the help to have the courage to ignore the appearances. If you think you are asking for help to get rid of the appearance, you are in the human dream. "I shall not fear what mortal men shall do to me," indicates there are appearances or mortal men but that we are not fearing them. This ability to withdraw fear is in direct proportion to our faith, faith without the word *in*. Have you perceived what I meant when I said that this is a difficult message to give or to receive, and that you cannot receive it while trying to understand it? The mind cannot grasp the intangible.

There was a mystic who wrote a paper somewhere about the 14th century which was known as *The Cloud of Unknowing*. A very fine edition of it is published by the Julian Press. In this, the mystic is referring to that state of consciousness where you *know nothing*. Your mind is not ignorant, but it is at rest. It is just an *unknowing*, and resting in no words or thoughts. This is what we call our high Infinite Way prayer. When you can rest in an inner communion, without words and without thoughts, you have attained the cloud of unknowing.

You are now abiding in God; you are communing with the spirit within you, you are one with the saints and sages of all time. The Master must have meant this when he said, "Abide with me . . . "[2]–not me as a person but Christ-consciousness. The only way you can abide in Christ-consciousness is to abide without words or thoughts, or faith in anything or fear of anything. Being, just being. God is being my being, but the minute I have words and thoughts I have a God and me unless the words are being poured into me, rather than thought by me. "God's thoughts are not my thoughts"; therefore, you must stop taking thought in order to receive God's thoughts. "My ways are not your ways"[3]; you will never know my ways while you are trying to know your ways. Abide in me. Rest in receptivity.

The world has been fooled; it really has been de-stroyed by a belief that there is a God somewhere that can be prayed to, to do something to you or for you, a God you can petition, or a God who will reward you. All of this has been a deception from which we are all suffering. You will see how difficult the transition is when you sit down for a moment of peace and realize, "I have faith," and then you have to cut yourself short right there. In what? In whom? For what reason? You have to refuse to answer. Remember, there can be no faith in anyone or anything, just faith that Being is *being*. "Nothing can be added to me for I and the Father are already one, and all that the Father hath is already mine. The earth is the Lord's and the fullness thereof. Son, thou art ever with me and all that *I* have is thine." What more is there than this divine *is*?

When the temptation comes of two powers, you have to deny both the evil and the good in order to remain in faith. "There is neither good nor evil. There is only the *I* that I am, without qualities and the only quantity is infinity. Appearances are erroneous, whether they are good appearances or evil appearances, because the only reality is the *I* that *I* am." This eliminates a future tense, and when you are neither living in the past nor in the future, you are living in the *I* and as the *I*, that *I* am.

Hope, expectancy, and what the world calls faith–this all has to do with a future tense. God has no way of operating except now, a continuing now. "Now is the appointed time,"[4] and this takes away from us the false sense of faith that God will meet our rent on the first of the month. It helps us to realize that God does not operate in the future, because that takes away from us the false sense of expectancy and the false sense of faith it gives us. "*I* will never leave you nor forsake you,"[5] so omnipresent *I* is a continuing experience, but not one that begins tomorrow. If faith has anything to do with anything beyond this moment it is not faith at all.

You may say that you will not have fruit on your fruit trees until next month; but I say to you–if the law is not operating in your trees now, there never will be fruit. It is only the operation of the nowness that brings fruit in its season. It is what is happening in the tree *now* that determines the fruit to be on the tree. So it is, that which is taking place in our consciousness now determines the fruitage in our bodies, in our pocketbook, in our family, in our life–next week, next month, next year.

As I lift up that *I* in me and abide in that *I* in me, rest and relax in it, I am abiding in my consciousness. The nature of *I* is consciousness, and that consciousness is the substance of every activity of my daily life. It is the substance and activity of my health, supply, home. Resting back in your consciousness without words or thoughts, this is the attainment of faith. Faith is the ability to rest back in your own consciousness without words or thoughts, without fears or hopes. Just being, restfully being.

You can know positively when you are not praying. When you have any thought in your mind of this world, then you are not in prayer. When you can drop all concern for this world and abide without words or thoughts in your own inner consciousness, you are in prayer and you are in communion with the source of being. This takes God right out of your mind and compels you to give up idols, the idols which men have formed for themselves and called God.

In Isaiah there are passages that warn the people about having faith in chariots and horses and soldiers. Twenty-five centuries later we no longer have faith in these, but in airplanes and bombs. In other words we have just transferred faith from one thing to another thing, instead of having just pure faith. No faith *in,* no fear *of,* and no freedom *from.* That is saying it shortly and sweetly.

THE UNFOLDING MESSAGE:
SPIRITUAL POWER

April 28, 1963
Halekulani Hotel

I AM SURE that when we first come to a study of this nature most of us are thinking in terms of the benefit that we hope or expect to receive from it. In one way or another I think you will find it to be true that the object in seeking any kind of a teaching was self-benefit or self-improvement in some form. It would be an unusual occurrence for anyone to go out and look for a teaching that would benefit the world, because until consciousness has been spiritualized, our interests are concerned primarily with ourselves and our families.

You would be surprised how many parents, hearing of this work, unite and ask for help for a member of their family who has a handicap of some mental, physical, or moral nature–but when we write back and say, "It will take your cooperation and study," nothing further is heard from them. In other words, their interest does not go even that far beyond themselves. This surely does not happen one hundred per cent, but there are many who write for help and never again answer when they learn that cooperation on their part is necessary. What I am trying to say is that to a lesser or greater degree we are seeking our own benefit.

As we come to this present stage in your spiritual unfoldment, we must know by now that we of this generation are going to benefit less from this teaching than those of future generations. By comparison we will benefit by only a few grains. Why? Because the coming generations will be born into a higher consciousness, a higher spiritual level of consciousness than that into which we were born. They will not even be brought up as we were, with the idea of self-benefit. This is becoming apparent in many parts of the world where we have contacts, showing primarily the benefit that is coming to the world through the unfoldment of our consciousness and the amount of world work we are doing.

This world work is not giving any of us the amount of benefit it is giving to the world. Pope John has made innovations which, if the world were capable of understanding them, would startle the world–indicating the degree to which he is responsive to whatever spiritual truths are active in consciousness. In his 1963 Easter message the Pope has done something never before done in the Catholic Church, and I give you now a quotation from a newspaper article by Walter Lippmann:

"In reaching out beyond the clergy and the faithful of his own church to all men of good will, including the declared enemies of his church, the Pope has based the argument of his message not on revelation and the inspired teachings of the church, but upon a philosophical principle. 'One must never,' says the Pope, 'confuse error and a person who errs. . . . The person who errs is always and above all a human being, and he retains in every case his dignity as a human person, and he must be always regarded and treated in accordance with that lofty dignity. . . . Besides, in every human being there is a need that is congenital to his nature and never becomes extinguished, compelling him to break through the web of error and open his mind to the knowledge of truth.'

The Pope's Encyclical seems to have been timed after deciding that the "moment has arrived . . . when it is honorable and useful" to restate the old philosophy for the modern age."

Although this tears at the very foundation of their church, here is the "divinity of man" even when he is a sinner, and here is the principle of impersonalization. The Master gave us: "Who made me a judge over you?[1] . . . Neither do I condemn thee[2]. . . . Thy sins be forgiven thee[3]. . . . Father forgive them, they know not what they do."[4] In other words, he used the principle of impersonalization. Why then are we beginning to hear a Pope of the Catholic Church giving us the Infinite Way principle of impersonalization which certainly, religion-wise, has not been used on earth since the Master's day?

It is not coincidence that the Pope's Easter message was given approximately the same month in which Bishop Woolwich's paperback edition of *Honest To God* was released. Neither is it coincidental that the subject of spiritual healing is becoming such an important subject in the churches today. Behind these, two things must be remembered: In the first place, the very fact that we have an Infinite Way must indicate that the time has come on earth for this transition in consciousness. Remember this–that we are by no means the creator of these world-wide conditions. No, it is all determined by transitional consciousness, and we are but the instruments for it. Secondly, as part of The Infinite Way message, we have almost from the beginning given the instruction that world work must be conducted. As a result, groups have been formed all over the world as a part of what is going on "behind the scenes" to bring to light the Spiritual Age.

In the earliest years of this century, the electrical wizard Steinmetz said the secret of spiritual power would be revealed in this century. Thousands of years ago it was learned that with the end of the Piscean Age, there would be the ushering in of the Spiritual Age. The Piscean Age has given us the great scientific discoveries and inventions, and it has given us the letter of truth. The Spiritual Age will give us the spiritual life of consciousness. By the letter of truth we include statements or quotations with which most of us were brought up, such as "Honesty is the best policy" and the Ten Commandments. In other words, because our natural human nature is completely enveloped in ourselves, honesty and integrity is not natural to us because it is not natural to human consciousness. All of our religions are aimed at teaching us to be good because it is not natural for human beings to be good. Instead, self-preservation is the first law of human nature no matter who gets hurt. We even had to be told to love our fathers and mothers—even that is not natural to human beings, and so it had to be drilled into us.

You feel the difference when you come in contact with people whom you would define as "good Christians." To them it is normal and natural to "love thy neighbor as thyself," for they have evolved out of that early state. Yes, there are many who have come to that place in their development; but stop for a minute: think about Christian church teachings, then take your mind back to the New Testament, and think of the passages of the Master. Then you will know what I mean by a Christian-consciousness. This is the consciousness that normally and naturally prays for the enemy and forgives seventy times seven. This consciousness has no trace of an eye for an eye, and a tooth for a tooth, nor has this consciousness a trace of revenge or punishment. This is a Christian-consciousness. As long as we have the Ten Commandments or the Sermon on the Mount, we still have the Piscean Age or the letter of truth.

In The Infinite Way we move from the Piscean Age to the Spiritual Age at any moment that our meditations contain no thought of self-improvement or self-betterment. This movement is made when our consciousness is open purely to receive the awareness of the indwelling Christ, but not for a reason. It is very much like the point brought up last Sunday on faith. We do not really have faith as long as we think in terms of faith *in*. It is a state of ignorance even to have faith in God, because that is based on the belief that there is a God who can do something and there is no such God. Pure faith is not ignorance but enlightenment as long as it is not faith *in* any thing. If at any moment we turn to God to fulfill a desire, even a good one, we are not yet in spiritual consciousness because spiritual consciousness is a consciousness that gives no power to anything or anybody. Therefore, this consciousness does not need a God-power. This is not doing away with God. It is a recognition that God *is*.

So it is that the real spiritual consciousness is the one that abides in the word and rests in the word. "They have only the arm of flesh.[5] And they rested in his word." They did nothing further than "know the truth," and then rest. "They have only the arm of flesh." This was what Christ Jesus was trying to teach when he said, "Resist not evil"[6] and "Put up thy sword."[7] Progress into the spiritual consciousness is a complete relaxing in God *is*. This consciousness is the God-presence and the God-power. The consciousness that does not fear external powers *is* the spiritual power. "In quietness and in confidence shall be my strength[8]. . . . Not by might nor by power."[9] A complete relaxing from power, or desiring power, or trying to contact power, leaves you in a state of *is* and this is spiritual power released.

As long as there are people fighting evil conditions, there will be evil conditions to fight because the mind believing in two powers is creating conditions of good and evil. These evil powers cease to be when you cease fighting them, when you withdraw power from them. "Pilate, thou couldest have no power over me unless it came from God!"[10] You see, our world work is not fighting evil people or evil conditions. To the contrary, it is withdrawing power from them and it is making of ourselves clear transparencies so the Christ can flow through our consciousness and dissolve the pictures of sense.

It is universal human consciousness that constitutes the belief in two powers and thereby creates the conditions in the world. It is an individual's recognition of the non-power of this universal carnal mind and its pictures that releases the Christ into human experience. Every time that we have an experience that proves the non-power of something that the world gives power to, we are not only lessening the universal belief, but we are making it possible for somebody somewhere to pick up what we have loosed in consciousness.

Do you realize that the fifty or sixty thousand of us who are studying The Infinite Way, and who in some degree are impersonalizing, are responsible for others picking up that very principle because there is only one consciousness? Many who read this are not going to believe that it was in the Pope's message, but the mere fact that it is there is proof that this principle of impersonalization is loosed in consciousness, and if we continue our work, it is inevitable that the principle will show up in one place and then in another. The children of future generations will wonder how anyone ever personalized because, when you perceive this, you will realize it really is a relic of the Dark Ages. Once you begin to perceive that the only power there is, is the power of your own consciousness, how then would it be possible to fear what mortal man can do to you? How can we speak of omnipotent omnipresence, and at the same time be subject to universal beliefs? In our writings we have the truth of this, but in our daily lives we have not even begun to scratch the surface of living it.

The only reason anyone suffers from anything is because of a universal malpractice. All the theories and beliefs of a mental or material nature comprise the carnal mind, and whatever we suffer from is the degree to which we have not realized the principles in our writings. All evil is the projection of the carnal mind, which is the belief in two powers, and our recognition of non-power is the antidote; our degree of awareness of this non-power is the measure of our progress into spiritual consciousness.

The development of spiritual consciousness begins when we release all concepts of God in the recognition that the *I* that is seeking God is God. Then, when we sit

down in meditation, we take no thought for any condition of the world or any person of the world and become
a state of receptivity as if to hear that still small voice.
"Who convinceth me of sin?[11] Who convinceth me of any
presence or power but the one which *I am*?" Watch this,
that you do not have "one" separate and apart from I
AM, or you are then out of focus. Watch that you do not
have concepts of God, not even up there in your mind,
because this is a projection of an image, which is idolatry.
Become free of all concepts of God so you can truthfully
say inwardly, "I do not have a God." This brings you
back to the subject of what we call higher prayer, which
is without words and without thoughts, but you cannot
pray this way while you are expecting something material
of prayer. If you want to patch up this dream, then you
will need lots of words and thoughts. The more these
Infinite Way principles are repeated back to you by
people outside of The Infinite Way, the more you will
know that our work is reaching human consciousness.

Probably all of the people in the churches who are
engaged in world-wide prayer activity are praying for
peace on earth. You know they must fail, because peace
on earth cannot be—not with man's consciousness as it is
now. That is why in our world work we are not asking
for peace. What good would peace be as long as consciousness remains at the human level? No, it would
only mean an interval between wars. Man's consciousness must change. Therefore, our prayers should never
be for peace or temporary good. World prayer should
be the realization of the non-power of the carnal mind
and the nature of God as individual consciousness.
When you can realize these two, you change consciousness; you even have a Catholic Pope directing his

message to the people outside the Catholic Church for the first time in the history of the world.

Those of us who still have problems might just as well realize that our consciousness is not yielding sufficiently. What good is it to try to change outer conditions? No, change consciousness first, and then the harmonious conditions will follow. So, when we are doing our world work, let us hold to our two major principles that God constitutes individual consciousness, and the carnal mind is not power but is the arm of flesh or nothingness. Then you will see people's consciousness changing, and you will see children born into a higher state of consciousness. They will be born into the consciousness we have loosed here on earth. Spiritual consciousness is one that is not warring with evil, nor is it recognizing spiritual power that can be used. It is recognizing spiritual power as a divine grace. Think a great deal on the term *spiritual power,* and try to get a clearer recognition of it. Remember that it is not a power over any thing or anybody–it is not a power to be used. Spiritual power is a state of grace.

Helpful quotations are the Master's "My peace I give unto thee, not as the world giveth, but my peace,"[12] and "My kingdom is not of this world."[13] Think of the mistake that the Hebrews made in expecting the Messiah to be a temporal power, expecting him to free them from Rome and from the Sanhedrin, their church. Christ is not a temporal power, spiritual power is not a temporal power. Check yourself to see how often you are trying to make the power of the Christ a temporal power. Seeing the mistake you are making will lift you into spiritual power.

THE WORD BECOMES FLESH

May 5, 1963
Halekulani Hotel
Honolulu, Hawaii

LAST WEEK IT WAS BROUGHT OUT that when we come to a spiritual teaching, we are really seeking for our own benefit. At first we do not think of our spiritual studies as having anything to do with the world; we are concerned only with what benefits we or our families will receive. This of course is natural and right because, until we ourselves have attained, we have nothing to give or to offer. If we do attain enlightenment, we soon find that it was not given to us for ourselves but for some God purpose. Be assured that whatever you receive from God is never given to you or for your benefit, because God is not so limited or so personal that he would give you a "pearl" just to wear on your finger. No, you will soon discover that whatever gift or grace you receive from God is given to you for a more universal purpose.

I will take you back to the day that started me on the spiritual path. It was a day of threatened war that brought to my thought, "Where is God?" I was not religious, remember, but everyone has heard of God and so where in this danger, I wondered, is God? This started a trend of thought that years later ended with the realization, revelation perhaps, that there is no God in the world and there never has been–that God is only where God is realized, and nowhere else. In other

words, where was God during all the centuries of the
Hebrews' slavery under Pharaoh? Certainly of all people
they prayed the hardest, but there was no God to take
them out of the horrors of life under Pharaoh. Yet, when
Moses attained his realization of God, that is where God
entered the scene. In other words, it entered through the
consciousness of Moses. Remember that Moses was not
seeking God for the Hebrews' sake. No, his was the cry
that is in the hearts of so many people: "Oh God, oh
God, where art thou?" But you notice that, almost as
quickly as he received his illumination, he was given a
mission to take the people out of Egypt. Moses knew his
lacks and limitations, but all were erased when he
realized, "The government is on his shoulders."[1]

No one should ever say the responsibility is on God's
shoulders until they have the conscious awareness of the
presence, or they will be very disappointed. I skip over
many generations in a moment to ask, "Where was God
among the Hebrews prior to the Master's mission?"
Certainly God was omnipresent, omnipotent, omniscient, but since this was not realized in the consciousness
of an individual, it was not in expression or in action.
Therefore, the Hebrews were again slaves–this time
double slaves, not only of Caesar but of their own
Sanhedrin. They were the victims of every possible false
religious teaching, and yet God did nothing about it.
With the coming of a God-realized man, the Master,
God does enter the scene and we witness a new era
ushered in which lasted three hundred years, in which
men really learned the nature of freedom, health,
harmony, and brotherly love, in which there was
"neither Jew nor Greek, neither bond nor free."[2]

It was shown to me that all of the praying that goes
on in this world is a waste of time and energy. All of the

prayer groups are just so much ignorance and superstition. They never stopped an epidemic or a war, nor did they prevent one starting. They cried "Peace, peace," where there is no peace. I am going to tell you why their prayers are wasted. They do not really mean them; they are honest only as far as their ignorance and superstition permits. When you pray for peace, you must be willing to give peace. If you are praying for peace and freedom and you want the intercession of God, you have to want peace and freedom for everyone everywhere. In other words, there must be peace on God's terms, not on our terms. There has to be a preparation for prayer, and this must consist of self-purification so we do not pray for "my peace" or "my life" or "my country." The laws of God are universal. God does not enter the world to answer prayer except through spiritualized consciousness, the consciousness of those who have attained spiritual awareness. So it is you must always have a Moses, an Elijah, an Elisha, a Jesus, John, or Paul. There must be a clear transparency through which God can work. There is success in spiritual healing only when there are those who know that the healing grace can not operate unless one has lost the sense of self. The greater the loss of the sense of self, the greater the healings.

After my first spiritual experience, the healing work began. I could and did bring about healings of a mental, physical, moral, and financial nature. I had not received any instruction, so I did not know how to impart spiritual wisdom to anyone. Soon instruction came, and it was to the effect that the secret of bringing God into individual experience—the secret of spiritual attainment—was in meditation and in no other way.

Now, meditation was a strange word to me and I knew nothing about it. When I went to investigate, I found no one else who knew anything about it, and in the libraries, I discovered that literature on meditation was almost non-existent. There were a few works from the Oriental standpoint, and a few pamphlets by Unity, but there was no instruction on meditation that could be adopted to Occidental use. The secret was lost in the Orient one-hundred and fifty years ago, even though there are a few teachers and mystics who know meditation; and so I had to begin with myself and instruct myself, or rather be instructed from within. You can see that I was not thinking in terms of the world, but in terms of myself and perhaps passing it on to those who came to me for healings. Who could have dreamed at that time that there was a world waiting to open itself to meditation?

Today we have arrived at a place where The Infinite Way writings are to be found on the book stalls of almost every protestant church, and they are being read and used. It is a literature that is being utilized on a worldwide basis, and is now being published in other languages. As the world becomes more and more conscious of meditation, more and more people will be bringing the presence of God into expression and will be proving that once the inner contact is established, "The Word becomes flesh."[3] In other words, the inner contact with God becomes the outer manifestation of human harmony, and the principle to be revealed is: "The Word becomes flesh," God becomes form, spirit becomes tangible as manifested form. And so, because of the inner, we have harmony without. It is not that God creates or sends the outer good—that is a fallacy. God appears *as* the good. It was very evident to me that, while sitting in meditation in my home or office with no promotion or advertising, God appeared to me as an overflow of patients and students, and an overflow of money with which to carry out the activity. "The Word becomes flesh."

Unless God becomes as real to you as I am real to you sitting here in this chair, you are missing the mark. If God remains an abstraction, or a hope or a faith, you are lost. No one is quite as lost as those who "have faith" in God, because there is no such God. God is spirit and the kingdom of God is within you, not in holy mountains or holy temples or merely in holy teachers. You must find God at the center of your being and experience God there. So, when God reveals itself to one person, see what it does to a whole world. The world is discovering through the teaching of meditation, that you have to "pray in secret" and leave the world outside. Get inside your own being until God reveals itself to you and you hear, "Be not afraid, it is *I. I* am closer than breathing." When this happens to you, do not think you are going to be able to congratulate yourself and say you are going to have an easy life. Certainly not. When the Christ comes to your consciousness, it is going to send you out on a mission somewhere, not to rest at home in retired peace.

Later on, perhaps four or five years after the beginning of my healing ministry, I learned that every metaphysical healing teaching in the world is based on a misconception, the misconception that the source of whatever evil is affecting you is within yourself and that you are responsible for the errors in your experience. This is the same mistake made by the psychologists today—never does this heal anything. One of the major secrets of healing work was given me then, and that was *impersonalization.* It was shown me how all error of any nature has its origin in the carnal mind or mortal mind.

It has nothing to do with you or me–nothing. Once we learn that the origin of all evil is impersonal, we begin to separate it from this world, and we begin to witness healings on a real basis. Carnal mind or mortal mind is really not a mind, but a universal belief in two powers; and as long as individuals look to a God to overcome evil, they will never be free.

Here again you have a principle that is being adopted more and more by practitioners and, as I read to you last week, the Pope felt called upon to revive this teaching of impersonalization. Do you see the far-reaching effect, when an individual reveals a principle? The principle was not given to me or for my patients, only that it might become worldwide. Certainly I had to go through years denying it; but again, another revelation came to my rescue: never to advertise, publicize, or promote. Sit and keep your principle in your consciousness and let those in the world come to you as they are ready. Then you carry on your work without opposition, and the truth you are willing to impart transmits itself by subliminal perception. In other words you have to live with it until it establishes itself.

In bringing the experience of pure meditation to yourself, remember that it is legitimate to think thoughts for a few minutes in what we call contemplative meditation. Silently we acknowledge the omnipresence, omnipotence, and omniscience of God, but this should only last for five or ten minutes, until you arrive at pure meditation which has no words and no thoughts. You will not attain pure meditation as long as words and thoughts are in your mind. Contemplation is permissible only as the introduction. But then we enter the phase of "Speak Lord, thy servant heareth,"[4] and we listen.

Meditation is only during that period where there are no words and no thoughts. Why? God's thoughts are not your thoughts, and you cannot receive God's thoughts while you are thinking. Also, your thoughts are not power.

It really shocked the metaphysical world when it was revealed in my writings that thought is not power. The power of healing, of supplying, of having happy relationships does not lie in your "right thinking," nor is it prevented by "wrong thinking." The power of God's grace is in God's thoughts coming into the consciousness of man. The individual successfully engaged in healing work is humble enough to realize, "Thank God I know that my thoughts are not power, but God's thoughts are, and when thy voice enters my consciousness the lame must walk." The metaphysical world was shocked, but it has witnessed the worldwide success of "thought is not power."

Then the revelation was given that prayer is not the words we think or voice—not even truths. Prayer is *hearing* God. That was one of the radical principles that did not receive widespread acceptance. I was very happy to find the principle in the Bishop of Woolwich's book, so now we have a church authority for it going all over the world. The very moment a Moses receives God in consciousness, he not only has a message but he has a power—the power of God working through him. Until that moment Moses was only a shepherd, nothing else. Afterward he had a mission and all that went with it. Saul of Tarsus was only a Hebrew scholar, but when the light struck him, he became a missionary who could support seven churches. "The Word becomes flesh." It is not that the Word of God gives anybody anything.

No, the Word becomes form. And, when you have the God experience, whatever form is needed appears. Think how terrible it would be if you went into prayer and asked for something. When you go into prayer without words or thoughts, "Speak, Lord, thy servant heareth," and the spirit touches you, the message, the mission, supply, and everything necessary to fulfillment appears.

That is the meaning of "In thy presence is fulfillment." There must be the experience; without the experience, this message would be only a philosophy. A living truth is something to be lived and proven, and this is not a living message until the experience takes place. Whether it is a Moses on the mountaintop who actually experiences God, or a Paul on the road to Damascus, or a John who received his revelation directly from Christ—the message will reach the world. Even if it took place 2500 years ago, the Word can never pass away. The Word of Christ slept for 1700 years, but it now comes alive again as only truth can and will.

Can truth die again? No, because this is the first time that truth has not been organized or promoted. Any time that this work is organized, the message must die. The only way a spiritual message can "live" is when someone receives it and says, "Go without purse or scrip," and those who succeed are those who have caught the vision. The moment you send someone out with this message without the healing power, he cannot succeed. You see I am always coming back to Moses, Jesus, John, and Paul. The moment the experience touches you, the message is yours by grace, and all those receptive will be led to you. You do not have to go out and seek them. It is legitimate for people to seek loaves and fishes at first.

We all did, but for how long? That is what is important. Remember always, when you have your mountaintop experience or realization, that you lock it up inside of yourself and "tell no man." We know nothing of Moses, how long it was between his illumination and the leading of his people out of slavery, but we do know that with Paul it was nine years before he went out on his first missionary work. The Christ must be taken into some secret and sacred place within you and hidden until it is strong enough. Only with your teacher do you share it. When you receive your light you hide it until it is so rooted and grounded in you that it finally comes out, first in little ways, and finally into a full mission.

Another facet of our teaching now appears in the Bishop of Woolwich's book: that no thought or idea or concept of God you can entertain is God. So, you might as well give up all your thoughts about God. They are only words and they will never produce any miracles for you. No word is ever God and no thought is ever God. What are you to do? Give up your words and your thoughts, and then you will be in the atmosphere of "God itself is in the midst of me," but it is not a word or a thought. "If you could name it, that is not it." Stop naming.

We read and we hear so often that God is love, and then people take that statement into their mind and they think they have God. They just have a shadow in their mind. God is an act. When a spontaneous act of love proceeds out of your consciousness, God has been there. Love is an act, a deed in a universal sense. The Master has instructed us that we do not profit from praying for our friends. God knows no difference between friends and enemies—they are one. When you do something loving for a friend or a relative, this can very well be personal sense; but when spontaneously an act of love takes place for the benefit of a stranger or the enemy, this is God acting through you. You have let yourself become an instrument. This is why there are so many stories of the stranger coming to the gate, and turning out to be the Christ. It was the *serving* of the stranger that made the stranger the Christ.

You can hasten the experience of God realization by increasing the number of your daily meditations, remembering that a minute or two or more is enough. Open consciousness for the experience, even if nothing seems to happen. Eventually something will happen and the more times you expose yourself, the sooner you will bring it to yourself. Remember the importance of inviting God without words or thoughts, and being still to listen. If you are a beginner you will usually find it necessary to spend quite a long time with books like *Practicing the Presence, The Art of Meditation,* and *The Contemplative Life,* because these books bring you into an inner atmosphere in which you can settle down and be still.

During this past week I have read the May *Letter* not less than ten to twelve times, and I am continually reading *The Contemplative Life.* Each time, an inner peace settles down over me. When you are in that inner stillness and peace, "In a moment that ye know not, the bridegroom cometh."[5] Our reading should be aimed at this inner stillness. When you have an inner experience, you have "opened out a way for the imprisoned splendor to escape" and this becomes a law of harmony to you, your mind, your body, your home, your business, and to any receptive member of your family. As you get into a teaching practice, it becomes a law unto your students and patients. They reflect the quiet and the harmony you have attained. Your attained consciousness becomes the law of those within your consciousness, just as the consciousness of Moses became the law of freedom to the Hebrews and the consciousness of the Master became the law of freedom and harmony to his followers. "There am *I* in the midst of you."[6] Here is a statement that is worthless as a quotation. It is only when the experience takes place that the assurance is given you that "*I* am in the midst of you."

One of the most sublime passages in Scripture is "Be not afraid, it is *I*."[7] As a passage it is quite meaningless. Only when it becomes an experience can you "walk through the flames." I try not to lay down laws, but I have no hesitancy in sharing my personal experience and so I will say this to you: Never give truths of this nature to people unless they have shown their readiness for it by their dedication. The world will tear you to ribbons. When you have people interested in learning truth, give it to them as simply and as gently as possible, but do not start anyone on this message unless you do as I do. I give this only to those who show their readiness by their dedication; and when it is published in books I am always safe because I know they are not going to understand it. No, they skim over the surface and do not know what they have read.

WE ARE GUESTS OF LIFE

May 12, 1963
Princess Kailani Hotel
Honolulu, Hawaii

THERE IS A PRINCIPLE OF LIFE not yet known to the world, but known to you through your studies of The Infinite Way. The effects of this principle have been known throughout all known time, but the principle itself has not been known. It is for this reason that, in reading history, you read of events that took place but you have no knowledge of what brought them about or how they came into being. An illustration of that is our Civil War. If you were to read the history books, you would believe that somebody so loved the Negro race that they were willing to die to free them, and somebody will point to Harriet Beecher Stowe and her *Uncle Tom's Cabin.* Others will tell you of the commercial war between New England and the Southern States and none of these are mindful of the fact that, starting with the Magna Carta of England on through the French, American, and Brazilian revolutions, consciousness had been aroused to this idea of freedom, liberty, equality, and justice. All of these events were but the out-picturing of a changed state of consciousness. You can go all the way back to Greece, the first country that ever experimented with the idea of freedom, and find how this longing in consciousness spread as if by subliminal perception and brought about the wars and agreements culminating in more and more freedom for people.

The selfishness of the average human being who has been brought up on the theory that "self preservation is the first law of human nature" is such that each tries to struggle to hold onto what he has, and perhaps get a little bit more. Therefore, the process of consciousness coming into expression in changing forms–better forms–is a slow one; and in the field of religion, the world has been more backward than in any other field of human experience. Until after the middle of the 19th century, religion was a total state of darkness and ignorance, almost without even the tiniest of lights. In the middle of the 19th century, some of the Oriental scriptures were translated into English and German and, later, into French. They took root in England and in Germany and the first spiritual light began to dawn. In the United States this never took root, although it was given to the States by Ralph Waldo Emerson in his essays, all of which were translations of Oriental scripture. There was the period of the Transcendentalists in New England and the start of Christian Science and Unity. All of this was the light casting its shadow into visibility and prophesying things to come.

The Infinite Way is the first of the purely mystical teachings of modern days, and with it we see that it also is "enlightened consciousness appearing in human experience as the consciousness of those individuals ready for it." An activity of God–truth revealing itself in human consciousness–is not limited to the few who write or read its message. Actually, we are but transparencies through which this message must reach the entire world. It was Victor Hugo who said, "Nothing is so powerful as an idea whose time has come," and it is true.

Impossible as it may seem, when an automobile is born in the consciousness of a gas-meter reader just barely able to support a wife, he receives all the money necessary to form the Ford Motor Company. So it is with an idea. If it is born ahead of time, it dies. If it is born at the right time, it carries with it all that is necessary for its fulfillment. As one of its foundational points, the message of The Infinite Way has no membership, no dues, no binding of anyone to itself—not only setting everyone free but maintaining their freedom. This now spreads further until we witness Bishop Pike of the Episcopal Church setting many of his people free of their superstition and ignorance, and Bishop Woolwich of England setting many more thousands free. And now comes word that, when the meeting called by Pope John comes to order this fall, it will be announced: "An endorsement of universal and complete religious liberty for all persons so that each man has the right to choose his own religion or even to have none at all. That both individuals and society should leave each one free to accept and fulfill his obligation to teach exclusively by the use of his own free will." I am sure you realize what a tremendous thing that is, especially in view of the Pope's statement in his Easter message that all evil must be impersonalized in accordance with an ancient philosophy.

To further show you the universality of this so that you will realize what has been given to us in these Sunday talks for the past two weeks, what you and I are receiving as benefits from our study or practice of The Infinite Way is far less in importance to what the message is doing in raising up the whole world. Of course, there is no Infinite Way separate and apart from your consciousness and mine. In other words, there is no Infinite Way hanging in space. All of The Infinite Way on earth is what is active in consciousness and whatever Infinite Way principles do not find activity and expression in consciousness are just not taking place in the world. Therefore, whether or not you believe you are getting all the benefits to which you are entitled by your study and practice, please remember that at best you are passing through this life, and therefore the major reason for your being here is for what you leave behind. Yes, what you take with you and what you leave behind, because it is of the spiritual nature that what you give you possess, what you hold onto you lose.

I am going to quote a few passages from a book, *Elements of Libertarian Leadership*, by Leonard E. Read. This book has a circulation among men and women, who like myself, have a deep passion for freedom. People are learning from this man and his associates that we do not gain liberty by fighting for it or by crusading. We keep it sacred and secret within our own consciousness, living it, and granting it to others, and thereby watching it spread worldwide. Just as we, by holding to our Infinite Way principle of freedom, not battling or fighting, but by keeping it secret and sacred and then sharing it with those who are led to it, have witnessed it on a worldwide basis. Here are Mr. Read's three cardinal points: A belief in the supremacy of an infinite consciousness; a conviction that the individual human consciousness is expansible; and a faith in the immortality of the human consciousness. I quote now from his book:

"We are truly happy only when we are in a perpetual state of hatching our own consciousness, opening to infinite consciousness.

Likewise infinite consciousness, at least as I conceive it, tries to flow into and through persons, manifesting itself as individual human consciousness.

We can refuse to be a member or a financial supporter of any voluntary organization that takes action for which we are unwilling to stand personally responsible.

The booby trap is the notion that vanishing liberty can be restored merely by an increased or stepped-up political activity."

No human footsteps, no crusades, no going out to overcome communism—this does not change a thing because it does not change the consciousness of the individual. So the secret of attaining spiritual freedom or economic freedom or political freedom is not in the physical work we do. No, it is in the degree in which our consciousness is lifted out of its humanhood, out of its belief that self preservation is the first law of human nature into the Master's idea of loving another as we love ourselves, but more especially to accept the revelation that "No man on earth is your Father. There is one Father and one great Brotherhood."

This brings us to an idea that came into my thought as I was meditating for part of our activity this week, and it came with the statement, "We are guests of life." You see, this world was here before we were born. We came into this world as a guest of a world that had already been established. Food was already in the larder, clothing was already in manufacture, there was wood and iron and steel for building and there were diamonds, rubies, and pearls for ornamentation. Everything was here for man's use. We were told, "Son, all that I have is thine,"[1] so it was put here for our use.

If we can understand ourselves to be guests of life, it is then not difficult to see what debt we owe each other. We know that if we were guests in someone's home a price would be expected of us. To the host, the hostess and the guests of that household we would owe gratitude, helpfulness, courtesy, cooperation, sharing, giving joyously, and receiving joyously. We would never have the feeling that we possessed anything in the home in which we were guests, but that it was all there for our enjoyment and for our practical use, and all without a charged price. What would be expected of us would be a spiritual price.

One of the most releasing experiences that can come to an individual is when we grasp the meaning of "The earth is the Lord's and the fullness thereof,"[2] that moment in which we realize how utterly ridiculous it is to believe that we possess something and that it is ours, or even that we have earned it or deserved it. We are guests of life and life has provided us with everything necessary to our fulfillment on the plane of the spiritual and the manifest.

Freedom is ours as a spiritual inheritance. Yes, freedom is ours as a guest of life. Certainly it must be evident that any guest is free to go, and to come, and to be. Freedom is a quality and an activity that is given to us as guests of life, and we need take no thought "what we shall eat, what we shall drink, or wherewithal we shall be clothed," because these also are ours as guests of life. This does not take place in the position of parasites who take all, because whatever we receive is for sharing, not for storing up "where moth and rust doth corrupt." "Freely ye receive, freely ye must give."[3] This is not saying that an individual can do this just because he feels it is right to do it or because he wants to do it. No, this is what takes place with the realization that we are guests of life, and not before.

A mistake has been made on the subject of tithing. Since it was discovered that those who tithe never know lack or limitation, it was believed that if you would teach this to people, they would always be prosperous. This is not true. Tithing is something that can only take place when individuals receive inwardly the realization of what great gifts of God they have received, and in gratitude decide to share some part of it. This sharing is just with the idea of thankfulness for the realization of God's grace, and it is for this reason that those who spontaneously come to tithe are always generously and abundantly provided for.

In the same way, improving ourselves humanly is permissible in its place because all human beings are born as animals with the animalistic instinct of self-preservation, but sooner or later they must come into some measure of refinement. This does not come naturally, and so every child must be taught the Ten Commandments. Only a few are born with the spiritual instinct of wanting to give. However, attaining obedience to all of the Ten Commandments is in no way living the spiritual life. The spiritual student's righteousness must "exceed that of the scribes and the Pharisees." It must exceed that of obeying the law; it must be an inner realization. That is why the whole Infinite Way teaching states in every book that the letter of truth, the specific principles we teach, are only for the purpose of bringing us to the experience. That is the reason we do not make rules. We do not say you should not smoke or drink or you should not commit adultery. No, we set forth principles of spiritual living and those who are led to them and respond to them find they are not smoking or drinking or committing adultery or cheating or lying or defrauding.

In this way then, we are not seeking to improve our humanhood any more than we believe that changing our political party is going to change our living conditions. There must be a change of consciousness. If there is a change of consciousness in the man on the street, this will change the nature of politicians. Putting politicians out of office is not the answer. The answer is individually rising above the belief of good and bad humanhood to the realization of spiritual identity. Then we will have different candidates without having to go outside our chapels or homes; in other words, by our inner realization.

The entire world does not have to be transformed. No, the history of the world is going to be changed by "ten righteous men" here and there. One pope is going to change the whole attitude and altitude of the world. One pope here, one bishop there, one priest here, one rabbi there, and one man in the business world, and all on the idea of freedom attained individually by spiritual means. It is not a matter of transforming the world, but of bringing to the surface one here and one there; to be lights in their communities, and these few will raise up the others with them.

Individually we must come to the realization that we are on earth as guests of life. Our purpose here is to dwell harmoniously in this spiritual household, this kingdom of God which is on earth, as guests, conducting ourselves along the lines in which guests conducts themselves. Then you will see that our entire attitude toward each other will change, but only after the experience has taken place within. It is like an alcoholic who would like to be free of alcoholism, but cannot be free until a certain moment when something takes place in his consciousness. Then suddenly he is free because now he has no power to be anything else.

For us then, the object of this work is not trying to improve ourselves humanly in any way. Our goal is God realization, and then automatically we become children of God, children of that one spiritual household. It is the experience of God in us that sets us free, but the point that I started with today and wish to conclude with is this: In attaining your freedom, your attained state of consciousness blesses those in your household or community who are receptive and responsive and, in some measure, sets them free. The greater the degree of your spiritual freedom, the more widespread is the freedom that you give. You may, through your studies and meditation, attain a degree of spiritual freedom that will enable you to be a spiritual blessing to members of your family or immediate neighbors. You may attain such a great degree of freedom that you may become a healer on a wide scale, city-wide, state-wide. It may give birth in you to some idea of commercial or political freedom and so be a freeing influence for thousands of people; or, you may go as high as Jesus, Moses, or Mrs. Eddy and bring about a whole world-wide religion. Who knows? But if you do, please do not organize it.

Always remember that the freedom that you crave in your heart everyone else is craving, but do not believe that anyone can ever be free through binding them. When you set anyone free, remember you are setting them free as the Catholic Church now says, "To have a religion or not have one." Set everyone free, and find that to a greater extent you yourself will be free. It was announced today that we are all guests of one of our students at this luncheon, and that is a sample of how we are guests of life. We do find ourselves to be guests, but this is when we set supply free and do not try to demonstrate it. Set it free. Let it be free. It is never necessary to demonstrate supply. It is only necessary to demonstrate our relationship to God and to life and "all things are then added unto us."

Every time you entertain a spiritual truth, you are in some measure attaining freedom, or life by grace, but remember you are doing more than this. Somewhere in the world there is someone attuned, and he or she is being set free by this realization you have had. I will try to explain it to you. There is but one infinite, unconditioned consciousness. Every time we individually receive an impartation of truth in our consciousness, it is likewise being received in the consciousness of others who are similarly attuned. In other words, all over the world at this minute there are people longing for freedom with all their heart and soul and mind and body. There are people who are turning within themselves, sometimes in prison, sometimes because they have no one or nothing to turn to, and thereby making themselves receptive to truth. In other words, they have created a vacuum and are attuned to the unconditioned consciousness. You can witness that this actually is happening. Everywhere individuals are receiving these impartations, and a bishop writes a book and says that prayer is not "speaking to God but hearing God." This is how these ideas are reaching human consciousness on a worldwide basis.

The history you are reading about in the newspapers is just the product of the karmic influences, good and bad, of past generations. The history in the making is what is happening to the world everywhere as a freeing nature, such as we are now witnessing on a small scale. People in the world are not aware of what is taking place now, but people ten or twenty or thirty years from now will be reading of these events in their history books.

Try to envision this "canvas" of life, so that you do not measure your spiritual life by what it is doing to you and yours, and for you and yours alone. Rather, see how the measure of spiritual freedom you attain is the measure of spiritual freedom that you are giving back to the world—hastening the day of its freedom. As guests of life we are really temporary visitors to earth. It is not given to us to own anything here, because we can take nothing with us when we go except the spiritual treasures we have laid up. Remember that every spiritual treasure that we will carry into the next plane of existence is a spiritual treasure which we leave behind. It is not finite—it is omnipresence itself. Once you have acquired the realization of a spiritual truth, it is yours throughout all eternity, but it is one which will remain behind in the consciousness of mankind to multiply itself. This is spiritual law.

The Word Becomes Flesh: Spiritual Responsibility

May 18, 1963

I GET A GOOD DEAL OF MAIL from people who say they want to "work things out spiritually," and I am very frank in saying that I do not believe many of them. They have difficulties that involve financial or legal matters but they do not want to take legal steps—they want to "work it out spiritually." They are just trying to evade a normal, natural responsibility. No one, from Jesus to Paul to Buddha, has ever claimed to work out spiritually something that involves someone else's morals or someone else's integrity; and, we have no right to take anyone on faith because he or she is an Infinite Way, Christian Science, or Unity student. It doesn't necessarily mean that they have attained the consciousness. Even if students have been in The Infinite Way classes, it doesn't guarantee their conduct. It isn't easy for all of them to keep themselves immaculately clear in their dealings with each other because of human temptation.

No one should choose a stock broker, real estate broker, or lawyer because he is an Infinite Way student. I do not care if he is an Infinite Way student or an atheist. If I am going to choose a real estate broker, I would choose him for his professional ability and integrity in his job; and that is the way I am always going to choose—by ability and integrity, not by his religion. Of course, if there is a competent real estate broker or lawyer available and he is a student, I would choose him, but I don't choose him *because* he is an Infinite Way student.

I not only have to tell that to you, but more especially through you to others with whom you come in contact. I don't feel you are going to go off the beam on this, but the more you are in this work, the more people are going to come to you for advice–advice on hotels, camps, stock brokers, and bankers. Sentiment plays no part in that with me. There are two standards in everything: integrity and experience, or ability. If they have that, they can have any religion they want. In every way that I possibly can, where there are legal matters involved, I have them legally attended to. In the matter of a will, real estate, brokerage, royalty contracts with a publisher, I have it taken care of with the best legal advice I can find. A lot of people may find fault with this way of thinking–I am one of those who like it.

What I am bringing out to you, but mostly through you, is do not take things for granted and say, "Let God do it." Do not overlook it in your business. Do not take people's word for something in matters of business–they may be here today and gone tomorrow. Use your God-given intelligence on the highest plane you can, but you haven't done this at all when you say "I am going to leave it to God." I do not say, "Oh, God will protect the working girl." I have seen too many working girls not protected, and too many metaphysicians buncoed.

Now let us be clear with this: As spiritual students, we must never do anything without turning within, and then we must listen. Train the student never to move or do anything without this inner guidance. No matter how good you are in anything, did you first turn within and get inner guidance? Do not assume God will lead us to anything, or do it for us, otherwise this whole contemplative life is a farce. I have found the secret is in the word *consciousness*. What I can become conscious of, that is what takes place in my life. Therefore, regardless of what I want guidance on, I have to see it in some way as spiritual demonstration of the presence of God.

What is the contemplative way? Well, this whole Infinite Way life should not be called that—although *The Infinite Way* was the original text book—but what The Infinite Way means is a way of life, or the contemplative way of life. Then this way of life could be lived by Jew or Gentile or Buddhist, because it would have no special religious connotation.

A minister asked me that the other day, "Do you call yourself a Christian?"

I said, "I must be frank, I do not call myself a Christian."

He said, "I gathered that from your books."

Part of the revelation I live by is to be found in the Hebrew scriptures, the Oriental scriptures, but I don't accept any of the leaders of those religions as being a Christ or a God. To me the spirit that operated in Jesus, Buddha, Paul, Elijah, Isaiah, Nanak, the Sufi, and Moslem leaders, is that same spirit (When you read the Sufi and Moslem mystical writings, you must see immediately that the same spirit produced them). It couldn't be just in one Christ, or in one Buddha. . . .

"Before Abraham was, God was."[1]

God has no religion, sect or creed. If I am not a Christian, Jew, or Catholic—what am I? I lead the contemplative life, the spiritual life, the mystical life. It means living a spiritual life. It means I do not go to a human source for authority—it means I turn within. I recognize there is a part of me which is a human being, and that "the natural man receiveth not the things of God[2] because they are spiritually discerned." How are you going to use your brain then if things are spiritually discerned? The second point I am making is let us forget sectarian religion and differences. See this for yourself that you are not so concerned with labels as to what your religion is or what it isn't. God doesn't have a denomination or a church. Let us think of our relationship in the real essence, the contemplative one, but then after meditation, "the Word must become flesh."

When the Master came down from the mountain top where did he go? Right down to the seashore, healing the multitudes and feeding the hungry. He came right down and put it into use. That is why he didn't mind mingling with the sinners and the tax collectors.

Lead the contemplative life, but then take every practical human footstep to let "the Word become flesh." Sometimes things are brought right to your doorstep. On the other hand, sometimes, as in the case of employment, it is in the realm of activity and you go and register for employment. That, then, would be right activity. It isn't that your good comes from those footsteps, but sometimes it comes through those footsteps.

How did Christopher Columbus know that the world is round, that there are continents beyond the horizon? In his day scientific teachings of his own university denied it—everybody denied it—and he affirmed it. How? He had to have an *inner* guidance. He had to have an inner guidance giving him such assurance that he could convince royalty to give him the means to carry it out,

in spite of all the teaching to the contrary. I always like
to think I was with Columbus in those days. While it
may not be true, it is part of my inner life that I *feel* that
I was with him on some of his trips, not as a man but as
a boy. It may only be that I feel his consciousness, but
anyway that is why I feel I like the sea. That is why I
have the conviction that Columbus had an inner assurance that the horizon was not the end of the world.

Where did Edison go for his inventions? Not to
books. Where did Steinmetz or Kettering go for their
inventions? No, those things are not written in books.

If I have to have a name, then call me a "contemplative." I can't think of being alone for a very long period
of time without a period of contemplation. When I
contemplate, something is given to me—something to
ponder. So it is, the source of my religion is to be found
within me, but I must go in to get it.

In living this life of the contemplative, you will find
that you are living a life attuned to an inner rhythm, an
inner grace. The more you listen, the more you contemplate within, the greater protection and guidance you
have on the outer plane.

God is the only real substance. You can lose anything
on the outer plane—your home, business or bank account, as during the depression—but if you have your
contact within, eventually all losses will be new profits.
In that way then, the contemplative way of life is the
most practical of all, because it turns in to the source;
but do not lose your balance. See that "the Word
becomes flesh," and as you practice this, it will not take
long until you find the wisdom of it.

We have experiences of people writing to say how
much happier they are since studying The Infinite Way,

even though their income hasn't increased. Perhaps they do not notice that pleasure bills are less, doctor bills are less, money for amusements is less. The income is not vastly increased, but there are a lot of places where the money is not going out. Even, as you know, in the beginning, practitioner bills may have been heavy; they are now lighter because we call on them less. Now our money fulfills a higher purpose because we are making contact with the only real substance there is–God.

Two things we have covered today:

(1) To separate yourself from the belief that you belong to any particular religious body, and see yourself as an individual leading the contemplative life, leading your life through inner guidance.

(2) Whatever spiritual inspiration you receive within, adapt it to your human experiences without. Above all things, this inner life manifests itself in human relationships with each other and at every level of life, regardless of what level it might be. In our conduct and attitude toward the one closest to us or the stranger, there must be the same integrity, the same tolerance, the same patience, the same forgiveness as with anyone else. This does not mean you must be taken advantage of–your inner wisdom would quickly take you away from those conditions.

TRUTH IS NOT FOR YOU ALONE

Now you have a responsibility, because as part of this group you are not receiving this message for yourself. I trust that you all know that anyone who is a part of this group for any length of time will be called upon. God won't let you store up this much spiritual treasure and not be called upon. Of those who have much, much will be demanded. The more treasures you lay up, the more you will be called upon.

If I set myself free from the world's problems, I have less of lack, sins, etc., but the strange thing is I am not doing it unto myself. Pretty soon someone comes to me, and then all the world beats a path to my door. I have witnessed it with myself and with my students.

When I touch the kingdom within, do not think God says, "Oh, Joel, I heard you." No, it is released in consciousness. The freedom I have has been shared with tens of millions of people around the world. Through whatever measure of freedom was given our teachers, others find a degree of freedom.

When you are leading a contemplative life, there is no such thing as leading a life for yourself. If you go off to a cave, pretty soon a shrine will be built around that cave, and millions will find freedom as they did with Ramakrishna. To Swampscott, Massachusetts, the town in which *Science and Health* was written, came multitudes finding health and other harmonies. Mrs. Eddy lived in a little room in a home there while writing *Science and Health.* The fact that an individual touches God, does not merely mean they will sit on cloud nine. In some measure others will be set free.

Through contemplation, you will gain a much higher awareness of the meaning of equality. Then you will see what the Master meant, that there is only one equality and one Father, and in our recognition of that, we set each other free.

WE ARE CONTEMPLATIVES

It intrigues me, this thought that evolves today. We are contemplatives. We merely use The Infinite Way books for guidance. We are really contemplatives. We could contemplate Emerson's essays, or we could contemplate the Bhagavad Gita. We are still living the contemplative life.

The observance of any holiday or holy day, feast day, rite or ceremony is usually believed to influence God. If we go through communion service, or observe any rite or ritual, we think that it gives us influence with God. There is nothing you can humanly be doing that will influence God. It can only be done by coming into obedience to God's laws. The Master's whole teaching is how to bring us into at-one-ment with God. Then you have attuned yourself with spiritual law. If you pray for the enemy, ask forgiveness, you are attuning yourself.

The minister I was with the other day said, "Prayer is fitting ourselves to receive the grace of God which is ever-present." I am really shocked when I think of people who pray for things without any idea at all of not changing themselves. Here I am leading my human life: "Now you come on down, God, and do something for me." God's grace cannot be added to what is done humanly. Individuals come for prayer thinking we would reduce the lump or stop the fever—then we would just be another form of materia medica. Yes, but that is not what we are praying for.

I have witnessed in my meditation, the usual change is a change in consciousness of the patient. Sometimes the person will say, "I have lost the fear, but the fever hasn't gone down." I am only interested in a change of consciousness.

So it is when you are working, do not allow patients to fool you when there is no change in the physical. That wasn't your function in the beginning. Your function is to bring the seekers into an awareness of God within—then, "all of these things will be added unto you." That is not what people are seeking. They are seeking an immediate healing and they will seek God after the healing. No one seeks God after the healing, because then the person is not seeking anything anymore. So again, that is the contemplative life when you are communing with God for no other purpose than communing with God—when no one expects to get anything out of it, only the unfoldment that comes.

Do you remember the story of the man who had lived a long, long life of devotion to other people? The story is told that an angel of the Lord came down and stood beside him on the street. The angel said, "God wants to reward you for all this devotion to others. What would you like?"

The man said, "What I would like most is that everyone who passes over my shadow is healed of all their problems, sins, and diseases, and that I never know who passed over that shadow."

This was the experience when the woman pressed through the throng and touched the Master's hem. You witness that everyone is healed of sickness and sin, but you have no awareness of being "spiritual." This tricks a lot of students who want to feel spiritual power, or who want to feel they are blessing somebody.

I never had a feeling in my entire thirty-two years of practice that I had healed somebody. I can only know it by the fact that people tell me they were healed. I, personally have nothing to do with their healing. I meditate merely for myself to feel the inner grace. Watch this very carefully—you will find many people want to be do-gooders and help mankind. We do not know when spirit functions; we are a witness and a transparency—a pane of glass through which the sun shines. Keep the personal sense of "I" out of it. When "I" gets in and makes us think we want to do something, it will not happen.

There is a spirit in you—"Thy faith hath made you free."[3] It is the individual's own faith, and sooner or later you will see that. Otherwise, why doesn't everyone receive the same degree of healing? According to your faith, so is it unto you. As we see this, we can really do greater works.

This does not take away from the fact that there must be an individual *you*—and without you, the healing probably wouldn't take place. That seems like a contradiction. In other words, if Moses hadn't received illumination, he couldn't have taken the Hebrews out of Egypt. Just as you might go to Jesus and have an immediate healing, you might go to one of his disciples and it takes longer. It is a matter of the degree of illumined consciousness.

Our teaching is based on God as individual consciousness. Without your consciousness, the works will not be done—your consciousness: not as a wielder of the power, but a transparency through which the power can function. It is almost a paradox with Jesus, Paul, Buddha—all of them very convincing in their argument, "I of my own self can do nothing."[4]

As Emerson says, every man is "an inlet to and an outlet for" God. Therefore, the only person who can prove he is an inlet to and an outlet for the divine source is the contemplative. There is only one way I am "an inlet to and an outlet for," and that is to consciously prepare myself for that flow. You are as necessary as can be as an individual "inlet to and outlet for" infinite divine consciousness.

The ego loses its sense of a power in having made contact with the life stream. In proportion to your receptivity, you will benefit by it, but that is also a grace. If you study ten minutes a day, that is the limit of your capacity. When it grows, you will spend two hours or five hours—it is all dependent on an inner grace.

Once you have learned these specific principles, put them out of your mind and you will draw on what you have stored up. After you have meditated, go out and do something completely different: go to a movie, watch television, or read good literature. "In a moment when ye think not, the bridegroom cometh." When you are not consciously thinking of God, at that moment it will come when it is needed. If you want to receive wisdom from a divine grace, the entire secret is that it comes at a moment when you are not thinking. Then as we live naturally, the divine grace establishes itself and it speaks for us.

An Idea Whose Time Has Come

May 19, 1963
Princess Kaiulani Hotel

ON MAY 12 WE STARTED off with this paragraph: "There is a principle of life not yet known to the world, but known to you through your studies of The Infinite Way. The effects of this principle have been known throughout all known time, but the principle itself has not been known."

The principle of which I spoke is that truth received and embodied in consciousness becomes known worldwide without any human effort or human striving. Just by abiding within one's Self with the revealed truth, it has a way of establishing itself. This does not always happen as quickly as we would like it to happen, but when we are dealing with truth we must learn that "a thousand years is as one day and one day can be as a thousand years."[1] There will be periods of thousands of years when little progress seems to be made, then suddenly in one day more progress is made than in a thousand years.

This was illustrated by the Civil War. The idea of giving freedom to the Negro was not really a result of the Civil War; in fact, the Civil War was a failure and did not give that freedom. However, the fact that it took place was in line with all that had been unfolding in human consciousness since the days of Greece, on up

165

through the Magna Carta, the French Revolution, the American Revolution, the Brazilian Revolution. All of this is the out breaking into human experience of an idea in consciousness.

I believe it was last week that we were given the quotation of Victor Hugo: "Nothing is so powerful as an idea whose time has come." Ordinarily this quotation is attributed to Ralph Waldo Emerson, because it was he who made the quotation famous. But strangely, in the editorial in this morning's newspaper it is correctly attributed to Victor Hugo, and in the correct manner in which we used it last week. In other words "its time has come," and nothing is going to stop the breaking down of racial prejudice. Furthermore, if you had access to mainland newspapers, you would know that this same experience is taking place on a much larger scale. It is not limited to our Southland, but extends to South Africa, the Congo, and other spots on the globe.

The idea of freedom, liberty, justice, and equality–this is the age in which "its time has come." Colonialism has to go, the holding in bondage of one people by another has to go; but unfortunately, the world–not knowing how to achieve this by spiritual means–has recourse only to the human means of force. To go out and fight for what we wanted and to fight those who wanted that which we had–this is all the world has known.

That another era was being ushered in is found in a little known statement of Mrs. Eddy's: "The time is coming when the thief will not have to enter your home to rob you. You will carry your goods to him." That is the era we witnessed in the United States beginning with World War I when, whatever the government wanted, it achieved by propaganda. It could set up a propaganda, invisibly, that inside of six months could make us cry for war. Mental powers can be used for good and they can be used for evil. A few years ago some tests were made with the mental power of subliminal perception. Through these tests it was discovered that the sales of Coca Cola could be increased sixty-four per cent in one day by reaching into the mind of man without his knowledge and directing him to go out and buy the product.

Actually, this use of subliminal perception at mental levels is an abortion of a true principle. It is a destructive effort that has behind it the reality of truth, which is the principle that I revealed last Sunday. The world has not known this principle, but today it is being proven by the few who have learned it. *An idea or principle revealed in consciousness, something real, something true, will manifest itself in tangible experience.* When the idea of freedom entered human consciousness in tangible form in ancient Greece, probably no one was sufficiently aware of the operation of this principle, or I believe that worldwide freedom would have been attained long before the Magna Carta. Instead, it has not been attained even up to this day. Actually we are losing more freedom today than is being gained and, if it continues for another generation, we will be back in the Middle Ages with no freedoms left on earth.

Therefore, if freedom is to be maintained in the world, it will have to be brought about through the conscious knowledge and practice of this principle. This requires dedication. It means being un-selfed, because ordinary human life is lived only for one's self and one's family. There is no higher vision beyond it. Very few can even take the action of going to the closet and sending out extra food or clothing to the poor. Without any effort, you will discover for yourself that almost all human experience is lived for the individual or his family, with only a tiny scrap left over for others. Therefore, it is meaningless for persons to think in terms of freedom for their country or for the world until they are ready to dedicate themselves to the task of bringing it into expression. This is why we read, "Ten righteous men can save a city."[2] There is not much use looking for the eleventh—the eleventh would be too difficult to find.

The principle is this: Freedom is of God. Freedom is not something thought up by man. It is a divine impartation that comes to the consciousness of certain men who are receptive to that idea: the men of Greece, the men of England at the time of the Magna Carta, and the men of Bolivia, Brazil, and France. In every generation there are certain individuals born un-selfed, with a love in their hearts that is not entirely self-love, a love that looks across the visible horizon and wonders, "What can I do?" To such people, divine impartations are revealed. Florence Nightingale comes to thought, and certainly Christopher Columbus freed the universe of its restrictions of time and space. Freedom is "a many splendored thing," and has many facets. So it is that here and there, individuals receive impartations from the infinite source which is divine consciousness, and this individual draws unto himself others. In this way then, the ideals that have been received are brought forth on earth. Remember that freedom can be political, economic, racial, religious.

Stop and think of The Infinite Way ideal of freedom. This includes no membership and no human ties or obligations, yet there is a spiritual bond that unites us in what is really an eternal relationship of love, sharing, and good will. Then look beyond the visible horizon, and see how it functions in one group and in one country after another. This is really one idea of freedom as applied to religious freedom. Then notice in last Sunday's message that a high official of the Roman Catholic church reports that it is the Pope's intention this fall to announce to his people that all must be free to seek any religion or none. See this high degree of religious freedom and remember it is not accidental that it comes at this time. It comes *after* The Infinite Way has demonstrated the close tie that binds people who are free and, therefore, this is another form of that same freedom. The editorial in this morning's newspaper which repeats "There is no greater power on earth than an idea whose time has come," and ends up by saying that the time for freedom of the Negro race has arrived, which was voiced here last Sunday.

No, this is not accidental. It is also not accidental that a book is written inside the church saying that prayer is not asking anything of God, prayer is listening, and that we must give up concepts of God for the experience. These are the fruitage of the truth that has been imparted to human consciousness from the divine infinite consciousness. Because we have been silently holding fast to it inwardly, teaching others as they are led to us, it is now finding expression everywhere. A truth that is given to me in consciousness, and which I hold sacredly within me and impart only to those who are responsive so that it makes a circle or flow between us, must eventually be established for all men on earth. The divine principle has within itself the power to establish itself, if it is held to sacredly and not forgotten.

Now we come to that most important subject—the contemplative life. The life we live as Infinite Way

students is really not a religious life as religion is usually
thought of. The Infinite Way may be called the contemplative life, or the life of a contemplative. This life is one
in which we ponder, meditate, and cogitate upon the
realities. It is a life in which we commune with our inner
or spiritual Self. It is a life which, by means of receptivity, makes us responsive to impartations from the infinite
to the individual.

This is a point to be remembered: When one individual receives a principle in consciousness, it has at that
moment been received in human consciousness. From
then on, it is available to anybody living the contemplative life. We can use electricity as an example. The
principles of electricity, discovered and received through
one individual, then became available to everyone else
in the world. So it is with a spiritual truth that is received
in the consciousness of an individual.

Let us take the word *freedom* in its widest sense, to
include religious freedom, economic freedom, political
freedom, racial freedom, even physical freedom, and
mental freedom. Then realize that these are the grace of
God, God's gift to God's kingdom, God's activity
operating in God's kingdom. Freedom is not of man—
man cannot create freedom. Freedom must be received
in consciousness because it is the only way God functions—*as* consciousness. Freedom is not to be begged for
or fought for—freedom is to be recognized.

"*Thy* grace is my sufficiency." *Thy* grace is man's
sufficiency. God's grace is man's freedom, liberty, justice,
equality. These are all qualities of divine consciousness,
omnipresent where *I* am. "The place whereon *I* stand is
holy ground." In these moments you will be looking over
the heads of those who are venal in their conduct, those

who are merely selfish, and those who are neither venal or selfish but who are ignorant. You will be looking over their heads and saying, "Thank God freedom is not at the mercy of any of these. Freedom is the gift of God, and it is God who establishes freedom on earth as it is in heaven."

We must reach the place where we can dedicate ourselves to something higher than our own interests. We must rise above self to the place where we dedicate some portion of our time to the cause of God's kingdom being established on earth—holding to the vision that has already entered human consciousness. Just remember, silently and sacredly, all freedoms are qualities and activities of God, as much on earth as in heaven, and then let this divine principle open up human consciousness here and there. Yes, when an idea's time has come, it does find a way to establish itself on earth.

As humans we are enslaved by words. A word gets a grip on us, and then we are the victim of that word. Among the words that have enslaved mankind are *he, she,* and *it.* These are really horrible words; in fact I am sure the devil has taken the form of he, she, and it. That is the way the devil appears; all evil is bound up in these words. But watch the difference when you can look over the heads of all the he's, she's and it's in the world and realize, "God is the source of my good. God is the source of my supply. God is the cement of my relationships" and, instead of getting angry at he, she, or it, get angry at ourselves for being enslaved by he, she, or it. This is another form of impersonalization.

If I look to the divine source for my good, my divine source appears as some he, she, or it of the right nature at that moment. If I am looking to a friend, a relative, a patient, or a student, I am looking amiss and I will some day be disappointed. But if I keep my vision above their heads, not looking to "man whose breath is in his nostrils," if I keep my vision on the divine source of my being, then "no weapon that is formed against me can prosper."[3] I can have all the he's, she's, or it's for sharing, but leaving them free to do their own degree of sharing or not. Sometimes living this way results in people being taken out of our lives. Sometimes this happens; at other times this does not happen, and they remain with us. That is when we have to rise higher and higher and be indifferent to their conduct. We must rise to where we can say, "None of this moves me. I am looking to the kingdom within me. I am looking within to my source."

Ever since I had my realization, "My conscious oneness with God constitutes my oneness with all spiritual being and idea," everything necessary for my good has appeared. Always when someone was needed for the good of The Infinite Way, that individual was raised up.

"God is my freedom, God is my life, the source of all I am and can ever hope to be. This was true before I was born and it will be true after I leave visibility." Perceive the bigger vision. You must place the world's freedom in the hands of the infinite. Take it out of the hands of man and say, "This world is not at the mercy of sin or stupidity." If we place the authority back in the divine consciousness, then this idea whose time has come will express itself.

There will always be an instrument of God on earth, because in every age there are people born who are attuned with their source. Look over the heads of men and women and see that of themselves they are nothing.

"All power is in the hands of the Infinite, the Eternal, and it operates through grace." Then witness this principle establish individual freedom at every level of human life through an inner communion with the spirit in which these truths are realized. Then we can take the larger step of establishing the kingdom of God on earth by the same means—the contemplative life. Recognize that *that* which is within you is greater than all that is in the outer world, rendering null and void the weapons of this world.

Review in your own mind how you have witnessed these truths that we have shared in these small groups appearing here and there throughout the world as if the world were aware of what we are saying, which it is not. I firmly expect to see the kingdom of God, the kingdom of righteousness, established on earth: "Not by might or by power" and certainly not for anybody's glory, but by the fact that these ideas established in consciousness—pondered, meditated upon, communed with inwardly—will establish themselves outwardly. Men here and there will voice these truths and, because these men are authorities in their fields, they will be believed.

The age of power has gone by. We are in the age of *spiritual power*, and spiritual power means non-power. "Resist not evil. . . . Abide in the word and let the word abide in you. . . . Be not afraid, it is *I*. . . . *I* in the midst of you am mighty." Think of the passage, "*I* in the midst of you am mighty,"[4] and then put up the sword. How do you make this true? By *knowing* it. The truth cannot make you free without your knowing it. You have to want to ponder truth, meditate upon it in your innermost secret sanctuary, and it will establish itself externally in miraculous ways.

Probably one of the major quotations to remember is, "Be not afraid, it is *I*."[5] This must be the first step. To be afraid means to empower something or somebody; it means to empower a he, a she, an it, or a they. To be not afraid means you have withdrawn all power from he, she, it, or they. *Be not afraid, it is I.*

During my business career I traveled a good deal abroad. When any inconvenience or trouble came into the experience of an American traveling, it was quickly resolved by saying, "I will call our Consul." In other words, the American government is responsible for its citizens, and miracles took place when the American Consul arrived on the scene. Just the words, "Call the Consul" did it, but this is not true anymore. Those days are gone. Now we are supposed to watch out that we do not embarrass the government or get it in trouble. This is good, because it was too easy to lean back on the power of the "red, white, and blue."

We must reach the point where we are Self-complete in God. Because "*I* and my Father are one and the place whereon *I* stand is holy ground." This is part of man's spiritual liberty, where man is wholly dependent on God's grace—only then has he attained freedom. He even has to know that if all his earthly good is taken from him, he still stands on holy ground and the lost years of the locust will be restored. Look over the heads of people, and see the spiritual grace that is omnipresence, and that is the source of all human harmony.

SPIRITUAL LOVE

May 26, 1963
Princess Kaiulani Hotel

IN THE JULY *Letter,* you are going to have the first three of this series of talks, and in following letters there will be more. You will remember that we started with the unfoldment of God as infinite divine consciousness. Because this same God, this same infinite divine consciousness is individual consciousness, we therefore draw forth our good by "opening out a way for the imprisoned splendor to escape." We do this not from the consciousness in a holy temple, or a holy city, or a holy savior, but from our consciousness, from the divine consciousness which is your individual consciousness and mine. That is why meditation is the entire secret of harmonious spiritual living–because meditation is retiring into our innermost being, praying secretly within ourselves, and then letting spiritual good unfold.

From this you catch a further glimpse that God never was a Jew, or a Christian, or a Mohammedan, or a Hindu–but rather that God is *spirit* and the spirit of God in you is the only God. Whether or not you were erroneously taught that you were a Christian, a Vedantist, or a Buddhist, you have learned that it is absurd to have any racial or religious prejudice for the simple reason that we all have the one Father. "Call no man on earth your Father. There is but one Father, which is your Father and my Father."[1] We all have the same God and, fortunately for us, it is "closer than breathing, nearer than hands and feet." This understanding, and this alone, can make for the "Fatherhood of God and the Brotherhood of Man." Otherwise we live our lives on the basis of tolerance and, if you were ever tolerated by anybody, you would know what a terrible word that is.

In all of the seventeen years that I have traveled with the message of The Infinite Way, only three men in the United States from the metaphysical world have come into spiritual fellowship with me. I have met only three with whom I could completely unite in spiritual fellowship, spiritual love, and spiritual companionship. Some of you have met the first of these, Dr. Irvin Gregg, head of the Divine Science Church and College in Denver, who with his wife is with us here today. The second is Dr. Sig Paulson, who is the head of Unity, and the third is Dr. Jack Addington in San Diego. Fortunately, all three are married to ladies who are also in complete union with us.

I mention this so that once again you may see that, where there is spiritual light, there is oneness and unity. Without it, there is bigotry, prejudice, or intolerance. Where there is spiritual light there is the awareness of the great truth that there is only one God, and that one "my God and thy God," and we unite in that truth. When there is spiritual understanding at the top of the religious movements of the world, there will be a spiritual union on the level of the lay members and not before, because the members of any religious group can never rise higher than their leaders. They never will go beyond whatever measure of spiritual freedom their leaders experience. On the other hand, when there is enough of this spiritual oneness among the leaders, there will be a complete oneness and this eventually will mean "peace on earth and good will to men." As you here know, two ministers of the Protestant world have come into the spiritual union with us. Of course this is only the beginning of what lies ahead of us if we unite more and more in spiritual oneness. Here is Dr. Gregg. . . .

"I have come to hear Joel this morning, and I know you have too. The last time we were here you were holding forth at The Kawaiian Village, but we have kept in close touch and it is wonderful to be among you and feel this rapport. We are very privileged to be here this morning, and our blessings are with you. "

For several weeks we have been bringing to light the different new phases of religion being adopted or approved of by various churches. We have had the Pope of Rome endorsing the impersonalization of error, and we have had the Bishop of Woolwich agreeing that no concept of God is God and that prayer is not speaking to God—prayer is listening. I have had a local minister of a large church here in Honolulu tell me that his concept of prayer as given to his church is "preparing ourselves to receive the grace of God that is already present." In other words, the wisdoms that have been known to the mystical world are being incorporated into the religions of today and within a generation or two will be the accepted religious teachings of the world.

Now comes some of the best news of all. Freudian psychiatry, which has always claimed that the baser nature of man governs him, now begins a change by the man who represents the head of Freudian psychiatry and who is professor of psychiatry at The University of Vienna. Dr. Viktor E. Frankel has written a book which is supposed to be psychiatry, in which it is now claimed that the ultimate source of man's own existence is what he must discover within himself. Dr. Frankel repudiates the basic Freudian concept that man's main concern is to "gain pleasure and avoid pain." Listen, and I quote:

"Life ultimately means taking the responsibility to find the right answer to the very real and concrete problems which are constantly being set before us as individuals.

No one can become fully aware of the very essence of another human being unless he loves him. By the spiritual act of love he is enabled to see the essential traits and features in the beloved person."

How could there be a spiritual act of love without being endowed with a spiritual capacity? Can a human being love spiritually? Impossible, because the human being is the man of earth, the creature "not under the law of God, and who receiveth not the things of God." Therefore, until an individual is spiritually endowed, he cannot know the meaning of spiritual love, nor is it possible for him to love spiritually. To love spiritually means to love without an iota of sensuousness and without an iota of personal sense. Spiritual love has no relationship to marital love, or parental love, or any form of human love. Spiritual love requires a spiritual capacity and, in light of this, Dr. Frankel has opened the entire world of Freud to the spiritual nature of man. Nothing but the spiritual nature of man is important—remember that. It makes no difference what religion you may want to follow, or what metaphysical approach you may be living. Unless you have the capacity to love spiritually, you are not on any religious or metaphysical path at all. Once you have the capacity to love spiritually, to understand the nature of man as being spiritual, it would not make any difference to you what religion a man has—or none.

What this means then, is this: Just as you have learned that you have to develop your spiritual capacities through your reading, your studying, through attending classes, through meditating primarily, now is the rest of the world going to learn that they cannot go into a church and pray to God and have their prayers answered unless their natures change. Trying to add God's spiritual good to a human being is nonsensical. Answered prayer comes only through spiritual discernment and that discernment is primarily one in which we recognize the spiritual nature of man.

We have a physical frame, a physical body. The higher we go in spiritual endowment, the less attention has to be paid to the body. So far as we have any knowledge, nobody has become quite so spiritual that he or she can ignore this body or its care; but it is nevertheless true that the higher we go in an awareness of the incorporeal nature of man, the more harmonious is the body and the less discord does it bring to us.

Never believe for a moment, as so many still do today, that you can be an ordinary human being and then turn around to God and say, "Heal me, and make me happier and more prosperous," and expect to be showered by God's blessings. There has to be a change of consciousness, a dying and a being reborn, a renewal of the mind, a "turn ye and live." Something has to give in every human before the divine grace begins to be made manifest in them and through them. It is an impossibility to remain the same human being and, at the same time, be the recipient of spiritual grace. There must be a fitness, a preparation for it, and that consists of this ability to love spiritually–but not because we merely want to or think we should. Ah no. *To love spiritually is a gift that is developed.*

For weeks now we have been bringing this up, that we who are studying together–though we are happy and pleased with every healing and every harmony that comes into our individual experience–have reached the stage where that is not the reason for our being here. We know now that our reason for being here is for the development of spiritual consciousness, resulting in spiritual love which is to encircle the globe. One of the strange things about this spiritual love is that it is actually the opposite of human love, and that is very strong medicine for many to take. There are many who like to believe that human love is a part of this spiritual love and it is not, although human love is hallowed when we are touched by the spirit.

You find that out as you go deeper into the spiritual healing work. Even those of you who have done a small amount of healing work have discovered that it does not help in the work for you to sympathize. As a matter of fact, any sense of human emotion you have about the patient or about the claim is a barrier to the healing work. I remember years ago when I heard so many people say that Christian Scientists are cold and unsympathetic. Little did they know how they were complimenting them, for it is indifference and lack of reaction that is the healing principle.

The healing consciousness is the one that is purged of the belief in the reality of all appearances. This came

forcibly to mind this week when I read the story from
India of three religious monks who, upon going to the
Ganges to bathe every day, hung their small amount of
clothing on the limb of a tree. One day they saw a great
big eagle swoop down into the water, come up with a
large fish, and fly away. One monk made a face at the
eagle and said, "You bad bird!" and suddenly his
clothing fell into the dust and blew away. The second
monk said in sympathy, "You poor fish!" and his
clothing fell off the limb and blew away. The third monk
just smiled—and his clothing continued to sway in the
breeze. In other words, the third monk understood the
nature of the carnal mind and its pictures.

So it is with us. When we ignore the appearances, the
pains, the lacks and limitations of our patients, and abide
in the center of our being in the full recognition of God's
love and God's grace, this brings about spiritual healing.
Sympathy plunges the patient deeper into his problems.
You come into this on the subject of prayer, and the
June 1963 Reader's Digest has a good one called "Help
Yourself." I quote:

"When I was young, I wanted everything and all at
once, until our old Scottish minister explained things this
way: One night he dreamed that he saw a new shop in
the High Street. He went in, and saw an angel behind
the counter. Nervously he asked what the shop sold.
'Everything your heart desires,' the angel said.

'Then I want peace on earth,' cried the minister, 'an
end to sorrow, famine, and disease. . . .'

'Just one moment,' smiled the angel. 'You haven't
quite understood. We don't sell fruits here—only seeds.' "

So it is that prayer ordinarily is for peace on earth, or health or supply, and God does not have these to give. Truth can only plant seeds within our consciousness, the seeds of truth and love and life, and these seeds produce the "added things"—the peace on earth, the healings, and the supplies.

This is the reason why, in our healing principles, we do not know how to stop pain or reduce fevers or lumps. Spiritual treatment is planting the seeds of truth in consciousness and, when consciousness responds, there are "signs following." So many forget that the ground must be fertile. It cannot be barren or rocky, and that is why everyone is not healed immediately by spiritual means. This is a spiritual ministry that plants seeds of truth in our consciousness. If your consciousness is fertile, you can have a quick and beautiful healing. If it is not fertile, keep on studying until your consciousness has been spiritualized and you have developed spiritual love.

When the churches can agree that prayer is "preparing ourselves to receive God's grace that is always present," and when psychiatry agrees that harmony is the result of spiritual love, you can be assured that the second kingdom of Christ has come on earth for the first time. There must be a development of spiritual love in our consciousness. We cannot tolerate, we must love, and no amount of human love will bring the desired results. Spiritual love is developed from the capacity to understand the spiritual nature of God and man, the oneness of all creation. You cannot humanly love the birds and the beasts, but you can spiritually love them once you understand that one life permeates them—the life which is God. Then you come into attunement and "the lamb will lie down with the lion." That will become an established fact on earth—but only through spiritual love.

You can watch the development and unfoldment of spiritual love in yourself as you come into a relationship with people from whom you want nothing and from whom you expect nothing. This is spiritual love. It seeks no return. In this relationship that is instantaneous and spontaneous between Dr. Gregg, Dr. Paulson, Dr. Addington and myself—and their wives—never once has there been a desire for anything. There is just a spiritual bond that, in every meeting, has been a sharing without a giving or a taking. That is the spiritual love that will enable the world to live in peace. As many of you know, I had this same beautiful relationship in England with Henry Thomas Hamblin. It is a spontaneous thing that takes place between people who can meet with each other without needing anything, who have attained the realization of their oneness with God and who receive everything they need from God—and so it is that this "love one another" comes into focus.

Week after week during these past months, our work has been bringing out this point of oneness, of union, of witnessing the world coming into agreement with these major points—so that in the end we can all say, "I live my life as a contemplative." Contemplate the spiritual graces within, then whatever religion you may call yourself in the without will be just a name, without a meaning.

Dr. Frankel, the psychiatrist, acknowledges that psychiatry has never been even one percent truth, that it has been one hundred percent erroneous. He does that in one sentence, when he says: "Sex is sanctified as soon as–but only as long as–it is a vehicle of love." That knocks out the whole picture of psychiatry as it has been known. You can see the straws in the wind, you can see where the world is heading. Even though the world reads the newspapers and reads about Russia and Africa and Cuba and the Southland, you can look into the next generation and beyond. It should not be difficult for you to be prophets, because these are the things that tell you where the world is heading. A thousand different religions, but all based on the one truth–spiritual endowment. It may take two generations to be fulfilled on earth, but by then we will all be back here to enjoy it! We may even remember that we helped to instigate it. So do not be too concerned if you are not finding immediate happiness or immediate success or immediate satisfaction, because on the spiritual path these are not to be attained. We are too hard at work to bring a new creation into existence.

Spiritual love is an awareness of spiritual power. Spiritual power means spiritual love, and it is not a power over anything. It is the power of oneness, understanding, unitedness. Spiritual power does not overcome anything. Spiritual power unites us in spiritual love, and in that consciousness there is nothing to be overcome. You will discover that spiritual power is not an overcoming power–it is a uniting power, the power of spiritual love which enables us to understand the spiritual nature of all living things.

TRUE PRAYER—
THE EXPERIENCE OF GOD

June 2, 1963
Princess Kaiulani Hotel

NOT ONLY IS OUR FAMILY growing in size, but it is getting to where it cannot be fed milk anymore—it must be fed meat. After all of these months that we have been together, we are going to be called upon to experience rather than to listen.

The function of ordinary religion is going to God to get something to improve one's life. It happened this way in the beginning and it is still happening in this way. Man, and I am speaking of mankind in the world, does everything he can to improve his humanhood. When he is sick he looks to all of the doctors and all of the surgeons and all of the medicines in order to be cured. Only when human effort fails and the doctors tell him there is no hope—only when he reaches the end of his rope and is desperate—is he willing to say, "I will try God." In other words, he is trying now to get from God that which he had been unable to get from man.

There are wars, and after man has suffered as much as he thinks he can, he looks to the government to stop these wars. Of course no government is going to stop a war as long as it has a soldier to put in the line. Then mankind decides it is going to pray to God for peace. You can take any phase of your human experience, your health, your supply, your relationships in the home, your business, and you will see that those of the world perform all of these things humanly until they find themselves in some desperate situation and then they pray to God. That this has not succeeded through the centuries has not discouraged them because they keep hoping that this time it will work.

You have seen pictures this week of the large crowds gathered in St. Peter's Square, praying that the Pope's life be saved. You can go back for a hundred years or more and find photographs of similar crowds in the Vatican praying the same prayer for other Popes, and it is going to be many years before these crowds wake up to the fact that there is going to be no answer to their prayers.

The reason for the failure to get peace on earth by praying to God for it, or to get health by praying for it, or to get wealth or happiness by praying for it is that, first of all, God does not have these things to give; God is not withholding them, and therefore God cannot stop withholding them or giving them. Next, there is no such God as these people are praying to. They are virtually praying to a hole in the sky; they are praying to empty space. Thirdly, the real place to go for what they are seeking is to the "kingdom within." This is where it is, "closer than breathing, nearer than hands and feet." But in going within for these things—health, supply, peace, happiness—do not pray for them as if there were some-body or something inside of you that is going to pass them out like a Santa Claus at Christmas. When we pray, our prayer must be for the experience of God. Where the spirit of the Lord is, there is our freedom from all discord, but only "where the spirit of the Lord is." Therefore, prayer must result not in getting things, but in getting the experience of the presence of God. "In thy presence is fulness of joy."[1] But it must not be a mental exercise; it must be an inner experience in which the presence of God is actually felt.

Just as people for centuries have listened to sermons on Sundays and sometimes on weekdays, and not found any divine intervention in their affairs, so have people read books, listened to lectures, studied philosophies and metaphysics, and not found their lives too much improved. Why? Because they stopped short of that which is necessary—the actual experience of the presence of God. If you ask "How may I know when the presence of God has been realized?" there is not one answer for everybody. There are several answers, any one of which may be the one for you.

The Bible says, "God is not in the whirlwind, God is in the still small voice[2]. . . . Be still and know that *I* am God[3]. . . . In quietness and in confidence shall be your strength,"[4] and in these you have a cue. Many of the great religious mystics have revealed that the secret lies in stillness and quietness and confidence, not on voicing prayers or thinking thoughts. Listening will eventually bring you to the experience of hearing the still small voice, and all the power of God and all the presence of God is in that still small voice. "When he utters his voice, the earth of error melts."[5] This is all it takes, the awareness, the "hearing in the ear." It need not necessarily be audible as you will discover, but in some very tangible way you will know when God speaks to you. You will never have to wonder if you were mistaken, because it is unmistakable when it happens. If an experience leaves you unsure, disregard it, because when the real experience comes it leaves no uncertainties. It is then that the world could threaten you with crucifixion or being thrown to the lions, and you would smile. When it happens you can never doubt and above all, there will be "signs following."

It is for this reason that so much of our work is devoted to, first, "practicing the presence of God," which is really an intellectual exercise. It means a fulfillment of that part of Scripture which says: "Trust in the Lord with all thine heart, and lean not unto thine own understanding[6]. . . . In all thy ways acknowledge him, and he shall direct thy paths."[7] In the 91st Psalm we find: "He that dwelleth in the secret place of the most High shall abide under the shadow of the Almighty. A thousand shall fall at thy side, and ten thousand at thy right hand; but it shall not come nigh thee." Or the 15th Chapter of John, "If ye abide in me, and my words abide in you, ye shall ask what ye will, and it shall be done unto you."

All of this is practicing the presence of God. Upon awakening in the morning we acknowledge "This is God's day and I am God's child, and both the day and I are God-governed." Then, on going to meals, is the acknowledgment "God's grace has set our table" and, when going out into our business or artistic or educational world, "God's presence goes before me, God's spirit walks beside me, and the spirit of God is within me." Or, when faced by what seems to be difficult problems, we relax in the assurance "He that is within me is greater than these problems. He performeth that which is given me to do. He perfecteth that which concerns me." And, when faced with an impossible situation, to be able to rest in the assurance that "God's grace is sufficient unto it." And then that final beautiful experience of going to bed at night and handing the world over to God and saying "God, take care of the world while I sleep. I have been so busy running it all day, but I am too tired to do it now. You take over!" Actually you can reach the point where this sets the stage for your being able to awaken in the morning and say "Keep the world today, God, while I just relax!"

All of this constitutes practicing the presence of God and is exemplified in the book *Practicing the Presence*. If this is faithfully performed, it naturally leads to a state of consciousness in which the mind can be at peace within you. It stops going around, and around and around, getting nowhere. You have built up such an assurance of a God who is closer than breathing that, regardless of where you may be or when, you can very quickly find yourself inwardly still, quiet, peaceful.

When this happens you are ready for the second step on the mystical path—meditation—which is covered in the book *The Art of Meditation*. First is the contemplative form of meditation, in which you sit for awhile and review within yourself the nature of God, the nature of prayer, the nature of spiritual existence, and then prepare yourself for actual meditation, "Speak Lord, thy servant heareth."[8] We are in a complete stillness, with our ears wide open, our mind alert, and in a state of expectancy and anticipation of hearing the still small voice. When we hear it, the earth of error—the discords, inharmonies, problems—will melt. They do not melt for the whole world, and not always for your relatives and friends—but for you. "A thousand may fall at thy left, ten thousand may fall at thy right, but none of these evils shall come nigh thy dwelling place."[9] "Leave all and follow me,"[10] and then of course you will be abiding with those who likewise have "left all."

The books we read and study are not power, nor do they have the power of God. They are to lead us back within ourselves to the experience and, after awhile, you find you only use the books for teaching others. It is the experience you live by, the actual experience of knowing God "whom to know aright is life eternal," and be assured there is no life eternal without knowing God aright.

With this we come into a spiritual revelation which has not been given to the world outside of the pure mystical teachings. Christ Jesus revealed it, and Paul carried the message. Seventeen hundred years ago it was dropped from all church teachings, although some churches are now beginning to reinstate it. I will give it to you from Bible passages, right from the mouth of the Master and the mouth of Paul. From the Master: "My kingdom is not of this world[11]. . . . My peace *I* give unto you; not as the world giveth[12]. . . . Resist not evil[13]. . . . Put up thy sword."[14] And from Paul: "The natural man receiveth not the things of God, for they are spiritually discerned[15]. . . . The creature is not under the law of God, neither indeed can be[16]. . . . If so be the spirit of God dwells in you, then do you become the child of God."

All of this must show you that, in order to experience God, we must leave this world and enter "my kingdom." It is only in my kingdom that you will find God. You will not find him in this world or in the creature, the human being. And so listen: There is only one way in which you can experience anything, and that is through your consciousness. Even your dreams are experienced in consciousness. Therefore, if you wish to experience God, if you wish to enter the kingdom of God, if you wish to be under the laws of God, you must attain this through your own consciousness—not in holy temples, not in holy Jerusalem, not in holy men. The kingdom of God, the realm of God, the experience of God is within you—and it is in your own consciousness that you experience it.

You see the depth of meditation that you must attain; but before you can attain it, there is a step to be taken and one we must take today. When you meditate, first agree that you are seeking nothing of this world, wanting nothing of this world. Agree within yourself that the purpose of this meditation, or prayer, or communion, is purely to receive God and the things of God, and the realm of God and his Son. If you receive the Son of God in your consciousness, you will receive the Son of God in your very body. Diseased flesh becomes healthy flesh if you receive the Son of God, and the only place you can receive the Son of God is in your own consciousness, the realm that is within you. That is why Christ Jesus taught, "Pray to thy Father in secret, and thy Father which seeth in secret will reward thee openly."[17] Remember—you have nothing to do with the "openly" part.

Dying daily to the things of this world is exemplified in this form of prayer or meditation in which we go within, and since we are going to a spiritual realm we are certainly not thinking of any material results:

I seek no earthly thing or thought or person. I know that God's thoughts are not my thoughts and I want God's thoughts, not my thoughts. I know that God's ways are not my ways, so I wish God's ways to be revealed in me. The reason that I cannot pray for anything is that I do not want my will to be done, even if it is a good one, and how can God's will be done if I interpose a desire or a will of my own. Therefore, I must come to the throne of God pure, with no desires of any earthly nature—no wish, no will. Let thy will be done in me. Let thy way be established as my way.

There is no greater help at this point than to consciously remember, "God is spirit." Therefore, be sure that you are expecting only spiritual grace, spiritual will, spiritual life, spiritual way. At this stage you have erased material ambitions, hopes, desires, and even fears. Yes, because at this point you know that "Where the spirit of the Lord is, there is nothing to be feared."

To come to this place in consciousness means that a great part of your spiritual journey is behind you, because you cannot attain this lightly, easily or quickly. You have been led up to this, as you will discover when others come to you for spiritual wisdom. You will learn that it is not an easy matter to say to them: "We are not going to God to have your fever reduced, and we are not going to God to get increased supply," for the answer you will receive is: "What then is the use of going to God?" When you have arrived at the place where you can accept such a statement, you have arrived at the place where you have given up human aspirations for spiritual revelations.

We do not become ascetics. In giving up the world it is not in the mistaken sense of asceticism in which, by depriving ourselves of everything pleasant, we believe we are pleasing God. On the contrary, be assured that God is only pleased in our joys—in our fruitage. We know this from Christ Jesus, who was sent to earth to "do the will of the Father," and the will of the Father is that we have health and happiness and forgiveness of sins and life eternal. There is no asceticism in the Master's teachings. He took only their sins—never did he take from anyone any form of good. Once you stop seeking in your prayers "what ye shall eat, what ye shall drink and wherewithal ye shall be clothed," you will find they are being added unto you. "Thy grace is my sufficiency in all things,"[18] only I must not seek sufficiency, I must seek grace.

For thousands of years men have prayed for an end of war, for an end of injustice, for an end of slavery, and disease. All of these human conditions are still going on, and those that are not going on have not been overcome by prayer but by men. Many diseases have been overcome and lost from the world because of medical and surgical discoveries, but you recognize the fact that Christ Jesus revealed that this could be accomplished without human aid. So we are not to be deprived of health, but we are to receive health through spiritual means. The Master fed the hungry. Therefore, we are not to be ascetics and give up food, but neither are we to earn it by the sweat of our brow. It must be revealed spiritually. We are to be deprived of all of our sins and sinful appetites by the benediction or grace of God—by a spiritual influence. And so we come now to this moment in which you close your eyes and acknowledge within yourself:

I am come to the throne of God, which is established within me—and to pray, not for any thing nor any condition nor any person. I pray only that God's grace be revealed, that God's will be done in me, that the way of God be opened up unto me, that I may come to know him aright and find life eternal—not necessarily that I have to live my eternal life on earth—but to live it in accord with God's will and under God's grace. I pray that I may learn to know and to love my fellow man and understand him spiritually. Regardless of any outer coverings, regardless of physical structure, racial or religious covering, I pray that I may come to know the man behind all of this facade. I pray to understand the spiritual nature of love, the spiritual nature of life, the spiritual nature of abundance, the spiritual nature of brotherly love, the spiritual nature of body—the body of God's creating, the temple not made with hands—the eternal body. I pray for the revelation of God's government on earth as it is in heaven. I pray for a revelation of the nature of the Savior. I pray for the revelation of the nature of spiritual power, spiritual presence, spiritual law.

Eventually you will see that, one by one perhaps, the nature of these spiritual realities will be revealed to you. And, with each one, there will be "signs following." There is always some greater peace, some greater health, some greater joy.

Be very careful that you do not, either consciously or unconsciously, pray for victory. Every victory means somebody loses. That means somebody else prays for a victory later, and so the turmoil continues. We are never seeking a victory. We are seeking peace, but the peace that is jointly or universally fruitful and beneficial. There never will be such a thing as peace on earth internationally as long as peace has a connotation of victory. In this same way, no political party will ever give this nation good government as long as we believe that good government comes through victory *over* or defeat *of.*

Whether you are listening to this, or whether you will be receiving it in the mail and reading it in a couple of weeks, this will be just a sermon or a lesson unless you make something more of it. The Master is known as a way shower, and so the spiritual teacher can be nothing more than that—one who shows the way. It is the individual who *walks* the way—and this will cease to be a sermon or a lesson only in that moment when you make it an experience of your own consciousness. One reason that many of these wisdoms were lost to the world, even after they were given to the world by the Master, is that hearing them once is not sufficient to enable us to "go and do likewise." One of the reasons these words will not be lost is that, in a week, you will have this printed and available to read over and over again until you can make it an activity of your consciousness. When that happens you will not need it any more, except to help somebody else.

Make the transition from being the "man of earth" to being "that man who has his being in Christ," or make the transition of being "unclothed" and then "clothed upon with immortality." This actually is an experience of your own consciousness and it is accomplished in your meditations when you surrender in your moments of prayer, the reaching out for health or wealth or companionship or home. Stop making prayer a merchandise mart and make of prayer the seeking of spiritual grace, spiritual wisdom, spiritual light, spiritual intuition, spiritual discernment. Then you will be obeying the Master who said "God is spirit, and those who worship him must worship him in spirit and in truth."[19] He thrust the money changers out of the temple, and we must thrust the merchandise out of our consciousness, out of our prayers, if we would move from this world into "my kingdom."

CHRIST: THE UNFOLDMENT
FROM WITHIN

June 9, 1963
Princess Kaiulani Hotel

LAST WEEK WE WERE LED to the unfoldment that there are two realms or worlds, "this world" and "my kingdom," and that, "my kingdom is not of this world."[1] Also, because of these months of our work together, we must now be having the experience of truth, rather than just lectures or classes about truth. In other words we want our work to be in the nature of an experience, not a philosophy. Unless we can experience my kingdom, we are just living in the language of words, thoughts, teachings, and philosophies.

In order to know the actual experience, you must begin by realizing that everything that exists in the external world had its beginning in the invisible—not just an invisible—but a very specific invisible consciousness. The consciousness of man, which basically is the consciousness of God manifested as the consciousness of man, is the invisible which is the substance and law of everything external.

We know that the Chinese gave us the wheel, and a wheel is the most important part of a civilized existence. Now go back to China in your mind, and try to realize the world without a wheel. Then ask yourself, "Where does a wheel come from?" From this you will have to see that it had its origin in the mind of man, but behind that mind of man is the God-mind functioning as man's mind. So man turns within to his consciousness and he receives an impartation—an impartation from the infinite to the individual. And once man has the idea of a wheel in consciousness, how easy it is then to go out and make that wheel in the visible. Follow this principle all the way up from the wheel to the airplane, to color television, to radar, and see that everything had to be imparted to man from something greater than his education or physical strength. First he had to receive all these things in consciousness; he then took the next step of externalizing them.

We have said in our work that there never will be peace on earth through any means as yet known to the human world, and the reason is this: You cannot have an externalized peace until there is the impartation of peace from within. You can measure this as you look in your home or in this group. How much real peace or brotherly love could we have in this room if peace and brotherly love were not already established in our consciousness? Could we rise any higher than our own consciousness? Certainly not. Then what establishes that peace in our consciousness that enables us to live in brotherly love with each other? I will tell you what it is: "I and my Father are one[2]. . . . Son, thou art ever with me, and all that I have is thine."[3] In the degree that we have learned that we do not need anything of each other, but can freely share that which has come to us as a gift of God without lessening what we ourselves have, we have realized the only basis for peace. As long as I have a conviction that I need something from you, I could not be at peace with you because unconsciously a protective mechanism would go up in you. I know God is the source of my good, therefore I can fully and readily share that which I have. It is because of this that you feel towards me what you do, knowing that nothing is demanded of you except that you live in harmony with your oneness with God.

Peace can only come to the world when the world becomes convinced that it need no victories, no conquests, and that if it does it will unfold in some natural and normal way. This consciousness of man from which he derives everything is God-consciousness. Therefore, the consciousness of man is infinite. I cannot go into my consciousness and want to draw out a wheel or a radio, because these originally were unknown to man, and so we learn to go within for grace. "Thy grace is my sufficiency, and the kingdom of thy grace is within me. The fullness of allness is within me—eternal life, immortality, infinity, harmony, wholeness, completeness." This is the nature of the infinite consciousness which is individual consciousness. Therefore, I turn within and seek thy word, thy kingdom, thy grace, thy spiritual treasures and this includes health. So we do not have to go outside of ourselves for health or wealth or peace, because all of these are embodied in our consciousness and we learn through meditation to *let* these splendors flow into expression.

Notice this: God knows nothing about sin, disease, or lack. If he did, they would be embodied in your consciousness as a part of omnipresence, and you could not escape them. The ministry of the Christ reveals that "I am come—this divine consciousness within you—that you might have life and that you might have it more abundantly."[4] *It* is come that you might be fed and have twelve baskets-full left over with every meal. *It* is come

that you might be forgiven for past ignorances. *It* is
come that you might have peace on earth. On the other
hand God does not know health or wealth, because to
know these he would have to first know sickness and
lack and then replace one with the other. God is infinite
individual consciousness, life eternal, without any
opposites. Therefore we do not draw health from our
consciousness; we draw our realization of the nature of
consciousness which is wholeness and grace. Grace is
not some degree of health. Grace is infinity and
eternality, and so this leads us to prayer or meditation.

In order to reveal the nature of the prayer that
"availeth much," let us go back to China again and think
of the man who received the impartation of the wheel.
Since he knew nothing about a wheel, he could not pray
to God for it. So, we must be safe in concluding that
probably the absence of a wheel was causing him a
problem and he may have sat down, as we do, and
turned within with the question: "How am I going to get
this load of dirt over to that field?" As he turned within,
he probably saw a picture of a wheel and received the
idea. When we pray we are just as ignorant of what we
need. You may tell your practitioner that you have a
pain or that your pocketbook is empty. That may be the
problem, but you do not know the solution nor does
your practitioner. So the only thing is to sit down and
pray, "Let thy grace be revealed to me. How love I thy
law," and an answer comes from within that has nothing
to do with the problem but is an inner peace, or an inner
joy or an assurance. When this takes place within, the
outer harmony is restored.

Notice this: In our prayer we did not go out into the
world to change anybody or to get anything. We went

within. If you observe yourself carefully in periods of prayer or meditation, you will discover that for a great part, you are allowing your thought to go to the outer and are thinking in terms of changing the external. It really is a tremendous discipline to arrive at that state of consciousness where you know that everything in the external belongs to somebody else, or like the farmer who is looking for the crops. We must never look for the crops. Our entire attention must be on the fact that, unless there is an activity of the spirit within, there never will be a crop. If I can abide in the remembrance of this invisible substance that is functioning within me, I will be able to wait for my crop, whether it is a crop of money, or a crop of health, or a crop of happiness or a crop of peace. It will come *if* I can keep my mind off of the crop, off of the without. The man who received the wheel would not have received it if he had known what he was praying for. The one thing Thomas Edison was sure of was that he was not looking for a phonograph when he discovered it.

There are many wonderful things in this world for us to enjoy. We need not be ascetics, if only we will not struggle for them in the outer and let them unfold from within. Bring yourself to that consciousness where you no longer pray for any effect, where you no longer pray for that which has form or being. Remember the function of the Christ is to break our attachment to "this world," to the outer realm, so we can enjoy it without being attached to it. You are not detached if in your prayer or meditation you have in mind something in the external that you are hoping to attain, whether it is a person, a place or a condition. You are detached only when you can close your eyes to this world, knowing that whatever the needs are, they will unfold from within. Then the hypnotism has been broken.

Practice shutting out this whole world when you close your eyes, and eventually there will be no attachment without, for person, place or condition. Now you can be centered inside and say:

Thank God the divine grace that is established within me is my sufficiency. All that the Father hath is mine by relationship of my oneness with my source. Thy Self within me is my bread, my meat, my wine, my water. Thy Self within me, which is really my Self, is the substance of all form, the essence of all outer being.

It seems impossible to the human mind, until you can visualize a little handful of seeds growing up into a whole forest of trees. Then you can begin to perceive how the spiritual essence within you is really the seed of all the outer demonstrations. This at the same time breaks the hypnotism that makes you believe you need something or somebody–and sets you free to live in an inner aloneness with God, even while companioning with the outside world.

To students who have been a long time on the path, this is going to lead to a higher step in the healing ministry. At present most people believe that they need the best available practitioner to meet their needs, and in a sense they do; but this is true only until you reach the higher realms where you acknowledge that there is only one Christ, whether that Christ is manifest as you or as me. Then you can begin to look to the Christ within the manifest realm or the unmanifest realm, because it is the same Christ whether there is a person attached to it or not.

"Before Abraham was, I AM with you." Christ must never be personalized. "Before Abraham was, Christ *Is*." All Christian religious experience is wrong, because it begins Christ with Jesus and ends Christ with Jesus. This is fatal. Christ is not a person and never was. Christ, being infinite, is your own consciousness so you never have to reach higher than your own consciousness to reach Christ. It is for this reason that we are taught, "Behold the Christ in everything and everyone." Christ is consciousness. Consciousness is God-consciousness individualized. If there were not a person on earth, there would be just as much Christ here, and remember that Christ is the "bread, the meat, the wine and the water." Christ is the forgiver, the mediator, the multiplier, and Christ is the divine consciousness. The moment you recognize this, you are illumined. The unillumined think Christ is in time and space. Illumination begins with the realization of "The place whereon I stand is holy ground. Christ is omnipresent where I am."

All of this must turn our attention back to the kingdom of God, the realm of consciousness, within us. The nature of our consciousness is divine spirit, and our consciousness is the source, the law, the essence, the "cause" of our crops. Then we will not look to anybody for anything. We will find everything within ourselves. As you drop the search for everything in the external, and attain the realization of the inner Christ, all the things appear externally as the added things.

Automatically this leads up to the dignity of individual man, without which you have neither Christianity nor true democracy. Nobody is holy except the individual. There is only one thing, one condition or belief, that can possibly lose for this world whatever amount of freedom and democracy it has attained, and that is the loss of the value of individual you. Perhaps some of you read in the newspaper this week that we are not to expect the church to take a stand for anything constructive, and gave the reason for it. This would be the loss of Christianity in the church, because the Master took a very strong stand for the dignity of individual man. "Know ye not that you are the child of God?[5] . . . You were not made for the sabbath; the sabbath was made for you."[6]

When man is willing to sacrifice his God-given heritage of individual dignity, and surrender it to a mass, to a leader, to a state, he deserves what he gets. We read of the many attempts to fight communism or state socialism, which is a doorway or entrance into communism. These attempts cannot succeed. As long as people want to surrender the rights of individual being, individual divinity, individual dignity, nobody can fight the inevitable. Be assured I am not saying that we are facing a hopeless situation. No, I am telling you that neither communism nor socialism has a chance to succeed because there are enough people in the world today who are standing on individual identity. Just be unconquerable within, and nobody can conquer you without. "Ten righteous men can save a city."[7]

Put up thy sword and stand silently, secretly, sacredly on the dignity of your individual being. Christ, divine Sonship, is your identity. Divinity is the nature of your being, and all you have to do is stand on that truth silently, secretly, sacredly, and the whole battle of hell cannot prevail against it. Why? Because you are not taking up the world's weapons.

Rest in this Word: "You are the Word, the Word made flesh, the infinite made visibly manifest." In this way you will discover that you are living a life in which you are drawing forth from the secret place of the Most High—from your inner sanctuary—the riches that are stored up in your consciousness by virtue of divine Sonship. We all have it equally; we experience it proportionately as we can stand on this truth in spite of appearances.

I — That Is All

June 16, 1963
Princess Kaiulani Hotel

GOOD AFTERNOON. First of all, to those of you who are here with us today for the first time, may I welcome you for myself and for all of us in this group.

You may perhaps know that we of The Infinite Way activity do not advertise or proselyte in any way, and there is a reason for this. We recognize the fact that we really have nothing to give, except to those who are led to receive it. In other words, whether or not you receive anything at all from the message of The Infinite Way is not up to us; it is strictly a matter of your own consciousness. You either recognize, receive, and respond to this message, or you do not. There is no power in the message itself, the power is in your consciousness. If the power were in the message itself, the entire world could be saved. We have been offered a gift of ten million dollars to put this message on television across the whole of the United States, but I cannot accept the gift because I do not believe the message in and of itself has that power. Only the consciousness of the individual is power, and whether a message meets your need depends upon whether or not you are receptive or responsive to it.

In the same way we could take the music of Beethoven, Brahms, or Bach, or the literature of Shakespeare. They are masterpieces, but does the world enjoy them?

No, only those persons in the world can enjoy them who are responsive to that level of consciousness. To others these masters have no value. We have great religious masters—Gautama the Buddha, Nanak, Christ Jesus—and we have many modern mystics from the 12th century to the present. You will notice that they are not saving the world, but they are contributing towards saving thousands of individuals who can receive them.

You who may be young students of The Infinite Way will certainly find us pleasant to associate with, although we are disciplinarians. We have no rules set down for the conduct of others, but we are very strict with ourselves. We insist on hours and hours of study each day, for ours is no pastime teaching, no small-change teaching. There are books to be studied, tapes to be studied, activities to attend. It really does demand all of you if you are to receive what we have to give. We recognize that during our span on this plane, we have more work to do than can be encompassed. Therefore, you will understand if we give our time and attention to those who are most generous in giving their time and attention to this study.

At first you may have some difficulty in understanding this message, more especially if you have a metaphysical background. You have heard the statement that "Truth is one," or "There is only one truth," and I will say to you that this is only true when you get into the higher realms of consciousness where you have transcended the letter of truth and can live purely by the spirit. Until that time, there are vast differences in the approaches to truth as presented by Christian Science, Unity, Religious Science, Mind Science, and even some of the independent or individual teachers. In other words, you may have worked from the standpoint that thought is power, and now you come to books in The Infinite Way that say thought is not power.

You must not accept a statement of that kind without understanding why the principle exists in The Infinite Way, otherwise you will not be able to properly apply the principle in daily living. Of course, I know that in the human picture we can entertain good thoughts or bad thoughts, and that the good thoughts are apt to do nice things for us and the bad thoughts are apt to do very bad things for us. However, that does not make them power in the way we use the word *power* in The Infinite Way. Our use of the word power really means an attribute or activity of God. Therefore, since there is only one God, there can only be one power. Since God is spirit, then the only power can be spiritual power—not material or mental power—only spiritual power.

As long as you are in the human scene, working only with the human mind, you can make a power of your mind and its thoughts. You can use them for good and you can use them for evil, as the world is doing all the time. The moment that individuals come into the atmosphere of The Infinite Way, you will find that they are seeking release from some physical or mental powers, and probably that is the only reason they come. Perhaps one in a hundred thousand is seeking purely the attaining of the mystical consciousness, but surely the rest of us are seeking release from some physical power that has gripped us, some material law that is influencing us, or some mental power that is holding us in bondage.

If you were seeking a power to overcome these material and mental powers, you would be seeking erroneously. You would be seeking amiss because there

are no such powers. Let us take the subject of warfare.
The world began by throwing stones at each other, then
sling-shots, bows and arrows, and spears, clear on up to
the atomic bomb–but they still have found no way to
overcome the atomic bomb. You can go on seeking
greater powers and find them, but you never will find a
way to overcome these powers until you reach that place
in consciousness where, instead of seeking greater and
greater powers, you begin to realize, "These material
and mental things that the world has accepted as power
are not power." Why? It is so simple. God, spirit, is
omnipotence–all-power–so there cannot be all-power
and material and mental powers.

When you come to The Infinite Way you come to a
place where you give up power, where you give up
seeking one power with which to destroy another power.
You give up seeking God-power. You come to a state of
consciousness in which you realize, "Because of God,
there are no other powers," and you learn to "Rest in
this word." This is exemplified in the Old Testament
where the Hebrews came to their prophet and told of
the great armies coming against them, and were given
the assurance, "Fear not, they have only the arm of
flesh.[1] We have the Lord God Almighty." And they
"Rested in his word" and the enemy destroyed itself.
The Master exemplified this in the New Testament
when called on to heal the cripple and the blind man,
"Pick up your bed and walk,"[2] and "Open your eyes."[3]
Nowhere does he claim to turn to God for a power. He
lives in the consciousness of God as omnipotence. "*I* am
the bread, the meat, the wine and the water[4]. . . . Fear
not, *I* am with you."[5] And remember that each one of
you has the same *I* within you.

Close your eyes, and very gently inside of yourself say:

I. *That is all.* I *is within you, so learn to trust it, but not as a power over anything. Just trust "*I *am with you*" *and rest, relax. "*I *am with you. . . . I will never leave thee nor forsake thee. . . . Fear not, it is* I*. . . . I will be with thee unto the end of the world. . . . I am come that ye might have life and that ye might have it more abundantly." Did that* I *live 2,000 years ago, and not today? Then what of the statement "*I *will never leave you nor forsake you"? Was that a personalized* I *locked up in the mind of Jesus, or was he declaring that "*I, *the Son of God, is within you"?*

So can you not see that some of you may have difficulty in making a transition in consciousness where you stop affirming truth and denying error, and reach that place in consciousness where you can relax and remember "*I* am closer to you than breathing, nearer than hands and feet, "Be not afraid, it is *I*." Every student has great experiences of healing and regeneration in proportion as he or she can relax in that statement, "Be not afraid, it is *I*. The only presence, the only power in the midst of you—closer than breathing. Be not afraid, it is *I*. Do not fight because when you are fighting you are fighting your imagination. You are fighting illusions, instead of relaxing and resting.

You may have accepted the belief that your sins of omission or commission, your sins of the past or your sins of the present, are going to interfere with your spiritual progress. The Master did not confirm that, or he would not have said to the woman taken in adultery and the thief on the cross "Thy sins be forgiven thee."

Yes, only do not go back and sin again. Always the karmic law of "As ye sow, so shall ye reap" is operating. This means that every minute of our lives we are putting into operation what will take place tomorrow, next week, next month. We are doing it by holding to fear, hate, injustice, malice, or jealousy instead of "Abiding in me and letting my word abide in you."[6] It is not easy to stop thinking worldly thoughts, and I do not believe anyone can do it alone. Only when you become aware that "*I* in the midst of you am divine grace" does thinking change from the material base to the spiritual base. The Christ, or the spirit or the presence of God—it forgives—it changes.

It is for this reason that we do not make rules of conduct for our students. They can ride to heaven on wings of glory, or they can travel in the opposite direction. We can only offer the cup of cold water, and then leave it to the individuals as to how much or how little they wish to drink of it. Something must be introduced into the consciousness of an individual to change it. That spirit is the spirit of God, which you will notice in our students as you mix with them. It is not human good in them—it is a spiritual presence which has been released.

Those of you who are in the Islands will discover that we have a wonderful activity here. It is one that has been going on for many, many years, one in which we have found understanding, peace, cooperativeness, and sharing among ourselves in so many different ways. Of course you will discover that we long to share it with those who seek it, but remember that we can only share to the degree of your receptivity.

Because we do not publicize our work, the question is raised many times why we do not make it available to the world if it blesses as many as we have witnessed it bless. We have even been asked to consider having a moving picture made of The Infinite Way activity, because the whole world needs it. Of course it needs it, but how much of it would the world accept? You remember the beggar addressing Peter and John, begging for coins, and the answer "Silver and gold have we none, but such as I have, give I unto you."[7] So with us. We do not have the silver and gold and the medical ability the world wants. What we do have is some measure of awareness of the fact that "God is the *I* at the center of our being." We do not have to worship in holy temples, nor do we have to appease or make sacrifices to God. We have only to "Abide in this word and let this word abide in us,"[8] and then accept that the evils of the world are the "arm of flesh or nothingness." Then rest—no crusading—just resting in it.

We do not go to God as if God were a Santa Claus with wonderful presents of health and supply and companionship, which we try to get him to release to us. No, this concept belongs to a bygone age. "It is my good pleasure to give you the kingdom,"[9] but there is a price: "Seek ye first the kingdom of God,"[10] and these things will be added. Trying to demonstrate these things will keep you out of heaven forever. The question arises over and over again, "Is it wrong for me to want enough money for my children?" or "Is it wrong to want to take care of my parents?" No, but most people are going about it wrongly. Seek ye *first* the kingdom of God, and all of these things will appear.

We ask all of our students to give freely of what they have received—to share—but to be sure that it is wanted. We have a monthly *Letter* that is sent only to those who request it and to no one else, and only those who request it every twelve months. Why? What use is it to send it to those who are probably not reading it? Every year we have to take four hundred or more names from the *Letter* list, names of people who are receiving it yet not reading it. Money is not a factor. The *Letter* is sent to those who contribute or to those who do not contribute. We do want to share, but we are eager that it reaches only those who would welcome it in the same spirit that we work to bring it out.

I hope I have made two of our principles clear to you today, and that it has reminded our own students of them—because without these reminders we ourselves can forget. One is the nature of God, the very *I* in the midst of you which you need not pray to or try to influence. Just "relax and rest in me." The other is the nature of error. You do not fight, rise above or destroy the evils of this world, but recognize them as "the arm of flesh or nothingness." Arm of flesh is a very good illustration. See this arm? This arm without *I* is an arm of flesh, and would probably stay in this position for a thousand years if there were not something called *I* to move it. You will discover eventually that all evil of any nature is dead flesh, unable to do anything unless I come along and fear it or hate it.

You will notice that this message is being written down and by next week it will be mimeographed. That makes it available to read over and over again, so eventually these principles really "sink from the head into the heart," from an intellectual acceptance to a spiritual realization. All of our monthly *Letters* from the year 1954 when they began, are in book form for the same reason. They constitute our lessons to students.

Every principle is set forth in these *Letters* so they probably become the most important part of our literature.

I will bring to your attention one final point. Everything I have said to you today is a waste of time without this added thing, statement, unfoldment: Within your consciousness is access to the heavenly kingdom, the spiritual realm, the realm of God, the atmosphere of God. "The kingdom of God is neither lo here nor lo there." The kingdom of God is not in a Bible or in metaphysics or even in mystical literature. The kingdom of God is locked up in your consciousness, and this is true with everyone on the face of the globe. We only have access to it through our ability to contact it. The whole function of The Infinite Way is to teach students—not these lessons I have given you today—but to contact the spirit within. These lessons are a part of the teachings that make it possible for you to meditate, and in meditating to make the contact with the source of life. Without this lesson you might find it difficult to meditate, but with this lesson today, you can close your eyes and remember this:

God is not afar off but within me, right here as I sit here. The kingdom of God, the kingdom of all-being, all-presence, all-gifts, is within me—closer than breathing—and its name is I. I *in the midst of me is mighty.* I *in the midst of me is the source of my eternal life, of my immortality. I need not fear the arm of flesh in any form—sin, disease, lack, limitation, loneliness—because now I remember "Fear not,* I *am with you." I can rest in this* I *within me. I know now what the Master meant when he said "Abide in me" and now I am living in this* I *within me. And also it says "Fear not,* I *am with thee."* I *am with thee and* I *will be with thee unto the end of the world. Neither life nor death can separate me from the love of God or the life of God. I can stop fearing death right now, for I will be as close to God in what the world calls death as I am at this moment. So again I will fear not what mortality can do to me.*

This is a contemplative form of meditation and you will notice that, as you become accustomed to this, you will quiet down inside. And eventually, instead of your making these statements of truth, these statements of truth will come from within you. When you begin to hear from within, you will understand why it is written "When he utters his voice, the earth melts."[11]

THE SOURCE

June 23, 1963
Princess Kaiulani Hotel

MEN AND WOMEN OF THE ARTS, the professions, the business world, of all religions, colors and creeds, must eventually understand that the power of life that flows in them has no art, no profession, no business, no religion— and yet it produces the very intelligence and inspiration in every activity of our human lives.

Artists, sculptors, painters, composers all acknowledge one source of inspiration. When you stop to think of the French or the Germans or the Russians or the Asians or the Occidentals or the whites or the blacks, you must know that the source of inspiration is *one;* and, when you have it, it reveals itself in whatever your particular activity may be. Let me illustrate: A man had an orchard of apple trees, all very fine apples and expensive on the market. But he had one tree from which he could derive no revenue, because the apples of this particular tree were of an inferior grade and were therefore unsalable. One year the idea came to him, "Why not graft onto that tree the limbs of some of the very good apples." He did, and shortly this tree was also producing good apples. In other words, the life that was giving expression to the apples was *one* life. You have witnessed this in so many different experiences. Whether it is music or art or writing, there is a source of inspiration.

In the religious world this source is called God, but it need not be called God because by any other name it would be the same source of inspiration. Some call it, religiously, the *Christ*. In the philosophies, and especially in mystical teachings, there are many different names for the source of inspiration or the source of power or the source of life. The first step that every one of us must know is that this source exists. You will not find this difficult as you notice the rhythm of the seasons, the sun, the moon, the stars, the tides, two times two always being four, like always begetting like. You know, of course, that there is such a law.

Even in what we call human creation or birth, you know right well that there is only one way to account for birth. In other words there are a couple of cells, but there is a force that acts upon those cells and changes them from cells to being. The next question is: "Where is it and how does it function?" Here of course is where the world has been misled for 4,000 years. It received all of its teachings along that line from the churches, and the churches never knew the truth. They had people looking for it up in the sky or on a cross or in some kind of a far-off God—and remember there was no unity where this God was. Every religion had a different concept of God, and God seemed to be every-where except where he is. Of course Jesus Christ revealed, not inside the temple but outside in the valleys, and by the sea, that "God is neither lo here nor lo there. God is not in holy mountains nor in holy temples. The kingdom of God, this source of inspiration, the source of power and life, is within you." For three hundred years his teachings had great effect upon the world, until it was decided to play down that teaching and put him up in heaven; and so for 1700 years we have been missing the mark.

If you want to contact the source, you must contact it within yourself. There is no other place to find it. The Church of England today is going through a shock because one of its bishops has written a book reminding that the church has been teaching erroneously by looking outside for God.

When you come to the realization of within-ness, eventually you are going to be tempted. Christ Jesus was tempted. After he had attained spiritual wisdom, he was still tempted to turn stones into bread, to perform miracles. But he was spiritually mature and he was able to say "Get thee behind me, Satan. My mission is to show forth the inner power—not my power but yours." When temptation comes you have to be able to stand fast, for it comes in the form of exalting the ego.

When you as an individual come to the realization that there is a power source, an inspiration source, and you begin to witness its fruitage, the temptation comes to use that power. That is where you can lose your entire demonstration of life. It is not meant that you use it, but that it use you. In other words, man is supposed to show forth the infinite wisdom, the infinite intelligence and the infinite love that is God. That is why the Master taught "You must pray in secret, not to be seen of men."[1] If you pray openly you receive the praise of men but you lose the God-power. The moment you take credit for anything that flows through you, you lose it. But, if you permit *this* that is within you to flow, it will make you great in the eyes of the world. The moment you achieve something, it is natural for people to start worshiping you and trying to get your opinions on anything and everything. Outwardly you cannot stop them, but inwardly you can realize "I know the source that is flowing through me. I know the source of all power, strength, wisdom."

As long as you know that, you will prove one of the greatest principles ever revealed to man, a principle which the world today is trying to destroy. That is your individuality, your strength, your power, and your integrity. Remember that you were born equal to God and equal to every other man. No one can maintain your integrity for you, your intelligence, your freedoms, your abilities, and skills except yourself. If I were to say that we are safe because we are a united group here, I would be deluding you. There have been united nations and united groups and united people, and they all fall, as they must.

Our concern at this moment is with individual you, because in the end a nation, a world, is only made up of individual you and individual me. Therefore, we must begin with the individual and we must understand our at-one-ment with our source which is within us, "Closer than breathing, nearer than hands and feet." It is the source of our good, and our recognition of our oneness with it sets us free. The mystical poet says "You must open out a way for the imprisoned splendor to escape." Only you can set it free.

If you will remember the foundational point on which our work is based, which is consciousness, you will know that nothing can take place in your life except through your consciousness. So it is that what you accept or reject in your consciousness determines what you are and what you will ever be. If you can be made to accept the belief that you are "a worm of the dust," you will not be any more than that. In other words your consciousness will give back to you what you can accept, but we are told "Ye shall know the truth, and the truth shall make you free." Remember that the truth cannot make you free—you must know the truth. In other words, you open your consciousness to truth, and your consciousness will give truth back to you.

If you are a Christian, accept "*I* and the Father are one and all that the Father has is mine."[2] And if you can accept that, then this source within you can begin to flow out as a talent or an art or whatever determines the nature of your life. If you limit yourself to your education or lack of it, your social status or lack of it, your economic status or lack of it, then that is what you will show forth. Instead, acknowledge "Son, thou art ever with me, and all that *I* have is thine,"[3] and you will begin to understand that the only reason you were ever created was that God would have an instrument on earth through whom to pour its qualities. You were not born to be subjected to anything or anyone.

Behind your birth is an infinite creator, and this creator must have a purpose. Therefore, we are on earth for a purpose, and that purpose is whatever purpose was in mind when we were formed. And remember that we are not limited to ourselves, because we were formed in the "image and likeness of God." The egotist says, "I am great," and he is cut down. The person who feels inferior says, "I am nothing." Both are wrong. Honor the creative principle of the universe by acknowledging that it had a purpose in creating individual you and individual me—it had a purpose in sending each of us forth into expression.

I can only live so that whatever gift is given to me comes through me to uplift one or more in this world, performing a God function, not a personal one. See that the purpose of what you are doing is that the creative principle may operate through you in order to benefit someone else.

When the Master takes his final leave of his disciples and ascends, he says a very strange thing: "Remain in this city until you are endowed from on high."[4] In other words, no matter what message you preach it is going to fall on barren soil unless you are "endowed from on high." Whatever it is you undertake to do, if you let yourself be "endowed from this source of inspiration within," then you will really discover what it is to have capacities beyond your own. The mass of people are really a herd, a herd of animals. They all have the potentialities of great beings, because they all have the same "gift of God" within them, incarnated within them when they were conceived. They are not taught this, so they do not bring it out; but during their lifetime some people awaken, each one in a different way. Some are compelled through problems to "turn and find the answer." Through an individual others are led to a good book. So, many people do awaken to "This that is within them"—some through religion, some through philosophy, some through art. It makes no difference what it is that awakens one, but fortunate is the person who is startled into asking "Why am I living? What am I accomplishing on earth?"

The Master made it very clear, not only that your praying should be done in secret so you do not gain the praise of men, but that your benevolences should be done in secret. There is a principle involved which I am sure he must have taught his disciples but which, for some reason, they did not give forth in their writings. The principle is this: "This source is within you, and

what it perceives in you is the way it acts through you."
Therefore, if you are praying rightly, then this inner
source is brought into action to answer that prayer. If
you are giving of your benevolences quietly, then this
inner source is coming into action. It is like placing a
seed in the ground and leaving it buried there. Nature
then goes to work on it and eventually the fruitage
comes forth. So, if we do not publicize ourselves in order
to gain approval, the law goes to work for us and we will
then understand "As ye sow, so shall ye reap."[5] There is
no greater law than that. In the East it is called karmic
law; in philosophy it is called the law of cause and effect.
All cause is within your consciousness, and therefore all
effect comes forth from you. Be prepared for some
failures. In interpreting this law of life you may have
some failures, but it is better to fail through your own
consciousness than depend on someone or something.

Keep yourself in the position "*I* and the Father are
one," and all I have to do is go within myself and draw
forth riches. We have introduced the art of meditation to
the western world and you are witnesses to the fruitage
of it because you know now that any good that is to
come into your experience is to come from that "Kingdom within you." Only through learning to live during
some period of each day in within-ness, can you bring
forth the entire riches, the entire splendors. Listening to
the music on the air today, you would never believe that
there is greater music in our consciousness than Brahms,
Beethoven, or Bach, and greater literature than Shakespeare.

Consciousness is infinite and there is only one
consciousness, but we individually have access to it.
Ralph Waldo Emerson made that very clear in one of
his essays: "There is only one infinite Mind, but every

man is an inlet to and an outlet for that Mind." If you wish access to the great treasures of consciousness you cannot go to a school in order to receive them. Schools give you working tools, knowledge, skills, but inspiration gives you the treasures of soul and mind. No, you must go within and bring it out of your Soul. In order to inspire, your life must be lived from the depths of your consciousness—then you will bring forth these treasures that will "glorify God and inspire men."

All forms of human union eventually lead to death and destruction. No longer can you depend on human union, human strength, human integrity. Those things that live come forth from within. Those things that inspire and illumine, that lead the human race upward, come from within. Anything of a lasting and beneficial nature must come through prayer, through inspiration, from inside the consciousness of an individual. The more you realize that the only thing of value in this world is the individual, the more will your capacities be expanded.

DISCOVERING THE SOUL

June 30, 1963
Princess Kailulanei Hotel

GOOD AFTERNOON. When we first come to a spiritual study it is only because some circumstance or condition of our life is in need of adjustment. We have not found the completeness of life, happiness, health, or some other aspect of fulfillment, and we are seeking the missing link. In other words, we are always wanting improvement in the human affairs of our existence.

During your Infinite Way study you will find some degree of improvement in your human life, but I can assure you that you never will find all that you are seeking humanly. It does not lie within the nature of a spiritual teaching to give you all of the human good things you think you would like. In some avenues of your life you will experience improved health, increased supply, or some other form of human happiness, but you will not find the completeness that you expected. About the time you actually realize that it never is going to happen, you will likewise perceive the reason, which is that you have been praying amiss. You have been trying to patch up or improve this human existence and that is not the function of any spiritual message.

From the message of every mystic it is very clear that the object of the spiritual path is that we may die to the human experience and be reborn of the spirit. We learn

225

that the spiritual kingdom, the real kingdom, the mystical kingdom is not of this world, not even when this world is healthy, wealthy, and wise.

On the mystical path we learn that there is a goal. This goal is not the metaphysical goal of better health, a nicer home, a better car, and more companionship. The goal is releasing the Soul from the tomb of human existence, more especially the tomb of the human mind. In your periods of introspection or contemplation check to see to what extent you are imprisoned in your mind and body. Notice how little you know except what is in your mind or body, and then you will realize that all human experience is a life of imprisonment.

Every human being who is ever born is in prison, the prison of the mind and the body; and during the normal human lifetime of an individual, he never gets outside of that tomb. As far as most humans are concerned, anything that is not in the mind or body does not exist, and this extends into the highest realms of the educated. In fact, very often the greater the education the greater the imprisonment.

Life understood is an adventure. It is like the baby starting to crawl who begins to find a world outside of its crib, highchair, or playpen. Even though the child does hit its head or burn its fingers, the world it is exploring is a fascinating place. But somehow or other, by the time children reach their teens, they have lost all desire for searching and seeking, they have lost all desire for adventure. There is an interval of sex curiosity, but when that is learned there is nothing further to be curious about. Life is then lived in the body and in the mind.

There are some, however—explorers, artists, adventurers—who do try to widen their horizons physically, mentally, and artistically; but only here and there have we had an occasional one or two or three who wanted to explore the realms of the Soul.

Just think of the word *Soul* for a moment, see how little you know about it, and remember that the rest of the world knows less than you do, because you have a great deal of the Soul in the writings you are reading and studying. The knowledge of the Soul, the life of the Soul, the wider horizon that the Soul encompasses is the greatest experience that can come to any individual.

The Soul is imprisoned in the tomb that we call the human experience—mind and body. If we are to experience the Soul we have to break through the limitations of the body and mind. This the Master called, "taking no thought for your life" but seeking the kingdom of God, the realm of God, the Soul.

See how we violate this by thinking of God or the Soul as having some function to improve our human life. The divine instructions are to take no thought for this life or any of its aspects—body, mind, or anything else. Seek an awareness of the higher realm.

The reason that the subject is so little known is that we speak of God as "God" and do not realize that God is the Soul of man. You can never find the kingdom of God until you have entered into the awareness of your own Soul. You can see that this is an adventure, because you have to leave behind the familiar aspects of life. You have to leave behind the things of the body and the mind and reach out into the humanly unknown.

Admiral Byrd had to leave familiar waters in order to reach the regions of the North and South Poles. He did not even know if there was a way back. That is why so many set out for those poles and never returned. They were willing to lose their human sense of life in order to venture into the heretofore unknown.

You will have absolutely no way of knowing what you are going to find when you reach the realm of your Soul, and you cannot even have a guarantee that you will get back. Those who have been that way before you have made no maps going or coming. Yes, we know that the way is the way of meditation, but a teacher can carry a student only so far into the practice of meditation and then the student is on his own.

Some become so frightened at the first glimpse that they never go that way again. You see, God is light, and to come face to face with that light is more intense than looking right into the hot sun. And so, if it has been frightening it takes an adventurous spirit to make more than one attempt. It is not that God is frightening, but that the human senses are frightened at the unknown. Actually there is nothing to fear.

As a rule it is so gradual that the entire way is a joy. Here and there will be experiences that are momentarily frightening because we expect something different. For example, we expect every day to be a joyous experience, whereas those experiences are few, and the experiences of barrenness, emptiness, and feeling that we are separated from God are many. Actually these are more necessary to our spiritual unfoldment than sitting on cloud nine, because without that complete barrenness we are a vessel already full and nothing new can enter. We have to lose our concepts of God and what we expect of God.

I wish I could use as a title of a book *Santa Claus God*, because that is what the majority of God concepts are. Be assured that we cannot enter the realm of the Soul with any such God in mind. Another thing: We leave behind all that we have heretofore expected of companionship in our human sense of companionship. We long to tell our companions what we are thinking and what we are doing, and we love to share our joys and successes, but that cannot be done on the mystical path because those who have not been there can have no way of being able to share it. Only rarely do you find a companion with whom you can share and even then you discover that there are some things that must forever remain hidden.

Does this not account for the Master's loneliness during his three-year ministry? When he wanted to reveal some of the secrets of the fourth-dimensional life he could only take three of his disciples with him. All twelve could never have been prepared to see that the men who lived five hundred years ago are not only living now but are standing right here with us and sharing with us their wisdom. He never told that to the twelve disciples—only to three, and I am sure there were some secrets he did not even tell the three. This is that aloneness that comes in this life, and we find we can share our accomplishments and attainments with only a very few.

This morning I was reading the 1962 *Letters*, and I noticed in one of them that I reminded the students that peace is now established on earth, but do not look in the newspapers for news of it, for it will be at least five years before they know it and report it. It has taken place invisibly and, little by little, will be made manifest outwardly until one day the newspapers will say, "Peace was declared yesterday," but what went on in the five or ten years before, when peace was actually established and gradually made manifest. Of that they can have no possible knowledge. I do not have to tell you how many signs there are now of this coming peace, except that it will be a few years before it will be reported.

It was in this same way in 1922 or 1923 that I saw as clearly as if it were already on earth the start of World War II, a war that actually started in visible form in 1939. Because no one would listen when I told it, I began a collection of books. I started with a book written by the man who was the Ambassador from Germany to the United States, and followed it with President Wilson's State Papers and went on through Churchill and some of the more prominent writers. From 1922 or 1923 to 1940, I made this collection of 267 volumes in which anyone could see that war had to happen. Since I have been here, I have presented those books to the public library.

The moment you enter the higher consciousness, you can see events of the present, the past, and the future. It is like standing on the eleventh floor balcony, where you can see in all directions for miles—to the right and to the left—but the man on the street is aware only of that which is taking place right before his eyes. From the higher realms of consciousness the past is visible and the present and the future, yet not as fortune telling.

You can go back to scriptural and other prophets and see how they knew of what was to come and what could be done to prevent evil from happening, but the evils did happen. Why? Because no one can believe that which they cannot comprehend. That is why you lose many companions on the spiritual path.

There is a practical reason for undertaking the spiritual adventure. With what we know now, it is possible to work behind the scenes and change the course of future events. This is known to the mystics who are now on the other side of the veil, and to the extent that they find men and women receptive to the spiritual urge or influence, they are able to give the benefit of their wisdom to those now on earth and to exert an influence which helps to adjust human affairs. Even without this, the adventure is worthwhile, because it frees our own Soul from its limitations. It frees our own life from being just a round of getting up in the morning, eating three meals a day, and going to bed at night. This in itself is a prison.

Man was not created to be a slave, physically, economically, or mentally. The purpose of man is to show forth the nature of God. Originally man was intended to be the instrument through which, or as which, God lived on earth. This is the meaning of the incarnation—God incarnated as, or in, individual man or woman. The Bible symbolizes man's lost way and shows that man can find his way back to the Father's house, to the divine consciousness and live as the heir of God with the purple robe and the jeweled ring. Man is the great glory of God.

Man was not meant to cry, and all tears are shed only because of a sense of limitation. Every tear we shed is proof of some form of limitation being experienced in our lives. Man was not born to cry. The more you search around in the body and in the mind, the more imprisoned you will become. If your doctor is a physical doctor, you will only have to talk with him for awhile to be convinced you are not a man but a machine that has to keep going. God help you if your doctor is a psychological doctor, for then you will be entombed in all of the error that has ever been discovered.

Do not think for a moment that you or I are free of the body or the mind. Rather we must understand that, through our studies, we are breaking out of the body and out of the mind and into the realm of the Soul. When we reach that realm, and even as we approach it, the mind and the body will be discovered to be more receptive to God government and require less and less of human attention. So do not let us be in too much of a hurry to legislate the doctors out of existence. Instead, keep your mind on your goal.

Eventually we will be released from this imprisonment by an act of grace. Something will happen to us. It will happen, not if we just sit around and wait for it, but if we keep our thoughts struggling upward. "Thou wilt keep him in perfect peace whose mind is stayed on thee . . . Acknowledge him in all thy ways . . . In quietness and in confidence . . ." And so, with these efforts of ours, we prepare ourselves for the act of grace that eventually sets us free.

You can see now the reason that angels are pictured with wings, and the reason I speak of soaring thoughts or mountaintop experiences or lofty heights of consciousness. When the Soul is released it flies upward, not in time or space, but in consciousness. It is no longer anchored to the ground; it is no longer entombed in body and mind. It is a soaring awareness, a soaring faculty.

Mistakenly it is thought that when a person experiences physical death, the Soul leaves the body and flies upward. The reason I say this is mistaken sense is that behind it there is the actual truth: As we die daily to the mental and physical sense of life, the Soul is released and flies upward. This is not the day of our physical death; it is the day we are released from the tomb of body and mind, and then the Soul is free. Because this is taught mystically, fundamentalists have made it a literal thing, just like Jonah and the whale which symbolizes our imprisonment in our human unbelief.

You know you have a body, and you know you have a mind, but you have not come to know *you* that has the body and the mind. This is the you that is the adventure of life, and the adventure of life is the awakening of this you. You are the Soul that lives. But first you must know you are the Soul, and then you must begin to explore, search, and seek until you find *Me*–until you find your Self–the real *you*.

MEDITATION IS THE KEY

July 7, 1963
Princess Kaiulani Hotel

GOOD AFTERNOON. The entire secret of The Infinite Way lies not in the books, but in meditation. In fact the secrets of life or the mysteries of life are not to be found in any book or in any message. If messages alone could give us the secrets of life, then Lao-Tzu, Buddha, Jesus, John, Paul, or Shankara have given us all of the secrets that have ever been revealed or perhaps ever could be revealed; but unfortunately, as Paul wrote: "The natural man receiveth not the things of God."[1] The natural man, the creature, is not under the law of God and that is why no message can reveal truth to you until such time as you are no longer the natural man, but have become the child of God—until you have attained spiritual discernment. There is not any message that can reveal its secret to you. There are people who have found a higher lifetime of joyous freedom through Christian Science, through Unity, through The Infinite Way. Why then has not everybody who has read their books attained this same freedom, and the answer is this: The secret is not in the books, the secret is within you and until you discover the secret within you, you cannot find it in any books.

The kingdom of God is within you. What is the kingdom of God, the realm of God? The consciousness of God, God-consciousness–this is the kingdom of God, this is the realm of God. The kingdom is not a temporal one. It is not built with streets, houses, or temples. The kingdom of God is a "Temple not made with hands, eternal in the heavens."[2] The kingdom of God is "neither lo here nor lo there." It is not up above you, nor beside you, nor beneath you. It is actually your own consciousness. This is heaven–this is the kingdom of God–this is the realm of God–and it is the only place in which you will ever find God. Do not look for God in a book or in a holy temple or in a holy man or a holy woman. This is folly. The kingdom of God is consciousness, but there is no consciousness other than your consciousness. There is no consciousness floating around in this room, nor up in a cloud. The only consciousness here is yours and mine, and the only consciousness on earth is the consciousness of mankind–and it is within that consciousness that you must find God.

It is for this reason that meditation is the key to the secret of The Infinite Way, because it is through meditation that we are led back to the realm where God lives. Within your own consciousness is where God is to be found. There are several things that make meditation difficult, until you discover a few little secrets of your own. Probably the major difficulty that we experience in our early days is that we do not know what God is. We have been taught so many concepts of God and we have had so few proofs of God, that we really do not know what we are looking for when we meditate.

It will make it easier if you will remember that God is the Soul of man. God is your own Soul and this Soul is not only within you, "closer than breathing," but it really constitutes all that is real of you. You might say it is your identity. "*I* am Soul," or "Soul constitutes *me.*" So if we say "I have sinned," what we really mean is that we have in some way violated our Soul—we have in some way violated our spiritual identity—we have acted in a way we find unnatural to us. In other words, as soon as I do or think anything I know to be not right, I know it because it is a violation of my true identity.

Now when I meditate, I can realize that I am not going anywhere for God nor am I reaching out anywhere for God. Thank God I have discovered that God is my own Soul. My very Soul is God, and since I cannot separate myself from my Soul, I can sit right here and turn within and develop a sense of within–ness. Now you see that I can commune with my own Soul, since I and my Soul are one. I and my Father are one. Yes, I and my Soul are one, so I need not reach outside of myself. Here I am with the outside world shut out, ready to commune with my very own Soul, that my Soul may impart to me its wisdom, its life, its love, its truth.

We are told that "Finally every man must be taught of God." Let us not make it finally—let us make it *now.*

I am to be taught of my own Soul. My own Soul is too pure to behold iniquity, therefore it has no remembrance of my past sins. It is meeting me on the level on which I am meeting it. I am coming to it pure—to my own Soul—pure in the sense that I have no hidden or ulterior motives. I acknowledge my past offenses and I am sorry, but let that all be bygones and let us begin over again.

Figuratively speaking I have taken off my shoes and my hat and, sacredly and secretly, I am seeking communion with my Soul.

This really sets the scene for you to have a beautiful meditation, with "signs following," but on condition that you do not violate the next lesson. Be sure you do not go to God for anything of a worldly nature. Do not go to God for supply or companionship or employment or marriage or divorce. Lift God up into a holier place than that of just a Santa Claus, and "take no thought for your life" or what you shall drink or what you shall wear. Just commune, as you would if you had the opportunity of sitting with your own mother. Just commune, that I may "know thee aright," that I may be a fitting instrument for thy glory. Give up the orthodox belief that you can pray to God for victory over your enemies, and come back into the mystical realm where "*I* and my Father are one. *I* and my Soul are one, and all that is stored up in my Soul is mine." Remember, my Soul has stored up in it only spiritual things like love, joy, peace, security, justice. These are God's gifts to man.

We are taught by the Master that if we live this mystical life in communion with the Father, all the "things" will be added unto us—and this is true. Enough supply comes to take care of us, and always with twelve baskets left over to share. And, in the mysterious ways that God has, we are led into a fellowship or a communion with those of our own spiritual household. So in one way we may say that we find our companionship. Those of us who meet here have discovered that we have a beautiful relationship with each other. There has never been an infringement of that relationship because it is entirely based on our coming together for the purpose of communion. See how simple meditation is when you recognize that the object of meditation is communion with your own Soul, which is in the realm of your own consciousness. Your own Soul is "the kingdom of God, the palace of God, the place where God dwells." And so no mental effort is necessary, no striving is necessary, no struggling is necessary.

The mystery that reveals itself eventually is this: When you make contact with your Soul, you do not use it or apply it or take thought about it. Your Soul becomes the invisible presence that takes the form of your outer life. But remember that you have nothing to do with it—you do not use, you do not manipulate—you do not imagine. You just "dwell quietly in your Soul." "Abide in *Me*"—that is all you have to do. There are no deep metaphysics involved at all, just abide in *Me;* there are no occult truths to know, just *abide in* Me. *In quietness and in confidence commune with* Me, *with your Soul, for* I *Am your bread, your meat, your wine, and your water.* I *Am even your Resurrection.*

This Soul with which you are communing is the power that restores the lost years of the locust. It is the power that restores your body, your business, your reputation—whatever it is you may have lost, and you do not have to tell it or inform it or plead with it or even tithe with it. It is really free, except for this price: Do not ask it for anything. Do not make a merchandise mart out of your consciousness. Do not try to trade with God. Make of your consciousness a holy place. Abide in the truth and let the truth abide in you, and be assured that if you commune with your Soul, it will impart truths to you to live with.

When I was first studying metaphysics, I was taught that "Thought is power," but I discovered that my thought could not make the sun stand still. And later I found that my thought could not even do lesser things, except to get me in trouble. It was the Soul within me

that revealed, "Thought is not power. *I* within you Am
the power, *I* within you am the resurrection, not your
thoughts." And then it gave me the quotation "God's
thoughts are not your thoughts, God's ways are not your
ways." There is only one way that you can "abide in
God's thoughts," by being responsive to the still small
voice that is within your own Soul.

I had been taught, when doing healing work, that the
patient's name and the claim must be taken into my
treatment. But the still small voice told me to "keep my
conversation in heaven." So, until you come to a place
where you can be taught of God, you can be taught
many things that are not necessarily so. That is why the
Master said "Why callest thou me good?"[3] It was not
that he did not recognize his spiritual identity, but he did
not want anyone to look on him as the final authority.
His mission was not to build up a name for himself. In
other words, "This message is not mine but his that sent
me."[4] Therefore, had he left his disciples in the position
of always "quoting our beloved Master," they would
have failed in their usefulness after his ascension. But
they remembered "*I* will not leave you comfortless. Turn
within and the comforter will be there to lead you and
protect you and guide you and deliver you."

So it is that every spiritual teacher today must show
forth in some degree the fruitage of the words he speaks
or else he is just a tinkling cymbal, a cloud without rain.
But, because the teacher can show forth some of the
fruits of the spirit, this must not permit anyone to lapse
into a state of inertia and lean on the teacher's consciousness. Use the teacher's consciousness only as a
bridge to reach the heavenly scene. Where is the
heavenly scene? It is within you.

You must realize that there is no way at all in which you can identify the Soul by any known language, or imagination, or vision. If such things were possible you would have finitized your Soul, and brought it within the realm of your mind. That would be impossible because God is your Soul, and so, spend no time whatsoever in wondering what the Soul is like. But eventually you will have an experience, and you will then know the Soul as well as we know each other—more so. To me it is always as if I could just rest my head back on a pillow of cloud and that is how my Soul appears to me. That is only how the Soul has defined itself to me—as an abiding place, a resting place, where I can be at peace, taking no thought for my life. But it is as real as if it were a solid object. When Truth reveals itself to me in this within-ness, it is never about anything that concerns my own life. It is always concerned with a principle of life. In other words, when it reveals something it is not for me personally, it is a universal principle which is available to all who are receptive.

The belief that God punishes was based on the fact that, when the belief originated, there was no recognition or awareness of karmic law or "as ye sow, so shall ye reap." As yet, the world does not recognize that it is not God who punishes and it is not God who rewards. It is the sowing we do that produces the reaping. Unless you understand this rightly, you could be led astray with that teaching. It requires interpretation, and the nature of the sowing and the reaping was revealed by Paul: "If you sow to the flesh you will reap corruption. If you sow to the spirit you will reap life everlasting,"[5] and the meaning is this: If you are living with your faith or trust in "man whose breath is in his nostrils," if you are living in fear of germs or bombs or bullets, if you are living with your faith or trust in anything of an external nature, if your thought goes outside of your own being and puts faith or fear in the external, this is sowing to the flesh. It has to do with form: if you have fear of, or faith in, anything that is formed, you are sowing to the flesh and you will reap corruption. If your faith is in money, some day it will not be there; if your faith is in a God "out there," you will be disappointed.

Sowing to the spirit is when you recognize that the Soul of man is God, and in the Soul of man are the issues of life. Everything that man will ever need will flow forth from his Soul, so put all your hope and your faith and your love in your Soul. This is sowing to the spirit, this is placing your hope, faith, and trust in that which you can never see, hear, taste, touch, smell, or think. It is placing your entire faith in that which is beyond the realm of thing or thought.

In mystical poetry you read that "you will never reach the kingdom of Soul until you go beyond words and thoughts." Words may be used as a preliminary step, but you will never reach the Soul realm until you have gone beyond the words and the thoughts and are resting in *Me,* resting in the Soul, and *letting* the words come through the still small voice. Open your inner ear and "Rest in *Me*–rest back in your Soul." And since "God is not in the whirlwind," which means that God is not in the problem, remember that "God is in the still, small voice." The very moment that voice begins to reveal itself within, you are being taught by God, fed by God, protected by God, and you can be in constant communion with God. "Let the meditations of my heart be acceptable in thy sight." They will be, if you keep all "merchandise" out of your thought.

You can always remember "*I* and my Father are one[6]. . . . Son, thou art ever with me, and all that *I* have is thine."[7] Then rest back, rest back and let "all that the Father hath" reveal itself to you. God fulfills itself through man when we know that God's ways are not our ways—and certainly let us not go to God with any thoughts. Realize, "The issues of life are all within my Soul. The length of my days on earth are determined by something that is taking place within my Soul. The measure of my usefulness to mankind is measured by some activity that is going on within my own Soul." My companionships, my student body, this is all being measured by an activity going on within my Soul, and I have no control over it. I can only be receptive to it as it unfolds.

Someday the businessman must learn, as some churchmen must learn, that there is no need for competition. Competition is a man-created activity, and there will be no room for competition or jealousy when we realize that the issues of life are determined by the activity that is going on within the Soul. "The activities of my life are determined by my own Soul and nobody can take it from me and that is true of every individual you."

It is so clear that if I have a relationship of *oneness* with my Father, what can possibly come between me and that relationship? The Master says "To know him aright is life eternal." To know him as the Soul of every individual is to bring about the demonstration of life eternal. And when you take the final step and realize "*I* am come that you might have life," remember that the *I* you are talking about is your own Soul. It is a storehouse out of which is unfolding, day by day, everything and everyone necessary to your experience—but you must be a beholder, as if you were watching God appear. And never use your mind to manipulate the human scene. *Be a beholder.*

REMOVING THE VEIL

July 14, 1963
Princess Kaiulani Hotel

GOOD AFTERNOON. Almost everybody comes to the study of The Infinite Way for the "loaves and fishes." Only rarely does anyone come to learn the truth of life; but sooner or later those who remain in this message are forced into making a decision: "Choose ye this day whom ye will serve," God or demonstration—seeking God or seeking through God to get more and better human good. As we seek and discover the kingdom of God, things are "added unto us" on the spiritual path, but by then we are no longer interested in the things.

We learn that Moses put a veil on truth and Jesus Christ removed it; but remember if Moses placed a veil on truth it must have been unveiled when it came into his possession or awareness, and of course it was. Truth had been revealed in Egypt, and because of this Egypt knew centuries of great prosperity and experienced the discovery of great natural laws. Moses received his earliest training in Egypt and, while he did not receive truth there, eventually he was turned in the right direction so that truth could be revealed to him at the right moment. Because it was revealed, it enabled him to be the means through which the Hebrews were taken out of slavery and brought into the promised land. He veiled the truth from the people, perhaps because of some early experience in trying to reveal it, or because his Egyptian training had convinced him that truth should be veiled.

Many Hebrew prophets between Moses and Jesus discovered the truth, but there is no known record of any of them, with the possible exception of Isaiah, making an effort to reveal to the people the secret. Jesus removed the veil and he was crucified for it. Authority, whether in the church or in the government, did not rest well if the people knew the truth.

That condition does not exist at the present time; the church today is as eager to know the truth as the people are. It is very much aware that at the moment it has not found truth, and so we witness many attempts on the part of the church to seek out and discover the truth in order to incorporate it into their teaching. No longer do they feel, as it was felt in the early Hebrew synagogues, that it is dangerous to discover and teach truth. I also believe there are officials of many governments who are seeking truth. In order to lessen the burden of government they would be happy to have their people learn even a small amount of truth.

Jesus unveiled the truth and then it was veiled again and has remained so, except in isolated instances and with very small groups. Egypt knew this truth several thousand years B.C.; Gautama the Buddha revealed this truth but it was again lost while he was still living on earth. Approximately seven hundred years later, Shankara rediscovered the truth in Buddha's teaching and revealed it in what is called Advaita. The only remnant of this teaching today is in one ashram located in India. This ashram is dedicated to the Advaita and can safely be called the depository of unveiled truth.

Jesus discovered the truth and unveiled it, but it was lost rapidly after the crucifixion. About one hundred years later John rediscovered it and revealed it in the Gospel of John.

About one-half of the Protestant authorities are in favor of removing the Gospel of John from the Bible. The truth is there but they cannot recognize it. Why? Probably the saddest revelation that has to be given to man is that truth can never be learned through the mind. Truth must be discerned through spiritual faculties. "The natural man receiveth not the things of God: for they are foolishness unto him: neither can he know them, because they are spiritually discerned."[1] Therefore, without spiritual discernment it is impossible to read either the Gospel of John and understand its unfoldment, or the Advaita and comprehend its meaning. It is like reading the story of Jonah being swallowed by the whale. One must either be a superstitious fool and believe the story, or be a skeptic and refuse to accept it. This is the way of the human mind which says: "I must believe it" or "It is too stupid for me to accept." However, if you approach that same story with spiritual vision, you will discern that Jonah was swallowed up by the darkness of his own disbelief or unbelief. Likewise unbelief would throw us into a very dark hole of Calcutta. Think where you would be if you were in disbelief of the truth of being and then you will be able to understand that story.

We are beginning to read books and hear sermons by ministers and bishops indicating that there is no devil, that there is no such God as the church has presented, and that it is nonsense to pray to a spiritual God for material things. Spiritual vision has entered the church and is beginning to reveal the spiritual things of truth.

Let us ponder some of the messages of Christ Jesus: "My kingdom is not of this world[2]. . . . My peace give *I* unto you, not as the world giveth[3]. . . . Take no thought for your life, what ye shall eat, or what ye shall drink; nor yet for your body, what ye shall put on."[4] Think of those combined statements and realize how, if you want to know the unveiled truth, you must first abandon all thoughts or prayers for your life. You must stop seeking material things. Everyone in the world is seeking peace. What kind of peace? They are seeking the kind of peace that this world can give: an absence of war, a greater amount of dollars or properties, a happier family life. Yes, these are the elements of peace that the world is seeking. If you want the unveiled truth—that is not the Christ-peace nor is it the peace that truth can give. *My Peace* is of an entirely different nature. *My Peace* is something that you cannot know or desire with your mind.

Or let us take this: "God is a spirit, and they that worship him must worship him in spirit and in truth."[5] If you are seeking the unveiled truth, you must ask yourself this question: "How do I worship in spirit, how do I pray spiritually?" You will see very quickly that worshiping spiritually or praying spiritually has nothing to do with the things of this world or the ways of this world. The woman at the well of Samaria says, "You Hebrews say we must worship in Jerusalem." To this the Master replies: "Henceforth you will not worship in Jerusalem or in holy mountains,"[6] and if you want the unveiled truth you must ask yourself: "Where shall I worship and where shall I pray?" Eventually you will discover this: Since the kingdom of God is within you, your praying and your worshiping must be done there—within you. This takes our attention away from

the outside world and it takes our attention away from
the things of this world. It also eliminates all human
saviors or masters and makes of them teachers and way-
showers. In other words we have discovered that they
are not necessarily the holy ground but, "The place
whereon *thou* standest is holy ground"–within you.

Eventually you will come back to that which was
taught in Egypt, that which was discovered by Moses,
Gautama the Buddha, Jesus of Nazareth, Shankara,
namely: *"I AM that I AM."* This is the teaching that you
will find all the way from Egypt right up to Shankara
and repeated since then by every mystic.

"I AM. I AM that I AM–*I* and my Father are one–
God the Father, God the Son–one." And so you have
revealed to you why you must go within–within you.

If you are to worship in spirit and in truth, you must
worship the presence of God that is within you. The
presence of God *is* within you. The Master not only
discovered the presence of God within himself and
within his disciples, he discovered it in the woman taken
in adultery and he discovered it in the thief on the cross.
There is no one exempt from the relationship of
oneness. "Thou seest me thou seest the Father that sent
me."[7] If you have spiritual discernment, if you are seeing
through spiritual eyes, you will know "The kingdom of
God is within me." If you ever discover this, it will be
only one further step to the realization that God has no
stepchildren, God has no illegitimate children. Therefore
God must be within all–sick or well, rich or poor,
educated or uneducated. Where you are *now,* the
kingdom of God is already established within you.

In the Hebrew teaching God is often referred to as
"Father," and Jesus carried over with him this Hebrew

teaching. So we still find God referred to as Father in the Christian teaching, and the Master did not consider it unseemly to reveal: "The Father dwelleth in you." This statement must have puzzled you many times, because it really does not mean Father in any way that we can possibly imagine. The Hebrews thought of God as Father because their concept of God was a punishing and rewarding Father–the disciplinary principle of a human father. Father must have had another meaning for the Master because he had discovered the truth that God does not punish and God does not reward. "As ye sow, so shall ye reap."[8] In the Hebrew faith it was taught that we must commit a sinful act in order to be punished, but the Master carried it a step further. He taught that even to entertain a thought of sin was to commit a sin. In other words to entertain thoughts of adultery was as sinful as to commit an adulterous act; to be angry with one's brother was as sinful as to commit murder, and so he gave birth to a clarification of karmic law: In other words, it is not only what you do but what your inner propensities are. This later led to "Thoughts are things," because on the human plane thoughts do have a way of becoming tangible form.

The Master knew from teaching in the monastery and by his own inner revelations that "The kingdom of God is within you,"[9] but he was also taught in the monastery and within himself by revelation the name of the Father. The name of the Father had been known to Moses, but Moses did not reveal it to his followers. Only the high priests were permitted to know the name, and this of course is what constitutes the veil. The veil is always on the truth as long as you do not know the name of God, and the veil has been removed once you discover the name of God because this discovery requires spiritual discernment. It is impossible to read books and discover it, even though it is there. Certainly it is in the Bible from Moses to Revelation, but few have discovered the name of God in it. The reason is that it is veiled. The name is not veiled—the veil is in the mist that covers the eyes, and this veil can be removed only through spiritual discernment—and so the entire secret of life is the name of God.

"To know him aright is life eternal," so if you have not found life eternal be assured you have not "known him aright." Jesus was crucified for revealing the name of God to his disciples and apostles, and probably to many of those in the multitudes. Today we will not be crucified for taking the veil away, but neither will we attempt to perform that service for the world. That will be done only for those who are drawn, only for those who in some way are led to where it is being revealed. There will be no more "walking up and down the seashore inviting everyone to listen." That day died with Christ Jesus. Whenever truth is unveiled, be assured it will be done without advertising or fanfare, and it will be given only to those who seek it. Of course they would discover it for themselves, because no one who ever decides to seek truth ever fails to attain it. This does not include all those who have come to metaphysical teachings, however, for those who have "sought the loaves and fishes from truth's table" have not received it.

At the well of Samaria the Master offers the woman water, saying: "Whosoever drinketh of the water that *I* shall give him shall never thirst again."[10] But he does it in a strange way: "I am not offering water to you but if you ask me, *I* will give it to you." Later his disciples came to him 'at the well of Samaria and, noticing he had not eaten a meal at noon, said "Shall we go to the city and get thee some meat?" "No, I have meat ye know not of."[11] At another time: "Know ye not, thou seest me thou seest the Father that sent me"[12] for *I* and the Father are one. And again, "Before Abraham was I am."[13] I know I am going to be crucified and leave you but still I am going to say to you: "*I* will be with you even unto the end of the world."[14] Jesus knows he will not be with you unto the end of the world, but "*I Am* the bread, and *I Am* the resurrection." And so the Master reveals that this God whom he has declared to be within you—this Father whom he has declared to be within you—has a name, an identity: "*I* have meat the world knows not of." "*I* can give you water, drinking which you will never thirst." "*I* will never leave thee nor forsake thee." Is there any presence or power but God that could utter such a message? Could anyone but God say to you: "*I* will be with you even unto the end of the world"? Could anyone but God give you "living meat and living water"?

When you learn this identity and the veil is removed, something very sacred comes into your life. It is something which, because of its sacredness, you will want to keep holy and secret. It is something you will never reveal to the ignorant or to the gross—you will never "throw your pearls before swine." Instead you will regard it as a treasure for which you can well afford to give up all you have. Many people really believe that truth should be free, but the Master did not think so: "Sell all that you have for this treasure. Leave all, even if you must leave father, mother, brother, sister."[15] It is worth it; it is greater than Aladdin's lamp.

When you discover *I* in the midst of you, there is no wishing or praying to be done. There is just a life of thanksgiving. It is never necessary to ask for anything you need, because the nature of *my* kingdom is omniscience—the all-knowing. It needs no assistance or help because it is omnipotence, and it is not necessary that you go anywhere because it is omnipresence. "Here where *I* am, without taking thought, *I* am in God. *I* and God—God and *I*—one." This kingdom is within you and a king is never outside of his kingdom; and God, being omnipresence, cannot get outside his kingdom because there is no way for God to escape out of you. He is locked up tightly because of oneness, and that one cannot be divided. It is invisible, indivisible, inseparable, but one—and *I* is that one.

Therefore, to worship in spirit and in truth, to pray the prayer of the righteous man that availeth much, means to go within—but leave all desires outside. We are not going into a merchandise mart, we are going in to tabernacle and commune with the Father within. And if we are wise we will do this many times each day and night. Ten seconds to a minute or two is sufficient. And then as time passes, we discover we are going within for two to three minutes and later for longer periods. But at present it is enough if, twenty times a day, I can just close my eyes and realize: "Thank you Father, thy presence is with me." That is worshiping the Father in spirit and that is praying; that is acknowledging the Father in "all thy ways." You have really summed it all up if, occasionally, you have looked down in the area of your chest and said: "Thank you Father, for thy omnipresence," or thy omnipotence, or thy omniscience.

"Acknowledge him in all thy ways."[16] To awaken in the morning and remember "God made this day," is really turning the day over to God. "It is not my day with my problems. No, this is the day the Lord has made and as far as I am concerned, Lord, you can run it." Then at breakfast: "Thy grace is my sufficiency. Thy grace put the cattle on a thousand hills and provided the iron and the coal and the diamonds and the pearls. Thy grace put birds in the air and fish in the sea." This is "acknowledging him in all thy ways"; and when leaving home: "Thy presence goes before me." That is all that is necessary to remember that God has gone ahead to make the crooked places straight and to prepare mansions.

As this practice becomes second nature, you are ready for a further step, a step that can lead to a wonderful change of life. It is a step whereby we no longer live by might or by power but by *grace*–where we live without taking thought, where we live by *thy spirit*. That step entails this: You must find a period of the day, either early in the morning or after your family has retired at night, where you can sit down and quietly and peacefully realize: "The Father within me, the *I* that *I Am,* can teach me, instruct me, guide me, lead me, protect me, speak to me–all through the still small voice."

Let me tell you something about yourself: This *I* that is within you was there before you had a form, before you had a figure. It sent you forth into expression. You would have been aware of it from the moment of conception had your parents known enough to realize: "We did not conceive this child. It was God's grace." And had they confided to you during the nine months: "You are coming forth as a gift of God and God will *always* be in the midst of you. Therefore do not violate God. Remember even before you are born, omniscience

is in the midst of you and always will be. It is this very
I of you, unborn child, that is sending you forth now on
a journey into this world whereby God may show
himself forth as you. It shall be your function throughout
life to let God function through you, and you can only
do this by being still and receptive, acting according to
God's will."

In this way you would have come forth not a creature, but the child of God. In other words, the entire
generation of mortality is done away with. As matters
now stand we must "put off mortality and put on immortality" because of the religious ignorance into which we
were born. So now we realize: "*I* in the midst of me sent
me forth into expression. This presence within me is
responsible for my being on earth, and the only reason
I have had problems is because I have been trying to
run my own life according to how I was taught."

I begin to die daily the moment that *I* begins to be
born within me, the moment I acknowledge: "*I* within
me, in the midst of me, is God. No wonder God is closer
to me than breathing, because *I Am* is God." Do you not
see why in the 15th chapter of John it is found: "If you
let *Me*–the *I*–abide in you consciously and if you abide
in this word, you will bear fruit richly."[17] Do you not see
why "If you do not acknowledge *I* in the midst of you,
you are a branch that is cut off, withers and dies"? This
should clarify for you also why obeying the Ten Commandments will never get you into heaven, but living in
the consciousness of *I* will always prevent you from
breaking any of the Ten Commandments. That is the
mystery of Godliness, of goodness, when you can say
with the Master: "Do not call me good.[18] The Father is
living my life and God's life includes no propensity of

evil. As far as I am concerned, the *I* is living its life through me and it is not good and it is not bad. It is immortality, divinity, perfection." That is where you reach the place or neither good nor evil–just God, spirit, being–without any qualities.

And so you see why, in the 5th chapter of Matthew, the Master has cautioned us to pray in secret where we are not seen of men. We are not to seek praise for praying, because praying must be something very sacred. Prayer is only concerned with how you and God get along together. It is the same reason the Master gave for being secret about your benevolences. If *you* are being benevolent, then you are really being self-righteous. Realize: "The good flowing through me is God in expression and I can take no praise for this. Therefore I *let* God express God's will and God's way through me." All of this is possible only when you have discovered the name and identity of God, and the very location of God's kingdom. Remember that your neighbors would never understand this.

Think how it changes the nature of your prayer when you stop looking out or up. Close your eyes and gently, "look down within," and *feel*. "Right here, closer to me than breathing, is the very source of everything I shall need in my outer life. There is even the "good pleasure" to give me the entire kingdom.

NOTHING CAN BE ADDED

July 27, 1963
Infinite Way Study Center

"OF THOSE WHO HAVE MUCH, much will be demanded."[1] It is inevitable that you who have had as much work with me as you have had, much will be expected. As visitors from different parts of the world come to Hawaii, they must naturally look upon you and wonder how much further along you are than other students of the world. In what way is that manifest? What have you to show forth, and what have you received? What great fruitage are you showing forth?

It is inevitable that from all over the world, people look at me and wonder in what way I am showing forth this truth and in what way my family is showing it forth. So it is asked—and more and more it will be asked, "In what way is this shining forth in the experience of the students who are receiving so much?" You must be prepared for this because it is natural. In order to bring forth spiritual fruitage it is necessary that you thoroughly understand what it is you are trying to show forth. There must be no question in your own mind.

In the ordinary religious life, the student is always seeking something. It is true they are seeking it of God, but this is not at all true in the mystical life. In the mystical life it is a continuous realization that "I already *am*." I am not going anywhere, nor am I going to attain more of God than I have, more of good than I have. I am rather "abiding in the Word." What Word? "All that the Father hath is mine. I am all that God is."

In other words, sooner or later you must come to the realization that God has fulfilled itself in you—not today and not tomorrow and not since you have studied The Infinite Way. "Before Abraham was, *I* am you; *I* am the fulfillment of you. Before Abraham was, *I* have come in the midst of you, that you might be fulfilled. *I* am come that you might have life and that you might have life more abundant."[2] It was true about you "before Abraham was"—not after you read a certain amount of books.

This message is not to make you spiritual, but to reveal the spiritual origin of your nature, the *I Am* nature of your individual being. Therefore, at some time or other you must find yourself in the position of Moses when he was on the mountaintop and suddenly realizes: "*I Am* that *I Am*. I already *Am*."[3]

I understand that, for awhile, you are studying with the hope of becoming spiritual—but sooner or later in this message there must come an awakening, as Paul had on the road to Damascus. It may shock you, blind you for a moment, but it must knock the wind out of you as you realize: "My God, I *am*." Then there is a relaxing, a resting, an abiding in this Word. "All that God is, I am." No more efforts to get, no more efforts to accomplish, and from then on the reading is inspirational. I have told you that ever since I have had the copy of *The Contemplative Life,* I have not been able to put the book down; I have not been able to stop reading it. I cannot truthfully say I am learning something from it, and I do not claim to be learning something new. But, after many years of study, the time must inevitably come when you read just for inspiration, for a depth of consciousness of that which you already know.

Jesus had the experience too, but it is not recorded what his experiences were. However, you can be sure at one time he was a carpenter and a rabbi, and then something happened that made him start preaching at the wayside, in the synagogue. He, too, must have had such an experience, but we do not know just when it happened. We do know about Moses and Paul, and we do know of John's experience on the island of Patmos when his eyes were opened: John spoke with the Christ and "his eyes were opened to God." That first light came, and the rest was just unfoldment.

This is what is meant in living The Infinite Way. This message is not so much a teaching as an experience. It is meant to bring the individual to an experience, an experience that changes his life from the "man whose breath is in his nostrils to that man who has his being in Christ." Whereas before you were trying to bring good into your experience, now you know "*It* abides in you and you abide in *it*." Everything from God *is*. Now you are prepared "to let the imprisoned splendor escape." Now you know the kingdom of God is locked up within you. You embody your good. You know that because you know *I*. "*I* am come that you might have life and that you might have it more abundantly." It is not that Jesus is within you; it is not that Joel is within you; it is that *I* am within you.

That *I* is not a limited person. Your external self is limited, and I will illustrate: At six years of age when you start school, you have no knowledge—but you have as much intelligence as you have when you graduate from college. Therefore, at entrance into school, you have the full intelligence that you have at any time during your lifetime. That intelligence will be the means with which you acquire knowledge. You have the infinity of life, truth, harmony, peace, and divine grace. Now all that is going to happen is that you are going to express it.

There was a time when education consisted of drinking in knowledge, and educators actually believed it was their function to push knowledge into the student. Today real educators know they have to draw forth from students what they want them to know. It is already stored up within and the real educator knows how to bring it out.

A time comes when you realize: "I and the Father are one," since before Abraham was. Now I do not add more to myself, I pour out. In humanhood I get; in Christhood I give, I express, I "open out a way for the imprisoned splendor to escape."

One of the great things that is revealed to you is that God-power is within you. It cannot be added to you. God-power is in you. God is omnipotent. When you catch this vision, you look out through your eyes and then you can smile. "I shall not fear what mortal mind can do to me, what mortal conditions can do. There is no power out there—none whatsoever." It also brings another realization which you may not like very well: There is no good power out there either. There is no power external to you that will benefit you or that can harm you: "*I* am omnipotent—all power."

Nothing out here, nobody out here, has any power over me. God never gave anybody power over me. As I embody that truth within myself, I am not only immune from all fears, I am immune from world beliefs.

And in the measure I realize this, I break the fetters for you, not only in this room but right around the world.

Our teachers in The Infinite Way have attained an experience that has set them free, even free of me, because they have attained their freedom in oneness with God. There is nothing of any nature that they need of me. "*I* in the midst of me am mighty. *I* in the midst of me am free." In the degree of their freedom, each one is traveling and setting others free. Before you travel you must be setting someone free in your household. The measure of your own freedom is the measure of freedom you can bestow upon others–but not until you have attained some degree of freedom can you free others. You must be coming closer and closer to the experience.

I think I have told you the story of the young student in India who went to his Master and said: "I know you are revealing truth to me, but I must know God face to face." The Master said, "I can take you to the door, but you must walk through." So the student was led to the first room and he looked around and saw a bronze figure of God. He pondered it and thought: "That cannot be God." Something convinced him that was not God. Then he found the entrance into another room of the temple and there he found a crystal figure of God. He thought, "Oh, that is more like it. But no, this could not be God." Then he found another entrance. He walked in, looked around and found himself alone! And now he realized nothingness. "There can be no other God but me. Thou seest me thou seest the Father that sent me; because I and the Father are one." If you had that realization could you fear people, could you fear bombs?

All the way back to Isaiah we read they put their faith in horses and chariots: Isaiah 31:1,3:

Woe to them that go down to Egypt for help, and rely on horses, and trust in chariots because they are many, and in horsemen because they are very strong, but they look not unto the Holy One of Israel, neither seek God!

Now the Egyptians are men, and not God: and their horses flesh, and not spirit: and when God shall stretch out his hand both he that helpeth shall stumble and he that is helped shall fall, and they shall be consumed together.

We put our faith in bombs and bombers twenty-five hundred years later.

What people have put faith into will always fail until they come to the room and are "all alone" and its name is *I*—then there is nothing to have "faith in"—just *be*. Then we will trust each other because we have learned: "I and my Father are one."[4] Therefore what have we to fear of each other? "*I* and your Father are one," so we need not fear each other or the world. And this experience must come to you.

Just as you are not going to fear anything from chariots to bombs, so you are not going to have faith in anything. I have faith that "I and my Father are one," and therefore I am in good hands. My faith is not in God. I just have faith—not in somebody or some thing. I have faith that "I and my Father are one." I have faith in the integrity of the source of the universe—not in government and not in law. How can I have faith in anything external? It is the faith that comes of the understanding that is incorporeal in my being, which *I* am.

Do you not see that if you meditate and want to pray properly, you must have no words or thoughts, no concepts at all? Just sit in a state of receptivity: "What am I waiting for? Well, we have been told, 'God is in the still, small voice, and when he utters his voice, the earth melteth.' " I am waiting for something incarnate in me. Jesus Christ taught that "The kingdom of God is within you." He did not make it up, it has been taught for years and years. Where did Gautama the Buddha receive it? Where did it come from? His own consciousness.

Know what you are doing when you are meditating. Be through with words that represent God and just be satisfied to sit in silence. *It is from within me that the spirit of God is flowing. It is from within me that his life and his love is flowing to the world. It is within me that all of these things take place.* Just sit quietly: "Be still and know that *I* am within you."

What do you have faith in? Have faith *in nothing*, and that is the principle that you carry home. Be still and listen for that still, small voice. Then you can prove living by grace. Live more and more by grace, with less and less fear in the external world and less faith in whatever it is that you have thought about God.

ABOVE KARMIC LAW:
PRINCIPLES TO LIVE BY

July 28, 1963
Princess Kaiulani Hotel

GOOD AFTERNOON. When I had been in the healing practice for about five years, I was taken very ill and the practitioner who was taking care of me reached the conclusion that I was not being reached and would probably pass on that night. To me it was particularly strong that it would be that night. In the middle of the night my mother and a favorite aunt, both of whom had passed on some years before, came to my bedside and told me they had come to "make my way across an easy one." They said it was a joyous experience and I was not to fear it, but being something new for me they were there to help. Suddenly I said, "No, Mom, I am not going. I have done nothing in this world to justify even the birth pangs that you had to bring me here, and I cannot go that way. . . . I cannot go without fulfilling myself. I have healed a few hundred people of their ills, but even though it were ten thousand people or three million people, that is no accomplishment. No, I must stay here and find a reason and a purpose for living." The following morning I wakened so much better that I was able to go to my office.

Then I discovered why I was not pleased for having healed a few hundred people, and why I would not have been satisfied had I healed ten thousand people. No, because I have never been interested in that phase of life. All my life my interest has been in principles, the principles whereby men can live more joyously. Not only the people who find my religion, but all men: the whites and the blacks and the yellows and the browns, the rich and the poor, the literate and the illiterate. I realized the only thing that can benefit people in the long run are principles to live by and from that time on, more than ever before I was consciously awake to the seeking of principles.

So it was, in late 1938 or 1939, the Voice told me that I must seek the secret of the impersonal Christ and impersonal healing. In 1941 I started out on a trip, seeking this secret. The trip was supposed to last two months; it lasted five months. You will notice in The Infinite Way writings that interest or attention is not primarily focused on healing you or improving your life, but in revealing principles whereby you can live better and live happier. Remember this means any *you* who finds these principles–any *you* anywhere in the world. When Christopher Columbus started out on his trip to prove that the world is round, he did not mean to earn a personal reputation or gain a personal fortune. No, his great discovery offended authority and he probably knew he would die in prison. Columbus set out to prove the principle that the world is round. So it is that we pay very little attention in our work to testimonies, except where a testimony bears witness to a principle that was involved; and so it is that our work actually is to set forth principles by which men and women can live–principles by which children can be brought up.

The reason it is necessary to continue the search for principles is that enlightenment, not only spiritual enlightenment but intellectual enlightenment, is comparatively recent. When we consider that there was not even an alphabet twenty-five hundred years ago, we know how few literate people there were and the advances in science are all comparatively recent. Even the telephone or the telegraph or the radio all came forth in this generation, and during my lifetime I have lived in a home with lamplight. So remember that though the world has started in this direction of enlightenment, it has not as yet even started in the direction of spiritual revelation. It is only at the beginning. Flying is so recent that I can remember when the Wright brothers flew their first airplane at Kitty Hawk, but in spiritual realization we have not even reached that point.

In the Oriental scriptures, which pre-date Christian scriptures, we have karmic law or the law of cause and effect as the major law or teaching. This law has held some parts of the East in such intellectual and spiritual barrenness that to this very day millions upon millions of people are making no effort to improve their lot because of the belief that it is their karma to "suffer it out" in this lifetime and possibly many lifetimes to come until it has worked itself out of their lives. Christian scriptures accept the teaching, "As ye sow, so shall ye reap," and there are millions of people with guilt complexes, because of some sin of omission or commission, who are unable to release themselves. Some are resigning themselves to sin or disease or sinful appetites or death because of a law of heredity—cause and effect.

The message of The Infinite Way would like to start you on a new path, not that it is new to The Infinite Way, but because you have never perceived this principle: There is no karmic law, there is no law of cause and effect–as ye sow so shall ye reap. These are superstitions and illusions of the human mind; these are beliefs created by men.

For generations there has been a belief–almost a law– that sitting in a draft or getting your feet wet would cause you to catch cold; but in the August 1963 issue of *Reader's Digest,* you will find a medical article saying there is no such law. In other words, catching a cold by sitting in a draft or by getting your feet wet is no longer official as a medical law.

If materia medica can change its mind about that law and other laws, we in the metaphysical world must admit that we to have been wrong about some of our pet theories. One of these is, "As ye sow, so shall ye reap."[1] Karmic law, or the law of cause and effect, or "as ye sow, so shall ye reap" is not a law–it is *dead* law.

Those of you who are hearing this message today, and those of you who will be reading this message when it is printed, will have the opportunity of putting this principle into practice. If it is true, it is a universal truth. It is not true only of Infinite Way students or metaphysicians or those who ask us for help. No, this is a universal truth which will set the world free. Just as materia medica is going to free the world of the belief that drafts and wet feet cause colds, so eventually will this spiritual principle being revealed today operate around the world and be applicable to free saint or sinner, black or white, or yellow or brown. This is the law.

You have the right to ask this question: "Has no one ever caught cold by sitting in a draft or by getting the feet wet?" Of course, millions have caught cold, not because of the draft and not because of the wet feet, but by being brought under the belief of that law. Likewise you have the right to ask the question: "Has no one ever paid a penalty for erroneous sowing?" Yes, because they were brought under that law. Every one of you has witnessed this law being broken over and over again. Every time a disease has been overcome by metaphysical treatment, the law of cause and effect has been broken. Every time you witness a disease of a hereditary nature healed, you have proven there is no such law. So you have already witnessed what I am bringing to you here today: that there is no law of disease, no law of cause and effect, no law of "as ye sow, so shall ye reap."

There is no karmic law except what men bind upon themselves by accepting. Should you teach your children that two times two equals five, I am sure you could get them to believe it and suffer from it, because they would have been brought up under that mistaken law or belief. We have been demonstrating this in metaphysics for ninety years, but never has it been spoken of in this way—to free all men everywhere of everything and release them into their birthright of divine consciousness, in which there are no laws operating on them because they are laws themselves! *"I* am the way, the truth and the life."[2] . . . *I* am the law. Until you are released into your true identity there will be laws operating on you, but they will not be laws, they will be man's creation—beliefs. Why do you think human sacrifices began? As recently as Hebrew scriptures, one of the prophets was ready to sacrifice his own son. Then came animal sacrifices, then sacrifices of crops, then money sacrificed to the church. We have gotten along beautifully without sacrificing human lives or animals or crops or money. If you are giving us money thinking it is buying you a place in heaven, keep it and save it.

Anything that comes to us should come as pure gratitude because there is no reward except that of sharing and the reward of inner joy.

Men have made laws and have made them binding upon you: religious laws, medical laws, legal laws, commercial laws, governmental laws. No one has a right to make laws for you, not even God. God is the law unto itself and unto its own life, lived as you and as me. Eventually this will lead you to what is undoubtedly the deepest revelation of The Infinite Way. It has its source in the revelation of Christ Jesus who voiced it in these passages: "Why callest thou me good? There is none good but one, that is God[3]. . . . The Son can do nothing of himself, but what he seeth the Father do[4]. . . . If I bear witness of myself, my witness is not true[5]. . . . I can of mine own self do nothing[6]. . . . My doctrine is not mine, but his that sent me."[7]

This is the principle: You must eliminate the word "I" from your life and in whatever degree you succeed, in that degree will you know successful and joyous living.

When I was in the healing work for a short time, and met one evening with a group of practitioner friends, the subject of love came up. This was a very strange subject to me. I could not understand love because I could not feel it. My friends said to me, "We look on you as one of the most loving people, Joel. You work so hard for your students and for your patients." I was unable to understand this either, because I certainly did not feel loving, and so for a long time I could not understand the word *love* or *benevolence* or *spiritual.* Certainly I did not feel spiritual and never have felt spiritual, but at least I now know the answer. When I had my first spiritual experience the personal "I" died. Certainly I am not loving or benevolent or spiritual; whatever qualities that may flow through me are flowing from the source. There is nothing personal whatsoever.

Many years ago during work in Portland and Seattle I wanted to give our students "the middle path" but resistance to it was very strong and two mothers showed me how impossible it was at that time. It was a time when everyone wanted to pray for peace so I said to them, "Supposing you know Russia was going to throw an atomic bomb at us tonight. Would you be in favor of our throwing it first, or would you allow them to throw it? But do not answer me now. Think it over until tomorrow." The following morning their answer came: "I could [refrain from throwing the bomb first] for myself, but not for my children." No, there can be no peace as long as there is war in the hearts of men, as long as the law of self preservation is accepted.

If you can eliminate the word I, you have no life to lose, including your children's. It is God's life and God can take care of its own. If you say "God is my life," you must trust your life to God, not to an atomic bomb. Neither can you feel that "we" are more righteous or more civilized. The word I must entirely disappear. You must be willing to give up the good as well as the evil—you must be willing to give up the rewards as well as the punishments. You must be willing to accept: "I live, yet not I, but Christ liveth in me."[8] I do not have to raise my hand in defense of my life, but I must not take credit for the good that flows through me, whether it is healings or whether it is dedication to this message. It is Christ living individual life; truth manifesting itself and projecting itself into human consciousness. We are fortunate that we can be instruments or avenues which show forth God's glory. "The heavens declare the glory of God and the firmament showeth his handiwork."[9] Much more are we the glory of God when "I" has been overcome. When the Master said "I have overcome the world," I believe he meant *I* have overcome *me* –the *me* who can be rewarded and the *me* who can be punished. Both have to go.

You cannot imagine how foolish the human scene seems when you are looking down from a spiritual height. We are trying to arrive at an agreement with Russia not to throw an atomic bomb, and one of the greatest objections is that we are not sure we can trust Russia. Yet Russia has never thrown a bomb and we have–twice! We have not even said we are sorry we threw it, nor have we said we would not throw one again. So here we are worrying about the other fellow and not looking in the mirror. This is the way the human scene looks, because it is based on the law of "self preservation is the first law of human nature." When ten righteous men begin to eliminate the "I," they will know there is no karmic law and there is no law of cause and effect binding on the Christ which *I* am –which thou art.

As you now behold evidences of sin, disease, lack, death, man's inhumanity to man, from the family circle to the international circle, quietly remind yourself: "There is no karmic law, there is no law of cause and effect, there is no 'as ye sow, so shall ye reap,' " and you will be nullifying it. You will be nullifying the human belief that there is such a law. As doctors will be telling their patients, "You can no longer catch cold by sitting in a draft or by getting your feet wet," so we can tell the world silently and secretly within ourselves: "There is no law of karma, there is no law of cause and effect, there is no law of 'as ye sow, so shall ye reap.' " This is just an ancient superstition and is not binding on spiritual man—and there is no other man.

Just as The Infinite Way has given to the world the re-statement that "God, spirit, is the only power," so does it give the world the two principles given you today—principles which are to release this world from domination of a superstition which has come to be law. We have been prisoners of the mind for generations, and the mind has bound us with laws, but there is only *one* law, spirit, which is freeing. Only one law is spiritual and that is the law of God or spirit, and that law frees you from the domination of the mind.

Moses spoke from Mount Sinai, Jesus spoke from the mountain from which came forth his sermon, and this that I have given you today has come from the mountaintop of spiritual revelation.

Becoming the "New Man"

August 4, 1963
Princess Kaiulani Hotel

GOOD AFTERNOON. There are some things which you may know but which you may not tell the student in his earliest months, or sometimes years of study, and the reason is this: Truth can be very upsetting. Yes, truth is upsetting and the first foundation of the message of The Infinite Way is this: Truth is something you must live with for a long, long time—until you begin to discern its meaning—and then share it only with those whom you ultimately feel are ready to receive it. Always remember that there is no absolute truth and no ultimate truth, because truth is infinite and you cannot embody infinity in your mind. No one can comprehend infinity and it is for this reason that you must accept the inspiration of truth, the letter of truth, as a stepping stone leading to the consciousness or awareness of truth.

There is a story told of the ancient Egyptian days where, at the Temple of Osiris, there was a covered plaque and above it the words *The Truth.* No one was permitted to look beneath that cover, but eventually one man did decide to look and it is said that he had a very sad end. The man who commented on this told what he imagined was under that cover and his imagination ran something like this: "Only a fool would believe that there can be a formula of truth. Only a fool would believe that truth can be embodied in any statement or formula, and only a knave would seek to find truth without the eternal struggle." This is of course true, and you have read in our writings: "You will never find truth in a book." No one can encompass truth in the Bible or in any book. Truth is infinite, and what is found in the Bible and in books is the revealed truth of certain individuals at a certain time and under certain circumstances, but this does not make the demonstration for you.

What I am leading up to is this: Let your manna fall day by day. Let the truth necessary for today flow to you from the kingdom of God, from the kingdom of divine consciousness which is within you. It is folly to seek truth for tomorrow, or for next week, or for next year when truth is omnipresence, omnipotence, omniscience. Therefore, whatever truth is necessary to you at any time is available at the time you need it. If you are in the desert without the Bible and without a book, or if you are at sea in a rubber boat without a Bible and without a book, despair not. All the truth necessary to save you is within your own consciousness. If you ever believe that either I or The Infinite Way books are necessary to your life and to the harmony of your experience, you will lose the way. The whole purpose of my individual ministry has been to reveal: "*I* am come that they might have life, and that they might have it more abundantly"[1]–not Jesus has come, not Paul has come, not Joel has come, but *I* am come, the *I* in the midst of you is come. It is for this reason that "Neither death, nor life . . . shall be able to separate us from the love of God."[2] God, truth, is omnipresence where you are and by its grace "manna falls each day." Do not believe that you can demonstrate more of truth than you can realize. Therefore, make the demonstration of truth a daily experience by turning within each day for today's manna.

The more you read scripture and the revealed truths of the great mystics, the easier it becomes to contact the spirit within you. When you read that there is only one power, it really does not remove all the other powers out of your life. Too many metaphysicians have believed that by reading so many pages of truth or by affirming truth enough times, it would come true in their experience. This is folly. As you read and ponder statements of truth such as: "There is one power" and abide with that truth, your fears of external powers become less and less, and this brings you closer to the ability to commune silently within yourself.

In the religious and metaphysical and mystical literature of the world, you will discover that one question appears more often than any other, one that has probably produced more agnostics and atheists than any others: "If there is a God, how can there be these horrors on earth: war, slavery, poverty, hate? How can these things be? That of course seems to prove to many people that there really is no God and, judging by appearances, they are judging very well. Of course there is a God, but there is no God in the human scene and this is one of the truths that must not be given to young students too soon. It not only shocks them but it creates a fear.

It was this very question that started me on the spiritual search: "If there is a God, how can there be these dens of iniquity in Paris, and the threat of war across Europe, and the poverty that is met with in so many places?" Eventually the answer to that question came to me and it forms the entire basis of The Infinite Way work. For many years I thought I was the only person who had discovered this truth, but later I learned that it was discovered in the Bible from Moses to Revelation. I also learned that the answer to the question was revealed only by Paul, and the answer was the same answer that I received: There is no God in the human scene.

Human beings are not God-governed and cannot be. Human beings cannot receive God, they cannot know the things of God nor can they be guided by God. That is why human beings are shut off from God and, being shut off from their source, they are subject to everything that is witnessed on earth. Have you ever seen men working in a coal mine? If so you will realize that there is no God watching that scene. Have you ever been in some of the dens of iniquity around this globe? Those of you who have must know that there is no God in that scene. Did you see London, Berlin, Dresden, Munich, Hiroshima, or Nagasaki after the war? If so, you would know that there was no God in that scene. Do you believe there was a God in those events? Yes, there was a God, but not in those scenes and not available to most of those people. Paul sums it all up for you: "The natural man receiveth not the things of the spirit of God. . . is not subject to the law of God, neither indeed can be."[3]

When this revelation was given to me it came as a shock, because what then is the next step? We have to pass over quite a few years to come to the answer to that, but the answer which came to me was the same answer that came to Paul, except that I was unable to understand it in his language. He said: "If so be that the spirit of God dwell in you [4] . . . we are children of God; and if children, then heirs . . . joint heirs with Christ."[5] This is a hard saying, for how do you get the spirit of God to dwell in you, and why are there so many who do not have the spirit of God dwelling in them?

To me the question was answered in a different way, but it meant the same thing: "There is a spiritual faculty which was incorporated in us, incarnated in us from the very beginning, before the world began." To Paul it was revealed as the indwelling Christ or the Son of God in man. To me it seems more simple to say the illumined consciousness of man, the enlightened consciousness of man. Robert Browning said, "There is a center in us all." This center may be termed the Christ, Self, the Son of God, Spiritual Man, the Buddha, the Light, the Enlightened One—but what it actually means is a spiritual faculty. With the physical faculty of sight we can see with our eyes; with the physical faculty of hearing we can hear with our ears; with the spiritual faculty we can know God.

The natural man can never know God, and the natural man is "every man" until that indwelling spirit in you makes itself known and felt, until you become consciously aware that there is more to me than what you are now looking at. What you are seeing with your physical eyes is the natural man, the animal man, the man who differs from the cats and the dogs and the horses only by the fact that he can reason—but he has all their instincts. If that is all there is to man, then the devastation that has taken place on earth since the excommunication of Adam and Eve from the Garden of Eden would go on forever, because this natural man lives by one code: "self-preservation is the first law of human nature." As long as man remains the natural man he will remain a predatory animal, which is why we are accredited with being of the animal race. We are not animals when we are letting the spirit of God consciously dwell in us, because we are then no longer governed by the instincts of the natural man.

When the spirit of God is consciously aroused in you, you begin to live the life taught by the Master, that of loving one another, of doing unto others as you would have others do unto you, but not by virtue of being a good human. No, you begin to live this way because it is the natural way to live. It is as if you were to say: "Do not call me good. I live yet not I, it is Christ living my life, and this good is being done by the Christ unto 'the least of these my brethren.'" Yes, the object or the goal of the spiritual life is to arrive at that place where the Christ, the spiritual man, the spiritual Son of God, is functioning as your individual consciousness. We demonstrate this only in part; we have not fully arrived. From the moment that you are first aware of an indwelling presence, notice the difference in your attitude toward everyone on the face of the globe. Then remember that it is not because you have become more patient or more benevolent or more loving, nor is it because you have decided to obey the Ten Commandments. It is because *that* which is now in ascendancy in you is "performing that which is given you to do," and is living your life.

With this revelation and realization, the next step is opened: "How? How do you become the child of God? How do you reach the place where Christ lives your life?" The answer I give you is based as always on my personal experience, that although I certainly remained a very natural man, at least there were these questions in my mind: "How do I become the other man? How do I reach it? How do I attain it?" From then on there was a seeking for the answer, a reaching out for the answer. "What is truth? What is God? How do I attain the indwelling Christ or the indwelling presence?" You must be driven with that desire, then read whatever is given you to read of a spiritual nature—study—ponder. In the end it amounts to breaking your head, screaming out to God sometimes. In my experience something unsolicited happened unexpectedly in a meditation with a practitioner and the "old man" died. It took place within a few minutes and it was an instantaneous death—and on the whole the old man has stayed dead. Then began the experience of getting used to this "new man."

You know, some of Paul's teachings are really my own life. "I knew a man once," he said, "whether in the flesh or out, I know not—a man who has his being in Christ."[6] This was the man I had to get acquainted with, the man who was no longer living the old life but was living a strange new life, so strange indeed that people coming to him were being healed of illnesses. He was a hard man to get used to and he was a hard man to live with, because little bits of that man of earth still stayed around to make the way very difficult.

It is not easy to say to students: "Just break your head until divine grace wipes out 'you' and rebirths *you.*" Even the Master was faced with these questions: "How can a man be reborn? Shall I return to my mother's womb?"[7] Of course not. "But how, then, shall I be reborn?" I know only two answers: First: Read, study, ponder, and live with whatever spiritual literature comes your way until you find the message that seems to be for you, then stay with it, and keep on praying for the day when the light will break. Secondly: If you can find a teacher who has received some measure of illumination, do all that is possible to receive whatever of light your teacher can awaken in you. These are the only two ways that I have witnessed.

The importance of what I am saying is this: Do not fool yourself into believing that, by your studies and by the truths you can voice or think, this alone is gaining you the kingdom of God. These are but the steps, and it is really through the measure of your inner dedication, meditation, and contemplation that you ultimately contact that source within yourself or are led to a teacher who can "help you across." The light that you yourself gain will be sufficient to help those who come to you, but it will not be sufficient to get them into the kingdom of God. That includes dying daily and being reborn, which each one of you must experience for yourself.

This of course leads us back to where we started. If you believe that there may be a long period ahead of you before you attain, you will entirely miss the mark. As of this moment you have to realize: "There is sufficient spiritual manna in my consciousness to serve my every purpose today." There is no use looking ahead to illumination or to initiation; there is no use looking ahead to being a master. All of this is a barrier to your spiritual development. Your greatest help lies in the recognition of the fact that there *is* daily manna, not ten years from now, but today. There is enough spiritual light, there is enough hidden manna within you to serve your needs *now*. Do not make the mistake of the ancient Hebrews by going out to "pick manna for tomorrow." It will wilt. Be satisfied that God's grace meets your need today. Look outside at the sunshine and you will see that you cannot capture the sunshine for tomorrow. Let it go. Do not try to capture the sun.

Embodied within your consciousness is a divine grace—the grace of God. It is not dependent on your being good or on your being spiritual, nor is it dependent on how many pages you read or how well you know the Bible. No, because it was there before there was a book or a Bible. The books and the Bible are merely to point your attention back within yourself to that which has been revealed to all mystics: "*I* have meat to eat that ye know not of [8] . . . *I* am come that they might have life, and that they might have it more abundantly . . . It is *I;* be not afraid."[9] You may be called upon to walk through the valley of the shadow of death, or you may be called upon to suffer lack or limitation of one kind or another. "Be not afraid. *I* in the midst of you am mighty. Therefore, turn to *Me* within you for today's manna. Thy grace is my sufficiency in all things." When? *Now.* In any moment thy grace is your sufficiency, and there is a sufficiency of thy grace within you at any moment of the day and at any moment of the night, if you will be satisfied with manna for today. Do not seek enough to make your whole life's demonstration at once.

It is for this reason that the subject of supply has been a terrible one for mankind. Without this spiritual faculty, you have to judge by appearances and if you judge by appearances you never can have enough. If you have enough for this month, what about next month, and what about next year, and what about when you get old? There is always the question: "How do I get more?" It is only with the coming of the spiritual faculty—it is only when you have inner discernment—that you learn the great secret which the mind cannot believe. God is speaking, saying: "Son, thou art ever with me, and all that *I* have is thine."[10] Only this can stop that mad rush to destruction, because now it is always possible to go to the source–that *I* within–for daily manna.

Sometimes a stumbling block arises because when you do this, the flow starts very quickly and very abundantly. It is at this point that you fail to take time to discover the next bit of manna which is that you have not merely been given a sufficiency, you have been given twelve baskets to share with "the least of these my brethren." Are we doing it? What about the distribution of the twelve baskets? "What we surrender, we have; what we hold in the grasp of possession, we lose. Every thing we release, we draw to us. Everything we loose, we have; everything we set free, we bind to us forever." This is spiritual law. If you receive forgiveness and do not give it, you lose it. If you receive love and do not give it, you lose it. If you receive gratitude and do not give it, you lose it because life–God–is an outflow, and only as we are letting the grace of God flow through us are we instruments of the divine.

These are some of the points that you are apt to forget. You must be reminded of them, as eventually you will find it necessary to remind others, until they too have become fully acquainted with the new man which they have become and who is now able to live peacefully with the spiritual facts of life rather than with the material concepts. Do you not see why many of our students miss the way? When students begin to have some healings, some forgivings or some supplyings, they must quickly realize that these are not the demonstration–these are the fruits of the demonstration. The demonstration is the consciousness of the presence of that indwelling spirit, and all the "things" are added unto us by the grace of that which has given us our hidden manna. As rapidly as possible stop rejoicing in your healings, or in your supplying, or in your happiness and rejoice in the source of them. Rejoice that Christ now lives your life.

THE NATURE OF SPIRITUAL PRAYER

August 5, 1963
Honolulu Infinite Way Center

GOOD EVENING. In an age like the present one, which seems dedicated to destroying the value of the individual and turning him into a mass, a herd, a horde, and making the individual a nonentity, ours are activities dedicated wholly to revealing the identity and the dignity and the magnitude of the individual. The Infinite Way is one of these activities and has for its basis: "I and my Father are one[1]. . . The place whereon *I* stand is holy ground."[2] There are other activities which are beginning to assert the value and the dignity of the individual, but The Infinite Way is approaching the subject from the religious standpoint–not from the standpoint of a religion, but from the standpoint of religion itself. The knowledge of God reveals the infinite nature of individual man. Since "I and my Father are one . . . He that seeth me seeth him that sent me."[3] That is how sacred the individual is. He is the showing forth of God; he is that place in consciousness where God shines through.

This late in the 20th century, only mass hypnotism could hide from the world the tremendous scope of the life and the activity of Lao-Tzu of China, yet there are many people in the world who are aware of the fact that Lao-Tzu gave the world one of its great spiritual teachings. Likewise, there are few in the world who do not know the Buddha, and hundreds of millions throughout the world live by the words of the Buddha, and hundreds of millions live by the words of the Christ. Christ Jesus was only one Hebrew rabbi among many, yet he was remembered and revered because of his recognition of his individual Selfhood and of the power *that* conferred upon him. "My words shall not pass away,"[4] not the words of the whole synagogue and not the words of the Roman emperors, but "*my* words"–the words of a simple Hebrew rabbi walking up and down the Holy Land.

When we think of electric lights, phonographs, and moving pictures we can only think of Thomas Edison. When we think of radio or television we can only think of DeForest. When we think of the telephone we can only think of Alexander Graham Bell. In each case one individual. Can you imagine that? Would you believe that any one individual could be born and so surmount the limitations of the time and the place of birth as to become known worldwide and be respected and revered? Any public library can give you a list of thousands of biographies or autobiographies, which will reveal to you that if there is anything important on earth, it is the individual who has a recognition of the force, power, and scope embodied in the consciousness of any and every individual.

That is why all of the movements, whether they are called communism or socialism or labor parties, are doomed to failure because an individual will always be raised up. When an individual is raised up, all the "armies of the aliens" cannot stop him any more than the Sanhedrin could stop Christ Jesus. Certainly, and not all of the ignorance and the superstition of the 19th century was able to stop Mary Baker Eddy. Have you any idea of the tremendousness of that one woman?

Yes, we could go through thousands upon thousands of biographies or autobiographies and prove one point: that no movement, superstition, ignorance, or tyranny will ever survive. Why? Because there will always be one Jesus or one Moses or one Paul or one somebody else, and that one will destroy the power of all of the armies of the aliens in any and in every form.

When Napoleon Bonaparte said, "Every soldier carries in his knapsack a marshal's baton," he was saying that every individual has within his own consciousness the power to be a leader or a savior or anything else that the particular time may require.

Whether you or I may be the individual needed in this age is not the question. At the very least, you and I embody the spiritual power to raise up the individual who is needed in this day or in this age. We may, any one of us, even be that one. If not, we do have the capacity to assure that in due time, the individual necessary to this day or age—and those to surround that individual—shall be raised up. This we have the capacity to do without might and without power, without taking up the sword. It may be that neither you nor I have the necessary amount of dedication and self-sacrifice to be that individual, but it takes so little to be one of those who contribute to the ultimate raising up of an individual or the bringing forth of the divine idea.

All over this globe there are individuals and groups praying for world peace, for an end of racial strife, and for an end of slavery—the enslavement of nations of people as well as the enslavement of individuals. To pray aright you must understand the nature of prayer and what you are praying for. During the years of the Civil War you can probably imagine how many people were praying for peace, particularly for a Northern victory because it would "free the Negro." The North had its victory but it did not free the Negro, so all of their praying was "praying amiss." In World War I many of you remember the prayers that went out for an allied victory. Yes, because such a victory would "end all wars, save Christianity, and save democracy." World War II was equally disastrous in spite of the prayers: futile, fruitless prayers.

As individuals we must be free of mass hypnotism and ask: "Why have there been these failures in prayer? What is necessary for successful prayer?" If only one individual can come to the realization of the nature of true prayer, be assured we will have peace on earth—not through victory, but through divine justice.

You who are embarked on this mystical path must understand that you cannot pray for victory any more than you can pray for another's defeat. In other words, you cannot pray to save your life or the life of your child at someone else's expense. There is no such God listening to these prayers. To begin to understand the nature of spiritual prayer, you must first of all recognize that all power, infinite power, resides within your individual consciousness, and just one man or one woman striking the right note of prayer can change the entire course of history as did Jesus, John, Paul, and Mrs. Eddy.

Have the courage to face this fact, that as a child of God you embody all of the power of the Godhead. You are the outlet for that spiritual power, but it is not a power to defeat anyone or to bring victory to anyone. Spiritual power defeats no one; spiritual power gives victory to no one. Spiritual power reveals "God is in the midst of you." Spiritual power reveals harmony, completeness, wholeness, justice, equity. Spiritual power does not defeat and it does not win—spiritual power reveals. Remember that.

In this same way the prayer, meditation, or treatment of a metaphysical practitioner does not destroy disease, poverty, accident, lack, or limitation. It reveals the illusory nature of these, and in doing so it reveals the omnipresence of God. Any spiritual prayer, meditation, or treatment that is aimed at overcoming sin, disease, or death is doomed to the same failure as the prayers that were uttered to give us victory or to overcome devils.

Understand the nature of spiritual prayer: Its function or purpose is to reveal God's grace right where the illusion, the discord, claims to be. When Pharaoh's army was in the rear and the Red Sea was in the front, God's grace revealed the "cloud by day and the pillar of fire by night."[5] In the experience of Christ Jesus, spiritual power fed the multitudes when there appeared to be a few loaves and fishes. Spiritual power healed the multitudes of all kinds of diseases, not by overcoming, but by revealing the harmony of God's being.

In your prayers and meditations for yourself, your family, your community, your nation, and the world, watch that you do not pray for either victory or defeat; watch that your prayers do not include as much as a trace of a desire for destruction. Instead, pray: "Father, reveal thy grace, thy peace, thy kingdom. Thy grace is my sufficiency in all things, not thy victories and not thy defeats. Just thy grace reveals abundance." Watch in your prayers, meditations, and treatments that you do not take up the sword, not even the mental sword. Watch that your heart and Soul is longing only to become aware of the presence of God, the grace of God, the kingdom of God, the peace of God.

The fault of all our previous religious praying was that we were praying for the opposite of that which we had. If we had disease we wanted health; if we had lack we wanted abundance; if we had sin we wanted purity; if we had danger we wanted security. Do you not see that all the things we wanted were material, and God is spirit? How can there be answers to such prayers?

That is why we call the nature of our work "the middle path," because we do not want the good any more than we want the evil. We do not pray to get rid of a material evil and we do not pray to acquire a material good. We go straight down the middle path and our prayer is: "Reveal the spiritual kingdom." What is this "my kingdom?" It is not just improved humanhood. There is a kingdom which may be experienced on earth which has in it no material evil and no material good. It has in it spiritual substance, spiritual law, spiritual life.

Let us take the word *life*. Suppose you had a sick life and you could exchange the sick life for a well life. The next question would have to be: "How old are you?" Oh, then perhaps you will not be around long enough to experience a well life! No, we do not want a sick life but we do not want a well life—we want *thy* life which is eternal and immortal. We know the world today is filled with those of mental unbalance but, if these people could be given a sane mind, again the question would have to be asked: "How old is that mind?" No, our prayers are: "Father, reveal that mind which was also in Christ Jesus—the spiritual mind."

Always, always we are praying that spiritual identity be revealed. When you understand this, you will begin to perceive the nature of prayer that can and ultimately will bring about a whole new consciousness on earth. It will not bring about another temporary peace treaty; it will not bring about a new division of power that will someday get out of hand. Leave that kind of praying alone.

Let your prayers be, first of all, the realization that the carnal mind is not and never was power, because it is not ordained of God. Then pray for the realization that the "mind which was also in Christ Jesus," the spiritual mind, the Buddha mind, be revealed as the mind of man. "Let thy kingdom be revealed on earth. Let thy peace and thy grace be established in the consciousness of mankind."

In your prayers, learn to walk right down the middle path, not wanting to establish human good and not wanting to get rid of human evil. Let your prayers be that the spiritual kingdom be established on earth as it is in heaven. If at this moment you do not know what the spiritual kingdom is, or if at this moment you do not have the nature of *my* peace, it matters not. You do know that it must be wonderful if it is ordained of God, therefore you can have faith and confidence in praying that Christ be established as the life and the Soul of man.

I must stress this point: If you allow your mind to wander into any vague hope that God is going to overcome the evils of this world, or that God is going to change the evils into good, you are just losing the value of the time you are giving to prayer. You must ignore both good and evil and set your goal on realizing the real nature of God's kingdom; and with all your praying you must remember that within your own individual consciousness is sufficient God-power to establish that prayer on earth. The Master revealed: "Where two or three are gathered together in my name, there am *I* in the midst of them."[6] Remember, one with God is a majority and your prayer is that "one." Never doubt that one moment of consecrated prayer can establish peace on earth. It can. It requires only one, when this one is sufficiently unselfed and is not praying for my country, my side or my city, but is praying for *My* grace, *My* peace, *My* kingdom.

During my years on earth I have seen a succession of Popes, but only one attracted the worldwide attention and the worldwide respect of Pope John. He had no more power than his predecessors and yet he will be remembered. He was a praying man, and prayer established him in the consciousness of mankind, and prayers brought forth from his consciousness whatever right idea had been expressed. This is the power of prayer in one individual.

Regardless of who eventually may be raised up to be the one through whom the kingdom of God is established on earth, I would like to be one of those who unite with others to raise up the one man or the one woman or the one idea that will captivate this entire universe. This is called impersonal prayer and many do not like this form of praying because to them it seems cold. You will never realize how warm it is until you enter into an inner communion within your Self, so completely unselfed that you are praying only that you may witness God's kingdom come on earth and God's grace established in the consciousness of man.

Your prayer, meditation, or treatment is the same in the meeting of your personal problems as it is nationwide or worldwide. Do not pray that your personal problems be overcome or that you be delivered from them. Do not pray that good health come to you to replace bad health, because you will then be right back in the old forms of worship. Regardless of the name or nature of your problem, take the middle path and pray: "Father, let thy light be revealed; let thy way be established in me; let thy will be done in me." Stay in the middle path! Just "thy grace, thy light, thy peace, thy will, thy kingdom," and let the heathen rage.

Spiritual prayer does not overcome and spiritual prayer does not win. Spiritual prayer reveals the nature of God and the nature of his man. Spiritual prayer reveals the nature of God and the nature of his universe. Spiritual prayer reveals the nature of God and his law. This is what we seek in prayer: *to know him aright.*

LESSONS ON GRACE

August 11, 1963
Princess Kaiulani Hotel

GOOD AFTERNOON. Every experience in The Infinite Way is meant only as a lesson. If we have meetings of this nature or of another nature, be assured they are of no importance except as a lesson. I would never have meetings in and of themselves, because they can become habit-forming. In other words students sometimes believe there is a virtue in attending them or they feel that by their attendance at meetings they become more spiritual. Once you have these mistaken concepts, the meetings have lost their value. During this year we have met at noon on Sundays in a room like this, or a more beautiful room upstairs on the eleventh floor, and also in another beautiful room on the shores of the Pacific. In times past, we have met in a tiny place here in Waikiki. Yes, we have met in many places and under many circumstances, and one of the lessons meant to be conveyed is this: You do not have to go to a holy mountain or to Jerusalem or to magnificent temple to find God. "Here where I am, God is," and this is true if you make your bed in hell. Yes, and it is true if you mount up to heaven and it is true if you walk through the valley of the shadow of death. "Here where I am, God is."

I hope those of you who have met with us here or elsewhere, in dingy places and in luxurious places, realize this: The meeting was only for one purpose—that we might unite to receive God's grace. It really makes no difference where we unite and it really makes no difference *if* we unite since "one with God is a majority"; and, "Where two or three are gathered together in my name, there am *I* in the midst of them." Our meetings are as irregularly conducted as you can possibly imagine; we meet sometimes here, sometimes there, and sometimes nowhere. We are held together by no human bond, no human tie, no human obligation—there is not even an obligation to attend these meetings. Even I hold myself without obligation to be here, should circumstances require me to be somewhere else. This too is for the purpose of a lesson, so that we do not subject ourselves to man and to habits, but that we maintain ourselves as subject unto God.

Here is another lesson: We owe man nothing—not to be anywhere and not to contribute anything. We owe no man anything. Our only obligation is to the kingdom of God within us, and this enables us to voluntarily unite outwardly, this enables us to share with each other voluntarily, giving according to our means of the moment. When you learn this lesson, you will then be living your life subject wholly unto God and, being subject unto God, you will be loving your neighbor as yourself. Why? Because in living a life subject to God, a love flows out from within you.

Today we have guests from Tokyo to Connecticut to Florida, but those individuals were not brought here by any human tie or obligation. They were drawn. Here again is our lesson: If you live and move and have your being in a desire to search for God, search for truth, search for God-realization, you will eventually attain some measure of God-realization. It makes no difference what you are doing as long as your heart and soul is at the same time engaged in this adventure—the search for God. For some this may prove to be a very short quest because they have been prepared by previous incarnations, and they step into this life ready to blossom. Others have a longer way to go. With some it takes ten or twenty, or even thirty years, before their consciousness opens into spiritual blossoming. Your function is not to question how long it takes, but to continue if you have that much courage and if the degree of intensity is sufficient within you. If it is, you cannot boast about it, because it is yours only as a gift of God. If it is not, you cannot condemn yourself, because some trees blossom in May, some trees blossom in November. Whatever it is that is the nature of your being, that is the time and the place of your spiritual unfoldment.

When spiritual light touches you, you will know it because of those who will be drawn to you for spiritual guidance, spiritual instruction, spiritual counseling, spiritual comforting, spiritual healing. Until this takes place it would be folly to do other than continue your daily studying, practicing, and meditating until the opening of consciousness takes place.

You have witnessed this here, and some of you have witnessed it in many parts of the world: It is always true that there are people who have come from far corners of the globe to attend these meetings. They have come at their own expense and they have not known what fruitage they would receive. The reason this takes place year after year in so many places is this: Whatever an individual comes for he probably receives, and then he is loosed, he is freed. No one is bound to me or to The

Infinite Way or to a membership. No one is under an
obligation to pay or to support—each one is set free. This
is another lesson. During my stay at home this year, so
many have come for instruction in healing, in teaching,
in conducting groups, and unless they go away with this
lesson learned, they risk their ministry. The lesson is
this: Do not bind anyone to you under any form of
obligation. Do not demand that students attend meetings
regularly and do not demand that they support this
activity regularly. Do you not see that you are only a
teacher or a leader if you have arrived at the consciousness which understands the nature of our work?

Paul says: "His grace which was bestowed upon me
was not in vain, but I labored more abundantly than they
all: yet not I, but the grace of God which was with me."[1]
Had I not recognized that no man could ever make up or
invent or imagine a teaching such as The Infinite Way,
had I not recognized that this message was given to me
by the grace of God, I could not have carried it all around
the world and I certainly could not have financed it and
yet not bound anyone into supporting it. It has been only
by the grace of God and that grace of God has been with
me since the first moment that I started out in a room
one-third the size of this room. The grace of God has
provided us with everything necessary to the fulfillment
of this message. It has raised up publishers, it has raised
up editors, and it has raised up all those necessary to
carry on the work. I have not done it; as a matter of fact
I have never made a human move in that direction. No,
and yet the grace of God has brought to me all that
constitutes the activity of The Infinite Way. This is the
lesson: Until you have "his grace," stay on and in the
search for God-realization. Look upon yourself as a

student, as a seeker; abide within yourself until that moment comes when the Christ announces itself in one way or another.

Through daily meditations renew the remembrance of that spirit of God, and never forget this: As the grace of God has drawn you to this room today, and as some of you have witnessed the grace of God drawing students together in every part of the world, remember that this is given to you as a lesson: "His grace which was bestowed upon me was not in vain." Without it Paul would have been nothing. Without it I could not have carried the activity of this work. No one ever carries a spiritual message or a spiritual mission without it. An individual does not need the grace of God only if he has no conscience; but to those who have been drawn to the spiritual path, there is no way to be really successful in any endeavor except as the grace of God touches them. Otherwise the Master would not have said, "I can of mine own self do nothing. . . . If I bear witness of myself, my witness is not true. . . . My doctrine is not mine, but his that sent me."

There is a grace which functions this ministry. It, not I, heals the sick, raises the dead, feeds the hungry. We are not miracle workers who go out and say, "I will make you healthy, wealthy and wise." No, but if we attain a measure of grace and you touch our consciousness with some measure of receptivity, you will be lifted up. If there is not that spiritual receptivity, you will have to wait until there is, because we have no power to change men's lives. The Christ has—when it touches receptivity. To those of you who do healing work, this will explain why you cannot always succeed. If you are conducting an Infinite Way activity, you are absolutely responsible to God—not to man—to maintain your consciousness at the highest possible level. Do not fret if it is not full Christhood, but you are responsible to maintain your consciousness at the highest possible level. Then, be as fair and as just and as willing to share as the Christ enables you to be. Do not sit around grieving that you are not healing everyone, but remember that it is the state of consciousness of the individual that determines the height to which you can lift him.

You who conduct meetings must go to those meetings completely free of having any ties on anybody. You must go there with no concern as to who is or is not there. In other words, the moment you allow your thought to go "out there," you have allowed yourself to come down to the human level. Only in this realization are you setting patients and students and everyone else free. "My conscious oneness with God constitutes my oneness with all spiritual good." You will then find that the passage which is in the front of every Infinite Way writing is absolutely true. There is no human tie between us, but there is a spiritual bond which unites us to a far greater extent than if we were to sign our names on a register or promise to be present at meetings.

In your ministry (and I am referring to everyone who is a student because you all face this ministry in your individual lives), you must understand the major principle in which is the major revelation of the message of The Infinite Way: You can neither heal bodies, nor can you reform people or enrich them or employ them. In other words your ministry is not with human beings. Let us go to Paul for a foundation:

"How are the dead raised up? and with what body do they come?

Thou fool, that which thou sowest is not quickened, except it die:

So also is the resurrection of the dead. It is sown in corruption; it is raised in incorruption:

It is sown a natural body; it is raised a spiritual body. There is a natural body, and there is a spiritual body.

Howbeit that was not first which is spiritual, but that which is natural; and afterward that which is spiritual.

The first man is of the earth, earthy: the second man is the Lord from heaven.

As is the earthy, such are they also that are earthy: and as is the heavenly, such are they also that are heavenly.

And as we have borne the image of the earthy, we shall also bear the image of the heavenly.

Now this I say, brethren, that flesh and blood cannot inherit the kingdom of God. . . ." (I Corinthians 15:35, 36, 42, 44, 46–50.)

Let us see this: If our ministry were to consist of the natural man, of the natural body, we would either be ministers or we would be physical doctors. Since our ministry is the raising up of the Christ, we have nothing to do with the natural man or with the physical body. We have found no cures for man's diseases, nor are we reformers of "bad" people. This is not our ministry. Our ministry is our recognition of this: When you were born you were the natural man who "receiveth not the things of the spirit . . . is not subject to the law of God, neither indeed can be."[2] We know this to be true just by looking out at this world and witnessing the disasters which take place in the experience of the "good" people as well as the "bad" people. Because we know the natural man is not "the child of God's creating," we have nothing to do with either his mind or his body. Our function is the recognition of spiritual man's true identity and of the nature of his spiritual body, a recognition that we attain only when our consciousness is enlightened.

Here you have the reason why we are not organized, and the reason gives us a lesson: What good would organization do to bring out your spiritual identity? No, you must learn that a spiritual message is to establish the death of that man who has to abide by human loyalties and bring about the rebirth of that man who has his being in Christ–to raise up his spiritual body, a spiritual body raised up by spiritual law. If you are abiding in the spirit, you will witness your body raised up.

We understand the nature of the individual, we respect the individual, and therefore we permit each person to develop in accord with his own nature. We do not expect any group of students to come into spiritual awareness at one time; our work is with individuals. It cannot be a collective work. If it were, I would have put an advertisement in the newspaper and invited thousands to come here today. It would have been of no use, because in the thousands would be only this same number who are here today, the same number who are ready to "hear." "Having eyes, see ye not? and having ears, hear ye not?"[3] Of course you have, and that is what has drawn you here, but it is not possible that each of you will understand the same amount at the same time. No, because our relationship with God is an individual one, and we attain one by one.

There is a foundation which has come to light recently in a different form than ever before. From the fruitage I think it is a much better form, and I want to share it with you as a lesson and as an experience to live with and to practice. In many teachings we have been taught that there is no use thinking of the past. There is no God in the past and so we might as well learn to let it go. Even if there was good in it, it cannot benefit us because it is past; and if there was bad in it, that too is in the past. In some teachings we have also been taught not to live in the future. However, at this point it becomes necessary not to just make statements, but to come into an understanding of why it is fruitless to live in the past with anxiety, or even with too much rejoicing. God cannot operate in the future. The only possible time that God can operate is now—only now. Try to get God to do something five minutes from now and you will see how useless it is. God is always functioning in the now.

Take this principle home and ponder on it: that God cannot do anything for you in the past or in the future. You must attain that conviction.

As you realize that you are living now, you will come to realize that it is at this moment that you must function by God's grace. Here we go back to Paul: "Thy grace is my sufficiency in all things."[4] When? This moment. How much? A sufficiency unto this moment. In this moment God's grace is functioning within you to whatever extent is necessary for you at this moment. You need not concern yourself with the past or with the future. Nature gives us enough air to breathe only for this second, and you know right well how impossible it would be to try to put your breath in storage.

You may have gathered the impression that there really are beginning students and advanced students, and this is the very place that you break down that belief. As far as God is concerned, it makes no difference. There is a sufficiency of God's grace where you are now to meet the need of this moment. Once you are anchored in that realization, you can go on with your studies and with your meditations and you make rapid progress toward the full realization of God. You have no problems if you have sufficient grace of God to fulfill you at this moment. In this moment God's grace is your sufficiency, there is enough of it present to meet the need of this moment; and, a week from now enough will be there. Always there will be the sufficiency of grace to meet the need of this moment and, on the spiritual path, you have no right to live one moment ahead of this moment. You plan meetings ahead or you make travel arrangements or you plan business affairs in advance. Certainly, but without burden and without problems because from one moment to the next there is sufficient grace to meet that moment. This is all you need–this is all anybody ever needs–enough grace for this moment. How can you be separated from God's grace? "Neither death, nor life . . . shall be able to separate us from the love of God." Neither sickness nor health can separate us because God's grace is omnipresence. How much? A sufficiency according to the needs of this moment. If you carry this remembrance into your spiritual ministry, you will remember that there is also a sufficiency of God's grace for your patient or for a hundred patients.

Always remember that it is the acknowledgment that brings the experience. If I acknowledge a sufficiency of God's grace in this moment, I have it! If I do not acknowledge it, I virtually deny it. Here again remember one of the basic principles of this work: "Nothing can happen in your experience except through your consciousness." Therefore, if you are not consciously aware that God's grace is sufficient unto this moment, then it is not so unto you. If you abide in this truth you will bear fruit richly. If you do not abide in this truth, and if you do not let this truth abide in you, you will be as a branch that is cut off. Therefore, the secret is acknowledgment. "Acknowledge him in all thy ways."[5] Acknowledge the presence of a divine grace sufficient unto this moment, and then stop taking thought for tomorrow. Your recognition of a divine grace sufficient unto the moment is your bread, your meat, your wine, and your water. "Man shall not live by bread alone"[6]—you must have that Word in your consciousness. You must be a law unto yourself by the truth you know and, if you are not as yet aware of the omnipresence of a divine grace sufficient unto this moment, become aware of it and live with it. Then you will realize how your life is lived not by might and not by power, but by grace. The Master is saying now: "Have *I* been with you so long a time? Has this grace been there all this time and you have not recognized it?"[7] Your recognition of it opens your consciousness for it to function.

Those of you with a ministry must assure your patients and your students that their salvation is not dependent on their becoming an advanced student. Their salvation is dependent on their recognition of this divine grace sufficient unto this moment. This makes it possible for students to be reformed, healed, lifted up in their first days of searching. God's grace is not dependent on processes. God's grace is not dependent on anything but recognition, and your responsibility is to recognize the function of a divine grace operating in your patients' and your students' consciousness as of this moment—sufficient unto the claim thereof and sufficient unto the need thereof. Otherwise you will be encouraging a belief that patients and students need you personally. You are not conducting a personal ministry; your ministry is the ministry of the activity of the Christ. How easy it is then to set them free in Christ.

In our meditations we ponder truth but we never repeat it as if truth were an affirmation. We ponder the principle behind it and then we turn within: "Speak Lord, thy servant heareth"[8]—then let God confirm it, let God put the seal on it.

ONE WITH GOD:
PRAYING FOR THE WORLD

August 16, 1963
Honolulu, Hawaii

GOOD EVENING. In the early years of our study of The Infinite Way, we must abide by the specific principles of this message very carefully, very closely and very intensely, because the study and practice of these principles develops our consciousness to where we no longer hate, fear, or love the human scene. We develop our consciousness to that place where we recognize that there is something greater than ourselves functioning within us. We of ourselves could never do the things that we are called upon to do. We of ourselves could not help people to overcome serious diseases, or to lose sins and false appetites, or to mold new dispositions. There is nothing about us as people that would ever enable us to do that for another. It is only when we have been touched by that which is transcendental, by that which is spiritual, that we can at least approach Paul in his statement: "I live; yet not I, but Christ liveth in me,"[1] or the Master's: "I can of mine own self do nothing"[2]–the Father doeth the works.

The study and practice of specific Infinite Way principles raises our consciousness because it helps us to overcome fear of anything in the manifest realm. It helps us to realize the non-power of what the world calls power. As we progress in this work through study and practice, and as some measure of the spirit of God enters our consciousness, we find ourselves called upon to help others. The others may not know why they come to us—it is something they *feel*, but they do come and they do ask our help, and generally we can give it. Usually, by the time they come asking for help, we have the spiritual endowment that makes it possible to give them their help.

Eventually this begins to dawn in the consciousness of every spiritual student, regardless of his approach: "If this that functions through me for the benefit of myself and others is so powerful, can it not then help the entire world? If I can pray for my neighbor and my neighbor benefits by my prayer, can I not then pray for the entire world?"

Praying for the entire world has been going on for centuries but it is only as we rise higher in the understanding and the demonstration of prayer that we will witness a greater fulfillment of spiritual peace on earth, spiritual harmony on earth. It is true that a great deal of the praying that has been going on for centuries, both in the visible scene and in the invisible scene, has had and is having an effect upon mankind. Thinking of the world from the standpoint of the consciousness of mankind, we must admit that the world is better today that it was a century ago. I am not talking about the effects out in the world that we are witnessing: the threats of atomic bombs and slavery of one kind or another. So, there are still areas of consciousness in which much room for improvement is needed. Let us put it this way: There is far less inclination to go to war, there is less inclination to stage the vicious strikes that were known forty years ago, and there is a greater inclination on the part of mankind to care for the less fortunate. Some of you may not believe this: In my own lifetime, orphanages and homes for the aged were horrible places. Orphans were put on farms to do hard manual labor; they were more than servants, they were really slaves. All of this has been done away with. In my own younger days, all that a workman had to look forward to when he reached the age of fifty or sixty, when he became physically incapacitated, was either to be supported by his children or be sent to a home for indigents. There were no benefits provided for him by the government or by industry, so never was it his fault that he became indigent. All of this has been changing. Yes, consciousness is at a higher level today than it was even fifty years ago, and far greater than it was a century ago.

Since it is impossible for the human mind to improve itself, it must be evident that the prayers of those who understand the real nature of prayer—both on this side and on the other side—must prevail. When I speak of those on the other side I am speaking primarily of the spiritually enlightened who have left this plane of life. I doubt whether any of you believe that Jesus Christ is dead, or that his spiritual function stopped at the crucifixion or the resurrection or the ascension. I cannot believe that you believe that the great contribution Buddha made, or the contributions made by John or Paul or thousands of others, stopped when they stopped breathing. What do you believe about yourself? Do you believe that all of the devotion and all of the dedication you have given to a spiritual study is going to come to an end? What then must you think of God? Those of you who are on the spiritual path are on it only by the grace

of God. Look around you out in the world at the billions
who are not on the spiritual path, and then you will
know that they cannot arrive there until they are
touched by the spirit of God. And when the spirit of
God touches them, they cannot stay away. Do you really
think the spirit of God makes us in some degree a light
to others, and then puts out that light? Impossible.

I know why the Master told us: "Lay not up for
yourselves treasures upon earth, where moth and rust
doth corrupt . . . but lay up for yourselves treasures in
heaven."[3] This is the answer: You must leave behind the
material treasures you pile up. It is true that it all gets
checked out at the probate court, but the spiritual
treasures that you have laid up in your consciousness
walk right out of here with you. In fact that is what
makes you *you*–just as the degree of your spiritual
understanding makes you *you,* and not the creature or
the natural man. You are what you are by virtue of your
attained spiritual consciousness, and you will be greater
than you are in the measure of your greater attainment
of spiritual treasure. You are not only going to give back
here on earth, but you will give back in multiplied
experiences when you have dropped whatever sense of
existence you still carry.

There have been and are people on earth who really
have attained an understanding of the nature of prayer,
and a great many who have passed from the visible scene
and are transforming human consciousness by their
dedication to prayer. It is for this reason that the world is
becoming more spiritualized. To become spiritualized
means to come into contact with spiritual consciousness,
and never believe that a piling up of years or a piling up
of centuries has anything to do with it.

Everyone who has attained enough spiritual endowment to help relieve the world of its pains, sins, diseases, lacks, and limitations must inevitably turn to the larger subject of world work or praying for the world. In this you must remember that you do not pray as others pray—that our enemies be defeated and that our allies achieve victories. You do not pray for the republican party or the democratic party or the socialist party, because all such prayers bring you down to the level of attempting to improve the human scene by utilizing your own human judgement.

In order to pray aright, you must not pray for any earthly conditions. Even though you should believe that you have a plan which would save the world, do not pray for it. There never has been a man on earth so good that he would know how to make laws which would benefit everyone. No one has been that intelligent. Humanhood is based on the law of: "Self preservation is the first law of human nature," so nothing of a human nature will save the world.

Only one thing will save the world and nothing else: the activity of the Christ operating in human consciousness. One thing and one thing alone can save your individual life and that is the activity of the Christ in your consciousness. That and that alone can bring you to the life that God meant you to lead when he created you in the beginning in his image and likeness. You have all witnessed good men who became bad, and intelligent men who lost their intelligence. You have all witnessed human good, but never have you witnessed human good working impersonally and impartially for the good of everyone. Man cannot become that good humanly, but he can when he is spiritually endowed.

You cannot pray for peace on earth, because you are praying for an effect. You can only pray that the kingdom of God be realized on earth as it is in heaven and then that realization will bring peace.

If, through your experiences with a spiritual message, you have had some proof or conviction that, in the presence of the Christ, the carnal mind is not power, then you can go on to the greater realization that the carnal mind is the arm of flesh or nothingness. If you can witness the carnal mind as nothingness, you should have no trouble at all in engaging in world work; and realize that there is only one carnal mind, whether it is manifesting as one individual or as a billion individuals.

When you can perceive that the carnal mind is non-power in the realization of the presence of the Christ, you are helping nullify it for the world. It is not enough to remember that the carnal mind is not power—it is not power only in the realization of the presence of the Christ. "One with God is a majority." Understand that the carnal mind is power on its own level of action. It loses its power only when it comes in contact with the Christ, with your consciousness. There is no darkness in the presence of light. "In thy presence is fullness of joy."[4] Wherever Jesus moved with his Christ activated consciousness, sin, disease, and death disappeared on his coming. So it is in some measure with each one of you. Wherever you move with some measure of spiritual endowment, some measure of sin and disease must walk out, it must dissolve.

Since we are agreeing that there is but one carnal mind, there is no reason why "ten righteous men" should not nullify the carnal mind of the whole world. Everyone is not receptive, but fortunately we do not have to wait for everyone. Be concerned only with this realization, that the activity of the Christ in your consciousness dispels the carnal mind. When I approach spiritual work it is not to change any set of human circumstances. My only interest is the realization of the activity of the Christ dissolving mortal sense.

Remember: There is only one claim—that the carnal mind has power. It not only has evil power, but sometimes it can even have a good power.

All the race movement in the world today is the result of spiritual endowment, because always there have been those who could say, "There is only *one.*" Because of these, we have had righteous prayer to stir up this racial situation and eventually lead us into the "tomorrow of oneness." All of the parades you witness are really the carnal mind trying to be good! It is not being good because it will not bring freedom. Freedom, equality and justice are only brought about by a change of consciousness—and so the real workers will work behind the scenes by realizing the activity of the Christ dissolving human beliefs, human theories, human modes, and human antagonisms. When you stop to think of the price that was paid in the Civil War to free the Negro and then realize how miserably it failed, you must understand that this was the carnal mind on both sides. Had God entered that scene there would have been freedom.

We are not going to pray for an end to racial strife, or that the world be humanly better. Our prayer always is the recognition of the non-power of the carnal mind, and the activity of the Christ in human consciousness. Then you will witness the changes on earth—but not through strife. If you lived in a southern town of ten-thousand people, and eight-thousand of these people were Negroes of little or no education, I am sure you can understand that you would have difficulty granting them equality. Yes, you might very well be on the side of those whom you consider the most backward of people. "What would you do?" you ask. If you were praying spiritually you would be called upon only for the recognition of the reign of the Christ—and then you would see the matter be taken care of and there would be a transitional change. Had the education of the Negro begun after the Civil War, who would care today if they did run the country? Once you let the activity of the Christ take over, in a generation or two it will prove that we are all equal. Then you will not really care who is governing your city or your country, because the basic patriotism will be the same.

It does not lie within our jurisdiction to decide these things humanly, but it is given to us to pray. It is given to us to pray that God's kingdom be realized on earth, that the activity of the Christ be made manifest in human consciousness, that the carnal mind be recognized for its non-power.

Let us localize this now into our immediate families, including our aunts and uncles and nieces and nephews—and we do not have to look far to see the carnal mind operating. What shall we do? Shall we start crusading? You know better than to try to change your relatives or to tell them what to do. That is not the way! The way for us is prayer, realizing the activity of the Christ in human consciousness, realizing the non-power of the carnal mind, realizing that the carnal mind has no law. We are not sitting in judgement as to who or what the carnal mind is. We are nullifying it by realizing that, whatever degree of it is still in us, it too has to be nullified.

Yes, we know from family life that the carnal mind is operating, and we know that it will continue to operate until "one, with God" realizes the activity of the Christ in human consciousness and the non-power of the carnal mind. The work must be kept on an impersonal basis. There must be no pointing of fingers at people or at ideologies. There must be no mental malpractice. There must only be the realization of the activity of the Christ and of the non-power of the carnal mind—and then let it be!

The carnal mind does not always act wickedly. President Harding was a very fine man and not a dishonest man, and yet corruption cost him his life. The carnal mind blinded him to what was going on and caused him to trust the wrong people. So even in a good man the carnal mind operated to make him careless and trusting. When we talk about the non-power of the carnal mind, let us be sure we also mean good humanhood, because that is the carnal mind too. How many times do you think good people are responsible for parasites? Yes, because in their goodness they want to help people, until eventually these people are no longer able to help themselves. This is the carnal mind acting as human good as well as human evil.

What we want is the realization of the activity of the Christ in human consciousness. So, in your world work, do not pray for peace and do not pray for equality or justice or prosperity or health. Just recognize Christ as the only power and the carnal mind as the arm of flesh or nothingness. If you understand that kind of world work, it will open up many ramifications of prayer for you. Take what I have given you tonight, and then let the Father reveal whatever else is necessary in the nature of prayer. This is merely to show you in general the nature of world work and, as you work with it, you can receive more specific instructions from within. Then you will be more deeply empowered from on high and that is what counts, not these words. The spiritual power that flows is what counts.

The one question this brings up is this: "Should these people not be out doing all the good they are doing?" The answer is "Yes, because that is the highest sense of service they have." Some of these spiritual prayers may be raising up these individuals who are out crusading. In other words, I do not think Florence Nightingale went out and did all she did just because she was a good human being. I believe that the spirit of God animated her at every step. I do not think that the men in the French Revolution, the American Revolution, and the Brazilian Revolution were all humanly good men. I think many were under spiritual orders and could not have done otherwise.

Whether we might be the spiritual power that raises up that seed, or whether we are one of the seed raised up to go out on the battlefield, we must not underestimate the value of those who are out on the front, more especially those who are out there under divine orders.

It Is *I*:
Nullifying the Carnal Mind

August 17, 1963

GOOD AFTERNOON. The work last night should provide you with a tremendous principle in the functioning of every detail of your life: in your family, in your business, in your profession. You cannot get away from the fact that the carnal mind is operating in every department of your human affairs. Therefore, just realize that it is operating, but always impersonalize it. In other words, do not try to find the carnal mind in "Bill Jones." It is always an impersonal operation even when it is appearing as an individual. On the human level it really is not possible to be perfect or to be all we are supposed to be. Therefore, when we are nullifying the carnal mind we are really nullifying whatever degree of it is still operating in us.

If you were to receive a warning that, at 12:00 o'clock tonight, there was going to be a tidal wave, you would have to admit frankly that you would not know what to do about it. The fact is that you do not know, nor does anybody else know. If such a warning came, the only thing you could do would be to get very quiet "in this minute," go within, and keep listening until something within you acknowledged itself. There would be no possible way of knowing how or in what way it would appear; in fact we might all receive different answers. For one it might come as "it is *I*; be not afraid," or "*I* will never leave thee nor forsake thee," or "Fear not, *I* am with you." It might even be that you would not get a message at all, just a feeling of inner peace. Then, whatever was necessary would follow. It might be that the tidal wave would not happen; it might be that you would be led in some way to move to another part of town; it might be that the tidal wave would be dissipated. In some way the situation would be resolved.

The point I am trying to bring out is this: When you are faced with a condition which you are not able even humanly to meet, there is nothing you can do except wait for the voice of God to announce itself. You will also find in the healing work that you will be called on for cases which would be absolutely ludicrous for you to believe you knew how to handle. Do you really think you would know how to handle cases of mongoloid babies, or insanity? Certainly not. No matter how experienced a practitioner is, he or she would not know what to do, and that would be the safest attitude to take. You would then sit down and you would not try to do anything—you would wait for God to do it. When you felt your feeling of release, your treatment would then be at an end. You might have to do it over and over again, but always your attitude would be the same: "Do not tempt me to *know* anything."

In this work you get calls from people who have "six fatal diseases," and who are dying from all six claims. To them and to their doctors it is all true, and to them they are beyond all hope. Unless you can acknowledge that you know even less than they know, you can be of no help to them. In Boston I had a case of a woman who came to me with thirty-two body cancers and I nearly laughed out loud. The reason I wanted to laugh was because, at that time, I had a case who had one cancer and I was sitting up all night with it. I want you to know that, in four days, not one of those thirty-two cancers was left. These cases come up all of the time—cases in which you would really have to be an egotist to think you could meet them. The safest thing to do is to admit that you do not know and then sit down and *let* something inside reveal itself.

When you see this, you will begin to understand what I mean when I talk about not living on yesterday's manna, not believing that the truth you knew yesterday is sufficient for today. During my entire practice I have never as yet allowed a truth to come into my mind today that might have helped a case yesterday or last week or last month. Each case is new to me and this is the safest way; otherwise, you are really depending on something in your own mind—and nothing in your mind has spiritual power. If you know the books from cover to cover, do not trust them for healing because this would be trusting an effect. In other words you would not be going to God, and you must not approach life that way.

A man just wrote me that he found The Infinite Way a year ago, and last October for the first time he had a paint brush in his hand and he has already sold a painting. This did not come from yesterday's manna. It would be impossible to turn within to your consciousness every day for a year, and not find something new flowing through.

Every single day, from the moment you awaken in the morning, you must treat this day as though you had never lived before and go within for something new. It may come through in a quotation you have always known, but you can be sure it will come through with power. Truth declared with your mind has no power.

What I really started out to say was this: The entire message of The Infinite Way (certainly the healing part) is made up of the nature of error, the non-power of error. Sometimes a young student will say, "How can you say that error is not power when I see so much of it around me?" Yes, when we say "Error is not power," it is an incomplete sentence. We should first complete the sentence by saying, "Error is not power in the presence of an illumined consciousness." Without Christ-consciousness, evil can go on and on and on. In other words a cold can become worse and end in death. So it is that the evils of this world can go on forever. There can be a Pharaoh in one generation, a Caesar in another generation, a Hitler in another generation—or strikes or wars—and you can go on to the end of time without error ever being overcome unless there is illumined consciousness to dissolve it.

My writings are probably full of this bad habit, that "error is not real and it has no power." That is an incomplete statement, because error does have power until it comes in contact with an illumined consciousness. As long as materia medica said that people could catch cold by sitting in drafts, millions of people caught colds. Certainly. Now materia medica reports that people cannot catch colds by sitting in drafts or by getting their feet wet, and so colds are on their way out. This is illumined consciousness. In other words darkness is now hitting up against light. There is no use saying there is no darkness. There is darkness until light is introduced.

Always remember that the appearances of evil in any form will dissolve in the presence of illumined consciousness. Illumined consciousness is of course not human consciousness with knowledge. Illumined consciousness is the consciousness that has received impartations of the spirit. Develop the attentive attitude of "Speak Lord, thy servant heareth." Then it makes no difference what the appearance is, as long as you do not try to meet it with your mind or with your knowledge. There is only one way in which error can be met–by non-resistance, by putting up the sword. Wait until your release comes within, and then watch it!

If you were to say, "There is something I know that heals," you can see how you would wreck yourself. There is only one answer and when you commence to perceive this, it changes your whole spiritual life. You begin in the morning to say: "I have no control over this day, and nothing that I know will control this day. I had better sit down and let the spirit of God be upon me." Then, when it comes through, you are fortified for that day. Instead of turning to yesterday's manna, sit down each minute fresh and let the spirit through. The voice is uttering itself constantly but, unless we are tuning in constantly, we are not going to get fresh manna.

You might as well make up your mind that, whether it is a simple cold or whether it is a cancer, you can do nothing about it. You might as well understand this in the beginning in order to get all traces of egotism out of you. Then you will discover the meaning of The Infinite Way principles. You will see then that they are principles that came to me in just this way–from within. By abiding in these principles they develop your consciousness to the place where you have no fear of the outer, and you will then see their marvelous function.

You do not want a religion king. You want a religious leader who will say, "If I go not away the Comforter will not come to you." Yes, let none of our leaders assume that they have authority. They can reveal principles and they can be of help, but their function is to build up students so they will be fed from within. Never is a leader to deprive anyone of this. Never.

The moment anyone believes that being an advanced student means having spiritual power and spiritual wisdom, they lose it. Spiritual power is God, and spiritual wisdom is knowing that you know nothing, and then going within. I do not know how people are healed and for this I am glad. If I was sure I knew, I would be sure I was wrong. We do not know how God works, but we do know that God does work by the effects. In the same way we do not know how nature works. I know nothing about spiritual healing–how it works or why sometimes it does not work. I do know this: There is a spirit in man and this spirit must be allowed to be released, and then the appearances dissolve.

Do not get the idea that error is not power. Just remember that it is not power in the presence of spiritual power. No form of error can survive in the presence of illumined consciousness. Illumined consciousness is really the release of that spirit within. The more we develop consciousness to the place where we can sit down in the face of any appearance and wait for the spirit to move through our studies and our meditations and our practice, we bring ourselves to the place where it can happen.

Think how you would feel if someone told you he really "knew the truth." Nobody knows what truth is, but if you are still enough it will come through and do everything for you. Do not even try to pin truth down into a statement or into a book. The safest place to be is that place where you know nothing. It is so wonderful to be taught of God each day, to know you know nothing and then be taught again fresh the next day.

Hidden Manna —
The Real Infinite Way

August 24, 1963
Honolulu, Hawaii

GOOD AFTERNOON. It is very noticeable that far too many students do not know what makes The Infinite Way, or why there is an Infinite Way message. If our students knew the answer, their progress would be very rapid; but, because they do not catch this major point, they struggle for years not knowing where they are going or why. That which started me on the spiritual path and which ultimately led to The Infinite Way, was the realization that there is no God in the human world or in any religious teaching as such. There is no God answering the prayers of people. For this reason, and for this reason only, there can be a world filled with all the things you can think of which constitute horrible world conditions. None of this would be if there were a God in the world. In the presence of light there is no darkness. You cannot have the presence of the Christ and have a sin or a death or a lack or man's inhumanity to man.

Eventually it was revealed to me that you cannot reach God through the mind, and that is why prayers as such are worthless except as one's blind faith might make of them a little power—just as it is possible to give a little sugar pill and stop pain. In this realization you must remember that this makes any religion or any religious teaching in and of itself nothing more nor less than a philosophy. The only thing that can make a religion a *religion* is something that brings the actual presence and power of God into concrete manifestation, and it is for this reason that we say The Infinite Way is not so much a teaching as an *experience.*

There are spiritual principles, but these do not constitute The Infinite Way. These are but stepping stones or bridges over which you walk. You have not reached the goal of The Infinite Way until you have the actual realized presence of God or activity of the Christ. It is for this reason that we cannot have outlined or formalized prayers or treatments. They are of no value except to quiet you. Your treatment is not going to help anyone until you reach that place of stillness where you receive a response from within. Therefore, the teaching of The Infinite Way is as valueless as any other teaching if it does not result in the actual experience of the presence of God, the feel of the presence of God within you. You can study the Bible and quote it and fall right into the ditch, if it does not elevate you in consciousness to where the actual meeting with God takes place.

No human being knows how to heal. No human being has the power to heal. No human being either knows or receives the "Things of God." Therefore, there can be no healing or real spiritual teaching until you are spiritually endowed, until the presence announces itself. Then you can sit back as a beholder and watch your life change. As you watch your life change you can say: "I did not do that." When you reach this place, you are then functioning in The Infinite Way. Now The Infinite Way becomes an alive religion, whereas before it was just a preparation.

People keep asking, "Why was this innocent child murdered or why was my dog run over when they did nothing wrong?" The world does not know the answer, but as students you should know that there is no God in the human world. Anything of that nature can and will happen until the child or the dog or the business or the profession or anything else is brought into the presence of one who is spiritually endowed. Then you can trust your child or your dog or your business or your profession because now the grace of God is benefitting them. It is the spirit of God itself. Until this is understood, The Infinite Way can mean nothing to you except as another teaching or as something nice to read or listen to and that is not its intent. The intent of this message is that every student shall reach that place in consciousness where the spirit of God is upon them and they can say, "I live; yet not I, but Christ liveth in me," or "Whereas I was blind, now I see." Then they can sit back and say, "I can fulfill all obligations"—not as if they were doing it but as if they were being guided, strengthened, and wisdomed from within, which they would be.

The principles of The Infinite Way, as they have been given to me, will definitely change your consciousness so that spiritual endowment can take place. Let me explain: The moment you learn that God or spirit is the only power and the only law, and you accept this even intellectually, you can at least meet a claim of bad weather by saying, "If God is the only law, weather cannot be law." Or, if you are faced with the threat of an atomic bomb you can say: "If it is true that spirit is the only power, then I do not have to worry about bombs." Or, in the case of a disease on the way, such as a flu epidemic: "What is that to me, since the spirit of God is the only power." Actually you may turn around and get the flu because intellectual acceptance is not the protection. However, if you persist in working with the principle of one power, eventually it will leave the mind and go down into the heart. When that takes place, then you can say, "Now I see."

There is not a person on the face of the earth who does not have a problem of supply. Even the multimillionaire has a problem of supply, if it is only concern as to how to meet his income tax. But when you adopt into your consciousness: "Man does not live by bread alone" or "Supply is not something material because supply is of God, and therefore supply is spiritual"–the fear or hatred or love of money evaporates. Eventually, then, you do perceive that this is a spiritual universe. When you stop the attempt to *get* material supply, it comes to you just by knowing that God is its source and God is spirit. As you take one principle after another and lose your fear or hate or love of the outer and can settle in meditation, you will find it much easier to say: "Speak Lord, thy servant heareth" and find yourself in a deep pool of contentment. When you are in this "deep pool of contentment," quiet, peace, the spirit moves and imparts itself to you. It may be in words, or in a deep breath, or in a feeling, but when it does, God is on the scene.

This is the function of The Infinite Way: to bring you to the place where you live by God, by the presence of God, not by statements of truth. The one demonstration you can make in The Infinite Way is the demonstration of the presence of God–that moment when you feel that "God is on the field." Then you are living by grace. Then you will realize: "Thy grace is my sufficiency in all things." Not that quotation, but the actual realized grace or presence is my sufficiency, and there is sufficient grace present to meet the needs of this moment. Everyone wants God ten years from now but, just as nature provides enough air in your lungs for this second, so God is sufficient grace for this second. As God's grace never stops, you always have enough grace for this moment. There is no future heaven; there is no heavenly heaven; this moment is the only heaven there is. The only heaven there is, is living in this moment, because only in this moment do you have sufficient grace to provide you with the spiritual bread, meat, wine, water—even resurrection. There is enough grace present in this moment to resurrect your body, your marriage, your fortune, your business—whatever the world says you have lost; and as you live in this moment, that grace becomes a continuing experience bringing about fulfillment.

Never ask this question: "Why am I in this trouble, or why did this happen to an innocent child?" You know the answer. There was no God in that picture or it would not have happened. Paul described it: "The natural man receiveth not the things of the spirit,"[1] or from the Master: "If a man abide not in me, he is cast forth as a branch, and is withered."[2] This is the man of earth; but the man who has his being in Christ toils not, neither does he spin, yet none are arrayed as beautifully in all the world's goods.

If you witness Infinite Way students going on year in and year out and not receiving fruitage or grace, you can know that they are just reading with the mind and remaining there. That is not reaching God. We are to live with a passage of truth until it becomes our own, and here is an example: "Thy grace is my sufficiency and there is a sufficiency of thy grace to meet this need." Then you could put away all of the books and all of the tapes until you could demonstrate that principle. Through the books and the tapes we present truth and, if you could take one statement of truth and demonstrate it, then the books and the tapes would have fulfilled their purpose.

We started out today by a reminder that there is no God in the human scene, that there is no way to reach God with the mind, and that harmony begins to come into your experience only as you attain the actual realized presence of God or spirit of God. In many of the metaphysical approaches you hear it said that evil is not power or there is no evil or error is not real or evil is not of God; but in The Infinite Way you must get out of that habit, because it is a habit which leaves you in the very error which you have been denying. There is error, there is evil, and that is why there is the search for God. Had there been no evils in the days of the Master, there would have been no Master on earth because there would have been no need of one. In fact every religion had as its origin the fact that there were so many evils on earth that people thought a new religion was needed. The true statement should be: "Temporal power is not power in the presence of the Christ or spirit," which means that evil or error of any nature is not power in the presence of the realized presence of God.

Let me prove this to you. Whenever you have been ill in your metaphysical life, the illness continued until you called your practitioner. The illness then either slowly or rapidly disappeared, indicating that there must have been something in the life of the practitioner which acted upon the evil, the ill. When sin or disease or death came anywhere near the Master, it was dissolved; but, if he was not around, the error kept on just the same. Yes, there will be evil, but not in the presence of the realized presence of God, the oneness with God. "A thousand shall fall at thy side, and ten thousand at thy right hand; but it shall not come nigh thee."[3]

You can sum up the evils of this world in the words *temporal power*, which would mean power of germs, power of dictators, power of armies, power of bombs. All that can be summed up as temporal power, and then you can realize that temporal power is not power when it is brought into contact with the spirit of God. Then you will know that, whatever temporal power is tempting you, you must bring the actual presence of God into the situation, whether you are so close to it that blinking your eyes does it, or whether you are so far away that you have to sit for days and nights until the spirit breaks through. If you are expecting any help until this happens, you are going to be sadly mistaken. Nothing happens to the errors that come into your experience until you have attained the realization of the presence of God—then temporal power is dissolved as darkness is dissolved in the presence of light.

This should give you such an understanding of the nature of the message of The Infinite Way that you will not rest or rely on any of its statements. Instead, you will know that they are to remind you to go within and bring forth the presence. You must actually experience God—then that invisible goes before you to make the crooked places straight.

The statement we had previously on grace, "There is sufficient grace present to meet the needs of this moment," brings up another subject. Let me illustrate: The question is asked, "What is truth?" I will tell you that no one in the history of the world has ever known what truth is because truth is infinite. Never has there been a religion or a teaching that was truth; but, like the omnipresence of sufficient grace to meet the need of the moment, as you turn within in your meditation, sufficient truth reveals itself for the immediate now. The infinite nature of truth means we can turn within and draw forth all the truth we need for any moment. Do not label any teaching "The Truth." Truth has been revealing itself through me all these years, yet it would be a horrible thing to say, "The Infinite Way is the truth." Truth must continue revealing itself one hundred years from now, but not the same truth that is in the Bible or in Christian Science or in The Infinite Way.

When you are dealing with your daily experience, you are opening yourself to an inflow of truth, but be careful not to depend on yesterday's manna. Go within for the inspiration of the moment—for this moment's manna—and then the spirit of God does the work. A statement of truth is not God. A statement of truth is the reminder that sends you back inside for further impartations.

If you will live constantly and consciously aware that there is a sufficiency of grace for this moment, or if you will live consciously aware that "I have hidden manna," and then go within for the flow, you will be living by grace. You must constantly know that you have this hidden manna, this "Meat the world knows not of." Do not depend on the statement, "Go within." Even if nothing comes, the contact has been made.

Be sure you never forget that the function of this message is to reveal to you that you do have an inner grace, a hidden manna, a "meat the world knows not of." Go within for the flow; then go about your business and, whatever your need is, the solution will appear in its own way. This has really carried me from the beginning of my work. Once touched by the spirit, I knew there was something within me that did the work. Everything necessary to my experience always appeared, even in time to correct my mistakes. You cannot avoid making a mistake but even if you do, this inner manna corrects it.

It is really very sad if an Infinite Way student does not catch this point, that there *is* an inner grace, a "meat the world knows not of," a hidden manna. Knowing this, you can always go within, wait for the assurance and then go about your business, knowing that something is going before you to make the crooked places straight. It is sad if students do not catch this. Nobody in the world has ever been born without this hidden manna—*nobody*—because God incorporated itself *in* man *as* man. Therefore, the only function of religion should be to acquaint you with that fact and to help you to raise up or release that spirit. When this happens, religion has accomplished its purpose. Then of course "Go and sin no more." After that there must be spiritual integrity or you have cut yourself off and human selfhood is the barrier.

Can you not see the sin of having anyone set up as a savior, whether it is Buddha or Jesus or anyone else? Can you not see the sin of believing that anyone of us is different from another, except in the degree of realization? There should be spiritual leaders, because in their presence temporal power does not operate. They can help in the overcoming of discords but only to a certain point, because "If I go not away, the Comforter will not come unto you."[4] However, no matter how advanced we become, there are times when problems can become so hypnotic that we ourselves may not be able to bring release and so we turn to each other for temporary help, for a lift. The Master was not ashamed to say, "Stay awake and pray with me,"[5] so there should be no hesitancy in turning to each other for help. I have no hesitancy whatsoever to do this when I need it, and I receive the help.

Religion is nothing to become sanctimonious about. Religion has to be a recognition of an indwelling presence, and then the ability to let it loose. There is nothing more sacred in the entire world than the individual. That means every individual, for it is every individual's function to attain his individuality and not keep it in a herd or a mass.

The students who have been with us here all year know that this has been a difficult year for me in which I have been going through a period of inner initiation waiting for a message. We have made no tapes this year except for four teaching tapes, and those were made in the actual teaching of those who were here for instruction. We made no other tapes because I recognized that the message which has been coming through each week was a "leading up" message, not a fulfilled message. During the last two to three weeks it all came to a head, and then it became clear that we are entering the consciousness that does not need words or thoughts. We can sit down to meditate and realize: "The kingdom of God is closer than breathing. I just have to tune in and listen. I need no words and I need no thoughts. I need only receptivity and, when the Word of God comes, the earth of error melts."

In The Infinite Way our dependency is on a hidden manna, a "meat the world knows not of," a presence you cannot define. You do not have a blind faith—you go within and bring it forth as spirit, then your religious life has been accomplished. Then forever after, you can say: "I live; yet not I, but Christ liveth in me." Because of the mesmerism of the world, you must go within twenty to thirty times a day. In other words you must get back inside where you acknowledge, "I have a hidden manna"—and then let it out.

It will not be long until someone will say to you, "What is it you have?" or "Can you help me?" No, it will not be long. Then you must remember to give milk to the babes. Do not give deep metaphysics at first. Give it gently, gently, and do not believe that you can lead anyone to this point in a year. Only a few are ready, because of previous incarnations, to catch this in a year or less. I can be very patient because I know that human wisdom cannot be replaced by spiritual discernment until onion skin after onion skin has been pealed away and they become transparencies. I can be patient with them until they have reached that place where self-preservation is no longer the first law and the first need. I know it takes patience on my part and I always hope they will have the courage to persist.

Miracles do happen, some far greater than you would believe if you heard of them. They are not due to a "miracle man"—they are due to consciousness and receptivity. Not even Jesus could perform miracles unless he was approached with receptivity. It really makes no difference what degree of spiritual height I attain—it can only affect you by the measure of your receptivity. That is why no practitioner can ever guarantee the measure of your healing or how long it will take, because it depends or your receptivity. No practitioner will ever heal everyone because there are those who cannot do anything but seek loaves and fishes and this sets up a barrier. The higher the teacher goes in spiritual realization, the greater will be the works, but only in the presence of receptivity. There is only one reason why healings do not come through. There is a barrier, a lack of receptivity–but be patient!

I could ask you a question: "If you knew this minute that the Russians were going to throw an atomic bomb tonight and the President gave you the choice of throwing the bomb first or waiting for the Russians to throw it, what would be your answer?" Your answer to this question would determine where you stand spiritually because, if you would choose to throw it first, you are still in humanhood, wanting to spare your life. Spiritual development does not include saving your life at the expense of another. Spiritual development recognizes: "Temporal power is no power in the presence of the Christ but, if it takes my human sense of life, I am not going to take the life of someone else." Why might it not stop a war if a group of people should say to the President, "Why should we save our lives?" As a matter of fact that is what would happen, should "ten righteous men" declare: "I am not taking someone else's life to save my own. I cannot see my life as being more precious in the sight of God than the life of the Russians or the Japanese or the Germans.

In your spiritual life you face this question to some degree every day. In other words, you prepare to send your child to school, but have you thought about the child on the other side of the tracks and have you made any provision for him? If not, you are still in humanhood. You cannot live in family selfishness and still believe you are living spiritually. These things resolve themselves when that spirit of God comes through, because then you cannot take any credit for being benevolent. You are not doing it, the spirit is compelling you. The Christians who were thrown to the lions were not courageous. It was the spirit of God that did it, for no human being could be that brave or that courageous.

We have arrived at a place in our work now where, if any of you are satisfied with anything less than the experience of God, you are satisfied with too little. Nothing should satisfy you but the experience itself, and you can accomplish that by turning within. It will come, and, when it comes, it must be renewed. Because of the hypnotism of the world, it must be renewed.

GROWING DAY BY DAY—
ATTAINING THE TRANSCENDENTAL
CONSCIOUSNESS

August 31, 1963
Honolulu, Hawaii

GOOD AFTERNOON. There are certain religions and certain religionists who call themselves fundamentalists. They believe that the Bible is the literal truth, that every word in it is a literal truth, perhaps because for so many centuries people have been taught that all or most of the Bible is the Word of God. Therefore, even the most enlightened people are often conditioned in their study of the Bible and thereby lose the way. I have witnessed that this is also true of Infinite Way students, but to a lesser degree.

Understanding the Bible is like understanding The Infinite Way. You cannot read the message of The Infinite Way with your mind because it was not written by a mind or through a mind. This entire message is a transcendental message that came through transcendental consciousness. To be understood it must be understood through transcendental consciousness—and this is also true of the Bible. The books of the Bible were not brought into existence by ordinary human beings; these individuals had access to the fourth dimensional consciousness or Christ-consciousness in Christianity, or the Buddha-mind in Buddhism. Both have reference to the same thing–the transcendental consciousness, or illumined consciousness. Therefore, the words never mean what they seem to mean and if you take them literally you will lose the Way.

It is for this reason that you have been given certain spiritual principles in The Infinite Way which, if you take them into your ordinary mind and work with them, will develop the transcendental consciousness until one day you can say, "Whereas I was blind, now I see." In other words you will then realize that you are not doing anything. It is doing it.

Because of the way in which the Bible was written, it is often said that Scripture is veiled or that those who wrote it hid the meaning. There was not so much an intention to hide the truth as there was this fact: The transcendental consciousness came through in a different form than the human mind could grasp. Therefore the Bible is not veiled when you read it through your higher consciousness, but first you must attain that higher consciousness. In the writings of all mystics it is true that to human sense the messages are veiled–but they were not veiled by the original revelators. They were veiled when they came through in transcendental form, because the language of the day must be used and this constitutes the veil. Remember this: Because a mystic has to reveal his message in the language of the day, this constitutes the veil.

Today we are going to take the monthly *Letter* for September, 1963 and try to unveil some of the Bible passages. I have been asked many times to do this in a book and I have refused. Unless it is done as I am going to do it in a small way today, students are deprived of attaining it for themselves. By giving students something to live with mentally, it then becomes just a formula. Today I am going to show you what you must do with every passage of Scripture in The Infinite Way, and, if possible, receive light on those passages which are not in this message—those on which I have not yet received my own light.

In the September *Letter* I have repeated a work given many years ago in Portland, Oregon, a work that bore great fruitage with a group of businessmen and women. This group met each day at noon for six days, and each day they were given one Bible passage to work with and apply for twenty-four hours. Wonderful results did take place, so I have repeated the exercise in the September *Letter* so that students can work with the passages and see whether something takes place in their experience which has not taken place heretofore. Remember this— if you take these passages literally, they will lead you into a ditch.

First Day: "Trust in the Lord with all thine heart; and lean not unto thine own understanding. In all thy ways acknowledge him, and he shall direct thy paths." (Proverbs 3:5,6)

Take my word for it, you will really fall into a ditch if you trust in the Lord with all your heart because that is what the world is doing. In the light of what you know, is there a Lord separate and apart from your own being? And the moment you read, "Trust in the Lord" did you instantly say, "There is no Lord to trust in except the divine consciousness which *I am*"? Therefore, the passage should really mean to trust the truth that God constitutes your consciousness and your consciousness is governing your day, your business, your home. Are you remembering that this passage also means "Lean not unto thine own understanding" but turn within and *let* the divine consciousness within you reveal its harmonies and its grace?

"He shall direct thy paths." Is there a "He"? No, your consciousness shall direct your paths. That which you are and that which *I am* is governing your life, that divinity which is the reality of you, that Son of God which is closer than breathing.

Do you not see how the Bible passage was veiled as long as you thought there was an entity somewhere who was going to direct your paths? The man who brought this passage through knew he was talking about the inner Self, but all the people knew was "Lord," or God or Jehovah. That was how it had to come through in consciousness and that was the veil, because there is no "Lord." There is only the *I* that *I Am.* In the moment you recognize that the *I* that *I Am* is one with God and has all that the Father has—and trust the Self of you to be the all-knowing, all-power, all-presence, you are abiding in this passage of Proverbs, where before you were trusting in a God who does not exist.

Second Day: "And Jesus answered him, saying, it is written, that man shall not live by bread alone, but by every word of God." (Luke 4:4)

"By every word of God." Again, if you do not take the word God and resolve it in your consciousness through the understanding that we are speaking of your consciousness, you cannot take the next step of listening for that word. Why? Because the still small voice is not going to come from heaven or from Mount Sinai—it is going to come from God. Where is God? Within you.

To spiritually understand this passage you must understand that the principle of life, the substance of your life, of your peace and your harmony, is the *Word*, and the Word is something that emanates from your consciousness to your conscious awareness. Do you not see how the truth is veiled when you say "every word of God," unless in your true spiritual discernment you have brought God down to where God is closer than breathing?

You must go a step further and realize that the word of God comes to you in your sins or in your diseases or in your deaths. Nothing can separate you from the word of God, because nothing that God has joined together can be put asunder. God is omnipresence, whether you are making your bed in heaven or in hell. Therefore, to read this passage aright really means to live in a continuous state of receptivity, whether you are being sick or well, rich or poor. Live in receptivity so the still small voice can impart itself. When you understand this passage and can say "I have hidden manna," you are home. You have made your demonstration because through this hidden manna you have access to the word and that is all the manna there is. It appears outwardly as the added things, but heaven forbid that you should look to it for the added things. You must look to it only for it.

Third Day: "Thou wilt keep him in perfect peace, whose mind is stayed on thee." (Isaiah 26:3)

Isaiah knew that this statement, the way it was stated, was not truth. He knew it had a hidden meaning. "Thou wilt keep him." Who is "Thou"–God or Christ? No, *you* is thou–and then you look down here somewhere in the area of your chest and say, "Oh! *Thou* is consciousness, my consciousness, the divine consciousness which God bestowed upon me in the beginning. That *thou* will keep me in perfect peace if I keep my mind stayed on this truth, the omnipresence, omniscience and omnipotence of this *thou* within me, this divine consciousness."

If you consciously let this divine consciousness live within you and then be receptive to the Word, you will be God governed. If you will keep your mind stayed on the omnipresence of the divine consciousness, its function is to speak to you as the Word. And, if you keep your mind attuned to the hearing of the Word, if you are trusting in the function of your consciousness and are trusting the consciousness of the Word that is to come to you, you are then living by grace.

Fourth Day: "Peace I leave with you, my peace I give unto you: Not as the world giveth, give I unto you. Let not your heart be troubled, neither let it be afraid." (John 14:27)

In the Christian world this means the peace that Jesus gives you, the peace that Jesus leaves you. You have to unveil the truth so when you read this passage you will say, "*I, I,* the *I* of me gives me peace–the *I* that *I Am* which is God–the *I* of my own being. This is the *I* that still gives me peace if I am in heaven or in hell or in death. *I* and the Father are one and neither life nor death can break that relationship because *I* in the midst of me is my creative principle–*I* in the midst of me is my Father–*I* in the midst of me is God."

Let no Infinite Way student ever say "I am God," because you will virtually be saying that your human piece of flesh is God. You do not say "I am God," you hear the still small voice within you saying "Be still and know that *I* am God." Then you know that *I is* God, and that is the *I* that gives peace to you and leaves peace with you. It is not the peace the world gives. No, the peace the world gives usually ends in heartbreak and if there is heartbreak there is something missing. What is missing? It is the peace that *I* can give you, a joy and a peace that bubbles up within you. God's grace is omnipresence so go about your business, do not outline, and let truth take form.

Do you not see why the world has fallen into a ditch by believing that "He" was Jesus? This is nonsense. *I* within you am God and *I* give unto you peace and joy and dominion as long as you look only unto *Me*–and then let it unfold. Do not try to influence it or it will show that you have not caught the message.

Come up. Come up from orthodoxy and metaphysics. Come up into mysticism and trust in omnipresence, omniscience, omnipotence.

Fifth Day: "In quietness and in confidence shall be your strength." (Isaiah 30:15)

You know what happens here, for you now say, "I do not know how to get quiet or how to be confident, so what do I do? I cannot pass over the fifth day, so how do I demonstrate this?"

The author of this passage is Isaiah, so you must turn around and say, "Isaiah, your consciousness is one of the greatest in the Bible and I rank you with Jesus and

Buddha. So, Isaiah, what do you mean by quietness and confidence?" Do not think that I have not turned within and talked this way to God or to Jesus because I have and, if I want to know what Isaiah is talking about, I must do this. Whether Isaiah hears me does not matter, because I know my consciousness is hearing me and it will give the answers back to me.

What has revealed itself to me in this passage is an unknowing. In other words do not try to learn to understand truth and do not struggle and strive. Do whatever you have to do and forget truth. When you can forget truth you have a good deal of confidence and the quietness will follow. When you feel you must struggle for quietness you are perpetuating your un-quietness. Very often the best spiritual prayer or treatment or meditation is to forget all about prayer, treatment, or meditation and go about your business. "In quietness and in confidence" really means to get away from knowing the truth for awhile and be still. It is not necessary to keep your mind filled with truth, because you are then back in the mental realm. You cannot become quiet or confident, but the Soul can give you quietness and it can give you confidence if you will relax from the mental exercise of knowing the truth and let your Soul take over.

You will discover this: As you have learned to work hard and long with the principles of The Infinite Way, so you must learn to stop doing this, sometimes for a day or two, and say, "Let me not trust in my mind. Let me relax in God." When these principles are embodied in you, your Soul begins to feed you, but until you really have that hidden manna, keep on with all of these principles that we are going through. Do not make it an eight-hour day; take time out to work in the garden, or read a good book, even perhaps a good novel. Never believe that The Infinite Way is trying to teach you to mentalize. This is necessary only when you are learning the truth, when you are feeding consciousness with the letter of truth. We want no student to live by affirmations and denials because that is not living by the grace of God.

Invite the Soul. Your Soul overshadows you as you sit or walk or sleep. Relax in it—without words and without thoughts. During these past months The Infinite Way message has been leading you to the place where you live without words or thoughts. The fruitage of abiding in these principles is a period of rest—and this is the true meaning of the Sabbath which Moses gave to the Hebrews. The Sabbath he gave the Hebrews was a period of rest forever. Labor for six days, yes, labor to know these principles. But then you come to a place of Sabbath which means for the rest of your days you live by the grace of God, by *My* spirit.

Eventually you come to a place where you do realize: "Oh! *I* is God, and the Word that it imparts to me is the bread, the meat, the wine and the water." You are then entering your Sabbath. When you have attained quietness and confidence, you have entered the Sabbath.

Sixth Day: "In the meanwhile his disciples prayed him, saying, Master, eat. But he said unto them, I have meat to eat that ye know not of." (John 4:31,32)

Do not go to the city, and do not go out and get meat. Rest in the Sabbath of "I have. I and the Father are one and all that the Father hath is mine." No words—no thoughts—no might—no power. You are in the conscious-ness of Sabbath and you need not go out and get meat for you have it. By what virtue? By virtue of "I and my Father are one and I know it." For six days you have labored to train yourself and study (the six days are probably many years), but there comes a "rest to my people"—there comes a Sabbath—and that is when you stop all of your metaphysical struggling. You stop and relax and let grace live your life.

So when you come to the sixth day of your exercise, just smile. "I do not have to pray for anything. I already have hidden manna the world knows not of."

Do you see how the Bible is veiled and how it takes a transcendental consciousness to unveil it? The mystics do not hide it—words hide it. There are some of you students here in Hawaii, and there are other students in California, Chicago, New York, England, Holland, Sweden, New Zealand, and South Africa who are in the six days of labor; but the few who have been listening with the inner ear to the messages of the last few months must be entering the period of Sabbath.

When a person is in the Sabbath he will say, "I do not know any truth. The only truth I know is what comes through today. I cannot live on the quotations of yesterday. As far as I am concerned, I am in the period of unknow-ing. I am living in the period of unknowing every day when I go within only to receive the manna for today—to listen for thy voice." You can recognize when a person is in the Sabbath because he realizes: "Thy grace is my sufficiency for this moment," and he is satisfied. He is resting not only in the assurance that, "Thy grace is my sufficiency" but, "There is a sufficiency of thy grace." You can tell when a person is in a consciousness of grace. He has settled into a consciousness of peace. The six days of struggle are over and "today I refuse to labor." Then, whatever is to come through comes through. Yesterday I was not able to even meditate for a message, so I decided that we just would not have a message for today!

When you hear it, and later read it, you will know it was not mine—I must have been able to be in the Sabbath.

Remember this: Your study has taught you that everything in The Infinite Way is a spiritual interpretation of Scripture. Because of this you can go back into your own consciousness and draw out the spiritual interpretation of these passages. It may come in a different form than I have given you today, but the principle will be the same.

Wherever you students are, those who are ready for the Sabbath, prepare for it by learning to rest back in this realization: "Let my Soul take over instead of my mind." Then, every time you go within, something new and fresh will come forth.

The consciousness which you are is infinite consciousness, and therefore you are growing day by day. The consciousness which you are is already infinite but day by day you are more aware of the infinite consciousness which you are. Infinite divine consciousness constitutes your being, and the life you are showing forth at this moment is the degree of the infinity which you are aware of at this moment. You may go still further to where you can say: "He that seeth me seeth him that sent me." That would mean you have come into the realization of your divine Selfhood, your Christ-being in its totality.

You who are sufficiently along on the path of The Infinite Way must now begin to realize that you have but one goal, the attainment of the illumined consciousness, which means the fourth-dimensional consciousness or Christ-consciousness or the Buddha-mind. Ascend into the mystical consciousness where you have but one demonstration to make. There is a transcendental state of consciousness which is beyond the human, but which takes possession of you at a certain moment. Knowing the truth intellectually ceases at some particular moment, and the transcendental state of consciousness becomes the individual consciousness and its function is a continuous state of impartation. You are always receiving from it and that is the meat or the hidden manna. Transcendental consciousness is not merely a term. It is your mind when it goes beyond itself, when something takes over. There was an absolute moment when Paul said "I live yet not I, Christ liveth in me." He did not mean that metaphysicians should make this statement—only spiritual illumination can make it come true. Let your goal be a single goal—*illumination*—and there will come a day when "that mind which was also in Christ Jesus" will not be a quotation. It is your living mind by virtue of its character, essence, and nature. This is The Infinite Way *goal*—attaining that mind which was also in Christ Jesus—attaining illumination, attaining illumined consciousness—and grace will then descend upon you.

Prayer of the Righteous Man: God Is

September 2, 1963
Honolulu, Hawaii

GOOD EVENING. Truth is a shocking experience and those who are not prepared for a continuous bombardment of shocks should not undertake the search for truth. Probably the first question that a truth seeker would ask himself is this: Why is there so little fruitage from prayer? Whether it is the Protestant prayer, the Catholic prayer, the Jewish prayer, the Buddhist prayer or the Vedantist prayer, why is there so little fruitage? If the search for truth were started in this particular year, the seeker would receive many shocks in reading magazine articles written by ministers telling why people are meeting in small groups to pray, why they are not meeting in large numbers in congregations, why they are seeking outside of their churches.

There is a simple answer to all of this and one that every religion should have been able to give. The prayers of human beings are not answered. The prayers that seek to improve the human scene are not answered. The prayers that are aimed at protecting our children or our friends or our relatives or our allies are not answered. Therefore, prayer as it is usually taught is unfruitful, unproductive, and unsuccessful.

From the beginning of time we have had warfare and from the beginning of time you may be assured that mothers have prayed for their children, but warfare with all of its destruction has continued. As a matter of fact, it is so intensified in this century that, not only are the boys who go to war endangered or destroyed, even the mothers who stay at home are in danger of being destroyed. Prayer has not altered that situation, nor has it prevented the intensification of war and the added destructive powers of war. Prayer has done very little on a national or international scale, and yet in the Bible we find, "The prayer of a righteous man availeth much"[1] and "I have not seen the righteous begging bread."[2] In the literal sense none of this is true because we have all witnessed righteous men begging bread, according to the human standard of righteousness. So, evidently the prayer the world understands is not the righteous prayer that availeth much.

First of all, let it be revealed for all time that God cannot be influenced by man's prayers to do anything at all under any circumstances and under any conditions. Therefore, praying to God to fulfill your desires is a waste of time and a waste of energy. Prayers for your children, your friends, your relatives, your allies are wasted prayers.

The prayer that has been found to be effective is the prayer in which you surrender your wishes, your desires and your will to God. It is the prayer in which you ask for no favors and no partiality. It is the prayer in which you open your consciousness in order that God may fulfill its plan in you or through you, that this presence of God and this power of God which you acknowledge may bless all, friend or foe, saint or sinner, white or black, bond, or free. Prayer must begin with this realization: "I pray that thy will be done and not mine. I pray that thy will be done on earth—not for the Americans or the British or the French or the Christian church—but that thy will be done on earth as it is in heaven."

The first element of prayer is humility. This is true whether the prayer is an individual experience in which you seek God's grace or in which you think of God's grace in connection with your daily life, your family life, your business or professional life, or whether you have grown somewhat above this personal prayer to the place where prayer includes your neighbor as well as yourself, your enemy neighbor as well as your friendly neighbor. Humility is important and the humility of which I speak is not a depreciation of yourself but rather an acknowledgment that you yourself have no power to benefit this world, even your family part of this world. Your attitude of prayer would be that God's grace, God's presence and God's power be released in the experience of this community, this nation, and this world. There must be an absolute conviction within you that your prayers are not going to save anyone, that your prayers are not power, but rather that your prayers are the instrument through which God's presence and God's power be released to govern mankind.

Before our last trip to New Zealand, we received letters advising us not to come on a certain date because there had been somewhat authoritative reports that there was to be an earthquake in the ocean which would set off a tidal wave scheduled to strike the center of Auckland. It so happened that the day it was to strike was the day of our arrival in Auckland. Needless to say, we did not change our plans, and needless to say, we knew we had no power over the earthquake or over the tidal wave. However, by opening our consciousness to the realization of omnipresence, omnipotence, and omniscience, the presence and power of God was released into the situation. The earthquake did happen out in the ocean, but the tidal wave was dissipated before it reached New Zealand. If our prayers were instrumental in any way in bringing about this demonstration, it was not that we or our prayers had power, but that the opening of consciousness to the presence of God brought forth the power.

This is the point I would make: God *is*. There *is* a God of infinite power, and that God is "closer than breathing." It is here and now in this room, but it is also here and now wherever you may be or wherever anyone else may be. The presence and power of God does not perform miracles until an inner stillness has been attained, and in this stillness the presence and power of God is released. "One with God is a majority" or "Where two or three are gathered together in my name, there am *I* in the midst of them"[3] or "Ten righteous men can save a city."[4]

The omnipresence of God you must accept. Then you ask, "If God is omnipresent, what is the explanation for so many catastrophes?" The proven answer is, the activity of God, the presence of God and the power of God is functioning only where God is realized. Therefore, in the absence of the realization of God, God is not functioning.

Out of one hundred thousand people traveling to Lourdes for cures, you read that only fifteen were healed. The activity of God operates only in the experience of those who open their consciousness to it. The fifteen were probably sufficiently enlightened to where they were not asking God to do anything but were presenting themselves to God in silence that the will of God be done. In an investigation of those fifteen cases, it was learned that they did not pray for themselves; they prayed for others who were worse off than they. In other words, "Greater love hath no man than to lay down his own life that another might be saved."[5]

I do not ask anyone to accept the revelations which have been given to me. I merely state them and offer them to anyone who feels an answering response and wishes to adopt them. What do you think would happen if any nation of people would say to its government: "Under no circumstances will we consent to the throwing of a bomb, even if we have knowledge that someone else is planning to throw it first. We cannot believe that our lives are more important in the eyes of God than the lives of the people of the enemy country." It is my conviction that should any nation make this declaration, war and the possibility of a bomb being thrown would end because bombs are held in reserve only as the result of fear. Because we fear for our lives, we would protect our lives at the expense of anyone else. Someone at some time must break the cycle of fear—the cycle of self preservation is the first law of nature. It may be the first law of human nature, but it is not the first law of God. The first law of God is, "Greater love hath no man than to lay down his own life that another might be saved." Only in losing your life can you save it.

I have witnessed this on an individual scale and, in some measure, on a collective scale. When an individual withdraws his enmity, the enmity ceases. I first witnessed this on a collective scale when I was called into a union situation where a strike could not be settled. I said to the union leader, "Do you really think for a moment that I can influence God to give you a successful strike? Do you really believe that my prayers would have the power to defeat anyone? If so, you do not understand the nature of prayer. I will tell you what will settle the strike peacefully and harmoniously for all concerned. As the union negotiator, are you willing for a settlement that will prove to be an actual blessing to the company as well as to your union members? Could you go into a meeting with your heart absolutely certain that you could settle for that which would be as fair to the corporation as to your union members?" This was his answer: "Perhaps some time ago I could not have answered in the affirmative, but I can today. Yes, I realize today that as men must live, so must corporations and businesses live, and I am willing to seek only that which is justice." Needless to say, the strike was settled amicably in twenty-four hours. I have witnessed the same result in families, where one individual was willing to surrender victory for justice.

When one nation in this world who has a bomb to throw will say, "We are not going to throw it," I know this alone will engender peace and will destroy the fear that is in the hearts of people and enable a world to function without the threat of atomic warfare. Remember this: We cannot advocate that any government attempt this, because it can only be attained on the same basis that you and I can attain it. When there is no enmity in your heart, no greed, no mad ambition, no lust for power or property, only then have we attained the purification of the senses that enables the spirit of God to function.

When we approach a healing ministry on the level of the individual, the community, the nation, or the world, remember to approach it first of all with no personal wishes, desires or motives. Approach it with the realization that our motive for prayer is that God's grace function. We are an instrument for God's grace only in the degree in which we approach prayer without an attempt to influence God or direct God, and can relax and abide in the assurance that God's will is good. "God has no pleasure in your dying. . . . God is too pure to behold iniquity."

God has never created a disaster. God has never created a sin or a disease or an evil of any nature. Therefore, with a full heart you can open your consciousness to the experience of God's grace—that "Thy will be done"—and then rest in that word. Rest and be a beholder and watch what things take form by virtue of God's grace. Surrender your will and surrender your desires, then bear witness and you will see what great things God does through the consciousness of those who open consciousness in this pure spirit.

God is not man's servant. God does not function to do man's will or satisfy man's wishes. Man, rightly, is a servant of God. Man, rightly, is a son of God and a son is not a dictator of the father. The son respects the father and lets the father have dominion. As you open yourself to God as a servant and as a son, you may be assured that God fills your consciousness. Then those who touch your consciousness are blessed to the limit of their capacity to receive. All who touch your consciousness will not be blessed, because many are seeking the loaves and fishes and not God. Many are not seeking the will of God; many are seeking that the enemy be punished; many are so busy praying for themselves that they do not even pray for their own friends. These find it difficult to receive blessing.

Once you actually perceive that there is a God and that God is available in your experience, once you learn to open yourself to God without a desire that a specific will or wish or chore be performed, but only that God's will and God's grace be done through you, then you will witness the miracle of prayer fulfilled.

I cannot go to God with a request that you be healed physically, mentally, or financially. I cannot go to God and pray for your employment or for your success. That would be as fruitless a form of prayer as we witness in the world in general. When you seek me for the benefit of prayer, that I may pray for you or pray with you, I have only one way of being assured that the prayer will bear fruit. It will bear fruit only in the degree that I open my consciousness–realizing God's presence, God's power, God's grace–and then be still until something within me indicates that God is on the field. I may not know what you are seeking prayer for, but I am always hoping that you are seeking the further realization of his presence.

God is light. Where the presence of light is realized, there is no darkness. If there is physical, mental, or financial darkness, be assured the presence of God dispels it. We need not fear to go to God in sin. As a matter of fact, the deeper the sin the greater the need for God. Acknowledge the sin and then open your consciousness to the realization of God's grace and be assured the sin will disappear and evaporate.

As you have learned in The Infinite Way, life would be a selfish experience if you spent all of your time praying for yourself or for your friends and relatives. Since you have experienced the fruitage of prayer, you must pray for the benefit of this entire world. When you do, be sure you are not praying for the Republican party or the Democratic party or the Labor party or the Liberal party. Be sure you are not praying for the allied nations and against the enemy nations. In the eyes of God this must be rank stupidity. When you pray, pray that God's grace be active in the consciousness of mankind. Do not make the mistake made in the religious world, that of praying for God to improve the human being or the human world. Pray that the Son of God be revealed in individual man; pray that the Son of God be raised up in individual man; pray that God's government reign on earth.

For a period of five or ten or fifteen years it is possible to have good government on earth, but it is never permanent. Why? Because it is not given to man's wisdom to govern impartially and with wisdom. Therefore, unless you are praying that God's government be revealed on earth, you are praying amiss. Remember this: Whether our administration is Republican or whether it is Democratic, exchanging one set of men for another set of men will not solve the problems of this world. When men are inspired by God, they govern well and it makes no difference who they are or what political party they belong to. When men govern by personal interest they govern poorly or, if well, temporarily.

The change that must come about from this period on is this: In your innermost heart your prayer must be that the kingdom of God be established in the hearts and souls of men; that God's government rule the consciousness of mankind; that all men subject themselves unto the wisdom and the will of God. If you and I cannot meet this requirement in our individual lives, do not try to pray this way for the world. First of all, place yourself in subjection to God. Pray that your Soul and mind and body be subject unto God. Pray that the will of God be established in you. Remember to repeat this reminder within yourself many times a day: "Let thy will be done in me. Let thy wisdom rule me. Let thy love flow through me that I may be wise, loving, benevolent, just." This is somewhat like Solomon's prayer when he took over his high office, that he be given God's wisdom. As you surrender yourself to God's government, to the reign of God, to the spiritual center of man that man may be spiritually inspired and God endowed, you are in some measure dealing more wisely, kindly, lovingly, benevolently, and more justly with your neighbor—and more forgivingly with your enemy.

Each one of you has been entrusted with a husband, a wife, a child, children, a business, or a profession. Something or someone has been given into the care of each one of you. Therefore, you must realize that, "I do not have sufficient wisdom to fulfill this trust. Therefore I open my consciousness that I may have the benefit of God's grace, God's wisdom, God's love, God's benevolence, God's justice, to fulfill the little trust that has been given to me." Some men have great trusts—whole nations are in their care. They have been entrusted not only with their families, but with our families. How much more, then, should they be subject to God's grace, God's wisdom, God's love, God's benevolence, and God's justice. As it is not given to many men in such positions to seek this guidance, it becomes necessary for every individual who has learned to subject himself to God's government to pray that the reign of God be established in all human consciousness throughout the globe. Then you will discover that an individual here and there will say: "Whereas formerly I was not thinking of justice for all, I now find myself thinking not only of myself but of all who come within range of my office." We cannot pray what they shall do, or when they should do it or how; we may pray only for the realization of God's grace, that the Son of God be lifted up in all mankind, that God's will be done on earth as it is in heaven. Then rest, relax, and be a beholder. We have no power to make any of this happen. Our only power is to pray, and then the omnipresence, omnipotence, and omniscience of God performs its function.

To rightly understand the nature of prayer is the most important function of any individual on the face of the globe. When prayer is rightly understood, it brings all of God's wisdom, power, and all of God's peace into this room—into your house, into your business, into this community, into this nation, and into this world. Prayer, which is the most important subject on earth, is the least understood subject in the entire world. We can afford to give all of our time to learning the nature of prayer. Learning to solve our problems will wait; learning the nature of prayer will not wait.

We learned about prayer through Moses who did not pray for a cloud by day or a pillar of fire by night, but received them. We learned about prayer through Jesus who never did pray to heal the sick, yet they were healed. We have learned of prayer through the Master who said, "Forgive seventy times seven that you may become the child of God."[6] We have learned that prayer really means we must love our neighbor as ourself. This is prayer, and we have witnessed that the love where-with we have loved our neighbor has been the "bread we have cast upon the water" which has returned to us.

When the Master said "My peace I give unto you,"[7] do you believe he was addressing that to all the sinners and all the saints, all the highs and all the lows, all the blacks and all the whites, all the bonds and all the frees? Of course. Therefore, as we learn in prayer to let the Christ-peace flow from us to our neighbor saint, our neighbor sinner, our neighbor friend, and our neighbor enemy, that is the measure of the peace that returns.

None of us has yet discovered the full secrets of prayer. If we knew only a little more than we do know, be assured our influence in worldly affairs would be greater than it is. The subject of true prayer has been absent from the world for seventeen hundred years, and only in this century has it been revived for study and practice. What has been called prayer has really been selfishness, superstition, and ignorance. The subject of true prayer is new. A few mystics in all ages have caught glimpses, but only in this century have we caught a wider vision of prayer.

Prayer is an activity of God, therefore its function must be to show forth the freedom of mankind. Never hesitate to be humble on the subject of prayer. Never hesitate to open consciousness to a greater realization of the nature of true prayer. The secret you must demonstrate is this: You do not pray—God does the praying. Your attitude must be one where you are open to the activity of the spirit within you; and, when you come into a consciousness in which you acknowledge, "I am not going to pray, God. I am here only to be the transparency through which thy presence prays, and thy spirit makes intervention with the spirit of man," you are going to witness the destructive influences of mankind nullified.

Open yourself consciously to the experience of being still and knowing that *I* is God and then letting it bear witness and perform its miracle. Perfect yourself first individually in prayer in the sense of being open, that God may pray or bear witness in you or through you. Be empty! Be so empty! It will bring upon you a sense of humility you have never known before. Then you will understand why the Master said, "I can of mine own self do nothing . . . the Father doeth the works." Then you will know that it is not merely a quotation. You will know Christ Jesus achieved that state of prayer in which he himself did nothing. He let the spirit of God bear witness with his spirit and perform its function.

When you witness that once, and experience some fruitage of the spirit of God bearing witness within you, you will say: "Praying without ceasing is not long enough. I must have even more time for prayer." You will then be able to see what happens on earth when God has an outlet.

Our Goal:
That Mind Which Was Also in Christ Jesus

September 7, 1963
Honolulu, Hawaii

Good afternoon. The papers we have done since August 16 are definitely of a different nature, and I am asking our teachers and practitioners to give class sessions on them to their students and patients. The nature of these papers would make it necessary for any of us to study them seriously in order to assimilate them. However, for those who are not teachers or practitioners, be assured that additional lessons on them would be very valuable in order to grasp the nature of these papers. Whenever I read the one of August 24, I cannot really believe it myself, and I read it two or three or four times a day. As a matter of fact I find it difficult to send out a copy without reading it again. I am sure that, if the message in the paper of August 24 could really be conveyed, our students would be *home*. Then, of course, there are those of August 31 and September 2. They are really beautiful, and I would not like to see them treated as if they were just papers, because it would deprive the students of the depth of consciousness that is revealed in them. Of course, there are the two new series of tapes which represent the fruitage of this year at home, which will undoubtedly be the study material for all of our students for a long time to come.

367

At the present moment I believe we are going to discontinue our Saturday and Sunday sessions on the last Saturday or Sunday of this month. If we do not do this, neither the papers or the tapes are going to be properly assimilated because I believe that the fruitage of our year's work here for 1963 is propelling us into something that has not yet fully revealed itself. Not only has the telephone not stopped ringing, but the mail is increasing faster than we can have it typed. Therefore, I think we should be able to get away somewhere early in October to be beholders and see what it is that God has in store. Since these messages really point to something of importance, we certainly do not want to miss it. There will be students visiting here throughout September and up to about the 5th or the 6th of October. Some were to have been here longer, but I have asked them to shorten their stay in order that students may have the months of October, November, and December to assimilate the papers and the tapes. Except for the Christmas and New Year Messages, the month of December is always a holiday month.

In the spiritual life you are never able to forget that you are not living your own life, and that you have no right whatsoever to consider what you would like to do, or when you would like to do it, or how. No, you do not have this right because always in the back of your mind is the reminder that it is God's life that is being lived and it is just your privilege to be at that state of consciousness where you can watch God live your life without interposing a wish or a will or a desire of your own. The average truth student is not at that stage of development because he has duties to his family, or his business, or his art; but, until such time as the spirit itself says:

"Leave all for me" or "Leave your nets," no student should ever forget his duty to his family, to his business, to his human interests. Rather, he should make his study and his meditations the foundation for the more harmonious functioning of these facets of his life.

It is only to some that the call eventually comes, "Leave your nets" and when the time does come it is unmistakable and it compels obedience. After that the nature of one's life changes. It does not permit the neglect or desertion of one's family or business obligations, but it should provide for their independent care so that one may be set free for whatever the call may be. Let no Infinite Way student believe that the call to "Leave your nets" is an excuse to desert or neglect one's duties or obligations.

The paper of August 24 reveals the mistakes that many of our students have made, are making, and will continue to make if they do not awaken. Unlike other messages, the message of The Infinite Way is imparted only through the fourth-dimensional consciousness or the attained measure of Christ-consciousness. Therefore, the teacher must raise up students to the point where they are able to perceive spiritually, because students do not have that capacity as human beings. For this reason one Infinite Way teacher, spiritually endowed, can handle not only a tremendous ministry, but the ministry grows until it seems to be almost beyond handling. However, those who enter the ministry before they have received the spiritual call make little or no progress, and the reason is this: The message of The Infinite Way did not come through the human mind, nor can it be imparted to the human mind. To the human mind this message is as foolish as the Master's saying "Go without purse or scrip."[1] The human being would want to know how he is going to afford to get there, but not so with the spiritual disciple. No, the spiritual disciple would not stop to consider how he would get there, he would just start traveling.

In my mail I often have requests such as this: "Please work for my supply." Let us stay with the subject of supply for a moment. I understand what is meant by the request because in metaphysics the request is legitimate, but remember that it is based on the belief that supply is "out here" and that my work will start it rolling. How then does one say to that individual, "I cannot work for your supply because you already have an infinity. I know why you asked the question—you thought money was supply so you used the word supply as a synonym for money. What you really meant was money, but money is not supply." How does one say that to a person?

All the money in the world cannot be used as food. Even gold mines cannot be eaten. No, money is not supply except in the human three-dimensional world, and even then it is here today and gone tomorrow. We are not dealing with money as supply. We are dealing with consciousness as supply; we are dealing with love as supply, gratitude as supply, benevolence as supply. How then can one "work" for someone to have them?

The ancient Hebrews were taught to tithe. In those days they knew that tithing was not for the benefit of the poor, and that those who received the money or the food through charity and benevolence received very little. In other words it was really just a temporary help for this week or this month. They knew that the purpose of tithing—of giving one's first-fruits unto God—was for the benefit of the tither, and Jesus confirmed this fifteen-hundred years later when he said: "Inasmuch as you have done it unto the least of these my brethren, you have done it unto me."[2] So, in feeding or clothing or healing or comforting "the least of these my brethren," are you doing it unto the poor? No, they are probably poor because they are poor in spirit and cannot understand. Whenever you "do unto your neighbor as you would have your neighbor do unto you," you are feeding your own self with charity and benevolence and brotherly love. In doing it "unto the least of these my brethren," you are doing it unto your self, your Christ-self.

How then could you work for supply for anyone? You could not say, "Give away all that you have." No, because that is not a teaching, it is a matter of spiritual *capacity*. There is absolutely no way to teach someone to "love your neighbor as yourself." Think of all the people who are being taught this in all of the churches and in all the religions throughout the world and then realize how few are applying it. You will then better understand the message of The Infinite Way. It is not possible to teach a person to love his neighbor as himself. It is not possible to teach a person how to be grateful. It is not possible to teach a person how to give up the law of self-preservation. It is not possible because the human mind cannot respond to these. Only a spiritual teacher who has risen to Christ-consciousness can awaken Christ-consciousness in their patients or students so that there can be a response, and it will not be done to anyone quickly. It is a slow process to bring about the transition in a human being to where he is no longer "the man of earth" but is "that man who has his being in Christ."

Therefore, only one thing should engage the attention of an Infinite Way student and that is the developing of his consciousness by any and every possible means, of raising the Christ above humanhood.

The need is that every Infinite Way student rise into spiritual consciousness, because the need in the world today is greater than it has ever been in the history of the world. Civilization could be wiped out. A book is to be published containing the lost civilizations of the world, and the volume is so large that it costs $28.50. It took all of these past centuries to wipe out a few insignificant civilizations and now, in one night, all the civilizations on earth could be wiped out. Yes, it could happen, even if it happened accidentally. Mankind is really past the stage where there is human help to save the situation.

If you were to review the history of the last twelve months you would discover that not one single person on earth has even proposed a plan that could save the moneys of the major nations of the world from being wiped out. Not a single person during the past twelve months has revealed one plan to change the situation in Cuba, South America, Vietnam. There have been more articles during these past twelve months revealing the terrible state of education in the United States, and there has not been one plan for improving it. No mention has been made of the food situation in India or China or Russia, and when was the last time that you heard a useful suggestion or plan to be used in capital and labor situations? No, only Mr. Kaiser can be given credit for the plans in operation in his plants.

From The Infinite Way standpoint, it is always good when you reach the end of your human resources because you are then either going to die or you are going to live. If you die it is not too terrible because you know you will have another chance. In the situation where there is no human help, you do have a chance to live a whole new type of life. Probably the nature of the world's problems will eventually compel someone to say: "Since there is no human solution, is there a spiritual solution?" A psychiatrist recently stated that he now realizes psychiatry cannot help and wants to see what spiritual resources can offer, or that Freudian psychiatry cannot succeed because it is atheistic and so psychiatry must now adopt God. This is why I say that the extreme in human situations often compels us to find a spiritual solution.

Whether the world ever comes to the point of seeking a spiritual solution, I can assure you that there are many more individuals seeking a spiritual solution than we can care for. Selling more books is not the whole answer. The answer is in the attained consciousness of those who can say: "Let me give you help." It might be sad if the world turned to us for spiritual help now and we had to say, "We are sorry. We know this is the answer, but our students are not ready." How long does it take a student who wants to attain spiritual consciousness? I can give you half the answer. A student cannot even start until his goal is no longer that of meeting his personal problems of health or wealth or happiness. The search for God-awareness must become the primary motive of study. Then the spiritual student is halfway home. He must decide that the goal of Christ-consciousness is his only goal, and having help for his other problems is secondary. It then might not take a student too long.

Attaining "that mind which was also in Christ Jesus" should be the primary goal. It is an interesting thing for me to watch this work and see some of the students who are beautifully attaining it, and then watch those who still want healings for minor physical claims and are complaining because they have not yet attained heaven. In other words, these students are still living for themselves and are making themselves the goal rather than having the attaining of heaven as their goal.

Read again the paper of August 24 and see what I mean by all of this. I am not trying to say that we should be concerned about the world's currencies or the world's health or even the world's peace. You would be misunderstanding me if you thought that was my concern. My concern is in lifting the world into the higher dimension of consciousness, where all the "things" of the world are added unto us: "I, if I be lifted up, will draw all men unto me" or "Ten righteous men can save a city." Let us hurry, hurry about this business of being lifted up, so we can lift others into the higher consciousness. Then these problems will solve themselves. Whether it is a community as small as this roomful, or whether it is an entire nation, the problems are all the same. The only reason we are not having those problems is that we are in a higher consciousness where we are not operating on the level of self-preservation or personal gain. We are not operating on the level of seeking anything on the human plane. We are at that consciousness where we are seeking the kingdom of God and its grace, where in our dealings with each other we have overcome greed, malice, injustice not by trying to overcome them, but by attaining the higher consciousness.

If we could solve all the human problems on earth, a new generation would start tomorrow with the same problems. No, our goal is lifting consciousness into the higher attitude and altitude and in discovering that there are no earthly problems in that consciousness. It is the consciousness in which temporal power is not power. Whether we are dealing with mental ills, physical ills, or financial ills, they are not power in the presence of spiritual consciousness. Therefore, in attaining spiritual consciousness, the harmonies will be revealed. Then you do not have heaven and earth, but heaven on earth.

The tape that we re-made today was an important tape: the 1961 Mission Inn Closed Class, "The First Degree of the Spiritual Path." This tape virtually had for its theme: "Our conscious oneness with God," and for the benefit of those who have either had the experience or who have asked about it I will say this: When we make the real contact, the spirit itself as well as our spirit have blended and become one. It is as if it were what the world imagines as the second coming of Christ today. Can you visualize Jesus coming down from heaven on a cloud, which is what the world visualizes? No, when one makes the real contact with the spirit it is as if there were an invisible spirit out in the world, and anyone who can attune himself to this transcendental *I* finds himself under grace.

That is what happens when students in difficulty reach out to me for help, either locally or ten thousand miles away, and in some cases, experience what looks like my physical presence. In other cases they just experience the presence of spirit and then find either a healing or instruction. What has happened is that, "I and my Father are one,"[3] which is the truth of every one of us. However, as you know, this truth is of no benefit to you until you become consciously aware of it. The whole world is one with God in all of its sins, diseases, deaths, lacks and limitations, all of which are removed when there is conscious contact with the spirit. Since this is a goal of life with me continuously, those who reach out for help have that experience because they have tuned in to the spirit of God which is the spirit of Joel—one. If they are far enough advanced they can attune themselves to the spirit of God at once, but in the meantime they can attune themselves to Joel and accomplish the same thing.

The earliest experience of a student is that in which he makes contact with the risen consciousness of the teacher, and he continues to do this until he has made conscious contact with the spirit itself. In turn he then becomes a teacher to students; but if the student has not made this contact with the spirit, and he breaks the contact with the teacher, the result can be disastrous. Whenever a teacher has the experience of a patient calling for help, getting results even before the message arrives, this is the risen Christ. "I and my Father are consciously one." There is but one consciousness, so now God-consciousness has become the consciousness of the teacher. Should a teacher violate this, he will lose it. Why? Once you come in contact with the spirit and then violate it, the penalty is great. Therefore, the spiritual teacher must always be in attunement with it.

The spiritual path has always been a difficult one. Once an individual has touched the spirit, people believe it is not possible to sin, and that is not true. There was Judas, Lot's wife who looked back and was turned into a pillar of salt, Peter who denied the Master, Jonah and the whale—the Bible is filled with those who succumbed to temptation. Although Jesus did not give in to his three temptations, they were there. While we are on earth there never is a time that we are outside the range of temptation, because temptation is subtle. It can appear through the prestige of wealth or the prestige of notoriety or fame, or it can appear as the temptation to wield power. Even if he is at the beginning level, the person on the spiritual path should become conscious of the fact that a wrong done by him is not the same as a wrong done by a human being. A wrong done under the robe of the spirit is a crime against it, and this is like hitting up against a brick wall.

Once conscious union has been attained by repeated meditations, then when someone reaches out to Jesus or to any one of us, they are touching that which we have touched and it is that which meets their need because that has become our consciousness. We have no other consciousness than that, unless we still have greed, lust, malice, criticism, revenge. The attaining of that conscious union is really bringing the spirit of God to earth. It is right here in this chair, and it is like an invisible cloud protecting everyone who consciously reaches out. If you are consciously aware of a transcendental presence, you have made it so unto you. If you are walking around in ignorance, it might as well not be there.

This teaching was brought down to us from the ancients and was revealed by the Master: "Thou seest me, thou seest the Father that sent me."[4] In his consciousness there *was* divinity. His consciousness was divinity. Every great spiritual teacher has proven the same thing. Each one has made contact with the spirit of God. Yet every responsible teacher has said: "If I go not away the Comforter will not come unto you. I do not mind helping you, but keep on and keep on until you have made your own attunement with it."

In the guru system of India, every student is taught that the mind of the guru is the teacher. Therefore, just to be under the teacher's guidance is enough to bring darshan or blessing. Yet the great teachers of India have acknowledged this to all students: "I am your guru, but this is a temporary relationship. The true guru is your own consciousness and it is within you. I am only leading you this way so you can see that the guru is me and thereby prove that the guru is you."

Therefore spiritual teachers have attained some measure of the Christ-consciousness—that mind which was also in Christ Jesus—and the degree of their fruitage usually attests to the degree of their attainment. Anyone who is at all successful as a teacher in the spiritual realm has attained some measure of that mind which was also in Christ Jesus, and the student contacting that mind receives his protection. It is like an umbrella—invisible. No responsible teacher should neglect to say, "I am willing to be your temporary guru, but if I go not away the Comforter will not come unto you. Be prepared. Be prepared, because one day you will have to be under the umbrella of your own consciousness."

THERE IS ONLY ONE
GOD CONSCIOUSNESS

September 14, 1963
Honolulu, Hawaii

GOOD AFTERNOON. I would like to ask a question today, and I am wondering how it will be answered.

Question: *We know why human beings are in trouble more or less, but why is it that animals are also in trouble?*

Answer: Because animals are in the same consciousness that we are in. Yes, there is one universal consciousness and, on the human level, it is the consciousness that is made up of both good and evil and it is the consciousness into which we are born. For this reason we have experiences of good and of evil and until, through a spiritual teaching, we rise out of that universal, mortal, or carnal consciousness, we continue to have experiences of both good and evil. In proportion as we rise in consciousness, the evils lessen and the good increases. Of course the ideal is that we eventually rise above both the good and the evil into the spiritual.

Animals are born into our consciousness and that is why, when animals are in the consciousness of humans, house pets are well treated but rabbits and the beasts of the field are hunted. However, when animals come into the consciousness of the spiritually illumined, then the "lambs will lie down with lions." Why? Because they have been lifted out of human consciousness. This is also true of plants and crops. When crops are planted they are planted in carnal consciousness; but when they are not fed by food alone, fertilizer, rain, sun, but by consciousness which is the substance of their being, there will be infinite crops which are not subject to human conditions.

It is for this reason that in a household where even one member of the family is metaphysically or spiritually inclined, both the children and the animals in that household know less of sin or disease or bad conduct than is the case if they are in a household of entirely human parents. What this means is this: The consciousness of *one* becomes in some measure the consciousness of all in the degree of their receptivity. In just one household it is possible to witness most members of that household doing well in a spiritual way, and yet have one individual not, because he is unable to be spiritually receptive.

Let us be very sure of one point, because the ultimate demonstration of The Infinite Way is based on this: When we have just one generation of serious Infinite Way students, the future generations will be born into the consciousness that we are establishing. The reason it will be more widespread than it has been in the past is because all metaphysical movements in the past have directed their truth at an individual's consciousness. In other words, truth has been directed at "you," whereas we in The Infinite Way recognize truth as being universal. If I am in meditation and a truth unfolds in my consciousness, I could not possibly be so egotistical as to believe that it was given to *me*. It was given to human consciousness through me. Truth cannot enter consciousness from the infinite and be channeled to any one person. Truth cannot enter consciousness from the infinite and be channeled like a telephone. So every time you meditate and receive a spiritual impulse, you cannot limit it to yourself nor can you limit it to where it will ultimately go. It has entered human consciousness through you and anyone in the world who is crying out with receptivity, "Oh God! Oh God!"—or anyone who is in serious prayer, could receive it.

If I sit at home and meditate: "My conscious oneness with God constitutes my oneness with all spiritual being and idea," someone arrives here from Tokyo or Florida or New York. I had not left my room, yet they found out about me. Every time you meditate for conscious union with God, conscious oneness with God, and an impartation comes to you, whether it is in the form of a truth or an impulse or a feeling of the presence, the spirit of God entered human consciousness—it did not merely enter you. You have no idea where that spirit of God was picked up and what its ultimate effect will be.

Always remember this: It is our expectation that we need only one generation of Infinite Way students with spiritual discernment. Let our students become aware of truth entering human consciousness, and the future generations will be born into Christ-consciousness. It is an idealistic vision to visualize an Infinite Way activity which has, as active workers, those who have attained consciousness—but with us it is a possibility because we do succeed or fail on our consciousness.

A mistake made in spiritual work is the belief that there is human honor or profit or both in being a teacher or practitioner, whereas actually it is the opposite. The person becoming a teacher or practitioner has more to lose than to gain, unless he has attained the consciousness, and the best way of knowing is the degree of healing, comforting, practice that he is drawing. No Infinite Way student should enter the healing or teaching ministry until demonstration proves the rightness of it. Consciousness is the secret. With it there is success; without it no one can succeed in this ministry. When a person comes into the atmosphere of a teacher who is spiritually attuned, he settles down in a calmness and a peace as long as the teacher's consciousness is as I am describing consciousness today. That babies be born into this new consciousness must be the nature of our world work.

This afternoon we are going to remake Side 2 of the 1961 Mission Inn Closed Class, "The First Degree of the Spiritual Path." When we talk about dying daily we mean losing the human sense of things. Then we have the consciousness where "there shall in no wise enter into it anything that defileth . . . or maketh a lie."[1] When Paul says: "The natural man receiveth not the things of the Spirit. . . is not subject to the law of God, neither indeed can be,"[2] he means that the human being could never behold the Christ, not even the Christ of Jesus. When anyone attains spiritual discernment, he not only looks at Jesus and witnesses the Christ, he is able to look at any one of us and see that we are the *I* of God. Anyone could see this, but only with spiritual discernment.

If you look at me with your human eyes you must not expect to see anything but a physical form, because you are looking through human awareness. If, in your meditations, you go deep enough and high enough, do not be surprised if you witness me as the Christ, as spiritual identity, because that is my true identity. When

I am in meditation and giving help to someone, I am always beholding the Christ in that individual. This is the only way in which spiritual healing can take place because it is the *modus operandi* of spiritual healing. The individual with spiritual discernment can even look at a cripple and say, "What did hinder you? Arise, pick up thy bed and walk."[3] He would not be saying this to a crippled man. No, he would be saying it unto the Christ whom he sees through spiritual discernment.

No man is loving–God loves *through* man. No man is living–God lives *in* and *as* man.

If I am holding you in my consciousness in this light, as spiritual, as the offspring of God, as the life, the law, the being of God, how then do you feel when you are in my consciousness? When I am releasing you from your sins and your fears by knowing that these are not of you but are of an impersonal antichrist, how do you feel? You cannot help feeling good. Then do you not see that this is your responsibility to the world? As you hold everyone in the world in this light, you are setting them free in Christ. When you are not doing this, you are really malpracticing and you are holding them in bondage to their own sins, diseases, and lacks.

Spiritual teachers and practitioners must live so as to keep their students and patients and families and enemies in this divine consciousness. The revelation of The Infinite Way is that freedom cannot come to the world until you are holding this world in this light as if you were the spiritual teacher and practitioner to this world, which you are. This is your function. You have no more license than I have to hold people in your thoughts mortally, and I have absolutely no right. Everyone who hears The Infinite Way is thinking of me as the consciousness through which this message came. So if I am not holding them in that light, I am failing as the instrument for The Infinite Way. So are you failing as students of The Infinite Way if you are not maintaining this universe in your consciousness in the same way. While we call this meditation, prayer, or treatment, it really is a way of life. It is a state of consciousness which must be lived twenty-four hours a day. Every Infinite Way student should have this as his goal, to accept the responsibility to die daily to material sense and be reborn of spiritual consciousness—and that means to bless the world that comes into your consciousness.

You might as well understand the nature of the activity of consciousness. I am not a physical being. I have a body but I am not a body. I am consciousness, and therefore you are embraced in the consciousness which I am. If I am aware of God as my consciousness and live by this principle, then you are embraced in God-consciousness. In other words, the consciousness in which I embrace you is my understanding of the spiritual nature of your being, of your life, of the law that governs you. I am aware of your spiritual identity. I am aware of your spiritual Selfhood. In high moments I am even aware of your spiritual form. As long as you are embraced in that consciousness, you are well, you are protected, and you automatically lose some of the carnal nature that may still be a part of your nature. Why? Because that light that *I* am dispels darkness. In other words, if there is darkness in any form of sin, disease, lack, unhappiness, it is dissolved in some measure merely by your entering my consciousness.

Temptation would cause us to let down; it would even say to some spiritual teachers or practitioners, "You can have a few off-hours." No, you cannot put on and take off this consciousness as if it were a stage costume. So it is with every student. In the early years of studenthood it is not to be expected that you actually attain and retain the full consciousness and the ability to live in and through it, but there are periods, especially during your meditations. Each of you as a student should remember that every succumbing to the temptation to "drop out" merely increases the load when you try to get back in. It is far easier to stay in than to drop out and then climb back in again.

Remember you are your brother's keeper, but not in the sense of having to support him financially. You are not your brother's keeper in that sense, but you are your brother's keeper in the sense of maintaining the highest state of consciousness possible through your studies and meditations. We do not want the children and the grandchildren of this generation to be born into the same consciousness we were born into. They will be, unless we present a higher consciousness for them to be born into. The responsibility is on all of every spiritual students, insofar as possible and as quickly as possible, to drop our concepts of man as being mortal—and our concepts of good and evil—and live in divine consciousness to the best of our ability. When we slip, climb back up as quickly as possible.

As you are in my consciousness and are looking to my consciousness to be your safety, health, supply, and protection, you must remember that all who are in your consciousness will likewise look to you for this. Everyone who is looking upon you with love is looking to you for trust. They may see it as human love and human trust, but you must see that whatever degree of human love or human benevolence you give to this world will not do too much. Therefore, what you have to give to this generation and to future generations is the maintaining of spiritual consciousness.

You cannot reach the realm of God except through silence. Eventually you yourself must adopt the realization that none of the activity of your mind will get you into the kingdom of God. Then you really will be *consciously* conscious, and the first thing you will become consciously conscious of is God, if it is only to instill in you a deep longing.

As a youngster I grew up in New York when the immigrants were coming in from Ireland, Germany, Holland, Middle Europe, and Russia. New York was called a melting pot, and indeed it was a melting pot of all races and all religions; but in these immigrants there was a deep hunger and a deep thirst for knowledge that could not be satisfied. Whether they were from Eastern Europe or from Western Europe, they took advantage of everything New York could offer them. We witness the same thing here in Hawaii with the Japanese immigrants who also have a hunger and a thirst for knowledge and education.

You are never going to attain the spiritual realm with any less of a thirsting and a hungering, because it is far more difficult to enter the spiritual realm than it is to enter the intellectual realm. As a matter of fact, it would be difficult, if not impossible, to take one individual out of a hundred and give that individual the kingdom of God *unless* he had a deep longing, a hungering, and a thirsting. As with Jacob, there must be a willingness to "wrestle all night" if necessary.

The metaphysical world got off to a wrong start by hungering and thirsting for *things:* for a better body or a better purse or a better home or a better marriage or a better business. In The Infinite Way we are trying so hard to have the world see that these things are "added unto us." They are not goals, but are the added things. The Infinite Way never had any intention of being anything but a mystical message, a message revealing the possibility of attaining its goal of conscious union with God, and the means of attaining it. During all these years the writings and the recordings bear witness to this: The Infinite Way is not a system of attaining improved humanhood; it is the attaining of the Christhood.

During the last two months we have taken the actual step of saying that attaining Christhood can no longer be "eventually" or "ultimately." It can no longer be a future goal. We have entered the period where, for Infinite Way students, Christhood is to be the immediate attainment. It is for this reason that lessons such as this are given to us. Who is the lesson given to? It is given to all those students who have been with The Infinite Way writings and recordings for enough years that the letter of truth is established within them and they can enter the period of opening their consciousness to the experience. For years you have read that The Infinite Way is not a message, it is an experience, but today you must realize that the time to demonstrate the experience is here for you. This is not so for beginning students; they may have to go through a period of preparation. However, it will not be as long as your period of preparation for this reason: The degree of your attainment lessens the period of their preparing.

Each one of you could take that word *I* and ask yourself: "Is there anything to me except conscious awareness?" In the physical realm you are conscious of your body and you are conscious of the body of others. You are conscious of the body of ocean and the body of stars, and you are aware of the body of edifices. Then you go up higher into the mental realm and find that you are aware of brotherly love, justice, mercy, benevolence, forgiveness, and you are aware of the ideas and ideals. Why not take the next step and realize: "I can be aware of the things of God because there is an area of my consciousness which is the child of God, otherwise I could not unfold it or disclose it."

Do not be impatient. The Way is straight and narrow but, knowing there is a part of you that is the child of God, you can afford to be patient. There is an area of divinity incorporated in your consciousness; there is an area of your consciousness which is heaven; there is an area of your consciousness in which an angel dwells. It must be loosed, it must be released, it must ascend.

Pay no attention to the mistakes of your humanhood because this will keep you out of the kingdom of heaven. Remember that you are trying to reach your divinity, that which never had humanhood. The Master revealed: "The kingdom of God is within you."[4] The realm of God, the area of God-consciousness, is within you. There is a spot within you that is called the kingdom of God, in which an angel of God dwells.

Do not try to understand this with your mind. Accept it and keep your inner ear open because it is in a state of receptivity, not in mental activity, that it comes. When it comes there is the same Christ that appeared on earth as a man called Krishna. When it comes there is the same Christ that appeared as Buddha, Jesus, John, Paul. It is the same Christ that has been revealed through the saints and the sages of all time because God has only one son. There is only one God-consciousness and that God-consciousness becomes you.

There are places on earth where men and women have had tremendous spiritual experiences: in the Holy Land, in Syria, India, Egypt. I have had such experiences in Scotland and Damascus where it is almost as if I was enveloped. I was in another world, aware of the spiritual universe. The reason is that as the infinite divine consciousness is released through an individual, it permeates the whole atmosphere. But, unlike the scent of perfume, it never leaves there because it cannot be withdrawn. This is a spiritual perfume, and once it is released it remains, and those who have attained this inner power of discernment feel it.

This is the same principle that I have described in the writings. As we enter some churches, we are automatically enveloped in a spiritual atmosphere or a sense of peace. It is not because of the edifice. It is because there has been a priest or a minister or a rabbi in whom this spirit of God has been released and we come into that released consciousness.

This is the responsibility that is upon you which I have spoken of before—to maintain the listening attitude. "I, if I be lifted up, will lift up this entire world back into the Father's house, into God-consciousness." Never believe for a moment that this world is going to be saved by any other means. This world will be saved by the "ten righteous men" who ascend to the Father's house and realize: "God consciousness is my consciousness." Then relax without taking thought and let that consciousness function every detail of your life.

THE ADJUSTMENT MUST BE MADE
WITHIN YOUR CONSCIOUSNESS—
A LESSON IN SECRECY

September 21, 1963
Honolulu, Hawaii

GOOD AFTERNOON. I would like to speak today about healing work. The minute you become aware of discords and inharmonies in any form, on the street or in the newspapers or in your family life, you begin to reach out for the healing ministry. You may not know how, but you are alerted, and from then on you will become aware of discords in the form of sins, diseases, lacks, inequalities, injustices and these are bound to annoy you. They cannot help but annoy you now, because you know something can be done about the errors and the inharmonies and the discords that you are witnessing.

The question then arises, "Do I know enough to be able to help in this situation?" Actually, it is usually in this way that you are ultimately led into the activity of spiritual healing. In other words, you are becoming very much aware of the sins and the diseases and the deaths and the lacks and the inequalities and the injustices, and as students you long to be able to do something about it. I am speaking only to those students who have had the experience of witnessing the errors and discords in the world and then being puzzled about what to do about it. That is the beginning of the spiritual awakening. Until then, no matter how much a person is seeking truth, there is no spiritual awakening because the individual is only seeking a solution to his own problems. From the moment that a student becomes concerned about what he sees on the street or what he reads in the newspapers and wants to know what to do about it, at that moment the real spiritual progress begins.

It is wise at that point to try to specifically do something about the errors of which you become aware, but it is important to remember that you are not to do anything outwardly, but you have to do something silently within your own consciousness. It might be compared to the experience of walking through a school building and seeing on a blackboard, 2 x 2 = 5 or 9 x 9 = 67. You would have no right to enter the classroom and change the figures on the blackboard, but you would find it impossible to pass by without inwardly making the corrections. Within yourself you would correct the mathematical error, within yourself you would substitute the correct figures.

From the moment that you become consciously aware of sin or disease or lack or limitation or man's inhumanity to man, you are called upon to make the adjustment within yourself. You are called upon to correct the appearances. You have absolutely no right to do this openly, because not all people want to be healthy or moral or anything else unless their particular way of becoming healthy or moral will do it for them. There are many people who would like to be healed of alcoholism or drug addiction, so long as they can stipulate in what way it is to come about. No, you have no right to interfere in the life of anyone unless help is requested by the individual, or by a guardian if it is requested for a minor. Always remember this point: You are not to intrude in the private life of anyone without that person's permission.

However, you are under a spiritual obligation to make the correction within yourself and, if they are at all receptive, they may experience a healing and very often do. Spiritually you may not "pass by on the other side of the road," to use the Bible story as an example. You must make the adjustment in your consciousness, because you are your brother's keeper. You are not your brother's keeper in trying to change his religion or his mode of life, but you are your brother's keeper by keeping his image and likeness straight in your consciousness. You have no right to let him live or die without knowing the truth, without making the adjustment in your own consciousness. This is called spiritual prayer or treatment. Remember: You are the keeper of your brother, but you are not the keeper of your brother's religious convictions. You must maintain the truth about him and his divine origin, divine identity, and government by divine law in your consciousness.

As a student of The Infinite Way, you cannot possibly fulfill yourself until what you are taking in is released. It would be like accumulating money and then locking it in a vault. As a citizen you would be worth nothing, because it is how you express and release what comes in that determines the quality of your citizenship. So it is that truth, taken in and not expressed and released, goes to seed and rots. Therefore, from the very beginning of a spiritual student's studies, every principle of truth that he learns must immediately be put into practice and into expression or it cannot grow. Every student, no matter how much a beginning student he may be, must find some way within himself to express every statement of truth that he learns. In other words, no Infinite Way student, walking on the street and beholding bad conduct or anything of an erroneous nature, is permitted to pass by on the other side. He must look right at the situation or the condition, and then immediately give the spiritual prayer or treatment within himself. Whatever the spiritual student witnesses of a negative nature, an evil nature, a sickly nature, an unjust nature, must be re-translated within his own consciousness. It is that which we have heretofore called "knowing the truth." You cannot pass by on the other side—in that direction lies barrenness. Whenever you perceive anything which is spiritually incorrect, the adjustment must be made within your consciousness. Re-translate the appearance!

We call this giving a treatment or knowing the truth, but it is a great deal more than that. It is really beholding this universe as it is, and it is by means of this practice that an individual ultimately becomes a practitioner. No one ever becomes a practitioner by deciding that this is what he would like to be, because on this basis he will never be successful. There is only one way in which a person becomes a successful practitioner and that is by practicing. The moment an erroneous picture presents itself to your eyes or to your ears, no matter what the picture is, you must make the adjustment within your consciousness. That is what is meant by "praying without ceasing." You cannot wait for someone to call and say, "I am ill." No, at every appearance of discord you must begin your treatment, whether you are asked for help or not. If you witness two birds fighting, surely you would not wait to be asked to give a treatment. This does not mean you should look for trouble in order to correct it, but it does mean that every time an erroneous picture strikes up against your consciousness, you make the correction within yourself and then go on about your business. Eventually, this practice brings about a change in your consciousness.

In your human consciousness you are living a certain pattern and you might walk along a busy street and not once see anything erroneous in your surroundings. If you did, you would probably just make some passing remark. As your studies on the spiritual path continue, erroneous conditions are shocking. I suppose it is like a mathematician who is shocked every time $2 \times 2 = 5$ strikes his eyes. So with you. Because you are abiding in the truth and inwardly spending so much time learning and thinking truth, the moment an untruth strikes your consciousness, it is as though it actually hit you. In other words, you are aware that some little thing is wrong, and suddenly now it ruffles your consciousness. That is your call to make the adjustment within. We have had many instances like this happen: After one of our classes in Seattle a young woman was going home on a bus, and on the bus there was an intoxicated and very annoying individual. Immediately she began to make the adjustment within herself and it was not long until the man spoke to her and said, "Thank you. I am sober now." How did he know? It all takes place in the invisible. Everything that takes place secretly of a truth nature will be known outwardly.

As you witness an accident, you realize: "There is only spiritual government and nothing ever falls out of spiritual government," and as you witness theft or drunkenness you immediately make the translation within your own consciousness. As you begin to re-translate appearances in this manner, you develop the higher consciousness and then every appearance that touches you is translated within you without your having a conscious thought. It is like those who go into the healing practice too soon and have to give so many treatments. Had they waited, knowing the truth would have become so automatic that the moment an error touched their consciousness, it would be adjusted automatically. In the experience of experienced practitioners, mental activity lessens and eventually these practitioners are hardly aware of the errors around them and yet the adjustment is made within them. It has become automatic. Eventually, practitioners do not even see or hear the errors that are brought to their attention; they just smile and the adjustment takes place.

If you start out as a student aware of discords and inequalities, and you make the mental adjustment by what has been called "treatment" or "knowing the truth," eventually you will be like the mathematician who does not consciously have to think: $12 \times 12 = 144$. By learning that $2 \times 2 = 4$ and $3 \times 3 = 9$, eventually it is likewise automatic for him to know that $12 \times 12 = 144$. So with you. After you have seen enough inharmonies on the streets and in the subways and in the traffic, and have known the truth, eventually the correction is made automatically like the mathematician and his $12 \times 12 = 144$.

That is what happens in the life of a spiritual student who starts out as a human being with a human mind, knowing the truth that is in books and absorbing it day by day. Gradually he becomes aware of discords in the form of the sins, diseases, lacks, inequalities, and injustices of the world and he learns to re-translate them immediately in his thought, never voicing it openly or outwardly. As the student studies and practices truth, and he does so more or less with the human mind, it filters back through the mind into his consciousness and eventually he does not have to speak it or think it, he just has to *be* it.

Eventually, you reach the place where you are not consciously declaring truth, and yet the moment an error strikes your consciousness, the adjustment is made. Now as you are called upon for help, you have very little conscious treating to do and very little knowing of the truth. You are at the place of the mathematician who can automatically say: "12 x 12 = 144." You have been through all the stages until finally you can just look out at error and make the adjustment with no effort whatsoever. At first you are mentally active in reversing the appearances, in knowing the truth, but eventually you do attain an actual consciousness that may not even see the error or be aware of it and yet your being there heals and corrects it. There actually does come a time in your life when you are not consciously aware of the discords around you and yet healings are taking place. Remember the experience of Jesus when the woman touched his robe? He did not know she was there, but she was healed.

This happened a great deal in New York and Chicago: People who had Jewish prejudices would often say, "I do not have any prejudice. I love the Jews." Immediately one knew they were prejudiced because the unprejudiced people did not have it in their consciousness. So with you. You do not deny error; it just no longer attracts your eye. There is an unconscious activity going on of knowing the truth, and that is the highest form of knowing the truth.

I must say this to you: You do not enter this spiritual life until you rise to that place where the conscious knowing of the truth has been subdued and you have actually attained the awareness. You are now not knowing the truth, you have become the truth and here is where in our work the active practice begins. I do not like to see students going into the healing practice too soon because it is too much of a mental effort and it is too time-consuming. When students are patient, abiding within themselves at the center of their being until they are called upon, they will never have to go through the affirming and denying phase and the knowing of the truth phase. They will just smile, and the work will be done. In other words, they have patiently abided until they know that all sin, disease, and death are illusions. Eventually realization dawns: "In spite of appearances, God constitutes individual being."

When students fail to take advantage of every opportunity to reverse appearances, they lose the opportunity to become the good practitioners who do not have to give treatments. It is only by the conscious reversal that all of a sudden realization dawns: "God constitutes the life of man." When students fail to do this for a long enough period, they will not become the fine and successful practitioners that they should become. Students should not go into the practice until they have arrived at that consciousness where they no longer have sick or sinning patients, but where they realize the spiritual nature of the universe.

Let me summarize: In the beginning you are accepting appearances at face value and so you must know some truth consciously. As you continue to work that way and if you are alert, you will reach that place where you immediately correct the error as soon as it strikes your consciousness. Then drop it. Eventually you reach the place where you do not even see the appearances, but they are corrected. Less and less error is coming to your attention, and more and more error is being healed by touching your consciousness. The healing takes place automatically. When humanhood touches up against the purity of consciousness which is no longer condemning or judging, that is what heals, reforms, corrects.

There is not a single one of you in this room who is not at the stage where, when you see or hear any form of error or evil, cannot realize within yourself: "It is not of God," and drop it. In this way you will insure that you are developing the healing consciousness because you are giving recognition to the fact that everyone in his true identity is the child of God and your recognition of that is what sets him free.

Last Sunday the title of our talk was "I As Consciousness." Close your eyes and very gently within yourself say "*I, I, I*." That *I* is God. You may actually think it is man, and because you were taught that it was man you lost your whole life's demonstration. That *I* is God, and that *I* contains within itself your life, your supply, your protection, and your harmony. In fact the whole of your life from now until eternity is locked up in that *I*, and minute by minute it is unfolding. As long as you think that *I* is human, your life will unfold as the opposite experiences of sickness or health, lack or abundance, good or evil. The moment you begin to live in the realization that *I* is God, it begins to unfold always as peace, joy, success, abundance, health, harmony.

Never forget that the minute you voice this you lose it. The minute you tell anyone, make up your mind that it will take you ten years to get back to where you are. You say, "You are voicing it, Joel." Yes, but there is a difference. I am not voicing it to you. I am voicing it to my Self. I am not even interested whether you are hearing it. I am voicing it to my Self, and the Self of me which is the Self of you will hear it. Therefore, even after I have voiced it, it is still locked up in me. I am voicing it only to you who have brought your Self here to receive it. I am not trying to sell it to you nor am I trying to convince you of it, but the minute you go out of this room and try to give it to someone, the minute you try to impress someone or convince someone, you lose it. Then why am I telling you? I am telling this to you because for years you have given evidence that you are seeking this revelation.

From now on, normally and naturally, you should have more spiritual experiences than you have ever had in your life. If you have had none, you should begin to have them because all our work now is at that stage. Keep the experiences secret and keep them sacred and they will multiply. Let them bear fruit. When others ask about the fruit, give them the books and give them the tapes, but do not give them your experiences. Let them come up the same way you did because that is what they must do; they must begin with kindergarten and go through all the steps.

At this moment you cannot possibly imagine what a tremendous experience you are going to be in your family, your business, your art, your profession, your community, and, eventually, the world as you commence to abide in the truth that *I* is God. The moment you can feel this, you will understand the revelations of Christ Jesus: "I have meat to eat that ye know not of ... It is I; be not afraid . . . I will never leave thee, nor forsake thee . . . I am with you alway, even unto the end of the world." Every time one of these passages comes to your attention and you realize: "This *I* is God, this *I* is my bread and my meat and my wine and my water," you break the whole attachment to this world. Then you will know why the Master said, "Carry neither purse nor scrip"[1] and prove that *I* go with you.

I is God and this *I* that I am declaring is omniscience. Once there was a youngster in high school whose teacher told him that he could never be a mathematician because his mind did not go in that direction and that, if he took up a certain subject, he would be excused from mathematics. This the boy consented to do, but one day he was very discouraged because he felt inadequate and different from the other boys and so he came to me for help. This is what I told him: "I is not man. I is God. Omniscience, the kingdom of omniscience, is within you and if you want mathematics, you must go within and meditate and realize that the *I* who is omniscience must have all of the mathematics there is in the world." In a matter of days he went to his teacher and became reinstated in his mathematics class. Furthermore, following high school he went on to graduate from college, where he was known as "Young Einstein." Yes, as long as you think that I is man, you are limiting your Self. Think! Think! Jesus Christ, Columbus, Edison, Mrs. Eddy. One individual. So you know they must have been something more than man. Why? Because the *I* of them is God and, as they learned to turn within, they were able to prove omniscience.

First, recognize that *I* of your being is God. Therefore, you can turn within and draw infinity forth from it.

Secondly, obey the primal principle of mysticism—secrecy!

"*I* have meat to eat that ye know not of. *I* have hidden manna. *I* will never leave me nor forsake me. If I mount up to heaven *I* goes with me. If I go down to hell, *I* goes with me. If I walk through the valley of the shadow of death, *I* goes with me. As I travel on the road in cars or in trains or in airplanes, *I* goes with me. *I* goes before me to make the crooked places straight. *I* goes before me to prepare mansions." Always remember never to reveal this secret except in teaching, and even then be sure that those you are teaching are not seeking this secret because of the loaves and fishes. Reveal it only if you are sure they are seeking the secret of life and are willing that the other things be the added things.

The reason there are secret fraternities is that, in the original secret fraternity which was Masonry, this secret of spiritual identity was known and taught to every Mason. For that reason Masonry became a world power for good. Later it was accepted more or less as a ritual and a ceremony rather than a spiritual principle, but all secret fraternities were founded on that basis.

If the secret is functioning in your consciousness, it produces fruitage. It is like a seed, and the moment you reveal it, it is as if you tore up the earth and allowed the seed to disintegrate. Plant secrecy deep with your consciousness and allow it to remain there. Only you can ruin your demonstration by outwardly sharing what you have no right to share.

Share the milk with young students, but then let them prepare themselves. Never hesitate to urge students to study the bound copies of The Infinite Way *Letters.* More profound teachings cannot be found in the literature of

The Infinite Way, because these books pound at basic principles. Do as much of that kind of teaching as you wish, but keep the secret of the mystical life to yourself. Teach the principles, share the books and the tapes, but please remember this: As you now come into spiritual experiences, you are only having the experiences because of your years of devotion. It is your degree of preparation that enables the rest to take place, so always remember that there are no shortcuts for your relatives and for your friends.

Secrecy is a spiritual principle. Secrecy is an actual substance that holds within itself your experience, so bury your experience in the principle of secrecy and just let the fruitage appear outwardly. *I* is consciousness. *I* is God. Consciousness is *I*. Consciousness is your real identity and the consciousness that you are right now has your life, your health, your success, your protection, your everything within you. Nothing can be added to you because the *I* of you is God and it is already the embodiment of infinity.

Go and tell no man that the *I* of you is God.

TWO COVENANTS

September 28, 1963
Honolulu, Hawaii

GOOD AFTERNOON. There are two covenants: the human and the divine, the mental and the spiritual, and there is absolutely no way for the human being to pray to God or make contact with God. The only contact there can be with God is in silence, and that does not mean the absence of noise. It means the silencing of human will and personal desire. Spiritual silence, "be still and know," has no reference to sound. Be still means to have no will or desire of your own. Keep your humanhood still and then be willing that the grace of God fill your consciousness. How it will appear in the outer form you will have no possible way of knowing. It really is a mystery, and how it is accomplished is an even greater mystery.

When the work of The Infinite Way started in California, none of us believed that it would ever extend outside of California. As a matter of fact it was a surprise when the work moved up as far as Northern California, and when we were functioning there none of us dreamed of going outside of that state. Actually it was a great surprise when I was invited to Portland, Oregon! And so it has been ever since—a surprise. Only an act of divine grace could have continued moving us from place to place to place, until the globe was circled.

When you go to God it must be with no thoughts and with no desire. You go to God to attune yourself to God's grace and, whatever form it takes, that is what you must follow. There will always be a divided world and an unsuccessful world as long as people are praying for things, conditions, persons. I know through the healing work that you cannot pray for persons. It has always been horrible to me to think of God healing Mrs. Brown and Mrs. Smith, but not healing Mrs. Jones. No, in healing work the person who has asked for help has attuned to your consciousness and, when you are spiritually attuned, they are spiritually attuned and receive the benefits of that attuning. It is for this reason that multitudes could be healed if the multitudes would assemble in the realization that the purpose of the assembling is to attune themselves to the spirit rather than to a teacher. You must forget who the teacher is and come together regardless of the name or nature of the teacher, not because you think a particular teacher is spiritual but because you wish to attune yourself. "Where two or more are gathered together" in thy name, in thy nature, in thy grace, you will discover that any teacher who has gone beyond the stage of praying for things, conditions, persons, will serve the purpose of bringing God's grace into visible expression.

Remember this: The human being receives no answer from God. "My kingdom is not of this world."[1] This has to be your major remembrance. Therefore, if you are going to God's kingdom, leave everyone and everything of this world out of your mind. Go to God with: "Thy grace is my sufficiency, but it is also thy sufficiency, in all things," and in the silence conscious-ness is filled with the spirit, and spirit is the substance of all form. Then you will find that the forms which are necessary to your immediate experience are revealed. In the case of Jesus he needed a donkey for transportation, while we in this age require airplane tickets or an automobile. God knows no difference. This sounds strange but it is true, just as God knows no difference between the English, French, or German languages. God is spirit and, when you receive God's grace, you interpret it in the way you know and understand. In other words your need is always met at the level of your immediate interpretation. Can you imagine God knowing the difference between a man's suit and a woman's dress? Yet as we live in attunement, somehow or other the men receive suits and the women receive dresses. It is our interpretation of the divine grace that is unfolding.

Many people believe they can pray when they go hunting or fishing, so their catch will be more abundant; either an abundance of animals or an abundance of fish. How can you possibly pray to God to destroy its own creation, yet such prayers are being uttered every day of the week in churches and in temples. You must change your concept of prayer and then you will find the way to bring the kingdom of God to earth, you will find the way to bring the kingdom of heaven on earth.

If you follow the subject of prayer, you will understand the real meaning of humility. Humility has no relationship to the word as it is generally understood, and humility must be understood in its right nature, before prayer can be effective. Humility is not a feeling or an emotion. Humility is a recognition of the truth that consciousness is the source and the activity of all that is. Therefore, the part that we play in prayer is an attentiveness to consciousness as if listening. This is true humility and this is the true attitude of prayer, because even without saying it, it is an acknowledgment that it is not the human sense of I who has power or who can bring health to anyone. But the consciousness which *I* am, expressing itself, reveals itself as harmony in any and every form. Prayer, which is without desire and without anything of a human nature, is this listening or attentiveness to that consciousness which is "closer to me than breathing"–right here where I am. And since I am listening, I will hear the still small voice or I will feel the presence. In some way I will usually know when the contact has been made, but it makes no difference if there is no answer. It is the attitude of listening that establishes the contact. The contact has been made and the fruitage will appear, whether or not you have any knowledge of an answer.

You can go a step further: If for a period of time, and this differs with each student, you will have ten to fifteen to twenty or thirty periods a day when you turn within with the listening ear, you will eventually find yourself in a state of consciousness in which you do not have to turn within and listen because you are always in. That is when you will discover that people will write to you for help and receive it, and before their letters are in the mailbox. Or they will think about writing or telephoning and, before they can do either, they are healed. Why? Just the thought of your name was enough to establish the contact. There have been occasions where people have met us and, although no mention was made of The Infinite Way, their lives were transformed.

Our function is to be sure we do not have any illusions about going to God concerning anything that has to do with the material realm, because God has no knowledge of such things. As you have these ten or twenty or thirty periods each day for tuning in to the activity of God, the activity of God makes whatever adjustment is necessary in your life. Sometimes you do receive health, supply, employment, or happy relationships, but that is because you did not go to God for health, supply, employment, or relationships. There is only one reason to go to God and that is for the experience of God. Then it performs its function and brings forth harmony into your experience, even though it is sometimes a complete reversal of what you had in mind.

Know this: You do not have spiritual power. No one has spiritual power and no one states it more clearly than the Master who said, "I can of mine own self do nothing."[2] It is the consciousness which *I* am, but this consciousness is "me and thee." This consciousness which *I* am, *thou* art, and it is because of this that one with God is a majority. One in attunement with spirit can bring peace and harmony to the entire community because the one that *I* am, thou art.

You may think this is easy to say and declare because we are all on this path, but I can say to you from experience that it is just as easy to say it to the men in prison because the consciousness which I am, they are. You are talking about the infinite invisible consciousness which you had not recognized and realized; but once you recognize and realize it to be the consciousness which I am, then the only power there is in the realization that this is a universal relationship.

It is only in the degree that we continue in our humanhood that we miss the full attainment of spiritual harmony. Spiritual harmony is a key, and do not forget those two words. You cannot pray aright if you forget them, because prayer must be the inner desire for spiritual harmony—not human harmony. How do you know what spiritual harmony is? It makes no difference what it is, but you can long for it and you can hunger and thirst for it, because you know it is better than even the best of humanhood.

In some of our work we have prayer from the standpoint of attitude and altitude, which brings us back to this: Prayer is an attitude and it has nothing to do with words or thoughts. It is the attitude of opening yourself to God, or of placing yourself in the position to receive God. There is an attitude, and it is also an altitude. True prayer has nothing to do with words and thoughts. It is the attainment of an attitude of expectancy, of oneness, of being—an attitude of being a transparency. The attitude cannot be voiced better than Samuel's: "Speak Lord, thy servant heareth."[3] These are not words; this is an attitude of prayer and it shows an attitude of listening, an attitude of receptivity, an attitude of humility. It is an acknowledgment that there is something above and beyond, yet "closer to me than breathing and nearer than hands and feet." Prayer, when it reaches its highest point, is really an attitude: "Let me be fulfilled." It is really taking the attitude of being the servant and it is taking the attitude of being the son. Both serve and both are obedient. The servant serves the master and the son is obedient to the father, but the Master and the Father are one. There is the attitude in which you have renounced human good and human expectancy. It is an attitude of renunciation of human desire. It is the attitude of expectancy of spiritual harmony.

"Thy grace is my sufficiency in all things."[4] No one knows what "thy grace" is, yet when you can take the attitude of thy grace and not know the form it will take, this is not only an attitude but it is also a very high altitude of prayer. It is a fulfillment of Paul's statement that we be unclothed of mortality and be clothed upon with immortality. You cannot be clothed upon with immortality while you are seeking more mortality, so here is another attitude of prayer: "Let me be unclothed and clothed." Immortality will never be proven by the age of an individual. Age proves nothing. There are those who, at one-hundred years of age, are living the lives of vegetables, and there are those who pass on very much earlier in life who have fulfilled their lives and who have been fulfilled. Prayer cannot even include a desire for more years on earth, because that too is of an earthly nature. Nothing of an earthly nature can enter your attitude of prayer or it will not be a high altitude of prayer.

To be able to close your eyes and open consciousness to "thy presence" or "thy peace"—this is the correct attitude of prayer. Then you become a beholder of life. That is another attitude, that of being a beholder, awakening each morning and wondering what things God has in mind. Get into the rhythm of being a beholder and you will find that the spirit fills each hour of the day with its activity, with some words of spirit. Unless you can believe that there is an invisible substance which we call consciousness and an invisible activity of consciousness, and that it is living your life, there is no way to become a beholder. There is no way to become a beholder unless you can perceive that there is an infinite invisible consciousness which I am, and which is living my life. Remember Paul: "I live; yet not I, but Christ liveth in me."[5] When you can once feel or witness that there is an invisible something living your life and producing things in your experience which you could not have brought about, you are living a life of praying without ceasing because you are always looking over your shoulder to see what is taking place. It is this invisible consciousness.

Until you can perceive that there is an *it,* you can not pray aright; but when you can close your eyes and know that there is an *it,* then you will discover that there are inner intuitions to follow and obey. Then all prayer becomes an attitude of listening, of letting, of watching, because from then on it lives your life. It performs that which is given you to do.

I had just completed a class in San Francisco and was returning to Los Angeles when I distinctly heard a voice say: "He performeth that which is given me to do."[6] At that time I did not know that this passage was in the Bible but, having a Bible Concordance with me, I looked it up and found the passage: "He performeth the thing that is appointed for me." Then another Bible passage came through: "The Lord will perfect that which concerneth me."[7] I had no idea whatsoever what was going to take place but when I reached my study in Los Angeles, I found a long distance telephone call awaiting me from Honolulu. It was from a friend who was very ill, asking if I could come at once. Yes, I could come at once because "He performeth the thing that is appointed for me." Shortly afterwards a telegram arrived: "Do you ever come to Hawaii? We have just found your books and would like to have instructions." My reply was: "I am on my way!" "He performeth the thing that is appointed for me." "The Lord will perfect that which concerneth me." Incidentally, that began my whole story here in Hawaii.

When you are living the prayer of just attitude, it fulfills itself. The same presence that makes the demand fulfills it. That is why the Master could say: "I can of mine own self do nothing. . . . If I bear witness of myself, my witness is not true. . . . The Father within me, he doeth the works." In other words it is not the human sense of I—it is that consciousness which *I* am.

Remember that the human being is the son of the bondwoman; but the moment you have no human desires, the moment you have the awakening which is a seeking of spiritual truth, spiritual grace, spiritual peace, then you are the child of the freewoman. Then you are under grace and there are no material or mental laws binding upon you. You are then living by grace, "Thy grace is my sufficiency in all things."

Spiritual Discernment

September 29, 1963
Princess Kaiulani Hotel

Good afternoon. Before we started on our 1959 lecture and class trip, I was instructed within that our students did not really understand the healing principles of The Infinite Way. For this reason I was to devote that year to giving them the specific healing principles of The Infinite Way as clearly as possible, because these principles are totally different from those of any metaphysical healing approach. This does not always seem apparent in reading the writings because we all use the words God, Christ, spirit, prayer, meditation, treatment. Therefore, unless a student is alerted, it is natural that he would not realize that these words have entirely different meanings in the message of The Infinite Way than those to which he has been accustomed. So I spent the year 1959 traveling the world, giving classes everywhere on the specific healing principles of this message.

In 1960, 1961, and 1962 I was given a specific subject each year, so that the students might eventually be prepared for the higher works. At the beginning of 1963 I had already arranged a very heavy schedule of lectures and classes to be conducted from January through May, but again I received inner instructions to cancel all of these plans in order to prepare the students for that which was to come. I remained at home, doing no

415

public work this year. I have been teaching four days a week, but I have been teaching only those who were invited to be taught, those who were the most ready, so that with them and through them the new work could be given.

Since the middle of August we have recorded on papers, and in two new series of tapes, the mystical message of The Infinite Way, the message that cannot be learned with or through the mind. The message first of all develops, and then governs, that part of man which we know as the Soul faculties, or spiritual consciousness, or the Soul of man. Every individual who has ever been born and every individual who ever will be born has a Soul, has Soul faculties, has a transcendental consciousness—sometimes called spiritual consciousness. In Oriental teachings it is called the Buddha-mind or Buddhi, but it all means the same thing: the transcendental mind or consciousness of the individual. You will recognize that Paul was referring to this when he said "Have this mind in you which was also in Christ Jesus."[1] You have probably asked this question many times, "How can I have this mind which was also in Christ Jesus?" If it were not possible, would Paul have given those instructions? No, the reason that you can have this mind in you which was also in Christ Jesus is because you have it. You were born with it, but having been born into materialism and into religions that never went into spiritual things, you were not told that you have this mind, nor were you taught how to develop this mind.

In the early days of metaphysical teaching in this country, it was revealed and stated in some of the textbooks of those days that truth must be spiritually discerned, but it was never taught how you would attain the power of spiritual discernment, where you would get it, or how you would develop it. With the human mind you never can discern spiritual truth; in fact there is no way to understand spiritual truth at all with the mind. With the human mind you can learn and even demonstrate a part of the metaphysical teachings of the world, because to a great extent these refer only to the mental side of life. In other words it is a mental activity to know the truth, declare the truth, or affirm the truth and deny the error. These are all purely mental activities.

Spiritual discernment, however, is a faculty of spiritual consciousness and here is a simple example: The Master says, "I am the bread, the meat, the wine, and the water; I am life eternal. I am the resurrection."[2] What do you suppose he meant by that? Surely you know he was not referring to baker's bread. You know he was not declaring that he was meat from a butcher's shop. You know he was not speaking of alcoholic wine and you know he was not referring to the water that is drawn from a well. That you do know. Remember what Christ Jesus said to the woman of Samaria at Jacob's well? "Whosoever drinketh of the water that I shall give him shall never thirst; but the water that I shall give him shall be in him a well of water springing up into everlasting life."[3] Yes, he was referring to the water that *I* can give you, so you know he was talking about a different kind of bread, meat, wine, and water. If you know what he meant, then you have the faculty of spiritual discernment. If you do not know what he meant, this faculty must still be developed within you.

He said, "I am life eternal," and then he died at thirty-three years of age. Actually this is not contradictory so, if you do understand that "I am life eternal," then you have spiritual discernment. In the New Testament you are taught that you must die daily and be reborn of the spirit. If you know what is meant by dying daily, then you have spiritual discernment; if you know what it means to be reborn, then you have spiritual discernment. If you do not know these things, you will never understand their meaning with your mind and you will never be able to demonstrate them. In the Hebrew faith of the Master's day there were two sins punishable by death. One was murder and one was adultery, yet the Master says this to the woman taken in adultery: "Neither do I condemn thee.[4] Thy sins be forgiven thee." If you understand this, then you have spiritual discernment. If you do not know why it is or how it is that you can forgive a murderer or an adulterer, you have not attained spiritual discernment.

The entire purpose of the Christ ministry was to develop spiritual discernment, because the Christ teaching is a violation of church teachings. In church teachings, regular attendance is demanded in the churches, the temples, and the synagogues, and the Master says that God is not to be found there. There are demands such as tithing and sacrificing in the churches, the temples, and the synagogues and the Christ teaching is that these are not right. If you can understand this, then you have spiritual discernment because Jesus was not telling anyone not to go to the churches, temples, or synagogues nor was he saying not to share literally with them. His meaning was this: "When you give, give from your heart, not because of rules or demands or regulations. When you attend services in a church, temple, or synagogue, go there in order to be two or more gathered together in my name for the purpose of uniting in spirit."

In the church, temple, or synagogue you can very easily be excommunicated for sin, but the Christ ministry is more concerned with sinners than with the ninety-nine righteous men, because the sinners have greater need of the spirit. I know I have more to give to the sinner than I have to the saint.

This year our meetings have been attended by those who were invited to attend, and undoubtedly more would have been invited had we known of more who were ready for the experience. This work now is recorded on paper and on tape. On October 9, Emma and I will fly to London, and there too our teachers, practitioners, and tape group leaders from all over England and the continent of Europe will be invited for a month of this same type of work that we have been experiencing here this year. Many of our teachers, practitioners, and tape group leaders have been here from the mainland to receive this work in Hawaii, and to return to impart it. After we leave England, those from abroad will be prepared to do the same work in their communities because it must be evident to you now that this work, which is so active on five continents and on many islands of the world, can no longer be handled by one teacher. Therefore, one teacher will function through the other teachers, practitioners, and tape group leaders so that the work can be carried forward into consciousness.

I want to sum up for you now the nature of this year's work so that, as you read the papers or hear the tapes, you will particularly notice these specific points. I am assuming that you who approach this work, due to the 1959–1962 work, already know the basic principles. Without these, I do not see how it would be possible to sufficiently develop, in a short time, the spiritual faculty necessary to the understanding and demonstrating that which has been given to us this year. I will illustrate that for you so you will know exactly what I mean: In The Infinite Way you have been taught that there are two distinct levels of life. One is the human, that which is made up of mind and body and which Paul refers to as "the natural man" or "the creature." You were born as this human being; you grew up and were educated as this human being, and you remained so until some experience brought about the transformation that lifted you into the stature that Paul referred to as "the Son of God" or "the stature of manhood in Christ Jesus" or "spiritual consciousness."

If you have studied the message of The Infinite Way well, you know why prayers are never, or rarely, answered. You know why it is that all the prayers of our chaplains are so fruitless on the front, and why all the prayers of our ministers are so fruitless at home. They do not know, but you know, that you cannot reach God through the mind and that all the prayers you can voice or think with the mind have no possibility whatsoever of reaching God or of being answered by God. You know from your own experience that praying to God for persons, things, or conditions is a waste of time. You know it is a waste of time to pray to God to heal you or to send you supply or to give you safety. Such prayers cannot be depended upon, which is why a man as high in church affairs as a bishop has told his church that, unless that kind of praying is stopped, people never will be brought back into the church. That is why you read of people forming small prayer groups, because they are not reaching God through church groups. If you have studied the books of The Infinite Way well, you know all this. You also know that there is a way to reach God and that there is a way through which prayer is answered. You know that, for you have witnessed it.

For years you have had the benefit of the letter of truth which, when consciously realized, has brought forth healings, improvements, and harmonies into your experience. However, perhaps you did not realize that something greater than these was happening to you. Your consciousness was being reborn. You were dying to the old belief that you could appeal to God. You were dying to the old belief that there were powers opposed to God. You were dying to the old belief that God caused any of the discords of this world, or was responsible for any of them, or could be appealed to to stop them.

When you were told during the war that we were fighting for Christianity and democracy, it probably did not strike you as strange that one of our major allies was Russia and that they were hardly fighting for Christianity and democracy. When the war was over and you were told that Christianity and democracy won, you probably did not think it strange that Russia also won. At least I do hope that, out of your studies, you have learned to think, rather than being a sponge who drinks in whatever is fed to you.

There are two levels of life: the human level which is made up entirely of mind and body, and the level which is the Son of God or spirit. If you have discerned that there is a "man of earth" and that there is "a man who has his being in Christ"—if you have discerned why it was taught that you must put off mortality and put on immortality—then you are ready to understand the message as you will receive it from now on. You will

now approach that time in your own spiritual development when you will be taught of God, as indeed everyone must be eventually. The Master provided for that by
saying: "If I go not away, the Comforter will not come
unto you."[5] The Master did not provide for his remaining on earth forever to be our shepherd. Therefore, in
the end every knee must bend, every consciousness
must open to receive instruction, guidance, protection,
illumination, from the Father within. Then eventually we
will all be able to say: "I am instructed, guided, protected, and illumined by God."

Let us take the subject of protection. I am sure that
most of you in this room have no fear of atomic bombs.
I do not see how you could have such a fear after being
with us this past year, because you definitely must have
attained the conviction that God *is;* and if God *is,* that
means omnipotence. Is there then any power to fear?
Each one must answer this for himself: "Is the teaching
of The Infinite Way truth or fiction?" No one can
convince you of this, either way. You yourself must have
an inner experience which is not a blind faith. Blind
faith has been a terrible thing through the centuries, a
blind faith because "my" mother or "my" minister told
me to have faith. Why not have our own convictions? It
must be possible for everyone on the face of the globe to
receive an assurance from God that there is a God.
"Fear not, for I am with thee."[6] What is this, fact or
fiction? Are we to accept the Bible as the word of God,
or as pleasant fiction? All the really great Hebrew
leaders, and all the great Christian leaders have been
able to say without exception: "Fear not, for I am with
thee. I will never leave thee nor forsake thee. I will be
with thee unto the end of the world. Fear not the armies

of the alien; they have only the arm of flesh," they have only temporal power.

As long as you are the natural man thinking with your mind, you cannot accept these passages of scripture and you cannot adopt them as your way of life. Even though the human race repeats scriptural quotations, you know the world does not accept them. Why? Because the passages of scripture were not made for "man whose breath is in his nostrils." According to the Old Testament you must live and move and dwell in the secret place of the Most High, and the Old Testament made it very clear that, "A thousand shall fall at thy side, and ten thousand at thy right hand; but it shall not come nigh thee."[7] The New Testament is equally clear that "He that abideth in me, and I in him, the same bringeth forth much fruit: If a man abide not in me, he is cast forth as a branch, and is withered."[8] That is what you are witnessing of the human world. The Bible recognizes two levels of life as we do. That level of humanity which is not consciously abiding in the word, and which does not consciously accept God as the life which is "closer than breathing," is cut off. The Bible also recognizes the second level of life—those who live and dwell in the "secret place of the Most High."

As you come to the state of consciousness revealed to us this year, and given to us as a mode of life, remember that God is the life of individual man or men, saint or sinner, Jew or Greek, bond or free. God is the life of every individual. When Moses received the name of God, the Hebrew followers who had been in slavery were certainly not prepared to understand that name. They could have misunderstood it so easily that Moses refused to allow them to know the true name of God, and they were given a substitute name. Only the high priests were permitted to know that name. We learn now that, one hundred years before the Master came to earth, there was another Hebrew master who was crucified because he attempted to impart this secret to the Hebrew world. For one hundred years the name was again secret, but then Jesus was determined to follow in the footsteps of this great master and he revealed the secret for three years until he too was crucified.

The importance of the name is this: Unless you know it, you never can fully relax the tension of living, nor can you relax in the spirit and be God-governed, God-taught, God-protected, God-supported, and God-maintained. Only when you receive the revelation of Moses and Jesus as to the identity of God, will you be able to realize why it was taught: "The place whereon thou standest is holy ground."[9] You now know why it was taught; you have had it all year. You also know why the Master said: "I will never leave thee, nor forsake thee."[10] You know the import of that, but you cannot know it with your mind. You will have to have the same discernment that Peter had when the Master said: "Whom say ye that I am?"[11] Peter answered "Thou art the Christ, the Son of the living God,"[12] to which the Master replied: "Flesh and blood hath not revealed it unto thee, but my Father which is in heaven."[13] Nothing in the mind could reveal this, it was the Father within, it was the divine consciousness. In other words, "Whereas I probably look and talk like a Hebrew rabbi, you have discerned that behind this face and this robe I am the Christ."

When people come to us in sin, poverty, and disease, the only reason we can help them without using material means is this same power of discernment. Through the natural or developed spiritual consciousness we know that you are not what you seem to be. We know you are not what you look like or what you sound like, because we have had the inner revelation that has disclosed your true identity. Whereas you seem to be a human being, we know that God constitutes your life, your mind, your Soul, your being. We even know that your body is the temple of the living God and that spiritual discernment is the consciousness that forgives the sinner, multiplies loaves and fishes, and reveals health instead of disease. It is not the words in a book that heal, transform, enrich, and that is what we have been giving you all year. It is the state of consciousness you attain through abiding in the Word.

No one could ever make up a prayer that would benefit you. No prayers ever written could do more than bring you human consolation because, if all the prayers printed had spiritual power, we would have heaven on earth. Prayers taken into consciousness can develop and enrich this spiritual sense and then, when spiritual consciousness is in bloom, life is transformed. To begin with, it has an effect upon your own life because the very moment your consciousness begins to lose its fear of everything and everyone in the external world by virtue of your understanding that the kingdom of God is within you, consciousness is enriched and transformed. The old fear consciousness dies and the new consciousness of realization is born. Every step of your study, practice and meditation peals off at least one onion skin of mortality, and in that degree reveals one onion skin more of your immortality until eventually enough mortality is worn away so your immortality becomes increasingly more apparent.

The Infinite Way is not a message that heals, saves, or
enriches you. The message can enrich and ripen your
consciousness and, as your consciousness comes into
bloom, it does the work. Your consciousness is the
Comforter when it has lost its faith and fear in externals
and has developed the realization that all power is in the
infinite invisible within you, here where you are.

The answer must be clear to you. "I and my Father
are one."[14] That would really be enough to develop your
consciousness if you did nothing more that live with that
one truth: "I and my Father are one." Now you can
relax your fears and your doubts; you can release
yourself from anxiety and concern because "Here where
I am, God is." "Son, thou art ever with me." Think!
Think what that does to you when you live with this one
passage for a month, or two, or three. Then you will see
that it is not the passage itself, but the consciousness the
passage develops. Scriptural quotations work only when
you take the passages into your consciousness and
accept them as applying to you.

When the name of God is revealed to you, you have
attained the stature of the high priests of the ancient
Hebrew faith. Jesus knew the name, John knew it, Paul
knew it, Elijah and Isaiah knew it. The disciples had a
great deal of difficulty with it because they had difficulty
overcoming their Hebrew orthodoxy, but the chances
are that at some time or other, Peter also must have
realized it. When you know the name, and you abide in
it in secret, and relax in it and let it be your protection,
your support, and your supply, the moment the thought
of lack or limitation arises you can smile in the realization: "I am the bread, the meat, the wine, and the
water." Or the moment some serious disease comes to

your attention, either in yourself or in someone else, you can again smile: "I am life eternal. I am the resurrection."

When death touches you or others around you, you can smile:

I can lay down my life. I can raise it up again. I can walk in, or I can walk out. If you destroy this temple, in three days I will raise it up again." Only with this can you completely repeat with the Master: "I have overcome the world. Rome, or the Sanhedrin may still exist for you, but for me I have overcome the world and nothing shall enter my consciousness that defileth or maketh a lie. Whether I live on this plane or on another plane, I will still live and I will be about my Father's business. I lived before I was born and I was about my Father's business before I was born. I lived on earth and forgot about my identity until I was awakened to it." Yes, I will never leave you in life or in death, so be not concerned as long as you know the secret name of God and the secret of the nature of God in you.

You could not possibly give this to a person who could receive it only with the mind. Most people do not understand immaculate conception, resurrection, or ascension—and you can see why. As a physical thing, there cannot be immaculate conception, or rising from a grave, or ascending on a cloud. Our friends would be foolish if they believed this, and I think the human part of the world who believes those things through fear or because they were taught them, are not completely mature.

In the moment that you understand the nature of the word consciousness, you will then know that the only truth there is is immaculate conception. We are children of God, and God does not need a wife. As a matter of fact God is not a male, so we do not need a female. Once you are free of the concept of a male God, you will understand immaculate conception. It will then be so simple. If you know anything, you know God is not limited so God could not be half of creation. You know God is spirit, not a body. When you understand God as spirit, you will understand that your life is spiritual and of God. Once you understand the infinity of God, you will know there was nothing for man to be made of but the spirit of God. You cannot understand this with you mind. You can understand it only when some measure of spiritual discernment has come to you and you can break through ancient beliefs about God.

Once again I am going to remind you that the real secret of the message of The Infinite Way is an understanding of the nature of God and the nature of prayer. Once you have those, you have The Infinite Way, but you will not receive them with your mind. They must be spiritually discerned, but when you do realize the nature of God and the nature of prayer, then you do have The Infinite Way and you can live it. Once this happens to you, you will discover a mystery: that no person is ever permitted to receive this knowledge or awareness for himself. It cannot be received in your consciousness if you are thinking what it will do for you, because God does not care any more about you as "you" than God cares about one orange tree as against another orange tree. God does not care any more about the piece of land called the United States than he cares about the piece of land called Russia. Therefore, once you begin to perceive the nature of God and the nature of prayer, remember this: All those in darkness who are desiring light will be led to you, and you will soon discover that truth has not been given to glorify you but to glorify God. The provision that comes to you from God is that you receive God's grace to glorify God—not man—and to show forth God's presence and God's power to those seeking light.

Those who are commissioned of God are commissioned to teach those who are seeking illumination. The human world would crucify you because no one can receive a spiritual message with the mind—only with spiritual discernment. When I was given the Message in 1946, the final words were these: "Never seek a student. Teach those who come to you," and this has been the nature of our work. I have never gone to a city without first being invited, nor have I spoken to a group in a church or in a metaphysical center unless I was first invited to speak. So as this message continues through teachers and practitioners, let them all remember this: You have not been commissioned to reform the world or to change the churches. You have been commissioned only to present this message to those who are seeking it and, as their consciousness is opened and benefits come to them, inevitably others will be drawn to seek it too. This is good.

There is a change taking place in the church history of the world and many churches are accepting truths and principles that are entirely new to them, and this is good. Let it come to them from themselves. Even if they seek and find the answer outside, let them seek and find it. Let us publish the truth silently and let it find its way to receptive consciousness. Then you will find you are blessing those who are ready for blessing. More than this you cannot do.

As you now study the papers which have been mimeographed since August 16 and the tapes since August 18, carefully watch every message that concerns the revelation of God and the revelation of prayer, because this is important. When you know God aright you have life eternal. How will you know? By the fruitage. To know him aright is life eternal and life peaceful and life safe and life harmonious.

With all your understanding, get the understanding of the nature of God and the nature of prayer. It is in true prayer that our oneness with God is made evident in life.

AN ETERNAL RELATIONSHIP

September 30, 1963
Honolulu Infinite Way Study Center

GOOD EVENING. You have an opportunity now to prove a major principle of The Infinite Way. Incidentally, reading about these principles or studying these principles is not of too much importance unless, in addition to the reading and the studying, you actually put them into practice, until you demonstrate principle by principle and very often one at a time.

We have been together for ten months and we have seen a lot of each other. We have been in each other's consciousness and we have experienced a great deal of love, friendship, sharing, companionship, and truth. Now it would appear that we will be separated for awhile. This always brings up feelings of sorrow or regret or sadness or some other negative emotion, and if you look at the situation humanly you might experience a day or two of sorrow. However, if you look at the situation spiritually, it really presents a tremendous opportunity.

What you have experienced of me is my consciousness of truth. You have brought yourself to me, but not physically. You have brought your self to my consciousness. Therefore I have been in your consciousness and you have been in my consciousness and what we have experienced of each other is this consciousness, this spiritual companionship. If you have been receptive and

431

responsive to what has taken place, you have benefitted by having been lifted higher into consciousness. Never forget this: I too have benefitted, because in the kingdom of God there is no such thing as a one-way traffic. In the kingdom of God there is a union. In the kingdom of God there is a oneness. In the kingdom of God there is a unitedness. Therefore, there has been a flow of consciousness among us and between us–from me to you and from you to me. If this were not so, if there was no receptivity on your part, the flow could not move out from within me because there would be nothing to draw it.

It is for this reason that all of The Infinite Way books have come forth from classes, lectures, and sessions of this kind. In other words, those who have been before me as students have drawn forth these messages that have become the books. It has been your receptivity that has drawn forth the messages, and so there has been a flow from me to you; but first there was a flow from you to me, the flow of receptivity and responsiveness which constitutes union, oneness, unitedness.

I would like to tell you that this relationship is an eternal relationship, if you will have it so. Knowing this, I will certainly have it so. Never, never will I be separated from my serious students. I will never be separated from you by time or space, nor will I be separated from you by life or death, because I know that all that constitutes me in reality is consciousness. Therefore, I can hold in my consciousness "my own," those whom I desire to be with, and those with whom I desire to companion. Nothing will ever separate me from the love of my serious students or from sharing with them. That is because, out of my lifetime, I have found that my greatest joy and my greatest fruitage has been from companionship with my serious students, those who live The Infinite Way, those who benefit by The Infinite Way, those who rejoice in their studies. These students have been my companions for many, many years. For many, many years these students have really constituted my family, my spiritual household. For this reason I have lived with my students very often early in the morning, and very often late at night, and very often in between. Where your treasure is, that is where you are going to be, and mine has been with spiritual seekers.

Since I am consciousness, I embody in my consciousness all that belongs to me, and since in the kingdom of God there is no such thing as time or space, this all happens *now* and this all happens *here* where I am. You may look outside and see a sign which says "Hawaii," and that is where I am and that is where it is happening, but if you look outside and see a sign which says "California" or "London," that is where I am and that is where it is happening. Why? Because it is happening in my consciousness, not in a city or a state or a country.

You are being given an opportunity to prove this principle: "Where I am, thou art." In consciousness we are never separated. We are all one in our spiritual identity, in our spiritual household, in our spiritual family. Therefore I benefit by your association wherever I may be. Open your consciousness and realize that I do not exist in time or space. The only place I can exist for you is in your consciousness and, if you let me out of your consciousness you have let go of me because all you can know of me is what you can embody in your consciousness, and this is not dependent on physical sense.

One's physical presence is not necessary and this is why we have what is called absent treatment. Prayer does not require the physical presence of the individual who prays or the individual who is prayed for. What is necessary is the realization that we exist as and in and of consciousness, and in consciousness we are one. We are not physical beings. We are offspring of God and we know it. That which constitutes the physical frame is only of relative importance; it is here today and sometimes gone tomorrow. There is no such thing as an eternal physical frame. Why? Because I am not a physical frame, nor are you.

I first received an inner vision of this while noticing a tree. The subject of immortality was puzzling to me, as I am sure it must have been puzzling and perhaps still is to some of you. Notice this in the life of a tree: A seed falls to the ground and that tree is born again. Yes, because the seed of that tree is certainly that tree. It is more of that tree than the trunk of the tree; but this is what I noticed: It really is not the tree or the seed which lives. It is the life of the tree which lives the tree and which lives the seed. And when the seed falls to the ground and is born again, the tree is born again because there is just the continuity of the one life. If you are life you are immortal. If you are body you die with the body, but this is not true. From the body goes the seed and becomes another body, but what causes the seed to leave the body and become another body? Life. As with the tree, it is not the body or the seed which lives. It is the life of the body which lives the body and which lives the seed. Life creates a seed, drops a seed, gives life to a new tree, but it is the same life—and so you have the life of a tree going on for a thousand generations and it will be the same life. Always it will be I, consciousness, life.

Eventually you will believe this if you practice our little exercise and come to this realization:

I am not this body; I am not in my feet, or my legs or my stomach or my chest or my head. I am not in this body. I am the life and the consciousness which functions this body, and the moment I throw off this body I pick up another one and always it is I, consciousness, life. Because there was so little population on the North American continent, it must mean I existed somewhere else. And because even Europe has only been settled in the last two thousand years and I have existed eternally, I must have existed in China, Japan or Africa—somewhere where there was population. The place makes no difference, only I, the consciousness I am, the Soul I am—the life I am. So it is that I, functioning now through this body, will eventually discard it and function through another body because the nature of I is consciousness, life.

Perhaps you have had these questions presented to you by people who have had no metaphysical background: "Will I be reunited with my family when I pass on?" or "Will my family be reunited with me in the next world?" You probably know my answer and it is always this: "It all depends on you and it all depends on them. If you want to be reunited with them, you will be. If they want to be reunited with you, they will be; but if you do not wish to be reunited you will not be, because you exist as consciousness and you can admit into your consciousness or drop from your consciousness whomever you wish.

This also takes place here on earth. Are we in touch with all of our relatives? No. Why? We have no interest in them and they have no interest in us, and so we drop out of each other's consciousness. There are loved ones from whom some circumstance of life, or some circumstance of death, has separated us. Be assured of this: No one who enters my life, my consciousness, will ever be

separated or apart from it, in life or in death, except those
with whom I have nothing in common and whom I am
willing to have dropped from me. By the same token they
are more than glad to drop me from their consciousness.

Have you ever received any benefit from each other
except a benefit of consciousness? Is it not consciousness
that has blessed us? What part of me has ever blessed
you except my consciousness of truth? What part of you
have I ever known except your consciousness, your love
for truth, your love for spirit? Therefore we are one in
consciousness and one we will ever be as long as our
interest is in truth, spirit, God, consciousness.

In the New Testament there is quite a bit about
healing "in the Master's name." You know there is no
such thing as healing in or through a name. You know
that a name has nothing to do with healing. What name
really means is identity or consciousness. The consciousness of the Master is a healing consciousness. Therefore
all healing is through the Master consciousness or the
consciousness of the Master, through a spiritual Master
who has "overcome the world."

This is very noticeable among those who heal by the
laying on of hands. Is there a difference between one
person's physical hand and another's? If so, what is the
difference? The answer is one word: *consciousness.* It is
not the hand that heals—it is the consciousness behind
the hand. Therefore there is truth in the laying on of
hands, not because hands have any power but because
the consciousness of the individual is empowered from
on high and the patient has accepted the religious
teaching that the laying on of hands plays a part in the
healing work. Had those engaged in healing been taught
in a different school, they would have known that the

laying on of hands is not necessary except under human conditions. It is not necessary for spiritual healing because it is not the hand but the consciousness of an individual that heals. However, sometimes another element enters which is the belief of the patient.

Likewise there are patients who have accepted the belief that they must be touched in order to be healed, and believing makes it so unto them. We in our work will not accede to that and so, if they must feel the touch, we will let them go to someone else who does engage in that form of healing. In the same way some patients come to us and insist that we give them a treatment when they are asleep, but I will not encourage the belief that there is a power which goes from one individual to another individual. In my work I abide by the truth of one consciousness, and that anyone who consciously reaches out to me, reaches me. Consciousness is the activity that heals and I am not interested in mental or physical oneness. Consciousness is the activity that heals whether the patient believes he must be asleep or whether he believes he must feel the touch.

An occasion of this kind is the right occasion to bring this subject to light so that, as we disappear from each other's physical sight while still on this plane of life, you begin to practice the presence of consciousness, the one consciousness which I am and which thou art. Then you will discover this: In your absences from loved ones for any reason, there will be no sense of loss or sense of separation because you will be able to say, "I have no physical relationship. Therefore my relationship is one of consciousness."

This prepares you for another day of separation, that which the world calls death. Each one of you must be prepared for the day when your loved ones will leave you, but this does not involve separation because that which we love of each other is not the body—it is the Soul, the consciousness. Not even in marriage is the body loved, not really. It is the individual who is loved, and an individual never goes any place because an individual is spirit, an individual is consciousness, an individual is omnipresence, an individual is here where I am and here where thou art, for we are one in consciousness. This is an experience that eventually must come to every serious student, because the greatest principle of life is revealed through this experience, the principle of omnipresence.

All the misery of humanhood arises from the belief that we are separate and apart from each other—from our friends, from our relatives, from our supply, from our home, from our employment, from our country. Every discord on earth arises from a sense of separation. The unifying principle is this: "I and my Father are one," inseparable and indivisible, and in my oneness with God I am one with infinity—infinite good—which must include companionships, relationships, supply, home, employment, activity, art. There never would be a discord on earth if there were not a sense of separation from God, but in our relationship of oneness with God we are one with each other and in no other way. If we become one on any other basis, it is not a permanent relationship.

Not every family remains together forever, and yet they would always remain together if that togetherness were originally based on the understanding of oneness with God. "My oneness with God constitutes my oneness with all spiritual being and idea." No one would ever be separated from supply if their supply were based on their relationship with Deity. When you understand that it is only your oneness with your source, with your Maker, that constitutes your oneness with supply, what happens is what would happen: "What God hath joined together, no man *can* put asunder." This is quite different from the marriage ceremony which says: "Those whom God hath joined together, let no man put asunder." Do you believe now that man has a power that can separate God from his own? This would be giving to man a power greater than God's.

Your supply is only yours by virtue of the truth that "I and my Father are one" and therefore you are heir to all the heavenly riches. In your understanding of that, no person or circumstance can separate you from your supply. Your relationship with God builds up whatever in your experience appears to be lost. "In three days I will raise it up," and three days means instantly. Why? "What God hath joined together, no man can put asunder." If God has breathed into you the life of God, then the life of God is the life of man and you can never be separated from your life not even in death, because I and my Father are one, I and my life are one, I and my love are one—indestructible.

All competition arises from the belief that I am here, you are there, and there is something out here that we both want. The sense of separation from God causes all competition and nothing else. In your conscious realization of your oneness with God, "all that the Father hath is mine" and you are in competition with no one. That which is yours is yours by virtue of your relationship with your source. Then you will be able to say with the poet, Burroughs: "My own shall come to me."

This all leads back to one of the major principles of The Infinite Way, one you have heard about so often: "My conscious oneness with God constitutes my oneness with all spiritual being and idea." Now what difference does it make where I seem to be or where you seem to be in time and space, or where your supply seems to be, since nothing has ever escaped out of my consciousness because God constitutes my consciousness. Physically there may appear to be an absence but, as long as you do not release it out of your consciousness, it is yours.

What is the greatest possession you could desire? What is the greatest of all possessions which, if you had it, would insure life eternal, life harmonious, life abundant, life joyous? What is it? Truth. Truth is more desirable than the whole earth. Truth. "Ye shall know the truth and the truth shall make you free."[1] Is there anything greater than freedom? Think of being free from bondage to sin, to disease, to lack, fear, hate, to discord. Think! Think of the word freedom and think what it means to be free, mentally, physically, economically, morally, politically. Is there anything greater than freedom? No, and the only way to freedom is through truth. "Ye shall know the truth and the truth shall make you free."

In the days of old, men acquired great wealth, military forces and armaments, and set out on a trip around the world to find the truth. Where did they find it? They found it within themselves. Where is the Holy Grail? It was back home in a tree in one's own back yard. Where is the blue bird of happiness? Where is truth—the truth that makes you free? God is not in the whirlwind and God is not in the storm. God, truth, is in the still small voice. Where then is the truth that makes you free? It is within your own being, within your own consciousness. Why is this? God constitutes your consciousness and the only place to find truth is within your own Soul, within your own consciousness. The sense of separation from truth brings upon you the sense of separation from life, peace, joy, harmony. Only when you realize that the kingdom of God is within you, will you likewise realize,"That which I am seeking I already am."

What else is there to the message of The Infinite Way except turning the student back to his own within-ness that he may find there the Holy Grail, the blue bird of happiness, the truth that makes him free. When you discover that you are one with the truth that makes you free, you will discover that you are one with your good in any and every form.

Do you not see this: Included in the oneness that constitutes your being, is God and man, Father and son. These are one. Therefore, turn within in the realization of that oneness. Turn within to our infinite divine consciousness which, in reality, I am and thou art. Recognize your oneness with your source. Then you will actually discover that you are never separate from love, from life, from abundance.

You will then know that in what the world calls life or death, "I am not body. I am consciousness, spirit, life, truth." You will understand that the seed of the tree drops into the ground and the life of the seed becomes the life of the tree again. Stop identifying yourself as the trunk of the tree or body, and identify your Self. Realize you are *I,* or consciousness, and that *I* goes on and goes on and goes on and becomes the next form of which *I* may appear.

A CHRISTMAS MESSAGE

December 22, 1963
Honolulu Infinite Way Study Center

GOOD MORNING. The Infinite Way has made a tremendous contribution to the world in the revelation that God is consciousness. Heretofore, God has not been identified in this way. Even though this does not make it possible to put your finger on God, it does give you the realization of why God is closer to you than breathing, and why whatever good is to come forth in your experience is to come forth from your consciousness. For thousands of years the entire world has been mistaken in believing that good must come from outside, that someone can give you your health or your supply or your freedom, whereas your own consciousness is the storehouse of all of this.

The Civil War did not seem to convince the world that you do not give freedom to anyone by going to war about it. What has happened is that we now have a second Civil War, but it is a difficult thing to erase from the human mind the belief that our salvation exists "out there" and that we can attain it by armies and navies and guns and water hoses.

Those who have eyes to see and ears to hear are beginning to realize that The Infinite Way contribution is this: Since God is consciousness and since God is the consciousness of the individual, you must seek your

443

good not outside from your neighbor or from your government, but from within yourselves by what you express. This is now becoming so recognized that many of the orthodox religious teachings are being changed to bring this into greater manifestation. So it is that, beginning in this present era, you will witness a change in every religion, leading the world back to the kingdom of God, the kingdom of power, the kingdom of grace that is within each and every individual. The greater our realization that we are living by grace and that this grace is established within us, the greater the contribution we can make to the world. This is our reason for being here. Remember this: What you and I can receive from our studies is only that we may have more to contribute to the world.

So as we go into this meditation, let us realize the major discovery of The Infinite Way—that of God as consciousness, as your consciousness, so that your life can begin to be more fruitful and that you stop wasting time with prayers and treatments. Let your prayers and treatments be the realization of this truth: The kingdom of God is already established within you and by not taking thought, it functions.

INTO THE NEW YEAR

December 29, 1963

GOOD MORNING. In meditating this morning, we will bear in mind that the subject is of course the New Year. We are looking into a new year. We are still back here in 1963, but we are at the tail end of it and we are looking into 1964, and then waiting to see if the prophecies will come true. There is a better way: Let us look into 1964 and, with our inner ears open and our inner eyes open, receive light, wisdom, and guidance for this that we are looking into. In other words, in order that we have a higher wisdom than human wisdom, a higher protection than bombs, a higher guidance than human prophecy, the only place from which all this can come is from the kingdom of God within you, individually as well as collectively. The kingdom of God is within you and it can reveal 1964 to you far better than any of our prophets can prophesy. It can give you a wisdom with which to live the year. It really can illumine and inspire your wisdom in lifting it up into a higher measure.

So, for the next fifteen minutes, we are going to look straight ahead into 1964 and let the spirit illumine it, not plan it, illumine it. Then, as you keep up this program each day and certainly preferably early in the morning, you will find that whatever illumination comes to you through this experience will be revealed to you each day. You will have a guidance and a protection from within you.

We will start now looking into 1964 without any wishes or hopes, just with the realization that whatever is to be in 1964 is to be determined by this spirit of God within us.

SILENCE! STILLNESS! QUIETNESS!

January 1, 1964
Honolulu Infinite Way Study Center

THANK YOU FOR THIS PARTY TODAY, and Happy New Year to everyone! I am asked very often, and especially by publishers, why I do not speak to larger groups and why I do not advertise and have more of the public come to our work. It is difficult to answer in a way that could be understood. To begin with, The Infinite Way is not a message that we can sell to anyone. It has to be sought, and the reason is that you cannot convince anyone of any of the truth that is embodied in the message. This is natural and it is normal, for "the natural man receiveth not the things of the spirit of God."[1] That means the mind can never understand the things of God. There is nothing about God or the realm of God that is common sense or reasonable to the mind. It might seem reasonable to you now but that is because you have in a measure gone beyond the mind, beyond common sense, and the spiritual center in you is opened. Even if it is open in a tiny measure, everything seems reasonable. But until that center is open, there would be no point asking you to hear this message because it would not penetrate.

In the original book *The Infinite Way*, from the First through the Ninth Edition, I paid lip-service to metaphysical belief by occasionally using the word Mind with

447

a capital "M" as a synonym for God. As you know, I took it out with the Tenth Edition and all later editions, but I would like you in particular to understand why that was done. The mind of man can be used for either good or evil as you well know. Many people are using the mind for evil or destructive purposes, sometimes merely for pleasurable purposes which certainly does not come under the heading of God or good. So you see mind could never be God, and God could never be mind. We are not so great that we could use God. Therefore the mind must be looked upon as a human instrument, an instrument for learning or for planning, and for some, for evil purposes. You must see mind as an instrument, and then you will not make the mistake of believing that mind is God or that God is mind. Because I was erroneously taught, in that same book I said that the mind (while not God), was an instrument through which you could reach God or through which God could reach you. That, too, was a mistake. If God could reach you through the mind, or if you could reach God through the mind, everyone would have access to God because man would have the mind with which to know God. Then you would not be able to say, "The natural man knoweth not and receiveth not the things of the spirit of God." You cannot reach God through the mind and God cannot reach you through the mind. Therefore Scripture says, "Be still. . . . In quietness and in confidence shall be your strength, your peace."[2] Silence! Stillness! Quietness! All of this really means the silence, stillness, and quietness of the mind.

The access to God is through spiritual discernment, and spiritual discernment is a faculty of the Soul, the spirit, which is within you. Therefore, since access to

God must be through the Soul, it can only be through silence, stillness, quietness. Then, "In the moment that ye think not, the bridegroom cometh."[3] In the moment when you are not thinking, the spirit of God, the voice of God, the action of God can take place within you. We read the books with the mind and we hear the tapes with the mind, but only in order that the message itself may quiet and still the mind and convince you of the need for that quietness.

Remember that behind the mind, there stands you. Take that with the word "I." Behind the mind stands *me*. I am behind the mind and I can think thoughts through the mind, or I can still the mind. Then, in the stillness, the Soul faculty is in action. It comes awake in you, it comes alive in you, and then through the power of discernment you can know that which is unknowable, see that which is unseeable, hear that which is inaudible. It is a state of grace attained through stillness. "Be still, and know that *I am* God."[4] Then be still and listen for the still small voice, the voice of God.

When you have thought about and pondered this daily for quite some time, you will understand what I believe is the greatest principle revealed in the message of The Infinite Way: "My conscious oneness with God constitutes my oneness with all spiritual being and idea." We call this the practice of meditation, or contemplation. Contemplation is a step before meditation. In contemplation you agree that the mind must be still so that you can listen and receive impartations through your Soul faculties. In order to receive these impartations you must be one with the spirit of God in you, the consciousness of God in you, and you attain this oneness through stillness.

In the beginning it is possible that you can hold this stillness for only five to ten seconds but, as you continue the practice, you will find you can hold it for a minute and that is really enough. Later you will be able to hold it as long as you wish or as long as there is a need, but only a minute accomplishes your purpose which is conscious oneness or conscious union with God. The moment I attain that stillness I am receptive, and my inner ear is open. And the moment I make that contact I know it because of a deep breath or because of some other manifestation. The moment I am one with it, I am one with everyone on the spiritual path and I am one with all spiritual grace, spiritual law and spiritual life that is in the entire world. It is for this reason that you need "Take no thought for your life, what ye shall eat, or what ye shall drink; nor yet for your body, what ye shall put on."[5] It is for this reason that you need take no thought for the human aspect of your life.

When you go into this meditation, clear out all thought of how you shall be healed, enriched, or how you shall be at peace with your neighbors. Drop all of this, for it is as foolish to take thought for these things as it is foolish afterward to give thanks for the new health or the new supply or the new business or the new friends. There is only one thing to be grateful for—that you have received the spirit of God. The palaces and the yachts can disappear as quickly as they came. By taking no thought for things and by centering your whole attention on this oneness with your source, what happens to the world of things makes no difference because even the lost years of the locust will be restored.

Remember, in attaining this oneness with the spirit or the source, you are attaining oneness with all of the spiritual good that is in the entire universe. If there is something in South Africa that is meant for your spiritual unfoldment, it will begin drifting towards you. Only take no thought about it. God does not read your human thoughts, so there is no use telling God what you want. This is a complete waste of time. There are mental practices you can indulge in and receive some temporary things but, as a rule when you get them, they could end up causing you harm.

If you are working from a spiritual basis, there is only one goal and that is attained without thought. It is attained through stillness. Then when you feel the deep breath, or the click, or some other manifestation that lets you know "God is on the field," or "God has reached me," you relax and go about your business. You must always remember that, having made contact with your source, you have made contact with all the spiritual activity everywhere on earth or in heaven—and some day even on some of the other planets.

As a human being it is impossible to have enough wisdom to know what to pray for. You cannot read the consciousness or spirit or Soul of God in order to know what God's plan is for you. If there were not a divine plan, there would be no you. Consider the over-populated areas on earth where human beings are kicked onto earth as mortals and where there is not even enough food to eat. Only the animal instinct to mate plays a part in that creation, and for this reason there is no God governing that form of life. You do not lift yourself above the level of that mortal creation where you are not under the law of God, until you yourself have attained the experience of conscious oneness with God by being still and letting the grace of God touch you. From that moment you are no longer a mortal. You are a child of God, under the law of God. Then you will find out that long before you were born, there was a plan for you.

We could use this as an example: A traveling salesman for a responsible firm is sent out with enough samples of merchandise and enough money to take care of the entire experience. In other words he is fully equipped to be successful and it is all taken care of by his firm. So it is with us. When we are realized as individuals on the spiritual plane, we go forth as the representatives of God. We show forth God on earth, and we are therefore equipped with the necessary intelligence, loyalty, health, peace, and grace—not by virtue of ourselves but by virtue of that which we are showing forth.

Remember this, which is the essence of The Infinite Way: No human being is ever showing forth God's guidance or God's protection or God's law. "A thousand shall fall at thy side, and ten thousand at thy right hand; but it shall not come nigh thee."[6] This thee is an individual who "dwells in the secret place of the Most High,"[7] in oneness with God. Again the Master says, "I am the vine, ye are the branches; He that abideth in me, and I in him, the same bringeth forth much fruit. . . . If a man abideth not in me, he is cast forth as a branch, and is withered."[8] The human race is that separate branch, and the only way to be one with the tree is through consciousness. You do not attain it by lip-service, or by rituals, or by believing, or by faith. Faith is a dangerous product. The secret lies in conscious awareness, conscious union, stillness, until you feel, "The spirit of the Lord God is upon me and I am ordained." When you can feel that, you can then relax and "take no thought for your life, what ye shall eat, or what ye shall drink; nor yet for your body, what ye shall put on."[9] Be assured that you will receive deeper thoughts than ever before, once you have relinquished "your thoughts." Then God's thoughts can come through, and God's thoughts are the productive ones.

Religion is not a teaching. It is an experience. Until you have experienced religion, you do not know what it is and, since the experience can come to you only through your consciousness, the need is for a greater stillness, even if only in one-half minute periods. Try to have them twenty or thirty or forty times a day until they begin to occupy one minute. As we sit here listening for the still small voice, in any moment in which we attain oneness with our source or God, remember we are attuned to everything that exists of a spiritual nature and this draws unto us those things necessary for our individual experience. The artist finds himself with new ideas or degrees of talent. The inventor finds himself receiving greater inventions or more of them. The writer finds himself with publishers and buyers of his books. The salesman finds himself in touch with buyers who can work profitably with him. God knows nothing of these things but, as you attain the Spirit of God, you interpret these in the terms of your own talents and abilities.

It is already being shown to us that *A Parenthesis In Eternity* is the book for the world. It is drawing to us and to itself those of a spiritual nature out in the world. *The Contemplative Life* is what is providing us with the working tools for our healing work, for our instruction work, and for the development of consciousness. We will be working with those two books for quite awhile. This year is different than last year. At this time last year we knew definitely that we were waiting for something to happen and we did not know what the message would be or when we would receive it. This year we do not know anything. This year we are looking into 1964 and it is just a big tunnel. Not a thing is revealed.

Take the attitude that you do not know God's will for you for today; that you are being still and receptive to receive God's grace so that you will be under the law and the wisdom of God throughout the day. Realize of course that, by this contact, you have also come into contact with all the spiritual grace necessary to your entire experience. You may be setting something into motion in Africa or England or here at home, that may take time. If you plant a seed in fertile soil, remember something is happening even if you do not witness the fruition for several months. So it is that your contact today may not mature for days, weeks, months, or even years. Take the attitude that you do not know the will of God, that you will be receptive and responsive to God's government, and that you will follow the leads that are given you. Remember, that in making contact with God, you have made contact with all spiritual being and idea. Then get up and go about your business even though at the moment it may seem like a wrong business. Keep at it until the spirit itself moves you.

There was a cartoon in the paper this morning where one of the characters went to the window and said, "It doesn't look any different outdoors. It still looks just like 1963." This is an Infinite Way principle too. There is nothing different outside. The outside is always the same. The difference is in our consciousness, and then whatever is different in our consciousness externalizes outside. If nothing takes place in our consciousness, nothing can change outside. Until your consciousness is deepened and enriched, your world cannot be deepened and enriched. Your world is always giving back to you the measure and state of your consciousness.

Three Lost Secrets

January 10, 1964

Good evening. For your meditation will you please ponder this: You have not come here to hear me, nor to receive a message from me. You have come here to be instructed by the spirit that is within you, to hear the still small voice that is within you, and my part is merely that you may be lifted up to the point of spiritual apprehension or spiritual discernment–not discernment of what I say but discernment of what is revealed within you. It is possible that something may come through my lips that may be the message that you will receive, but do not be surprised if you hear something tonight and discover later that I never said it–if you are not here to see or hear a man but to receive the grace of God. Because if two or more of us unite in this meditation, we will be lifted up to that point of spiritual discernment; then the voice can speak, either through my lips or it may speak directly through your consciousness.

I would like to talk tonight about three lost secrets. They are not lost in the sense that they have been lost to consciousness, but they have been lost from mankind. The only reason you have them in active form today is through revelation because, although they exist as written words, they are passed over as if they were not major factors–and they are sadly misinterpreted. Let us take first, secrecy. Secrecy is one of the lost principles of life. What we call benevolence or charity or brotherly love is the second lost secret and, through these, we will come to the third.

You must remember that there are two major forms of life, just as there are two major forms of religious life. One form is that which you meet in all religions; it is the religion of the Old Testament, the moral law, the Ten Commandments. It is the Old Testament teaching of "love the lord thy God" and "love thy neighbor as thyself"—to which has been added ceremonies, rituals and rites. This, you might say, is a beginning form of religion, ideally adapted to those coming out of ignorance and superstition and a more or less animal way of life. Obeying the Ten Commandments develops moral responsibility; it sets man apart from the animals. To love God originally meant to love, honor, obey, and respect law, and to "love thy neighbor as thyself" needs no explanation. This is an ideal form of religion for those beginning on the religious path. The next highest step in religion is the one just now beginning to be revealed to men and women throughout the world, and it is embodied in the revelations and teachings of Christ Jesus. This, however, must be understood from the standpoint of the Master's consciousness, otherwise it is misinterpreted and the word becomes lost.

We will start with the word *secret*, or *secrecy*, or *secretness*, and you will admit that even humanly a person who is capable of keeping a secret is admired and respected because it is not the ordinary status of mankind. There are not too many people who can keep a secret and, when you find one, you find a man or woman inevitably loved and respected. You must go beyond the human ability to keep a secret and reach the place where you understand secrecy and what was meant in the Master's teaching: "Go and tell no man what things ye have seen."[1] Do not let it be known how smart you are. Go and tell no man. When you pray, pray in secret, not to be seen of men. When you do your benevolences, do so in secret, not to be seen of men. Why? Why go and tell no man? Why pray in secret? Why do your benevolences in secret? Ah! Here is actually one of the deep, deep secrets of the spiritual life, the harmonious life, and the reason that you must understand is this: The kingdom of God is within you. Therefore, the relationship between you and your Father must be one that takes place within you. The moment you start to talk to anyone else about it, you have turned your back on the Father within you. You are then communing with a man, not with the Father within you.

For prayer to be effective, it must be communion between you and the Father which takes place within you. It must be treated as you would treat a seed you have planted in the ground, covered up, and left there. You do not open and expose that seed every day and then cover it up again. No, you leave it secretly and sacredly in the womb of the earth. So it is that communion with God takes place only when you have closed the door to the world and opened the door to your inner consciousness. "I stand at the door and knock."[2] In other words, the Father within is always at the center of your being, knocking at the door of your consciousness, and it is only when you close your eyes to the outer world and turn within that you are opening the door of your consciousness to admit the Father. Then in that inner sanctuary, in the temple of your own being, in silence and in secrecy and in sacredness you commune with the Father.

You wish ultimately to hear the still small voice. There is no use telling your neighbor about it, firstly because your neighbor may not have heard of such things. Secondly, even if your neighbor were a fellow student, he could not do anything about it because it is you yourself who must hear that voice which is within you. Therefore, it is folly to speak to your neighbor about knowing God aright or hearing the still small voice. In the present understanding of the world, it is not wisdom to let the world know that you even believe that God can be met face to face within you, or that you can commune with God, because the world as a world is not yet ready for such revelations. Ah, yes! We offer a cup of cold water, a book or pamphlet, but if the individual does not respond, we drop it there. When we have secrets to share, we do so only among those who have indicated that they too are seeking the spiritual secrets of life.

If you wish to admit the Christ, you must go into the silent, sacred, secret sanctuary—the temple of your being: "Speak, Lord, thy servant heareth,"[3] and enter into a listening communion. Eventually the wall will be broken down, the veils will be removed, and you will find yourself in communion with God. But remember that this must be your secret as far as the rest of the world is concerned. It must be a sacred subject within you. Listen to this: "Thy Father which seeth in secret shall reward thee openly."[4] Do you not see what happens if you do not keep your secrecy between you and the Father? It would be the same as if you exposed your planted seed to the air and then closed it up again. Nothing would happen to that seed! So it is that the "seed of communion" is planted deeply within your own consciousness and then, if you expect an answer, keep it secret and "The Father which seeth in secret shall reward thee openly" and fulfill your outer experience.

You violate this if you think you are going to pray or commune, and then perhaps "get a little help" from your fellow man, neighbor, or friend. Do you not see that this is not the purpose of the spiritual life? The purpose of the spiritual life is to be in such intimate communion that it can fulfill its promises: "I am the bread,[5] the meat, the wine and the water . . . I am the resurrection[6] . . . I am come that they might have life, and that they might have it more abundantly."[7] Accept these promises secretly and sacredly, keep them locked within your Self, and then watch the Father who "seeth in secret" manifest his grace openly and outwardly.

A student wrote me last week that she had moved to a new city and was planning to look for employment soon. On her third day in that city a firm telephoned and asked her to come to work and she wrote that for the first time in her experience, she realized that one does not have to seek employment. The answer is this: The experience would not have happened if this student had not been aware of the nature of secrecy and at least to some extent, was not looking to human help for her demonstration.

Nothing is impossible, but the question is, do you understand the nature of secrecy and the reason for secrecy? Do you actually understand that omnipresence means that there is an all-knowing presence within you—within you, remember, "closer than breathing, nearer than hands and feet"? Do you actually, consciously, know that there is an all-knowing wisdom, an infinite wisdom within your own being whose function it is to know your needs in advance and whose function it is to "give you the kingdom"? Do you actually know that you are not dependent on man whose breath is in his nostrils? If you have come to the realization that the kingdom of omniscience, omnipresence, omnipotence is within you and that there is this ability to commune within, you can then rest in the assurance that you need speak no outer word.

Spiritual teachers know the degree of progress that students are making and know when they are ready for further steps. One of the ways in which they know is the ability to observe that the student speaks less and less and listens more and more in the within. This is one of the signs of progress on the spiritual path because, just as the student learned that man does not live by bread alone, so he comes to learn that man does not live by affirming God. Rather does he live by every word that is revealed in this inner communion within himself, and this word he receives within is the bread, the meat, the wine and the water which he can only receive in quietness, secrecy, sacredness. This word is really the fountain of life, the fountain of youth. It is the cattle on a thousand hills, and it is the bread of all the bake shops in the world. This will explain to you why so many people who have received illumination like to retreat from the world to a monastery or a convent or a cave, because once they have made contact within, they have access to a whole new area of consciousness and a whole new mode of life.

In 1954 I started to write a book, and today I found the manuscript and discovered that I had only written one and one-half pages. But I have the title: *Between Two Worlds.* When you turn to this inner life and make your

contact, from then on you are living between two
worlds. You are living in this inner world and you are
living in the outer world, and most of the time you are
between the two. It is not always pleasant, but that does
not make too much difference because the fruitage of
this way of life is so tremendous.

One of the lost secrets is the nature and function of
secrecy and its purpose and mode of operation. Once
you have this understanding, you have one of the major
secrets of the spiritual life. Another lost secret is the
secret of benevolence. Again, in the human world a
person who is benevolent or charitable in his efforts to
help meet the needs of others and provide for the things
that others lack, is also honored and respected. This
again is just an outer human form and it is not the secret
of benevolence. The secret of benevolence is this: "Son,
thou art ever with me, and all that I have is thine."[8] God
has endowed you with his love, his grace, his peace.
Think! Think! "My peace I give unto you: not as the
world giveth."[9] *My* peace. Do you see how the two tie
together–secrecy and benevolence? Think what it means
to be driving on the road, shopping in the market, or
doing business in your office, and at the same time, in a
little corner of your consciousness remembering: "My
peace, the Christ peace, give I unto all who are within
range of my consciousness." *My* peace. How much peace
have I? Infinity. All. All that the Father hath. All of the
Father's grace and all of the Father's peace is mine to
give, to share. Therefore, in secrecy I give God's grace
and God's peace. To live this life of secrecy and benevolence soon manifests itself in the pocketbook, so we are
not only able to give God's grace and God's peace, but
also of God's abundance. In giving, the Master again

cautions secrecy because there must be no sense of needing or desiring recognition or praise. In giving, the truth has been realized that it is God's grace, not yours or mine. This is likewise true of money, since neither you nor I can manufacture it. Whether you are sharing the spiritual word in consciousness secretly, or whether you are sharing dollar bills in secrecy, remember that it is all God's grace, and you are but the transparency through which it is manifesting.

It becomes necessary to ponder and meditate on the subject of secrecy and benevolence from a spiritual standpoint, and come to this realization that since all that the Father hath is yours, you can say with the Master, "My peace, my abundance, my grace, give I unto thee." But secretly! Checks must go back and forth, but it can still be done without an attempt to receive credit or attention or praise.

This leads naturally to the third lost secret. If I can commune with the Father within me, then the Father is not a man, the Father is not a person. The Father must be spirit, consciousness, something of an impersonal nature which means not a person. If it is possible for me to commune with the spirit within me, it must be equally possible for you. Remember this very carefully: Whether I have no religion or whether I have a Christian, a Jewish, a Mohammedan, a Buddhist, a Zen, or a Taoist religion, it makes no difference. The same spirit must be within each and every one of us. It must be that impersonal and, even further, it must be as much within the sinner as within the saint. Therefore, it must be available to the sinner as to the saint, to the atheist as to the believer, to the highest or the lowest, to the black or the yellow or the white or the brown. It must be impersonal, even though it does function within us more or less personally because it involves a personal relationship between "I and my Father." There is a man called Jesus who says: "I can of mine own self do nothing."[10] Then he speaks of "the Father that dwelleth in me, he doeth the works."[11] So with Paul. There is a Paul who has a "thorn in the flesh" and who acknowledges he has not "fully attained," and yet there is the same Christ within who can do "all things."

The third lost secret is this: Within individual you and individual me, individual he and individual she, saint and sinner, religionist and non-religionist, there is this presence, power, spirit with which we can commune in silence and in secrecy. All of this is lost to the world because they are worshiping something external to themselves. In a symposium recently held, a large collection of ministers of various churches agreed that the major foundation for morality is that "Jesus is God." This is the very belief that cheats the world of God's grace, the peace and the morality that could come to the world if it could be revealed that the presence of God is within you and that, if you wish to sin, so be it unto you and the penalty thereof. Knowing this truth, it is hardly likely that the sin will remain. Where the spirit of the Lord is realized, there is purity and divine grace. When you have closed your eyes long enough to realize that this spirit is within you, then open your eyes and realize that the same spirit is within all. You must acknowledge that Jesus did his mighty works, and Paul, through the spirit of God within them. And if you have any knowledge of other religions, you will know that Gautama did all of his mighty works through the same spirit of God within him. You can go through the lives of thousands of spiritual lights who have contributed to the world and who have said, "It was this indwelling spirit which performed that which was given me to do."

This secret was known to the ancients who lived in their temples separate and apart from the world, and it was for this reason that it is embodied in the teachings of Masonry that no Mason may invite another man to become a Mason. Anyone who wished to become a Mason must ask someone to propose him. Why do they have this rule? Because they know this secret; that they must keep locked up within them the great secrets. And, as we seek those secrets, we are "answering the knock." Keep the secret of secrecy, benevolence, and the nature of God locked up within you. Share it secretly. Find a dozen periods a day in which to be silent and to say to all in this world: "My peace I give unto you. My peace, the Christ peace, I give unto you. Blessings! Benedictions!" Then, when you are asked, share in proportion to their ability to carry away. Give the milk of the word to the babes, and give the meat of the word to the mature.

Every time that you share a spiritual truth, a book or a pamphlet, every time you make a contribution to any cause, remember consciously that you are not doing it for them. You are doing it out of the infinite nature of your own abundance. Sometimes parents actually believe that what they are doing is for their children, and it really is not. They are doing it for the fulfillment of their own nature. The mother has a mother-nature and the father has a father-nature and, if parents were not constantly giving, the mother-nature and father-nature would go unexpressed and would dry up. So it is that the mother-nature and the father-nature must continue to give and to share with their children. On the wider scale you will learn that all of us dry up unless we share. We will dry up our God-nature which is infinity. The secret of giving is that you are not giving for another but for your Self. The Master voiced it: "Inasmuch as ye have done it unto the least of these my brethren, ye have done it unto me"[12]–for the fulfillment of *My* nature.

Remember, "Do unto others" but realize that in doing so, you are giving out of your infinity. And combine your secrecy and your benevolence with an understanding of the reason for it. The kingdom of infinity is at the center of your being and, as you commune with it, it pours itself abundantly and your function is to pass it on.

COMMUNICATION OF ONENESS

January 19, 1964

THIS MORNING WE HAD tape number 2, Honolulu Infinite Way Study Center 1964, and the subject was "Spiritual Attainment Through Contemplation, Meditation, and Communion." When we reach the final lesson on that subject, we will reach a place that can only be attained by the preparation that takes place leading up to that final lesson. Without adequate preparation, the final lesson can never be demonstrated and the final lesson involves the word *omniscience*. This means an all-wisdom, all-knowledge, and of course includes omnipresence, so that we have a lesson which says: Because of omnipresence, omniscience is always functioning. You have to remember that when you meditate, pray, or treat (whichever way you are thinking) in The Infinite Way, you must start out with this realization: Since omnipresent omniscience or omniscient omnipresence already knows everything, you cannot inform Deity, you cannot tell God, you cannot ask anything of God, you cannot desire anything because you are always faced with omnipresent omniscience, the all-knowing. You have already trained yourself in this form of meditation, prayer, or treatment, so that regardless of the situation or the appearances, you can sit quietly listening until the still small voice utters itself, or the awareness of peace descends, or some other sign is given that "God is on the field."

In our final lesson on this subject we cover a wider territory. How do animals communicate with each other? How do fish and birds communicate with each other? There has to be a communication between them. With some birds there is always a leader that goes before them, taking them to the north or taking them to the south. Surely birds have no way of knowing such things, so there must be a communication that puts them in their rightful place in line in the safari. Consider dogs and cats at play. There must be a communication that lets them know they are at play and are not out to kill each other, and I will tell you now that the mode of communication is not a conscious one. The birds and the animals do not know how to communicate; it is an activity of consciousness that operates through them. You may try to tell animals that you are friendly and mean them no harm, but they do not understand your language. There is only one way you can communicate and that is if you are harmless. Then you do not have to tell them; you just have to *be* it, and then this being transmits itself to them.

Let us assume that today is Sunday and that tomorrow is going to be Monday, which it is, and we admit that we do not know God's plan for us tomorrow–where we shall be or what we shall do. Humanly we assume that God wants us to do tomorrow what we did today or last Monday, because humanly we are living on yesterday's manna and we would not enjoy being taken out of our routine. Therefore our mind is set on doing next Monday what we did last Monday, and doing this year what we did last year.

But we on this path have decided that we want to be God-governed, and this means a degree of inner communion which is a complete be still, quietness, peace.

With no communication on your part to God or to man in the recognition of omnipresent omniscience which is also omnipotence, you let it function. When you have arrived at that place of recognition that God is on the field, you are a beholder and you are then curious about tomorrow and you awaken with this sort of an idea: "What hath the Lord done for me today?" or "What hath the Lord done today?" You begin a whole new activity of consciousness, that of a complete settling into omniscience–omnipresence–omnipotence and then letting it function. This sets up a communication of oneness, not only with God but with all spiritual being and idea, so that out of the universe is drawn to you that which is to be a part of your fulfillment, whether it is recognition, reward, activity, new ideas, new business or new people. Why? Because a contact of communication has been set up between you and the universal consciousness and that communication reaches its own level, just as a telephone conversation reaches only the number that is being dialed.

In this same way we communicate with animals, vegetables, minerals, birds, beasts, insects, or fish, but in absolute stillness in the recognition of omnipresent, omnipotent omniscience. The first thing you know, you will find everything and everyone coming your way without fear. This is of no particular importance except as proof of the principle. I was in this kind of a meditation in the prayer garden of the Victoria Truth Center, when robins and sparrows flew right around me, touching my shoulder and even my head, and then flying off again. This had never happened to me before, and the only reason for the function of it was in that moment I was in attunement with all the world. Another time

Emma asked me to treat a bird in her home that had been injuréd, a bird which had never noticed me before. After that the bird dashed for my shoulder the minute I walked into Emma's home. The same thing happened on other occasions when I was asked to help animals and afterward met them, showing that a contact had been made in consciousness, which was why they benefitted by me. Remember this: No contact was established with the bird or the animal, but by absence of the effort to make contact.

The same thing has happened throughout the experience of The Infinite Way. Since I had no idea what its unfoldment should be, the only thing I could do was to enter into the same form of communication, becoming consciously one with my source and then being a beholder and watching as everything came into line, realizing that a spiritual contact had been made in Africa or England or Australia or somewhere else. The contact was not made by me. No!

This is the difference between the White Brotherhood and the Black Brotherhood. This is the difference between mystical truth and mental science. In mystical truth you know that of yourself you can do nothing and be nothing, but that in the stillness you can contact omnipresent omnipotence which is omniscience. And, it performs "that which is given you to do." In the Black Brotherhood the individual knows what he wants, and then draws you mentally, as advertising does, bringing something or someone to you whether or not it is good for you. However, the moment you relinquish the power of the mind in that direction, the power of the mind becomes illumined to help you perform your function. But it deprives you of something: personal sense.

Ultimately those students who are participating in our work will have to be led to the surrender of themselves in the recognition of omnipresent, omnipotent omniscience, relaxing and resting in it, and then being a beholder of it in operation as it becomes the means of communication.

I will use one more illustration: You may have read the news story which let the people in the northeastern part of the United States know that it was going to be a severe winter last year by virtue of the fact that the animals had heavier fur and had laid up more food than usual. What animals do is instinctive, but where does the instinct come from? It is an activity of consciousness that works through them, and without their knowing it they were automatically growing heavier fur and storing up more food. Consciousness is operating because they are taking no thought about next winter.

Humanly you cannot stop taking thought about next winter or next year. You have had too many centuries of training. The only way you can accomplish it is through your meditations, whereby you can at least have periods where you drop thought and let the divine consciousness function. It will not be accomplished one hundred percent, because you have not attained taking no thought one hundred percent for your safety or your security or your old age, and all of those thoughts hinder its operation in your experience. They do not hinder the operation of omnipresent, omnipotent omniscience—they hinder it in our experience. Omniscience is operating on a worldwide basis, omnipresently and omnipotently, but the world is not receiving it because it has the barrier of the human mind which is taking thought.

When formerly answering my mail or phone calls, if a student said, "I have a cold" or, "I need a job" or,

"Business is bad" or, "I have family trouble," I would reply that I would take care of it, assuming they knew and understood that I was going to take care of a spiritual realization. However, since I discovered that they were perfectly willing to stay in the attitude of problems and demonstrations, I stopped that practice about a year ago. It is a form of metaphysics I do not understand. All I can do is try to lift you into a spiritual consciousness where you become aware of the presence of the Christ. I can do nothing about those other things." You can see that even if taking thought did serve as an introductory way to get you on the spiritual path, it has to be abandoned before you can make spiritual progress. When there is a group of students in different parts of the world who are living in this attunement, the kingdom of God will be brought to earth more rapidly because they will be instruments through which it will take place.

I had an experience when I lived and practiced in New England. A man bought a dairy herd, and within six months he was getting twenty-five percent more milk without making any human changes. It came about through the power of prayer, and I certainly was not praying for more milk. My prayer was the realization of omnipresence, omnipotence, omniscience, which affected everything within range of my consciousness, including the cows. Then, instead of merely living by the food they ate and giving milk in proportion to that food, they were being fed by the spirit. Cows shall not live "by bread alone," any more than man.

You can see now why tape number 1 and tape number 2, Honolulu Infinite Way Study Center 1964, will have to be practiced diligently in order to lead up to this ability to be still and let divine consciousness establish the communication through you, in you, for you, without your taking thought. This is the ultimate of meditation.

MEDITATION: GOD FULFILLING GOD

January 26, 1964

YOU NOTICE THAT I have a meditation before I talk, and one thing you can be sure of is that I am not meditating for myself. Meditating almost day and night for some part of every hour, my own needs and the needs of The Infinite Way are well taken care of. Therefore my attitude is usually this: Whether there are just two or three or four of us meditating together, whether I am meditating for this Sunday noon group, for our Sunday morning group, or for any lecture or class, the object of meditation is the realization of the Presence.

What I would like you to see is this: Right now there are twenty-four of you sitting here in front of me, and since I do not have the faintest idea of what you may need or desire, the only way in which I can pray for you, meditate for you, is to forget you individually and collectively as people–forget your needs or your desires–and turn in for a realization of the Presence, for the realization of divine grace. As I succeed in attaining that awareness, the presence of God is consciously realized and then every one of you who is receptive to the will of God must find yourself benefitted in some measure.

This would probably not be true if you were outlining the form that God's grace should take. If you were expecting God to remove your pains, your sins or your lacks, perhaps you would not receive anything from my

477

meditation. If your desire was also for divine grace and you had completely wiped out of your thought any form of grace that you wanted to receive, you would then be receptive to the Presence that I had realized, and you would receive God's grace in some form. It may not be in the form which you expect, because as a rule we entertain our own opinions or concepts of what constitutes fulfillment.

We do not sufficiently believe that the kingdom of God is utterly different from what the Master called "this world," and even when our students pay lip service to the statement "My kingdom is not of this world,"[1] either consciously or unconsciously or subconsciously they still have an idea that "my kingdom" is going to fulfill itself in some way of "this world." There does not seem to be sufficient recognition of the fact that there is a "my kingdom" entirely different from anything that the mind of man can know, or that the grace of God takes forms completely different from what we think. One of the greatest barriers to demonstration is the fact that we have in mind some human or material form of demonstration, instead of going to God completely in the "unknowing" and with the attitude: "Thy grace is my sufficiency in all things."[2] Like so many people who pray, we think that "Thy grace" is my sufficiency in bringing me the things of this world, and it does not say that at all. It says: "Thy grace itself is my sufficiency . . . Thy wisdom is my sufficiency . . . Thy gift is my sufficiency . . . Thy will is my sufficiency . . . Thy way is my sufficiency." Accept that and then rest in it.

An article appeared in a recent magazine which was entitled "Man Is Not Entitled to Happiness." The whole essence of that was that man is not happy until he is getting his way, and his way is what he thinks of as constituting his happiness. Is he entitled to that? No! Only yesterday I received a letter from a student who wanted to know if she should not perhaps give up The Infinite Way because "she has not been healed yet, and she has been 'trying' for several months." I do not know what to say because there is no sign of her willingness to do God's will. There is no recognition that consciousness must be changed before there can be an external change. It is so very evident that she is expecting God to do her will and in the time she outlines. There is no such provision on the spiritual path.

The spiritual path is one of dying and being reborn. The spiritual path is one of molding yourself to God's will. The religious path is getting God to do your will and the metaphysical path seems to be following right along with that, but it is not right and it cannot possibly be successful. There are too many people saying that they have been in metaphysics or in truth for ten or twenty years, that they formerly had wonderful healings, but that it "does not work" anymore. Certainly. There has been no change in their consciousness, and what benefit they did receive was from their teacher's or practitioner's consciousness. Eventually the healings had to stop because the consciousness of the patient or the student had not changed.

Following through on this morning's tape number 2, side 2, Honolulu Infinite Way Study Center 1964, "Illumination through Meditation," see what happens if you put more effort into accepting omniscience, omnipotence and omnipresence when you meditate, and break the habit of reaching out to God to do your will or fulfill your desires. God does not fulfill you. God fulfills itself as you and as your experience—if you give God the opportunity. God's function is to fulfill itself and, if you and I leave our selves out when we go to God, God will fulfill itself in our individual experience.

The trips that I have taken around the world certainly have not been God fulfilling any desire of mine, because it never entered my mind to have any such career. It is God fulfilling itself. If any one of us ever succeeds in getting God to do something for us, it would prove that God is a monster. No, there is no such thing as God doing something for you or for me. God is fulfilling itself. If we are satisfied with God's fulfillment of itself, the most wonderful things are "added unto us." As soon as we inject "I" or "me" or "mine" or "my child" or "my neighbor," we lose God. Deny thyself. This does not mean to deny that there is a "you." Just deny your own desire and your own way and let God have its way.

You see the importance of meditation. Until now these things have not been written in books, so the only way you could have learned them would have been through meditation; and if we had learned meditation from childhood, we would all be "taught of God." Some day that will be the truth. The only reason there are not more mystics in the world, more people having mystical experiences, or more people being taught of God, is because there are so few individuals who are going to God with a completely open consciousness. We have been erroneously taught that some activity of the human mind is prayer. In the church it was the prayer of petition; in metaphysics it was the prayer of affirmation. The activity of the human mind is taking thought and we were told: "Which of you with taking thought can add to his stature one cubit?"[3] Taking thought is only the preparation to getting ourselves into the attitude of receptivity. Then taking thought stops and an attitude and an altitude of receptivity must follow. We are then God-governed.

REALIZING THE NON-POWER
OF APPEARANCES

February 2, 1964

HUMAN EXISTENCE IS GOVERNED principally by emotions, and if you analyze your relationships with your family, your business associates, your friends, and your enemies, you will notice that very little reason enters into the relationships. It is mostly emotion, which is why most people lose money in speculation, because emotion controls them more than reason. When emotion controls you, you have no opportunity of benefitting by principles of life.

When you are facing a situation and withdraw emotion long enough to realize the impersonal nature of the appearance, you immediately begin to dispel it. The natural tendency is to personalize and that is why it has been said, and rightly so, that it is unwise to discuss either religion or politics. The reason, of course, is that emotion enters in and makes it virtually impossible to talk about these subjects objectively. You would very quickly see what I mean if you could be in England during a pre-election campaign and witness how little emotion enters into the speeches by political candidates. The arguments are always aimed at the candidate's proposition, not at an individual. This is approaching politics with a minimum of emotion and a great deal of objectivity.

In the same way we think of disease, sin, lack, and limitation as having to do with a person or persons, and so we center our arguments mentally against a certain person or a certain political party or that church group or that race, and this has been the error that binds men in slavery. There is no possibility of freedom from the human emotions and human passions except by the realization of the impersonal and invisible nature of error which may be operating in and through a person or a group. You do not cure a tree of its illness by cutting off its branches. You lay the axe at the root. Likewise, if you want to cut off the operation of evil in your individual or collective experience, you also have to lay the axe at the root and stop fighting the forms of persons or groups or ideologies. Lay the axe right down at the root, which is the impersonal source of evil or the belief in two powers. There is the root.

If you had a conviction of one power, "no evil would come nigh thy dwelling place." There would be no evil to fight or remove or rise above. You could then resist not evil and you could put up your sword, just by the recognition of the non-power of the appearance world. This too would reveal to you, as it has to me, the nature of spiritual power. Spiritual power operates when there is no belief of an opposing power. That is why so many mystics have lost the way. Even though they have realized God, they have not realized the non-power of appearances and have therefore thought of God as a power *over*. The second chapter the Bhagavad Gita of India recognizes this where it tells us: "He who is slain and he who slays are both in error." Certainly! Such a thing cannot be if there is only one power, for that power is life itself maintaining and sustaining itself. To be slain or to slay another is to believe in two powers—life and death—material force. The Master recognizes this in his passages: "What did hinder you?. . . Resist not evil[1]. . . . Put up thy sword."[2]

There was a mystic who lived about 1500 B.C. or perhaps earlier, who revealed the nature of his own initiation by telling of all the discords that he met on the spiritual path which tried to keep him from the ultimate realization of truth. He revealed all of the terrible ordeals and the temptations that he went through. The temporal powers of his land tried to have him slain in order to keep truth from the religious people of his era. His goal was continuously thwarted and in many ways his life was threatened. Attacks were even made on his reputation in order to discredit him, but he survived all of this and came into his full realization. He then revealed that none of this happened externally. It all happened in mind; it was his own mind warring against his spiritual nature.

I often have students say they would like initiation, but experience proves that ninety-nine out of one hundred would fail if it were offered to them. Why? Because every initiation ends with the death of the one going through the initiation, and ninety-nine out of one hundred would stop there and say, "That is the one thing that I cannot do." Some give up on the path when they have to give up the externalized forms, yet none of this is actually taking place externally. It is just an activity of your own mind being externalized in your experience—but it is not being externalized "out there." The enemy is within us and the enemy is the antagonism to truth. How many people are there who will accept this fact, that their failures in life are due to themselves and not to anything or anyone in the external?

So a student who is well along on the path must expect that trials are going to be more severe than for the beginner, because the further you go the closer you come to the realization that it is a battle within and not outside. Whether the government or your wife or your husband or your friends or your neighborhood objects to truth, the responsibility is yours. These are only good excuses, because in the final analysis you had no right to tell them what is going on in your consciousness. When you learn this, you will learn to be still and work out your religious initiation within yourself.

In this message you have it that God is impersonal being—but how long it takes to accept the fact that God is my being as well as your being, and that God is your friend's being and your enemy's being is the difficulty that constitutes part of the initiation. In the same way, in this message you have that all error is impersonal. There is no lack or limitation anywhere: not in the middle of the ocean or the middle of the forest or the middle of the wilderness. Nowhere is there lack or limitation; but until you see that, because of the impersonal nature of God, omnipresence means fulfillment here where I am, you cannot even enter in. In the same way, until you stop blaming someone or something and realize that what you are fighting is the arm of flesh or nothingness and that you never did have a chance for victory, you cannot enter in.

Think what life would be without victory and without defeat, and then you will see how quickly you can lose emotion because emotion deals with victory and defeat, accomplishment or lack of accomplishment. If you are impersonalizing, then you have nothing to accomplish. You cannot win and you cannot lose. You can only *be*.

The reason that we have the death of Jesus, the resurrection from the tomb, and the ascension, is the same reason that we have these experiences in the lives of the spiritual Masters of all time. In Egypt, in Persia, in the Holy Land, all the way back as far as the Book of the Dead, there has been death, resurrection, and ascension of a Master. Death, resurrection, and ascension is not meant to personalize—it is meant to symbolize. What good is the death, resurrection, and ascension of a Master except as an example? As someone to worship? No! Jesus was, I believe, the sixth or seventh spiritual Master who, it was claimed, was immaculately conceived. It was claimed that Lao-Tzu's mother carried him in her womb for sixty or seventy years. This is not personalization; this is symbolization that man is a fully matured individual when he comes to earth. The story of Buddha's conception and birth is almost identical with that of Christ Jesus. It might have been one and the same, so it was not meant to personalize but to symbolize that all birth is immaculate. It has to be if God is your Father, and resurrection is an experience of every human being. Ultimately everyone must be resurrected out of the tomb of personal selfhood and be realized as the Son of God, as incorporeal being. And eventually everyone must ascend above corporeality into incorporeality, not by physical processes but by an activity of consciousness. It all takes place in consciousness. Consciousness must lift the man out of the tomb, not a body. Even a sick body cannot make itself well. It has to be lifted up by a change of consciousness. Poverty will not get rid of itself. An activity of consciousness has to change the picture.

At this point a question always lifts its head: "What can I do to bring about this harmonious conclusion to the initiation? What can I do to perfect myself?" The answer is this: Recognize that God is spirit and acknowledge that you are seeking only a spiritual demonstration. Stop thinking in terms of a spiritual God who will perform some material good. Stop thinking in terms of a God who will do something for a person. There is no such thing. There is no such thing as a God who will heal me or you or your patient or your student. That is going back to paganism. God is the impersonal life of all being, but God is spirit, and so your entire consciousness must be on the nature of the kingdom of God: Seek ye first the kingdom of God, the nature of spiritual grace, the nature of the gift of God. Then when you are absent from the body, when you are absent from taking any thought about the externalized forms, "the bridegroom cometh." The eternal mistake is trying to connect a spiritual God with a material universe when "My kingdom is not of this world." Do not try to make a spiritual God maintain a human body or a human home or a human purse or a human business, and in the moment ye "think not" about persons, things or conditions, and continue to abide with *me*–continue to abide in the Word–spiritual harmony comes and it brings the outpicturing of harmonious human conditions.

This will make clear to you the Eastern teaching of non-attachment. Many religions have misinterpreted it. Non-attachment means to take your thought away from this material universe. Live in the spirit, and all the things will be added unto you. Some have taken it in the literal sense: "Get rid of everything and live in sack cloth and ashes." That is not it at all! You do not get and you do not get rid of. We are talking about non-attachment in the sense of not trying to connect Self with material world. To be attached you would have to have a human relationship or a human membership; but to be non-attached means to have no human relationships, and yet the spiritual relationship is one of love and in it there is no lack and there is no depletion. When you try to finitize it and put it down on paper, you lose it.

How many times have you heard this: "The laborer is worthy of his hire."[3] That is not true because you immediately set up a relationship of a human nature, whereas "love thy neighbor" takes care of the entire situation without an obligation. There is no obligation on your part to love your neighbor or to be charitable for the sake of the poor. No, you love your neighbor and you are charitable for the fulfillment of your own nature. It is folly to believe that you are doing something for them. Whatever you are doing you are doing for your own nature. If you accept the belief that you are doing something for another, you will be paid off in that coin. Acknowledge that you are doing something for your own fulfillment.

I have witnessed this so many times when I have written a check for a community cause and then was told that I was doing it "for them" or "for the boys." No, I know better! This just fulfills me. I have no illusions on that score, but it is the same with every phase of life, including your relatives. What you withhold represents a lack in you. What you give represents a measure of fulfillment in you. No, if you think you are doing anything for someone else—this is ego. In the early days when I could give very little of a material nature, I used to think: "What good is this tiny little one dollar or five dollars or ten dollars?" I awakened later to realize that, as far as the world is concerned, it is very little, but I am giving it for the fulfillment of my Self. Carry that out and you will see that when you forgive you are not forgiving someone else for a wrong. They may go out and do more wrongs, so it will do them no good. No, forgiving is Self-fulfillment.

The work we have been doing since the first of the year has a cumulative effect. The fact that we have heard these principles over and over again presented in different ways, is having a cumulative effect in your consciousness so that if we keep it up long enough there will be a change of consciousness. Remember, the more of these principles you can work with consciously, the more years you save of the struggle. These principles must be remembered, consciously taken into meditation, and then they must be lived as you come up against a problem which is a person, a condition, or a circumstance. Then remember that it is a picture, behind which is the arm of flesh, or nothingness.

Beyond Metaphysics — *I AM*

February 7, 1964

GOOD EVENING. Most of our students are having quite a difficult time making the transition from metaphysics to mysticism. Some have not even realized that there is a difference, that they have to die out of their metaphysics in order to be born into realization of their true identity—and here is a question that helps us very much in starting out on this subject:

Question: *My understanding is that mind is a human instrument. It can be used for good or evil. Here is a quote from your writings: " 'I' am behind the mind and 'I' can think thoughts through the mind, or 'I' can still the mind." Now who or what is 'I' in this statement?"*

Answer: It must be clear that it cannot be God, because you must understand that God cannot think. God cannot start anything and God cannot stop anything. There is no beginning in God and there is no ending in God. In metaphysical teachings it is said that "God thinks and we think after God." Of course that is not any more true than the fact that God punishes or rewards. God does not do anything. God is being, but God is *being* the same now as a million years ago, and the same as a million years from now. "God changeth not." That is why in theology there have been so many quarrels about how old the world is. Did God create the world ten thousand years ago? We were told so, but the truth of the matter is that this world never was created. There never was a beginning and there never will be an ending, for "God changeth not."[1] He does not start anything and he does not stop anything, and certainly God does not think any more than the principle of mathematics thinks, or the principle of science thinks, or the principle of chemistry thinks. The principle of all being certainly does not think. It is. It never *thought* 2 x 2 into being because there never could have been a time when 2 x 2 was other than 4. It never thought H_2O into water, because H_2O never could have been anything other than water.

This brings us to our subject: There is *I* which is God, but if you will remember the work which we have been doing through 1963 and up to the present, you will notice that I have been carrying you beyond metaphysics into the original revelation of The Infinite Way which is mysticism. The reason it has taken so many years to reach this point is that most of our students came out of metaphysical movements and had to be taken from where they were in order to reach where we are now, because it was only last year that I was given the word to work with our students and lead them out of their metaphysical consciousness into the mystical.

In the metaphysical you have to become more loving, more grateful, more honest, more patient, or more peaceful, and all of your studies are intended to produce this result in you. In the ancient wisdoms this was called the First Degree. In the wisdom schools they began to teach the initiate, to mold his character into greater integrity, greater loyalty, greater fidelity, greater love of

God and love of man—obeying the laws, loving thy neighbor as thyself, developing benevolence and charity. All of this is in the First Degree, even teaching reliance on God, faith in God. If you follow yourself through your metaphysical days, you will discover that was exactly what happened to you.

When you came into any of the metaphysical teachings, you may have been mentally, physically, morally. or financially ill; you may have been impatient, short tempered, bigoted, biased; you may have had severe likes and dislikes and oh! so many other human failings. But if you were faithful to any of the metaphysical approaches to life, it would not have taken more than a few years for your entire nature to have changed. You must have recognized this, and surely others must have recognized this in you. In other words we could say that your humanhood has been greatly improved. You are now obeying the Ten Commandments—in fact you may even have gone further than the Ten Commandments. You may have come to where you truly love God with all your heart and soul, and you may even have begun to love your neighbor as yourself. If so, you have come far on the metaphysical path, but you are a long, long way from the mystical path. In fact if you reach that place, you will have to leave your metaphysics as far behind you as in metaphysics you left orthodoxy behind. Why? Because all of this time in metaphysics I have been a human being going from sickness to health, from poverty to abundance, from hate and animosity to "loving God and loving my neighbor as myself." So the I that is behind the mind in this question tonight is the human I, which, through metaphysical study and practice, has been raised to the point where it is not capable of thinking or being evil, but is now "loving God supremely" and "loving your neighbor as yourself."

Now we come to that in the message of The Infinite Way which consists of *I is God* or *I Am that I Am*, and therefore I do not "take thought for my life, what I shall eat, or what I shall drink; nor yet for my body, what I shall put on."[2]

I *have meat the world knows not of."* [3] *As a matter of fact* I Am *the meat. "I am not resurrected*–I Am *the resurrection. I am not conscious*–I Am *consciousness. I am not spiritual*–I Am *spirit. I do not have life eternal nor will I ever gain it*–I Am *life eternal. Therefore I do not think. In silence the light that* I Am *shines.*

Remember how many times you have read or heard me say, that I have never given a treatment to anyone at any time under any circumstance? Of course, because I would then be a human being giving a treatment to another human being for that human being's benefit. Metaphysically this would be acceptable, but mystically the treatment would be this: "Arise, take up thy bed and walk[4]. . . . Neither do I condemn thee."[5] Why? Who is this *thee* but *I?*

Let me illustrate this by taking a subject that is bound to be universal for a long, long time to come, until this mystical consciousness is attained. We will take the subject of lack, or abundance, or supply, call it what you will. What it means is that there is a belief of insufficiency of something, and so you are turning to truth to meet that need, to reveal abundance in place of lack. Once again The Infinite Way says, "You cannot meet a problem on the level of the problem." Therefore, you

for me, so you see mystically you have to change your life to one of inner awareness so that you are attuned to whatever it is that is God's will for you, God's plan. That is all that God is going to perfect in your life–not what you wish or desire, but that which is appointed for you. Then you do not have to take thought for the success of any mission, business, or activity in which you may be engaged. You have only to live in the inner communion so that the will of the *I that I Am* can be performed through you.

When you grasp this you will understand why it makes no difference if you had not been born into this experience, nor does it make any difference if you pass out of this experience, because the *I that I Am* is eternal and "He performeth the thing that is appointed for me"–not on my birth date, but in the beginning. Eventually you must understand what the Master was revealing: "I and my Father are one, not two, and *I* am that one." Remember this: If I were to say that Joel is that one, I would be leaving you all out and as an egotist I would probably burn in front of you. No! *I* am God, every I in this room or in a gambling house or in a brothel. *I* is God. I must realize that and then live by prayer. But by now prayer is without words and thoughts. Why? Because have I anything now to attain or achieve? No! *I am.* My prayer is merely a communion without any desired goal, because *I am.* I am about my Father's business. "I and my Father are one"–now. "All that the Father hath is mine"–now.

I embody the resurrection, and so I am going to take you back to an exercise we have had several times in my class work, in which you ask yourself: "What is God?" If you answer "God is love" you are wrong. If you answer

"God is life" you are wrong. In other words you go through every synonym you have ever heard in the Bible, in metaphysics, or in mysticism, until you do not have one word left in your mind, not a single concept of God. Then you will find yourself face to face with God, but not as long as you have a concept. Why? Because you would be depending on a concept only. In fact as long as you are depending on a God, you will fail. Why? Because *I* is God and there is no other beside that. Therefore, if you would like to depend on truth, there is only one truth to depend on: *I* am the truth.

Do you see why, when you reach the mystical, there is no truth to depend on? There is no such thing as a word or a passage or a message that you can rely on. You cannot even rely on Infinite Way passages. They were not meant to be relied on; they were meant to reveal the truth. Relying on a passage is only for the very beginner, not to rely on, but to learn from. Anyone who depends on a passage is depending on a straw. *I* am the truth to depend on, the fact that *I* am the truth. "I and my Father are one," therefore there is no need for a dependence. Why? Is there something you need or would like, or wish to attain? Not if you understand that I is God. The only truth there is is I *am*. I *am* truth. I *am* the way. I *am* life eternal. When I am in communion, there is a movement from the I that I Am that flows through me as action, as being. So we could say with Paul: "Christ liveth my life" or, "He performeth the thing that is appointed for me," because it is *I* performing it *as* Joel.

If you will go back through The Infinite Way, you will discover, "That which I am seeking I *am*." If you pondered and meditated with that statement until realization came, you could tear up the books, for you would be living it. "That which I am seeking I am." What will I seek? Truth. I *am* the truth. I *am* immortality. I *am* life eternal. Does that clarify the statement, "I am come that they might have life and that they might have it more abundantly"[11]? *I* am come. Dwell in the *I* that I Am, for that *I* in the midst of you will live your life abundantly and graciously.

Again I quote: "The way that provides not for the wayfarer is no way to fare upon." What is the way? I am the way and if I, the realization of my true identity, does not provide, then I had better give up all of the revelations of the Master because the way he reveals is the way of I. That is the way that is revealed in The Infinite Way. You will find it in every Infinite Way book and in every chapter. *I. I* am the way, and as long as I abide in this, the *I* provides my wine, and my meat, and my water. The Infinite Way reveals that thought is not power. Then why take thought? Now the time is here to take the way of *I.* When you take this *way* you become a beholder of God in action, a beholder of your life as it unfolds.

Now you realize why it is given us in this message that our benevolences, our charities, are never done for the sake of the poor. There is not enough money in all the world to overcome the poverty of the world, because the entire human mind is a state of barrenness. Benevolence and charity, loving your neighbor as yourself, is not done for your neighbor. It is done as a fulfillment of your nature. *I* cannot withhold. *I* must forever pour itself out, not for the sake of anyone, but for the sake of its fulfillment. Do you not see that the earth is full of God's bounty? The sea and sky and the air is full of so much we do not even know about at the present time. Is God giving this to us? No! God is pouring this forth as the fulfillment of the nature of God. And so with us. If you are living on the human plane of life, that is the fulfillment of your nature. If it were not your nature, you would not be it; but if you are living from the standpoint of *I*, living in the mystical life, you will never believe that you are good or spiritual or moral. You will be able to say with Master, "There is but one good."[12] The *I* of my being is fulfillment itself. I am not fulfilling myself for you. No! It is Self-fulfillment because that is the nature of God. For a human to take credit for it would be the height of egotism.

When you come to this place of recognition, there is bound to be a question that will arise in your thought and I hope you will always know that the answer is in the chapter "The New Horizon" in *The Infinite Way*, and in the book *The Thunder of Silence*. The question that arises is this: "Why then 'this world' with its sins, diseases, deaths, lacks, and limitations?" The answer is a state of hypnotism brought about by the belief in good and evil. It is a form of malpractice, but a form of self-malpractice.

No one can be malpracticed by anyone but themselves. Self-malpractice consists of believing the appearance. The moment you accept the appearance at face value, the moment you accept good and bad appearances, you are malpracticing yourself. When you see someone who needs healing, enriching, or reforming, you are indulging self-malpractice and the remedy for malpractice, even self-malpractice, is just this recognition. Then drop it! Recognize it for what it is, as the Master recognized the temptations. When the three forms of temptation came to him he just dropped them because the devil was but an appearance in his own mind; self-malpractice—a belief in a selfhood apart from God. In the measure then that you are tempted with appearances, in that degree you have not attained full Christhood. It is nothing to be ashamed of, because no one has attained the fullness of Christ and remained visible. But at least when you are faced with a temptation to believe that "out there are human beings," you are indulging self-malpractice and in that degree you pay the penalty.

That brings us to this question: "Why then do we teach, since there is no one to be taught?" The answer is this: We are not teaching. *I* am the truth and the light and *I* just cannot be hid under a bushel basket—and if I did not speak these words, the stones would. There are sermons in stones. As humans we are not necessary to the world because the *I* that *I Am* will always be manifest. "Before Abraham was I am,"[13] and "I will be with you unto the end of the world."[14] If you go looking for Jesus "before Abraham was" or in the present day, you are about to have a long search. But if you will search for *I*, and search in the right place, you will find *Me*, "closer than breathing and nearer than hands and feet," because the kingdom of God is within you.

It is not easy to stop thinking in terms of human beings. It takes the grace of God to make the transition, but at least you must realize that you would not be hearing these words and you would not be responding to them but for divine grace. It is true that not all who heard the Master speak rose to the demonstration, and perhaps not all who hear these words will. But, perhaps later! I feel I must have heard these words from the

Master, but could not rise to the demonstration. But I finally made it!

There was a story of a great Master walking through India who came to an earnest spiritual student who said, "Oh Master! Will you tell me just one thing? Will you tell me how many lifetimes it will be before I attain illumination?" The Master prayed and then he said, "I am told it will be just another one or two thousand lifetimes before you attain." "A thousand or two thousand lifetimes!" said the student. "How can I stand it?" The Master walked on and came to another student and this man asked him the same question: "How many lifetimes will it be before I attain illumination?" Again the Master prayed and he said: "Do you see that tree? As many leaves as there are on the branches—that is how many lifetimes it will take you to attain." And that student jumped up and down and said, "Only that many? How fortunate am I!" What difference how many lifetimes, for what else have we to do?

CHRIST COMING INTO ASCENDANCY

February 9, 1964
The Halekulani Hotel
Honolulu, Hawaii

IT IS PRESUMED that Jesus was admitted to the Order of the Essenes shortly after he was twelve years of age, or probably in coming to manhood in the Hebrew faith at the age of thirteen, and he was graduated when he was thirty. In all of the wisdom schools a normal period of study would be from six to nine years. You may wonder at that and why it is that our students go through a week or two of classes and then expect to be graduated as ministers or healers. The secret of course, is that it is not the knowledge that you acquire in class that qualifies you for a title or an activity, but the material that is given to you in class is meant to be the substance that forms the new consciousness, that which enables you to die and be reborn. This is illustrated in tape number 4, side 1 of this 1964 Honolulu Series, in which we have had a different unfoldment each week leading up to this last one—and yet all of this is meant only as the substance with which we are to work to form the new consciousness.

In the First Degree, which consists of the earliest years in your wisdom school, you are taught a reliance on God. In fact you are really taught that there is a God, and you are taught the nature of God and the nature of your reliance. Then you are taught a moral code such as the Ten Commandments. Through this study and practice you learn how to love your neighbor as yourself by being honest in your dealings, generous, loyal, faithful, benevolent, forgiving. It takes several years of practice before you can really say, "There is greater integrity in my human relationships, family relationships, business and community relationships. There is a greater sense of benevolence and mutual helpfulness." It takes time to bring yourself to the top of that First Degree.

Of old there was a Second Degree, which we can eliminate today because we are living in a state of society that embraces the Second Degree. It has to do with education, culture, art, science, mathematics, but in the days of the wisdom schools none of these were available to the ordinary person. In fact not many could either read or write, even if they were available. Therefore, those who went to the wisdom schools had to spend quite a few years in which they were taught mathematics, science, architecture, and cultural subjects. Today we can eliminate the Second Degree because in almost every major country these are available to the people from the time they are infants. So it is then that you can now go directly from the First Degree to the Third.

The Third Degree is where you forget everything you learned in the First, because now you are not going to be loving or charitable or honest. Now you are going to be nothing and you are going to let the spirit of God be everything, functioning through you. Now you are going to say, "Why callest thou me good?"—you are going to say, "Do not praise my intellect." In other words, you are taking no thought; you are letting your life be lived by the spirit of God in you. Saroyan said: "I find lately I am not living my own life. Something else is living it and I go along for the ride." So now there is no longer any reason to have faith in God or to rely on God, because there is no personal sense of I. Then you discover that in the Third Degree you are developing this inner capacity which has been called the Christ in you, the Son of God in you, the spirit of God in you, the inner Self, the real Self, the super Man, the divine consciousness. In the degree that this is developed, your outer world changes because you are no longer seeing it either as a good human world or a bad human world. Through this developed consciousness you are now beholding the spiritual creation which God created "in the beginning, in his own image and likeness"—where there was light before there was sun, where the food was in the ground before the seeds were planted, where there was a man before there was a married couple. This is the world that is only beheld by those of spiritual vision, and that is why Paul could say: "God's word is foolishness unto man,"[1] and it is! How can the third-dimensional man believe that man is not created of flesh but out of the word of God? How can the third-dimensional man believe that you can have food before you have seeds or light before you have a sun?

You cannot give the Ten Commandments to people and then believe that they have already accomplished the life of obedience to the Ten Commandments. That takes a long, long time. You cannot take nine of those Commandments away from a person without someone saying, "You mean it is alright to commit adultery or to steal?" It takes quite awhile to understand that you do not mean that at all, that in this higher consciousness there are no such temptations, and no such situations could arise. There has to be a long period of practice of the Ten Commandments, of developing charitable instincts, forgiving instincts, and tolerance.

There is another long period when the nine Commandments are taken away and you are left with only two, before you can adjust to living a life that is spent in communion with God and you can say that all relationships are a communion with your fellow man. Then when you come to the "dying" process before you enter the Third Degree, and receive a lesson like this tape number 4, remember that it is going to require a long period of adjustment before you can stop enjoying the mountains and the seashore as they appear to be and begin to discern them as they really are. It will take a still longer period before you can stop enjoying the good people and criticizing and condemning the bad people. Yes, it takes quite awhile before you can go right down the middle path and see God's man as Man.

Right from the beginning of The Infinite Way to this moment, you will notice that we have no titles and diplomas. Why? Because from the start of my ministry more than thirty years ago, I saw that the only ordination that counts in this world is the spiritual ordination–the descent of the Holy Ghost. Those who merely receive diplomas or titles have no capacity as such to go out and heal or teach. The only healing consciousness there is is the one that is endowed from on high, the attainment of spiritual discernment, and classes can only give you the tools with which to mold your new consciousness.

I think it is safe to say that this first side of tape number 4, 1964 Honolulu Series, gives you the working tools with which to develop the spiritual power of discernment or the capacity of spiritual discernment. There are some students already at such a point of attainment that just hearing a message like this is all that is required to lift them right out of mortal sense into spiritual discernment–that is somewhat like reading in the newspaper that "a new star was born last night in a theatrical production." It is so easy to forget to look back over the years and take into consideration the amount of study and practice the actor put in which eventually entitled that individual to stardom. You may be sure that if anyone is lifted in a given moment from mortal sense to the divine, there has been a period of preparation preceding it–probably a period of many years and perhaps many centuries; and then, just at "that moment," came full flowering.

For most people there is a long period of study of a message of this kind, and then long and arduous practice of these principles. Then all of a sudden "in a moment ye think not," the light shines. In other words, "Whereas I was blind, now I see."[2] There is then a stilling of all of the mental senses, a rest, a "Peace unto our people."[3] You then look out and no longer see a world that needs to be healed, changed, or reformed. You now see God's world breaking through the crust of humanhood.

When you witness these battles in Africa, India, China, the Southland, remember that what you are witnessing is Christ breaking through into visible form and expression. You are not witnessing any evil. The evil was in the days of "peace where there was no peace," the days in which some people lived in subjection to other people, when so many lived without benefit of the opportunity for education. Those were the days of evil when seemingly there was peace in the land, but actually those were the days when the inner warfare was taking place which has now erupted.

If you could have seen in my childhood days in New York City the eagerness of the children of immigrants to be educated, or if you could have witnessed here in Hawaii the second generation of Asians who arrived in the Islands with the same eagerness to take advantage of the opportunities for education and achieved it, you would then be able to see that those were the years of inner warfare–but it was driving those immigrants in the eastern states and here in Hawaii. In those areas the opportunity was freely offered and so the transition from ignorance to intelligence, from lack to culture, was achieved without wars. Also, remember that the same urge was driving the people in our American Southland, in India and China and Africa, but the urge was repressed and therefore had to break out into open warfare.

This is actually good warfare, not evil, because it is the Christ of man breaking out against authority in order to find expression. These are the good days in which we are living. It makes no difference that some are losing their lives or their health or even their sanity in order that their children or their grandchildren may be free. Why? Because those who are making the sacrifice will be back here on earth to enjoy the fruitage, just as some of us have perhaps given our lives for freedom and equality and are back on earth where we can enjoy it.

At one time the religious world, the church world, rejected every spiritual revelation that came to earth, and rejected many of the revelations of a humanly cosmic nature, just as they at one time resisted the ancient mathematicians and seafarers. Today we are in an age when there is no resistance to truth, and just as our immigrants in the eastern states and in Hawaii were freely given the opportunity for education, so the churches of today are freely accepting the new-old revelations and are not preventing the people from hearing, receiving, and accepting them.

So you see there is a warfare going on within each one of us, a warfare which took the place of wanting cultural education or artistic education or musical education. At another time it takes the form of wanting spiritual education. It is the same battle, the desire for light against the limiting sense of darkness, but the nature of consciousness is such that in the end it over-comes all obstacles. If a boy wants music and cannot find it at home, he will even run away from that home in order to attain it; and, those who yearn for spiritual light will do likewise. Why? Because this capacity of spiritual discernment must come to the surface in this age. Since these teachings are coming after a period of seventeen or more years, this transition will be an easy one to some of our students. For others it will be difficult and they will have to practice the lesson for a long, long time—and sometimes painfully—until the power of discernment is attained. And some will not get it at all. "The way is straight and narrow and few there be who enter."[4] Fortunately the world is further along the path, so there will not be as few as there were two thousand years ago, *if* they can discern.

Whenever you are going through a period of unhappiness, illness, lack of peace, of prosperity, or frustration, remember that this has nothing to do with your outer world. You will be tempted to believe that the external world is causing the difficulty, but this is not so at all. If you can discern that this represents a battle going on within you, you will quickly achieve victory just through the ability to discern that no person or condition or situation is doing anything to you. This is a battle within you in which your higher self is seeking ascendancy over the mortal sense into which you were born. This is the Son of God in you struggling to come into manifestation and expression. "I must not seek victory over outer conditions or persons, but rather let the Christ of me come into ascendancy, and it will be the light revealing that there is no darkness." In the South the Blacks are fighting the Whites for something the whites cannot give them, and that is the ascendancy of their higher self. It is the same in Africa, India, and China. They do not realize that what they are battling for no man can give them. Each must attain for itself. In Cuba the people were fighting for freedom from their capitalistic masters, and look what they got.

We still cannot cast our pearls before swine, but we know now that we are in a position to teach those who are receptive that the battle can never be against people or conditions or things. The battle must always be within yourself until your real Self, your spiritual Self, is risen. Then you will find that this outer world is already heaven. When you are tempted to believe that you are fighting a sin, a false appetite, a disease, or lack or limitation in any form, please relax at once and realize that is not true. The battle is your Christ-self trying to break through into manifestation; and as you relax from the struggle and stop fighting evil—as you "put up the sword" and rest in quietness and peacefulness—the Christ will come into ascendancy.

Do you see why the Master said, "I come not to bring peace but a sword"[5]? That Christ does not come in you just to lift you onto cloud nine. It comes to tear you away from that self that must die, even when it is good. When you are going through difficulties it is so important to remember that it is the Christ that is doing it, not the devil and not satan. The Christ is doing this in order to take you out of fleshly peace, temporal peace, even out of fleshly health.

INTO THE MYSTICAL CONSCIOUSNESS

February 15, 1964
Honolulu, Hawaii

GOOD AFTERNOON. Our 1963 work was to make the transition from metaphysical consciousness to mystical consciousness, and as you study the four tapes of the 1964 Honolulu Series and the papers so far, you will discover that we have been consciously making that transition and should either have made it by now or be right on the verge of attaining.

There is one final step you can take that will help you complete your realization, and that is this: Look out of this window and select a tree or a group of trees, and behold that there is a law of life functioning in that tree—from the roots out to the fruit on the branches. Take it very slowly. Look down into the roots beneath the soil and you will soon agree that the roots are drawing unto themselves from the surrounding earth, food which has been formed of the rain that has fallen, sunshine, fertilization, and that out of these surroundings is sent up into the trunk of the tree and out into the branches all that is necessary, not only for the sustenance of the tree, but for the forming of the leaves, the blossoms, and the fruit. All of this is possible, not by virtue of the roots or the surrounding earth, but by virtue of an invisible life force acting in and through the tree or upon it, producing the effects that are probably visible through a high-powered glass.

513

The miracle of this exercise is that you have been a beholder, but in no way have you had any part in what you beheld. You did not bring it about, you did not start it into action, you merely beheld, and by your beholding came into the awareness of that which has been taking place out there in those trees before we even came into this room. What is the miracle? You do not set God at work or to work; you do not bring the power of God into any situation. God was there before you, because of omnipresence. It makes no difference if you had a wrong thought this morning or if you committed a wrong deed yesterday. It has nothing to do with what is going on in God's universe because it is not your purity that makes God work. It is God's function. God's grace is not dependent on how good or how spiritual you are. God's grace is dependent on how good God is, and any saint or sinner can behold God at work once their eyes are open to omnipresence.

Think a moment. If the particular tree you are beholding is barren at the moment, what kind of a treatment will you give it to make it fruitful? In mysticism you will not give it any treatment. You will know that, regardless of appearances, omnipresence means that God has been at work "since the beginning" and "unto the end of the world." There is no presence and there is no power to prevent the activity of God. Scripture says, "Who shall hinder him?[1] . . . Who shall prevent?" What shall prevent God? Therefore, the life of a mystic is the life of a beholder, one who through spiritual discernment sees God at work. "What did hinder you," in spite of appearances? "Neither do I condemn thee," in spite of appearances. It must be spiritual discernment that enables you to look at a barren tree and not give a treatment, as if you are greater than God or as if God could be made to start some benevolent action today. "God is the same yesterday, and today, and forever. . . . Before Abraham was, I *am* with you. . . . I will be with you unto the end of the world." See how all this breaks down appearances, yet it does not change God and it does not start God in action. It brings the awareness of omnipresence, omniscience, omnipotence, and knowing this truth sets you free. Every problem has its foundation in the belief of the absence of God, and most prayers are aimed at bringing God into the picture, which is impossible. "Before Abraham was" and "Unto the end of the world," God is. The beauty is that, in spite of appearances, nothing else *is*.

If you wonder why it takes a long time to attain the mystical consciousness, remember that it takes as long as is necessary to develop the consciousness that can look at barrenness and see God at work, without attempting to "make it so." Suppose you are looking at a tree that appears to be dying. Remember that this is the place in which this principle is even more necessary than when you are looking at a healthy tree where you can readily agree that God is functioning. Now, through spiritual discernment alone, you have to agree that there is no evil, no death, no destructive power, and therefore there is no need for a God to change anything, improve anything, or heal anything. So whether or not that tree dies is up to who is beholding it. The one who can behold that tree and can smile because of the spiritual discernment of seeing God at work will watch that tree be raised up into life. The beholder of God in action bears witness to God in action.

I have said in some of The Infinite Way books, "Why did they have to go to Jesus two thousand years ago? Why did they not go to the Hebrew rabbis?" Or, "What was the principle that enabled Gautama the Buddha to set up healing ashramas all over India?" Have you ever asked yourself, "What was the principle?" The Hindus do not know the principle, but I know it: "'This world' is an illusion." You do not change or improve or heal an illusion; you recognize it, and that recognition is the illumined consciousness. No one has an illumined consciousness who prays to God to do something, for "God is no respecter of persons"[2] and "God is the same yesterday, and today, and forever."[3] Was it God who forgave the woman taken in adultery? If so, why did he not do it before Jesus got there? Did God lift up the thief on the cross? It was the illumined consciousness of Jesus. Of what does illumination consist? Illumination consists of spiritual discernment that sees through the appearances and sees omnipresence, omniscience, omnipotence.

To a great extent then, it is the consciousness of the practitioner that determines the healing. There are exceptions because there are those who are not receptive, not through any fault of theirs and not through any lack of desire for God, but because of some innate quality of consciousness. But for the most part, perhaps eighty to ninety percent, the nature of the healing is dependent on the consciousness of the practitioner. "I, if I be lifted up, will draw all men unto me."[4] In other words if I clearly discern the illusory nature of the appearances, healings take place. If I try to reach out to God, God help the patient because millions are doing this. You all know that there are some practitioners who have beautiful results when you take it over one hundred cases. You also know that some, even if they had two hundred cases, could not be successful. Why? Because of the state of illumination, the degree of illumination. Of what does illumination consist? Spiritual discernment that does not react to appearances but can rest and say, "What did hinder you?" or "Arise, take up thy bed." The difficult part is this: God is always God, but not separate and apart from my being, or your being, or his being, or her being.

So then it is your degree of awareness that determines the degree of harmony brought forth. It has nothing to do with God. God is absolute. It has to do with your awareness—it is the state of the individual's consciousness. Mortality is a myth, and by calling it mortality you are impersonalizing it. Whether you witness sin, disease, death, lack, or limitation in any form it is mortality, it is mortal sense. If God did not create it, it has to be a myth. If you would read this in its fullest form, I urge you to study the chapter "God, the Consciousness of the Individual" in *A Parenthesis In Eternity*.

You must see this: What has created The Infinite Way and carried it around the world but the consciousness of *one* individual? All that Jesus brought to earth was the consciousness of one individual. All that Buddha brought to earth was the consciousness of *one* individual, and it is the consciousness of *one* individual that is taking you out of metaphysics into mysticism. So the consciousness of *one* individual must heal. Further, it is a myth that there is a supreme being who "sits up here with good and evil in its hand." That is why we say in the message of The Infinite Way that there are two major points: The nature of God and the nature of error. If you know the nature of God you will know that God is omnipresence, omniscience, omnipotence. If you know the nature of error, the error will dissolve.

Why do we need teachers and why do we need masters? We do need both. Why? Because we need the consciousness of the individual that has attained the realization of the nature of God and nature of error. Jesus gave us the nature of God as *I*, Buddha gave us the nature of error as *maya*, or illusion, and both of these combined in me to bring forth this message. One without the other would not have accomplished it. I have said this so often, "You cannot use spiritual power, because there is none to be used." Spiritual power is recognition.

Question: *You spoke about stilling the mind. Can you give us more help with this?*

Answer: Trying to still the mind is a dangerous practice and, if I did use those words, what I meant was this: Do not let the mind reach out mentally to a God to do something, which is why I used the illustration today of the tree. When you are watching that tree your mind is beholding, it is not trying to do something. In other words the mind is doing something, but it is doing something by beholding, and that is a quieting process, not an active process. This is the difference between beholding, which is an activity of the mind, and reaching out to God by taking thought. Do not let the mind do that, but instead settle down and let the mind behold. This is the attitude we use in healing. When someone asks for help, instead of the mind of the practitioner reaching out to see how quickly he can heal the patient or get God to do something, he lets the mind settle back so he can behold God in action. If the practitioner can get quiet and not try to stop the pain or save the patient's life, and behold God in action, the appearance will dissolve.

That is part of the experience of the whole mystical life in which no matter what you are doing, you are never looking at people as male or female. The ordinary person is looking at this world and seeing male and female with whatever reaction that has on them, but in the mystical life you see men and women but it does not register to you in that way. In other words it makes no impression. One cannot afford to see students or patients as attractive women or beautiful women or plain women. You train yourself so that your attention is always on listening. That is what I mean by stilling the mind, but I really do not mean stilling it in the usual sense because that can be dangerous by getting you into the occult. This is why I do not believe in long meditations, because eventually the mind gets into the mental strata which consists of good and evil. By stilling the mind I mean not *using* the mind.

Let us take the subject of eyesight. You see through the eyes, but you are not really using your eyes. If you try to use them you will quickly see that you are feeling pain. No, you do not see by the eyes, you see through them, and you do not hear by the ears, you hear through them. It is the same with the mind. The moment you start "using" the mind, you are making a creative force out of it and are thereby misusing its function. Remember, you think through the mind. So the step from metaphysics to mysticism is accomplished in proportion to the degree in which you can become a beholder.

You use the mind only in the sense of awareness, never in the sense of power. When I can be still and receptive, no matter what is "out there," the awareness of spiritual reality will come into me. My eyesight may see the same things for awhile, but someone will soon say, "I feel better," not because I did anything, but rather I had the attitude of a composer. What is a composer's attitude? *Listening.* The mystical mind is not used; it experiences. I remain perfectly quiet, and my mind interprets to me what it sees. If I am thinking humanly, I will see male and female, tall and short. But, if I am using the mind spiritually, I do not see this universe humanly. I see what the Soul reveals, which is the spiritual identity, yet it is nothing that I can describe. You must never still the mind, but you must let the mind become still through making it your interpreter. Joan of Arc was asked, "Does God speak to you in French?" to which she replied, "I do not know whether he speaks to me in French, but I hear him in French." In other words we know God speaks in the language of spirit, but we "hear it in English." The mind is interpreting it to us but without any activity on our part.

You have a fourth-dimensional consciousness, but in most students it is used only slightly or not at all, and the work you do in studying and meditating is for the purpose of developing that fourth-dimensional consciousness. It might be compared to the student who is studying music. He cannot ever make his fingers play. It is consciousness that does that. So, by developing his musical consciousness, his fingers then fly. So, it is with you. Your studies and your meditations are meant to develop your consciousness and your body and mind then work automatically, without any conscious volition.

Here is an illustration: I suppose to me the greatest passage of Scripture is, "I have meat"[5] or "I am the bread,[6] the meat, the wine and the water." What makes these passages so important when humanly they do not even make sense? Because they have significance to me and the reason is that to me it means that when God made me he incorporated in me everything I shall need unto eternity. He embodied everything within me, or the power to draw it forth as in the example of the root of the tree. With every appearance of a claim I can close my eyes and say "I have meat," and that breaks my attachment to this world and everyone in it. Why? Because of an experience. In my early years I too depended on God for supply, and I depended on patients to be the instruments through which supply would reach me. After awhile this did not work because it is not truth, but then the *I* dawned: "*I* is God. *I* is the Christ. *I* is the source. Then *I* is fulfillment and *I* do not need God or man." It makes no difference what kind of a claim can arise of insufficiency or limitation in any area, that word *I* pops up in my consciousness and then all attachment to this world is broken.

Everything is embodied in the *I* that I am and whatever is necessary to bring about healing is embodied in the *I* that I am. God fulfills itself as my being, so I need not reach out to God. I reach within to the *I* that is "closer than breathing" and then be patient and wait. I am not stilling mind, but I am getting very still while I am listening. Then the fourth-dimensional consciousness is on the scene, and if it has to do something, it will.

Always remember that no matter what language I use, I do not mean to still the mind by disuse but by using the mind in a different way. It goes back to the Master's statement: "The Father within" or Paul's statement: "The indwelling Christ." These both mean that within your consciousness is this presence and power, and how else can you go into your consciousness except in quietness and receptivity, and then let it come forth as bread or meat or resurrection or life eternal.

The Menehune of Hawaiian legend is definitely the Christ. It is something other than human, which in your need supplies you and satisfies you. Angels are the same thing. An angel is just the mediator fulfilling your needs, but it is the presence within—Master, Presence, Christ, the Buddha-mind. You have the illustration in the fairy tale, "Aladdin's Lamp." That is the meaning of Aladdin's Lamp. Just rub it and the genie appears, but be sure that what you are wishing for is spiritual or you are in witchcraft. The danger of all of it is that, whether you are thinking of Menehune, angels, Aladdin's Lamp, or Christ, you are thinking of something other than an activity of your own consciousness. You are expecting God to do something after this prayer, or after this treatment. You cannot expect the Christ to do something. Christ is a revelator revealing omnipresence. The fact that in the spiritual kingdom there is only *now* is proof that a prayer cannot do anything one hour from now. A prayer should reveal that which is.

Actually then, you only enter the mystical estate when you know the identity of the *I* that I Am. Am I a man desiring or requiring, or am *I* spirit already fulfilled? While you are under the law through the Ten Commandments, you are being improved and reformed and spiritualized, but when you are under grace, I am that *I Am*—and it means I am neither bad nor good.

Whatever spirit is, I am. I am neither young nor old. Whatever spirit is, I am. I am neither rich nor poor. Whatever spirit is, I am. I am the way, the truth, and the light.

God has fulfilled itself as me. This breaks all the attachments "out here," yet provides twelve baskets to share because if I do not share it, I am cut off from God's kingdom. Again, I do not share in order to please God. I must share as the fulfillment of my Self. In your humanhood you are usually good only because you are afraid of the penalty for being bad. That is natural to all human beings; but in the mystical life you are good, not for a reward nor for fear of punishment, but as fulfillment of your nature.

You have to work with every one of these principles. When the *I* first revealed itself to me when I was going through a period of lack, supply did eventually come, but there were months and months during which I had to remind myself each day, "I have." Your consciousness is being transformed from "I want, I need, I wish, I desire," to I have and why I have. Your consciousness is dying to its man-being and is being *reborn* into its Christ-being. *I,* Christ, is quite different from I, Joel—so I, Joel must die so that *I,* Christ can be born.

YOUR DOOR TO INFINITY

February 16, 1964
The Halekulani Hotel
Honolulu, Hawaii

IF YOU REMEMBER what we had this morning on tape number 4, side 2, Honolulu Infinite Way Study Center 1964, there is only one thing that can be added to that and I will not have to say too much about it because we had the subject recently, and that is *secrecy*. The vital art of this practice is the ability to keep it locked up within you and perform it and practice it without ever speaking of it to anyone. Never under any circumstances let it come through your lips until such time as you have completed the demonstration and are fully living in the consciousness that enables you to automatically turn within every hour of the day, every quarter hour of the day, and realize that right here where you are, in the midst of your meal, at any moment, you can turn within and you will be flooded with whatever you need: inspiration, light, wisdom, principles, courage, foresight, judgement, integrity. Whatever it is that may be the need of the moment, you just have to blink your eyes and immediately *I* have access to all that God has.

When you are demonstrating this in your life and the fruitage is apparent, then you can begin to teach it and impart it to others, but not before. If you try to tell it or teach it before you have demonstrated it, you will be telling something to someone else that you have not proven; you will lose your self-respect by setting yourself up as a teacher of something you do not know, or pretending that something is a principle which you have not demonstrated. At first there will be those who will tell you that it is selfishness, that you must give everything you have. No! Just because you know about it does not mean that you have attained the consciousness of it. Spiritually, never give that which you have not attained. If you learn of a principle that seems reasonable to you, practice it until your life shows it forth. Then when someone is led to you, you can share it because it will then multiply itself. The more you teach what you really *know*, the more it will multiply itself, but what you try to give another before you are ready, diminishes, and you have less of it.

Do you not see why I had to sit with this message as a practitioner in an office for sixteen years before I could teach it and before a book was written? There were sixteen years of practice before the first book was written, and then no one could deny or refute the principles of The Infinite Way or they would have been in the position the church was in when it said the world was not round after Christopher Columbus returned from his voyage. Yes, there were sixteen years before the first book, and then another seventeen years in which the message has gone around the world.

That is how you must be individually, until it is such a part of your life that it is a very living witness of it. Until then, do not teach anyone because you have nothing to teach. Spiritual teaching comes out of an attained consciousness, not out of an intellectual knowledge. Anyone with a quick mind can read these books and memorize these principles, but there is no power in reading or memorizing. One reviewer of a recent Infinite Way book said there is one thing that has to be said about this message: "The author himself is convinced that it is truth." Back in the old days I used to write articles that were called didactic. Why? Because I stated principles with positive conviction, which is the only way in which spiritual teaching can be fruitful. Until you have arrived at the point of conviction, do not try to teach—for the only worthwhile conviction is that which is based on demonstration. "By their fruits ye shall know them."[1] Until then, stay alone, even if you have to wait for sixteen years. A strange thing about truth is that it really does not have to be spoken. Once you have an inner conviction of it, it shines out of your inner being to those who are receptive.

This brings us to what might be called the very height of mysticism: Spiritually you are imparting only when you are in silence, when there is no activity of the conscious thinking mind taking place. You can prove it in this way: Take plants or birds or animals or infants, and sit by them in an absolute silence, not attempting to impart with the mind or through thoughts, but with an active receptivity: "Speak, Lord, thy servant heareth."[2] Then hear! As you sit in that listening attitude, with no attempt to impart, you are imparting it. You will notice that you have better crops and that the birds and the animals and the infants respond. Eventually you will also find adults who are responsive and receptive.

That is the reason I have a meditation before my work: to create a mental vacuum where I am not trying to impart any thoughts, and where members of the class or audience are not listening except within themselves, but not to me. When I have that vacuum, the imparting takes place and, no matter what I say, they receive truth. On some of the recent tapes we have noticed that I have spoken mistakes in the very reverse of what the truth is, and as far as I know only one student caught it. Why? Because students heard the truth in spite of the "lie" I was uttering. That is why there are people who cannot understand the language we are speaking, and yet who catch the message. As a matter of fact we have had deaf people who responded to the message when they were unable to hear, and the reason is that spiritual impartation is clearest when there is an absolute silence and a receptivity. You can bear witness to this yourself. If someone tells you he is spiritual, it would be impossible for you to believe him, yet there are those who have not even thought of such a thing and about whom you have said, "Oh! They are spiritual." Do you know what I think about "honest John" or "honest Bill" or "honest Jack"? *Silence* speaks the loudest. "What you *are* speaks so loudly that I cannot hear a thing you say," and in a spiritual message that is absolute truth.

Jesus says: "Thy sins be forgiven thee,"[3] yet you would probably have to spend a great deal of time trying to explain to someone why you are forgiving them. Jesus says: "I will take you into paradise this very night,"[4] but you would probably have to give a treatment that lasts an hour. Think of a mystical treatment: "What did hinder you?" and then realize how much time is wasted with treatments, all of which proves that it is not the treatment that is important but the *consciousness* behind the treatment. Then a smile should do it!

I am sure there can be no greater form of practice than what we have gone through for the past eight weeks, leading up to this morning's tape. When you reach the point where you know that your own consciousness is the access to infinity, you have the whole secret of life. Then there is nothing to do but practice. Once you are assured that you do not have to go to holy mountains or to holy temples, that infinity is "knocking at the door of your consciousness" and you have only to open that door, how much further can you go unless someone could take you by the hand and take you into heaven. Recognize that your consciousness is the door to the infinity in which you are living.

I live and move and have my being in infinity. I dwell in that secret infinity, so there is no place to go.

Close the eyes and open the ears, and remember that it does not mean you always have to physically close your eyes. Learn to be receptive to it with your eyes open, even when you are driving a car, and have the infinity of protection.

I had an experience that went into the supernatural. Perhaps I should not admit it, but I was driving a car ninety miles an hour on a highway. A car was parked on the side of the road where the driver was changing a tire, another car was right beside it going forward, another car was coming toward me, and I was traveling ninety miles an hour. I was absolutely blocked, and all I know was that my ear was open and all of a sudden I was through those cars and in front of them. It happened on a highway in the western states, and certainly you know that conscious thinking would not have given me that protection.

Infinity embraces us and sometimes that is called the Robe. This is the meaning of the Robe of mysticism. It means you are cloaked in it, covered with it, embraced in it. Another mystic called it "The Cloud of Unknowing." Of course unknowing is based on the truth that you know, but you do not have to know it forever and forever. You have to learn it so that you know it, just as you had to recite the alphabet and the multiplication table. Once you know that your consciousness is the door or the access to infinity–infinite supply, infinite love, infinite joy, infinite life, infinite peace–you will no longer look to "man whose breath is in his nostrils" and no longer will you fear "what mortal man can do to you," because figuratively speaking you will close your eyes and get into that silence of listening–and then watch the grace of God take over. In time it gets to be spontaneous. It acts to provide for you before you know you have a need, but "go and tell no man what things ye have seen."[5]

The day will arrive when someone will come to you and say: "Your life is a miracle. Tell me how you did it." Then you can begin to impart, but be sure to caution about secrecy. Aligned with secrecy is sacredness. Do not ever allow anyone to treat you as if you are a human being. Maintain the dignity of your spiritual Sonship. Let no one get too personal or too intimate: "Thus far and no further. Come out and be separate."

There is another spiritual principle: "What you hold yourself to be, that you are to others." If you are holding up to this world the image of your Self as you believe your Self to be, then the estimate you have of yourself is the estimate the world puts on you. If the world is not according you sufficient dignity, it is because you are cheating your Self in your own estimation and then the world does likewise. People who have titles such as doctor, minister, rabbi, priest, or professor are always held with a measure of dignity unless they themselves let down the bars. Then the dignity they had through their titles breaks down. "What you *are* speaks so loudly I cannot hear a thing you say."

When you know who you are, you do not need either a title or an outer robe. Even with these you could not hold sufficient dignity any longer than you hold within yourself the right estimation. It is a very sacred thing that happens to you when you know you have access to God. It sets you apart because you have demonstrable proof that you have access to infinity through your own consciousness. Then you understand what a great person you really are, one who is a dweller in the secret place of the most High. It does not mean you are aloof. No! You are in the world but not of it.

Regardless of how long it may take, make up your mind that your inner consciousness is the means of your access to God, and keep practicing it until you have demonstrated it. When you make that discovery you will really find that "man is an island"—an island bounded by God.

IMPERSONALIZATION AND SILENCE

March 15, 1964
The Halekulani Hotel
Honolulu, Hawaii

REMEMBERING THE SERIES that we concluded before we left on the trip to California, when you enter meditation and close your eyes to this world, remember that you are now in the corridor—or at least you are behind the door that opens to infinity. Through your consciousness you have access to the spiritual infinity of God, the kingdom of God, the realm of God, the world of God, the activity of God, the substance and the law of God. All of this is within you and yet the Master says "I stand at the door and knock."[1] *I*, the infinity, the kingdom, the realm, the world, the activity, thence, the law of God am closer to you than breathing, awaiting your invitation to enter—not to enter from outside because the kingdom of God is already within you, but to go from the center of you to the circumference—from the inner to the outer. This active meditation is really the opening of an inner door.

In Los Angeles we started off with the dedication of a new study center, the one that has been opened by Mrs. Muhl. It is small, seats about forty students, is beautifully furnished, and will give an atmosphere for those out in the valley. California is certainly thriving; we had close to five hundred students in the Los Angeles class and close to four hundred in San Francisco.

World work gets a great deal of attention in California, but you can see that world work is only going to produce fruitage as students can rise above their personal convictions. This presents a problem because we must in no wise lose our convictions. In other words it would be wrong to lose our convictions of what we believe to be right politically, economically, commercially, and internationally. When you come to world work you have to be in a position of being able to completely put those aside, first by acknowledging that no matter how much you are convinced that you are right, perhaps you are wrong.

Let me illustrate: In my early years in the business world I was naturally a voter of the Republican ticket in national affairs because in those days it was inconceivable that the Democratic party could select an adequate candidate for the presidency. When Al Smith came along with the liberal ideas of social security, although the program he had in mind was wonderful, it would have been impossible to sell businessmen on the idea. It was so contradictory to the old status quo that we could not be convinced of the rightness of it. In other words, we were wrong, and so, if we were praying about it, the height of our prayer would have been: "Oh God, help us maintain our status quo!" I know what I mean when I say you must have convictions, but you must also acknowledge that they may be wrong or they may be outmoded.

When you go into prayer you do not try to change a bad condition into a good one; you have to be high enough so you can go down the middle and say, "What I am looking for is a spiritual idea or plan." You witness this in the work we have done in dealing with strikes. Spiritual work on a strike problem cannot be undertaken by thinking in terms of a human solution to the problem. When you are no longer interested in a solution which would be beneficial to one side and can go straight down the middle, then out of that pure meditation an idea would evolve which would be absolutely beneficial to both sides.

So it is that the world makes this mistake: A member of the conservative party in England goes on the air and says, "Even though we may lose, we know God is on our side." Germany goes to war and says: "God is with us." Americans go to war and say "Democracy and Christianity are on our side." Is it not clear that you cannot approach any subject of this world spiritually with a preconceived opinion of right or wrong? Then when you open your consciousness to a spiritual solution, it comes forth in a human way that you could never have thought of or planned. All over this world there are prayer groups praying for world peace, and I do not think I am exaggerating when I say that ninety-nine percent of it is a waste of human energy. Why? Because they are all going to a spiritual God to find a human solution based on their ideas of the rightness of it. Until you understand that God is Spirit, you will never be successful with prayer—whether on the personal level, the national level, or the international level. When you come to the conclusion that God is spirit, you will then seek the intervention of spirit, and you will watch in what way it unfolds humanly.

If you can do that you will be more successful in spiritual healing, because spiritual healing is a wonderful subject if you can rise above the desire to heal someone, if you can rise above pity for an individual's diseases and pains, if you can rise above the desire to get someone out of his distresses. Even if you succeeded, ninety-nine out of one-hundred would go back into something worse–but where there is a transformation of consciousness, that is something else.

I will go back again to my first spiritual experience. Frankly, I contacted the practitioner only to be healed of a severe cold. That is the reason I went to see him, and I was sure I was going to get rid of the cold through prayer. That, and that alone, was my motive. However, he did not understand prayer in that way because, when I left his office, I could no longer smoke and I could no longer drink or play cards or bet on the horses. All that left me. He had been praying in the sense of wholeness and a transformation of consciousness took place. The cold was gone but that was the smallest part of the demonstration.

Now we come to the major point of this entire subject, which is the ability to impersonalize. Let us see it in this light: God has never made any one of us greater than another. We all have equal capacities. I do not mean that we have all brought them to the surface, but we all have the potentiality of infinity. There could be no such thing as a God if one were better than another, because that would reduce God to the level of man. This is one of the subjects that is now giving so much concern in the church world.

The new manuscripts reveal that Jesus was not born of a virgin, that he was not physically resurrected after his death, and that he was just a man who, after spending eighteen years in the Essenes group studying their scripture, went out to teach them. By his elevation of consciousness, some of the miracles of spiritual healing took place, healings which we do not call miracles today. It is also revealed that he was always talking in mystical language when he said: "I am the bread" or "I am the door" or "I am life eternal." In other words he was not referring to Jesus Christ, he was referring to the Christ of Jesus. It also shows clearly when he was speaking about baptism, that no man can be baptized of water. The church is now faced with the problem of how to introduce all of this without causing a major catastrophe in the world. I think they have agreed on a gradual introduction into Scripture and that by gradually teaching students in theological seminaries, it will gradually reach the children of the next generation so that truth can be taught more or less as we teach it.

When Jesus says: "Call no man on earth your father,"[2] he is revealing that the creative principle of one is the same for all. Therefore, we must all be equal, but not in forms of expression. We have beauty, but beauty is not found only in a rose. We can see beauty in a stone or in a piece of wood or in a rock. It makes it impossible to say that one form is more beautiful than another. So with us: We have to see that intelligence is God bestowed, but we will not all use the same amount of intelligence. In other words, the amount we express is determined by the amount we draw forth, because it is all stored up within us.

Here you come to the transition out of metaphysics, where for the most part you were concerned with effects: demonstrating health or supply or purity or the overcoming of false appetites. You cannot bring that state of consciousness into mysticism. In mysticism you can live only with the attainment of "that mind which was also in Christ Jesus," the attainment of the Robe, the Whole Man, and then let it wash out the impurities. This takes you into the realm of *I, Me, My.* You cannot get away from those three words in mysticism because, until there is a recognition that there is an *I* "standing at the door of consciousness," until there is a recognition of a *Me* within, until there is a recognition of *My* kingdom, *My* peace, *My* grace, there is no possibility of entering the mystical kingdom. When however there is that recognition, consciousness is immediately opened to receive it and eventually you come to that place where you can say with Paul: "I live, yet not I, Christ liveth my life.[3] It is that indwelling presence that is living my life."

Many who review my books and who know nothing of mysticism think this message is an escape, living in a mythical kingdom. We know it is not that at all. Opening ourselves to this inflow gives us a keener ability in the marketplace, in the arts and professions, because this fourth-dimensional activity not only activates us but motivates us to lose interest in "our" benefits. Our thinking then becomes in terms of the universal good rather than of the person.

You are reading about a greater degree of harmony in the relationships between the Catholics, the Protestants, and the Hebrews: not on the level of the average citizen, but on the level of the higher church authorities. This is the reason behind it: In our writings you notice that I use the words Messiah and Christ as synonyms. In fact, when, in my talks with members of the Hebrew synagogue, I was asked what they lacked and I said "Christ," they were shocked until I brought out the fact that Messiah and Christ are the same. It is now official that, since 2,000 B.C., Christ and Messiah mean the same thing. It is in the new revelations. Furthermore, it is now becoming clear to those who are familiar with what is taking place that Judaism and Christianity are the same thing. They all stem out of the Old Testament. Their realization that in truth there is but one religion, will begin in minor ways to change their attitude towards each other, and later it will reach down into the masses. Eventually we will see the end of religious bigotry, not because man is getting better, but because he is receiving more light or spiritual truth.

To me the greatest part of the new unfoldment was that it completely revealed the correctness of the "two men"–the man of earth and the spiritual man, and the nature of that which brings to light in him the spiritual man. Even the metaphysical world has not accepted two men. No! "You are spiritual and you are perfect," which is ludicrous when you witness whom they were calling spiritual and perfect. In the New Testament, man is identified by Paul in his two-fold nature, as the "man of earth" who must "put off mortality and put on immortality,"[4] and this, we are told, is by a transformation of consciousness. Then there were the two means, as it is in The Infinite Way: Either direct intervention of God as in the case of Moses on the mountaintop, or through the intercession of a spiritual teacher.

As I said on the tape this morning, I have never been able to prove anything I have revealed. Therefore, this message has had to be presented without proof, as a set of principles, as a way of life, with a proof resting on your individual demonstration. What it has done to my life will not convince you. It is no proof until you yourself experience the proof. For this reason you cannot advertise or proselyte, because you have no proof to offer. Yet, by your living of these principles without speaking of them, others do witness what takes place and are led to you. That has been the secret of our work.

There are not too many authors whose books have sold beyond the million mark, and yet this author did, without advertising or proselytizing. Why? Because the message was felt. Someone out in the world felt it. I am illustrating for you the principle of the invisible. You do not have to speak truth; you do not have to advertise truth. You have to live it, and then it spreads out from you without your even being aware of how it happened.

None of us know why people are influenced in this direction. The only thing we do know is that it is not humanly induced. It is so with salesmanship and also with principles that are necessary to your particular work. You would be surprised how little needs to be spoken about, except when the way opens for the right words to be spoken. Until then it has to be held in consciousness.

The greatest power on earth is the power of silence. You cannot express spiritual power in words or thoughts, nor can spiritual power be brought through with words or thoughts. Only through silence when the senses are at rest can spiritual power come through. That is why, whether you are in prayer for some individual concern of your own or for another, or whether it is on the wider level of state or world, the rehearsing in your mind of these basic principles is only a step leading to a period of absolute silence in which that invisible spirit, whatever its nature may be, can come through. If you are not careful you will be trapped in the belief in temporal power, the power of numbers or the power of some human "do good" activity.

We are about to enter a period nationally which, if it is allowed to run its course, will have very injurious effects on the nation for the next twenty years or more. That is the period in Congress where we enter the subject of Civil rights. It is purely a political matter on both sides; neither side is deeply interested in the Negro.

On both sides it is a political matter, like a ball game where the Negro is the football. Under the guise of doing good, they will throw this ball back and forth and the Negro will be more despised than ever. Feeling is more intense in the South today than it has been in recent years because of what has been stirred up. There is a rightful solution to that problem, but personally I do not think anyone concerned in it has a rightful solution. That can be brought to light by prayer, because nothing is beyond the realm of prayer. In this period that lies just ahead, remember this: Instead of trying to work out the rights and wrongs of it, open yourself to a spiritual grace. In this way we might be able to introduce something that will change the picture.

Someday it will have to be proven that "ten righteous men" can save a city. When? I do not know, but it could be today. Spiritually it is still true that you must put up the sword. Spiritually it is still true that, "if you live by the sword you will die by the sword." Therefore, if the prophecy of Steinmetz is to come true that in this century spiritual power will be proven, this is the time to prove it. Spiritual power means introducing the spirit of God into the situation–not to prove right or wrong–and then letting the chips fall where they may.

Recently the people of India who represent Advaita, which is the absolute teaching, recommended the Infinite Way books. I had a letter from one branch of it saying that, while they are advocating my books, they are still in disagreement on one subject, which is that of spiritual healing. Their attitude is fatalism, to accept things the way they are. In our work we do not agree that God creates or even tolerates good and evil. Even in their prayers they go to God with a concept that either good or evil is all right with them, because they believe that good and evil has a part in the spiritual kingdom.

This question faced me thirty years ago, and of course you know the answer is very clear in these writings: "God has no pleasure in your dying[5] . . . God is too pure to behold iniquity."[6] In other words there is no such thing as evil in the consciousness of God or in the creation of God. Therefore, we are dealing with something of an illusory nature, and when we come to it, we find there is nothing there. This is quite different from letting God have the credit for it in both cases. I could not *know* this because there was no place in which to find it out. Therefore, it was necessary to go to the Spirit with a complete freedom from concepts for the purpose of enlightenment and then receive the truth that in the presence of God there is fulfillment and freedom—freedom from any sense of limitation.

Make this an important part of your prayer, meditation, or communion: Do not have any "golden calf" on your mind; do not have any images or reliances. Just have an open consciousness, a receptive consciousness, and then what comes is the "signs following." The signs following testify to it and to its rightness. If you get any answer that is universally blessing in nature, it is from God, because neither the "devil" nor personal sense can be responsible for pure, universally good action.

THE BREAD YOU CAST
ON THE WATERS

March 22, 1964
The Halekulani Hotel
Honolulu, Hawaii

PROBABLY ONE OF THE GREATEST revelations of The
Infinite Way is this: No amount of truth can benefit you,
no matter how profound it is. You are benefitted only by
your realization and your utilization of truth. Truth will
not set you free. "Ye shall know the truth," and this
means *know*. In the same way, every effort you make
towards acquiring truth brings truth nearer home to you.
I try to tell students not to depend on my books and not
to depend on my tapes, because in and of themselves
they have no effect. I have seen this happen in the lives
of thousands of people who have read the books and
heard the tapes. On the other hand, with hundreds of
students I have witnessed a wonderful effect. What is the
difference? Do you practice it? I know of people who
receive gifts of books and write to me and say: "I have
read your book and it is beautiful!"

The effort you put into acquiring truth determines
what you will get from it. "The bread you cast on the
waters is the bread that will return unto you."[1] I never
want to see an Infinite Way student turned away for lack
of money, but neither do I want to see students continued in charity, because it will not demonstrate the

543

principle of The Infinite Way. The Infinite Way is very clear that the secret of supply is giving, and I am not talking only about money. You do not get from The Infinite Way what you do not give. In our capitalistic days anyone could be successful by working hard enough, because life gives back what you put into it.

In The Infinite Way I have witnessed so many people listening to lectures, reading books, going to classes, and accomplishing nothing. Why? Because they put nothing into it. I know that the whole secret of life is outpouring. This is true in any branch of life, whether you are studying an academic subject or whether you are studying a spiritual subject. Throughout my Infinite Way experience I have tried to see to it that every one who contributed to its activity received something in the nature of reimbursement. In other words, I have never allowed anyone to work for The Infinite Way and say, "It will not cost you anything." No, otherwise a hierarchy of special privileges would be set up.

I could follow that up with our subject of this morning's tape: When an individual has been touched by the Spirit, you do not have to teach this to him and you do not even have to tell this to him, because one of the signs of spiritual endowment is gratitude. Many times people write and tell me they want to come to Hawaii to study with me and I write back and say, "No." When they discover someone else came here, they want to know why, and I tell them, something guided me, that they were not ready. There are several signs that indicate when a student is ready. Most of the signs are not tangible; it is something you feel, and one sign is always that there is gratitude, there is a love, there is a sharing. A teacher can always tell when a student is beginning to be inspired by the spirit because the student's nature changes in that regard. Where formerly he may have "paid a bill," now he shows signs of a tenderness where gratitude is concerned. In other words, he could no longer be ungrateful any more than he could be immoral.

It is for this reason that we do not teach anyone to be grateful or to be moral. We do not tell students they must stop smoking, or stop drinking, or stop anything else. That is none of our business. Our business is to impart the spirit, and let it do the purifying. Likewise, we cannot tell students to be grateful. All we can do is bring out the principle, and show them the basis from which we are working. A person who is spiritually endowed automatically finds supply. Actually, it is a miracle to watch this. Therefore, the object of our work is to impart the spirit, not to change humanhood. In the same way it is no use teaching anyone to be honest. For three thousand years the world has had the Ten Commandments. Our function is to impart the spirit. I would like every Infinite Way student to see that we are not trying to improve any student's humanhood. We are not concerning ourselves with whether they are moral or whether they are grateful. What we are concerned with is this: Are they seeking spiritual light? Then we can impart, and this is the major theme of The Infinite Way, the impartation of the spirit. This takes care of everything else that is necessary.

In the age of metaphysics it has been the normal thing to give testimonies and to make promises. Many in the New Thought movements merely promise they can demonstrate anything they want to demonstrate, but you know it has not worked out that way, and the metaphysical work has shrunk. We have come into an age, inaugurated by The Infinite Way, in which it is revealed that you cannot go to God for "things." Things will be added, but the moment you go to God for things, you have lost it. The Infinite Way has to base its teaching entirely on spiritual wisdom, spiritual consciousness, spiritual grace, and then let it unfold and reveal the testimonies. I may have made a million dollars or I may have attained health, but that does not mean you will.

Is it not clear that the demonstration of spiritual harmony is an individual matter? Reading the books and hearing the tapes and attending the classes will not do it for you, and no longer can you believe they will. We know that the only demonstration that can be made is a change of consciousness. Therefore, health and supply is an individual demonstration of consciousness. In other words, even if a hundred of us attained these, the one-hundred-and-first might not. This is our function, that the material state of consciousness die and the spiritual state of consciousness be reborn. If we can succeed with that, all the rest will be added. If we cannot succeed with that, we cannot add the things.

The Infinite Way stands alone in this, that it cannot promise anything to anyone. But, if you are seeking a change of consciousness, that we can help you with. What it does for you I have no way of knowing, because with each one of us, the moment we touch the spiritual path, we have to be purged of whatever illusions we have. Some of us look on certain means of income as natural, and we have to lose that. Others look on health as natural, and we have to lose that. In other words we are always losing our material sense of things and being reborn into the spiritual sense of things. No one remembers more than I my own period of severe lack, but no one could be more grateful today than I am because out of that experience came the principle that is the foundation of The Infinite Way. Furthermore, I know of no other way in which it could have been revealed except by forcing me with my back to the wall. Some of us are obstinate, and we have to have our backs to the wall.

We have a fund through which libraries, colleges, universities, and seminaries receive free copies of Infinite Way books if they wish them. Any library, university, or school of philosophy in the United States and Canada may have our books, and all we need to know is that they desire them. We have students who like to contribute to this activity. In England, we have a fund which comes out of our Infinite Way fund, and four of our English editions are likewise available there. In addition, there are some countries where funds cannot be sent out of the country, and students receive free books. There must always be an activity of that kind in The Infinite Way; you might call it benevolence if you like. However, never must that give you any false notions on the idea of benevolence.

If you read this paper up to this point, a question is immediately going to strike you. You know that nothing can be accomplished without the attainment of spiritual consciousness, so the question is this: "How do I attain it, or how do I attain more of it, or how do I attain it more quickly?" Unfortunately we have to listen to the Master when he says, "The way is straight and narrow, and few there be that enter."[2] Yes, unfortunately, but you know he was wise because he knew that it is not easily attained—and you can see the reason. The moment you think of attained spiritual light, some reason enters your mind by which you hope to benefit from it. That is the barrier. Someone wants it for health, or for supply, or for companionship, or for peace on earth, and that is the barrier.

That is the meaning of self-surrender. Self-surrender does not mean one-half the things most people think it means. It only means surrendering the things you think you want. Whatever you are looking for in life, surrender it, because it is a barrier to the major attainment. If I go to God because I want health, wealth, or because I want something else, I am going to God as a beggar for one thing, and then I am accusing God of withholding.

The secret is this: The gifts of God are not material. That is the secret. There is no way for a human being to know the nature of God's gifts, because the human being has only to look around to see what others have and judge by that—and that is not the nature of the kingdom of God. "My kingdom is not of this world."[3] One of the greatest helps in healing others is having a conscious remembrance of that when you go into prayer. Think what would happen if you could eradicate from your thought the kingdom of man and go into your meditations in the same way explorers originally went to the North and South Poles, not knowing what they would find. If you could go into your meditations knowing, "I do not know what to pray for, because I do not know what the kingdom of God is like and I do not know what God has to give," you would have great success.

Very often it really shocks me when I am called on for help in serious cases and I remember that God does not care two hoots. I think of all the people dying from accidents or cancer or polio, and God doing nothing about it. Yes, it shocks me, but out of that shock comes the ability to say: "I do not know what I am going to

You for, but here I am." Think how useless it would be to go to God to save someone's life when others are dying untimely deaths. Think how horrible it would be to go to God for supply for someone, when hundreds of people are starving. If you can eliminate from your thought the idea of saving people's lives, bringing them supply, or getting them out of prison, and can realize: "Thy grace is my sufficiency, and I do not know what thy grace is," the miracles take place in your experience.

It helps me to know that God is spirit, because then it frees me from all attempts to draw forth anything of a material nature from God. God is spirit, and then I have to rest on that. Whatever God's grace is, whatever God's gift is, it must be spiritual. It appears to us, when it comes, in some material form, but you know it is not material. It appears materially because we still have enough material concepts of the spiritual kingdom, but it is not. It is not that a sick body has been made well; it is that the body of God has been revealed. In our ignorance we say, "My body has been made well." No! We have received God's body. And if you could only see supply the way it is, you would know it is not money. You are still "painting spiritual gifts" with a material form. As a matter of fact the kingdom of God is incorporeal; therefore, God's gift is incorporeal. When you say, "This is more or better matter," you have not recognized: "This is still spiritual, in spite of appearances." There was a man in whose heart a small valve disappeared, and the doctors said no man could live twenty-four hours without it. He lived over thirty years! Why? He was not living through a material heart, but through the grace of God which did not need a material heart. And one of our patients who was blind has complete eyesight today—but has no eyes. She "sees without eyes." Why? She received God's grace of sight—not in the form of physical eyes.

FREEDOM IS AN ACTIVITY
WITHIN YOUR OWN CONSCIOUSNESS

March 29, 1964
Between Two Worlds
Honolulu, Hawaii

THE HUMAN BEING LIVES in a world of material sense, and this means that his measurement of life consists of amounts, weights, degrees, abundances, limitations. One of the first things an infant learns is that two things cannot occupy the same space at the same time. In other words, when he hits his head against a table he discovers that either the head or the table belongs there, but not both. As we grew up we measured everything in that manner; in relationship of power we ascribed good power to some germs and evil power to some germs. We ascribed powers of good to some individuals, powers of evil to other individuals. Therefore, in the materialistic sense of life we are always conferring powers upon some one or some thing. The entire human experience is made up of this combination of good and evil, externalized good and evil, and we give power to everything external to ourselves. As a matter of fact we seldom reserve any power at all, any dominion to our selves. Practically everything good comes from someone or something, and practically everything evil comes from someone or something, and we are either the beneficiary or the victim. Rarely do we acknowledge

551

that we have dominion. This is the materialistic concept of life.

As you come to a mystical teaching you begin to reverse this, and as a rule you start with the word God. Not only do you begin to give more power to God and less power to the external world, but you even give power to God "over" the external world. In other words you turn to God as a power over disease, and all orthodox religion is built on that premise because all of their prayers are for healing or for well-being. Unlike the metaphysicians, they do not have the same faith that it is going to happen, but orthodoxy does give lip service to the belief that God is a power over disease. It is in this same way that families ask for prayers of ministers for their sinful relatives, thereby giving power to God over false appetites and other sins. Then you start to give power to God over lack and limitations, turning to God to help you attain your daily bread, and so you have now begun to acknowledge that, although evil has power, there is a something called God or truth which, under certain circumstances, has power over those evils.

You are now living between two worlds, the world of material sense whereby you give power to persons, things, and conditions, and the world of spiritual awareness where you begin to believe that there is something greater than those external powers of evil. And so you begin the search for God or truth, but always you are living between the two worlds, part of the time in the world of acknowledging the power of mind and matter, part of the time living in the world of accepting God as the greater power of the two. It is a volleying back and forth.

The recorded history of the world shows that there have been very few people who ever got out from between those two worlds, and the reason is this: You cannot get out unless you have a revelation within yourself. Moses may prove the non-power of Pharaoh, Elijah may prove the non-power of his persecutors, and the non-power of lack, and limitation, Jesus may prove the non-power of sin, disease, and death, but their realization does not get you out. You read about it and you say, "How wonderful!" and then you wish you could go and do likewise, but you cannot and the reason is this: You have not rightly understood that only God can get you free. You have thought that sitting at the feet of the Master would get you free in spite of the fact that it did not free the Hebrew people who sat before the Master. No, and it did not free the Buddhists who sat before Buddha, nor did it free the Chinese who had the opportunity of knowing Lao-Tzu. However, you believe that hearing truth or reading truth is going to give you your freedom and it is not.

This error has been perpetuated by the churches because they seem to give the impression that if you attend church, support it, become baptized, or observe the holy days, you will attain your freedom. This has never proven to be true. No religious activity has ever freed its people. As a matter of fact what it has done is to bind them more deeply in bondage, because the ultimate truth is that you can only be free by the words of God. Man must live by the word of God. Is not the word of God the truth that comes forth from my lips? Yes, to me it is, but to you it is only the way. It is setting forth the way in which you can be free, but it cannot promise you your freedom. Yes! You may experience temporary health and temporary freedoms, but this is not the freedom. The freedom can only come from God, and that can only take place as an activity within your own consciousness.

In some of our classwork we have had experiences in which students have attained their realization and their freedom and have had the feeling that I did it for them—and I did not. It was their responsiveness in their consciousness because, had I done it for one, I would have done it equally for everyone. It would be my greatest joy to see everyone on the face of the earth free this minute, but I do not have that power. The grace of God operates in my consciousness, and then each student receives it in proportion to his own readiness. This is the reason that some students have tremendous experiences with their first meditation, and some, five or ten years later. It is usually a gradual experience, because it is very difficult to receive truth in one glimpse and live. The shock would be too great, and so a transition of consciousness takes place. In those moments when I could be still and receptive to the still, small voice it was given to me that the way is meditation. Then I knew that this was the way in which ultimately everyone could be set free who could have sufficient patience—with meditation.

I would like you to see what sometimes happens with sudden revelations. I had been giving a class in Victoria, B.C., and was on my way to California for another class. I took the plane to Seattle and, while waiting in the Seattle airport to catch another plane, an idea struck me out of the blue. It was so powerful that I immediately took out paper and pen and began to write. I wrote one and one-half pages, and I entitled it "Between Two Worlds." That was twelve years ago, and I was never able to go further than those one and one-half pages until yesterday morning on Maui when the whole secret flooded me. Remember, this was after twelve years of waiting! Each year I took out those pages and read them, but nothing further would come.

I know meditation opens consciousness and I know that prepares the way for you in your consciousness to receive it. When Peter recognized Jesus as the Christ, Jesus answered: "Flesh and blood hath not revealed it unto thee, but my father which is in heaven."[1] And when he took the three disciples to the Mount of Transfiguration, why did he not take the twelve? He knew that only three were prepared to see that all the Hebrew prophets were right there on the mountaintop, even though they were supposed to be dead and buried. Only three disciples could recognize the truth that there is no death. Perhaps if we could have the transfiguration experience, we would hear him say: "These men never lived in the world. They lived in your consciousness. Therefore, you are witnessing only that which your consciousness can embrace."

In this period of living between two worlds you are faced, as the Master was faced, with temptations. We hear about his three temptations, but actually every experience he went through during his ministry was a temptation. Whether he saw an insane man, whether he saw people who were "an hungered," or whether he saw a withered tree, they were all temptations. What manner of temptation? To judge by material sense. What about Peter's mother-in-law who was "old enough to die so why not let her die peacefully"? Yes, judging by material sense, but in his ascended consciousness, having seen God as the Father, Peter knew there could not be a material daughter. In other words the temptation to see an old woman had to be translated. And as you go back and see that God is the substance of all form, then you have God as the substance of the seed, right up to the "old" lady—and you then have the old lady as ageless as God. If you could see that, she would be healed.

That happened to me in California. I was called to visit a woman in her eighties who was dying, principally of the belief of old age. Her family were metaphysicians and they wanted to see life proven. I visited her and sat with her for quite a while, and she rose up well. I was then asked, "She was not going to do anything more on earth, so why did you do it?" My answer was this: "I was interested in proving that God is the life of individual being. My business is to prove it, but what she does is her business." God does not need to be proven but I had to prove it.

Therefore, in this period of living between two worlds, you are going to be called on to face temptations, as we were called upon to face a tidal wave several nights ago. In your material sense, a tidal wave is a destructive power; but, since you are between two worlds—even before the tidal wave strikes—you are going to have to see a picture of it in your mind's eye. Face it!

Is there a material universe, or does that tidal wave represent a material sense of universe, and is it not the truth that consciousness is the only cause, the only law, and the only effect? Therefore, consciousness must be the substance of the waves, not only consciousness but *My* consciousness, since there is no other. Do I have a destructive power in my consciousness? No! Having realized the spiritual nature of the universe, there is nothing in me that wants to destroy anyone or anything, and I realize that my consciousness is not even mine but

God's. Therefore, is there anything destructive in God's consciousness?

In orthodox religion you were trained to believe that God causes storms and fires and desolation, that these are "acts of God." If you are living between two worlds, you have at least come to the point where you understand that the creative principle of life could not have created anything destructive to itself. You would otherwise be leaving out the element of truth and love, making God less than man or putting God on the level of man. Therefore, since you are between two worlds, there is enough material sense left in you to be tempted by the appearance of the tidal wave. However, there must be enough elevation of consciousness to be able to sit down and realize: "What am I accepting? Am I accepting external powers? Am I accepting power in things, or am I accepting that all dominion is given unto *Me*–and this means individual consciousness? If all power is in individual consciousness, then all power is good and there is no power external to it." Then you can rest!

The next time you may be faced with an epidemic, and the next time with an election, and since you are living between two worlds, you will acknowledge that there is a temptation to believe that there is a destructive or evil power in the infection or the contagion or the election. Then also there is enough elevation of consciousness in you that you can sit down and look it in the face, as Jesus looked at Pilate and said: "Thou couldest have no power over me,"[2] over man, over the world, since all power, all dominion, is the consciousness of mankind. "No weapon that is formed against thee shall prosper,"[3] if you have learned not to take up the sword.

Why do we have a double-edged sword? Because the sword we are pointing at our neighbor's throat has a reverse side which is pointed at our own.

While you are living between two worlds, acknowledge that material sense (the material sense of life) says there is a power in the body—power to be healthy or to be diseased or to be sinful. Then draw yourself up into your higher consciousness and realize that it is only material sense that is telling you this because in the Garden of Eden there is no power, there is just pure being. Material sense has hypnotized you into accepting the belief of three score years and ten, a few more or a few less. But if you look out at this world, do you see anything destructive to you and to your body? It is only your acceptance of an aging power, a deteriorating power, that makes you subject to it, just as you formerly believed that you would catch cold by sitting in a draft or by getting your feet wet. Now you know that even the medical profession says that cannot happen.

By your higher consciousness you know that there is no influence out here in the air that is aging you, but you will not prove this except in proportion as you open your consciousness several times a day to the realization that your consciousness is an access to infinity and infinity is flowing in you and through you and as you—*now*. You are not influenced by the thoughts, opinions, and concepts that are floating around in the air in human belief, but you are subject only to the still, small voice. Do you not see that you then build a consciousness in which you specifically open yourself to a divine inflow of truth? Then you discover that man really does live by every word of truth that flows into your consciousness.

Hearing this message and reading it is no different than a lesson that is given to you in a schoolroom. You have to take the lesson home and study it, assimilate it and practice it until it becomes your own. My telling you that your consciousness is an inlet to and an outlet from infinity is of no more benefit to you than when Ralph Waldo Emerson said: "Your mind is an inlet to and an outlet from the mind of God." It is true. He gave the truth, but it has to be practiced until the experience happens and you begin to live it. Then you will come back and listen for more, but by then you will be receiving it from the same source from which Emerson received it.

A responsible guru will tell his students, "I am your guru and you listen to all that I tell you. You follow my precepts and you practice my lessons, and you give your loyalty and your faithfulness to me; but remember that I am only your guru because the voice of God is speaking through me, and the true God is the voice of God when it speaks to you." He does not want to hold his students in bondage to being students forever; he wants to see them go out and be gurus.

So it is that we want to see this entire world receptive and responsive to the still, small voice, to receive the word, and therefore we say: "What has been given to me has been given to me by revelation, but do not be content until you too are receiving it by revelation, because you must live as I live—by the word of God." Then the new generation will be brought into the world with that, and we will not have to take them out of material sense nor will they have to live between two worlds. They can be brought up in spiritual consciousness.

In facing the temptation that there is an external power, go back instantly and realize that consciousness is the basic substance, cause and law of all creation. Therefore, all creation manifests its qualities, character and nature because creation is the heir to all of those. This shows you why you do not need God over error.

THE MAN WHO HAS HIS
BEING IN CHRIST

April 5, 1964
Between Two Worlds
Honolulu, Hawaii

THE SERIES OF TAPES we are working with now is called "The Oahu–Maui Series" because some of the tapes have been made here at The Infinite Way Study Center, another message was made at The Kapiolani Center on Oahu, and still others were made on Maui.

Those who have worked with this series should now find it easier to bring about that transition in themselves from the man of earth to that man who has his being in Christ. This entire series has to do with that subject. Part of the series is entitled "Between Two Worlds," and the two worlds revealed are the world that is made up, on one hand, of personal sense–man whose breath is in his nostrils, the natural man, the man of earth–and on the other hand, the Son of God, the man of spiritual discernment, the man of Christ-consciousness. We were born as the natural man, but we have been told that we must die as this man and be reborn of the spirit so that even our prayers will be "in spirit and in truth." Through this series you have learned that, as long as you are judging by what you see, hear, taste, touch, or smell, or even think, you are in the world of the creature, "the natural man (who) is not under the law of God, neither indeed can be."[1]

Think what that means. As long as you are judging by appearances, as long as you are seeing good and evil, believing in good and evil, you are not under the law of God. Shocking as that may sound, you may as well accept it. When you make the transition to the man who lives by "every word that proceedeth out of the mouth of God,"[2] you are then forming no judgments, but rather you are creating a vacuum within yourself resulting in an attitude of listening so that divine judgement may be rendered. Then you will discover that you never hear or see good or evil, but that the man and the universe of God's creating is revealed to you.

Remember that it is not that you are seeing many things and many people as evil or erroneous and are beginning to declare that they are all good. No! That is just mythology. You are not to call the human scene good any more than you are to call it evil. That is the mistake of metaphysics which says, "I am spiritual" or "You are spiritual" or "He is spiritual" when all the time we know better inside because, even though we may not be able to read the thoughts of others, at least we can read our own. We do not change from seeing a lot of evil to seeing everything good. No, we stop declaring either good or evil and allow the judgment to be rendered within us. Then it will be neither good nor evil, but spiritual. The one world is the world of human judgment based on appearances and the conditioned mind, and the other world is the world that is revealed to us when we no longer form any judgements.

Recently I read a very interesting book written by a brilliant man. What made it interesting to me was that the author named about fifty men and women in contemporary history and gave his evaluation of them and, by reading what he had to say, I could have told you the author's religion, race, and profession, even if I did not know who the man was. Why? Because everything he wrote revealed the concepts of a particular religion, race, and profession. On the other hand one half of the world would believe the opposite and his opinions would have been ridiculed by a different religion, race, or condition of politics. Therefore, brilliant or not brilliant, when you evaluate humanly you are doing it through the conditioned mind, the mind that has been conditioned by nationality, race, religion, and politics. Even if you could evaluate those people correctly from a human standpoint, you would be adding nothing to the sum total of peace on earth or good will among men because there would always be the conflicting views—and this could probably be another source of enmity and war.

Now comes the difficult part of setting aside your views, opinions, and concepts, and turning within and letting the "Spirit bear witness with your spirit."[3] Then it is that you learn something entirely different about these same people, but it is not only people—there are the so-called powers. In this world we have two powers, good powers and evil powers, and because of the evil powers we invented a God to try and overcome the effects of them. For thousands of years we have tried to get this man-made God to stop wars, contagions, infections, epidemics, droughts, poverty, storms at sea, and plagues on land, but this God is just a golden calf and we know it by the lack of fruitage.

If the evils of this world are to be overcome, they are not going to be overcome by this man-made God of religion, but each and every evil is going to be overcome by the power of spiritual discernment. This inner discernment enables you to see that "The earth is the Lord's and the fullness thereof,"[4] and there cannot be anything destructive in it. This is the spiritual discernment that enables you to see that the people you have called good or bad are neither. They are children of God and the qualities and activities are those of God, individually manifested and expressed. Be assured it is only through spiritual discernment that you will be able to see that there is no evil in man and no evil on earth, and that there are no destructive powers in heaven or on earth or in hell.

Those who are not ready for the transition may hear these words or read them, but nothing will follow. Those of you who are ready will accept this message, live with it, and practice it until the ability has been fully developed to look out on this world of man, things, and conditions, without that word "I" beginning to form its judgment. Rather, you will say to this personal sense of I, "Be still . . . Be still and know that I am God," and then listen to the word, to the judgement of God that is uttered within you, and thereby behold this universe as it is, in the image of God. Through spiritual discernment you can see as you would like to be seen, you can know as you would like to be known, and then you really see two worlds: This world and *My* kingdom. You will then be able to understand why the Master could always say: "Father, forgive them; for they know not what they do."[5] You can then really see that they were handled by the personal sense of I, self-preservation and self-glory. You will then also be shown that it is nonsense to believe that all men are created equal. All men are not equal. Some are just lazy good-for-nothings who deserve all they get, until they awaken. Some are just unfortunate that they are not in a position to learn about truth. The only equality there is is the Son of God, and the only equality we are going to find and the only justice we are going to get is when we stop evaluating by human standards and begin to discern spiritually.

These two worlds have never before been revealed in this lifetime. Although it has been revealed in different ways by the Master and by the Buddha, unless you found the original manuscripts, you would only catch glimpses but you would not have the real principles stated. However, you have it clearly stated now. There is no devil to handle you and no God to help you. There is just this: Are you living through personal sense or are you developing spiritual discernment?

I AND MY FATHER ARE ONE

April 12, 1964
Between Two Worlds
Honolulu, Hawaii

OUR SUNDAY MORNING tapes are still on the subject of "Between Two Worlds," the world of material sense and the world of spiritual consciousness. You are reminded that there are two worlds, although one of these disappears in proportion as you attain the consciousness of the other one. As you die daily to "man whose breath is in his nostrils," you are being reborn into the Son of God. But here you must remember, and I say you must often remember and consciously remember that there are not actually two worlds. There is only one, the world of consciousness or spirit, but there is a false sense of that world which you entertain and that false sense constitutes the other world—the world of material sense.

I spoke this morning of Dr. Loren Eiseley's article entitled "The Uncomplete Man," published in *Harper's Magazine*, March, 1964, in which he tells of a revelation he experienced on the nature of the body which corresponds to what we have been teaching for more than thirty years. In this article, Dr. Eiseley says that all evil is based upon the belief that we are man. In other words, we are not man, and even Scripture says: "Know ye not that you are Gods[1].... even your body is the temple of

567

God."[2] We are really spiritual, offspring of spirit, and that which constitutes our material sense of world is this belief that we are man.

You will remember our exercise in which you stand slightly in back of yourself with the word *I*, and look down at the feet and realize: "These feet are not me, they are mine." You then go up to the knees, the hips, the waist, the chest, the shoulders, the neck, the head, up to the topmost hair of the head, always declaring: "This is not me, this is mine." Then, as you go up and down that body mentally, at the end of the exercise you realize: "*I* am not in this body, but there is an *I* separate and apart from body which is the owner of this body—and therefore the body in and of itself is nothing. *I* am the law unto it." This world-famous anthropologist looked at his body and said: "Ninety percent of this body is water and salt and a few minerals and none of this has intelligence." In other words he had been led to the same revelation as that of The Infinite Way: "This is not *me*. This is a handful of water and salt and minerals." I have no idea how far he has carried his discovery, but our work continues: I said, "Since you (the body) are flesh and bone, or water and salt, you do not have the power to cause a disease or to perpetuate one." Do you not see that, were it not for false beliefs, the body would be as ageless as *I* am? When you can see the body in that light, either as "flesh, blood, and bones, without intelligence" or as "water and salt and a few cents worth of minerals, without intelligence," you are no longer in material sense because you are not judging what you see, hear, taste, touch, or smell.

This awareness can come to you only through spiritual awareness, never through material sense. Therefore, only to that degree are you living in the higher world. There are times when you are apt to "bump your knee" but, if you can quickly jump up into *I,* the pain or the bruise will disappear instantly because the body in and of itself cannot be hurt, bruised, or destroyed. If you are sowing to the flesh, to the belief that intelligence is in the flesh, you will suffer the bruise, the burn, the hurt. However, if you can jump up quickly into *I,* the body responds because *I* is invisible and the body is but the form. When you jump up into the *I,* you then reap spiritually because of that. If you believe there is life and intelligence in this body, this water and salt and minerals, you will reap what you have sown, which is the belief in material sense.

A few months ago I said to you that the children of this generation, or the following generation, will be born into spiritual consciousness. This which we are imparting in The Infinite Way also comes through a world-famous anthropologist, and through Dr. Von Braun who says the substance of matter is mind. Mrs. Eddy saw that years ago: that all is mind and its manifestation; likewise, every New Thought teaching is based on that statement. As far as the human world is concerned, the world of the five physical senses, this is true—mind is the substance of matter. However, this is still the world of the five physical senses, because it is only when you go beyond the mind that you are in the real world. While you are in the realm of mind, remember you can have a good body or a bad body, a well body or a sick body. Since mind and matter are one and you can have good or bad thoughts, material thoughts or spiritual thoughts, true thoughts or ignorant thoughts, can you not see that it is just a question of "sowing and reaping?"

You do not bring forth perfection unless you rise above the mind of good and evil, into the realm of consciousness where you find oneness. Why? Because spirit is the invisible consciousness and it has no qualities. *It* is just spirituality. *It* just *is.* H_2O is neither good nor bad; it just is. Negative and positive electricity is neither good nor evil; it just is. Only thinking can make them good or evil. Human ignorance in the form of religious superstition makes the marital relationship good and evil, good if someone says mumbo jumbo over a couple, evil if someone does not. The mumbo jumbo–the wedding ring and the marriage certificate–does not make the marriage good, nor does the lack of it make the marriage bad. The truth is that marriage is neither good nor bad. When accompanied by love it is a spiritual relationship, and when there is no love it is really an illusory relationship. In other words mumbo jumbo just makes marriage legal, not happy. As long as you are in the realm of seeing good and evil, you are forgetting the voice of God saying to Adam: "Who told thee that thou wast naked?[3] Who said there is something wrong?" The world of material sense, with its good and evil, must be put off. But remember this: No amount of studying is going to put it off and no amount of instruction will put it off. The only thing that will put it off is realization. When you take a truth into your consciousness and abide with it and let it abide in you until a moment of realization, with every such realization you have to put off some measure of mortality. You have not put it off with the mumbo jumbo of speech or thought or college degrees or diplomas, but only in the measure of realization.

In your meditations, close your eyes and take the word *I,* and then realize the invisible nature of your Self, of the *I* that I am. Realize that your body is visible but *I* am not visible. And then remember the passages of Scripture: "I am with you always[4]. . . . I will never leave thee or forsake thee[5] . . . I am the bread, the meat, the wine and the water . . . I am come that you might have life, and that you might have it more abundantly[6] . . . . I am eternal life . . . Closer than breathing, nearer than hands and feet am *I*–the infinity, the Master, the Father within." Then you look at your body, your business, your marriage, or your home and you say: "Of yourself you are nothing. This *I* that I am–this is the law and the substance and the cement and the food that feeds the body or the business or the marriage or the human relationships."

Sooner or later temptations will come, as they came to the Master, in the form of lack. Suddenly the mind begins thinking of dollars, as the mind of Jesus turned to the thought of bread, but he quickly recognized the nature of material sense which says power is "out there" in bread. What was his answer? "Man shall not live by bread alone but by every word that proceedeth out of the mouth of God."[7] You, too, must jump up into that higher realm and say: "Man does not live by money. Man lives by every word of God, by every spiritual impulse I receive in consciousness." Certainly it appears outwardly as money or muscles or functioning of the body. The realization of *I* does bring forth fruitage on what we call the material plane, but it is not the material plane. Even body, or money, must be an instrument of God. Body or money, separate and apart from consciousness would be exactly what Dr. Eiseley said: "A lump of water and salt and minerals," or a piece of paper in the pocketbook. What gives money its value is the spiritual value of confidence, faith, agreement. A promissory note is no better than the character of the individual who writes it. Therefore, to look upon a promissory note as if it had value is nonsense. If you will think of money, property, goodwill, trade, as the outer manifestation of consciousness, then these things will have the quality and the quantity of consciousness, which is infinity. If you see them as something separate and apart from consciousness, they become worthless.

When a thought comes into your mind, train yourself to weigh it in the light of the two worlds: "Is that a material thought? Am I placing power in something or someone external to the *I* that I am? If I am placing confidence in good or bad powers, or in fear, if I am implying an external power in germs or in infections or in the calendar, if I am imputing power externally, I am living in the world of material sense, material values." But when such thoughts come to you and you reinterpret them: "No! I do not live by bread or by property, but by the will of God. I do not die by the power of accidents or germs or heredity; I die in proportion as I withdraw power from that external realm. I die to my human-ness, but I am in that degree reborn into my spiritual Sonship." As soon as you can draw back the power into the *I* that I am, fear of this outer world disappears.

When it is said that you must overcome death, it does not mean that literally. It means you must overcome the fear of what the world calls death—passing from this plane of experience. This passing is the normal functioning of every individual who has ever been on earth, so how foolish to fear the experience as though everyone before us has come into harm! Overcome the fear of death by realizing: "I do not have a life of my own because all that I am is God expressing itself as my individual being, and I leave God to perpetuate itself."

Judging by appearances, a tree perpetuates itself when it drops a seed, which takes root in the ground and then comes up as the tree again. In the human sense we perpetuate ourselves though our children, but this is really an illusion. God is perpetuating itself as your child or as your grandchild. Just as life is being lived on a universal scale so life lives itself as individual being. Then actually the seed of the tree dropping into the ground is really God perpetuating itself. There is no human way of overcoming what the world calls the delinquency of youth or the delinquency of this generation, and psychological attempts will make matters worse. There is a spiritual way of overcoming, which is this: Instead of seeing your child as "my child," if you can really see God as perpetuating itself as individual experience, this will change the entire nature. I am sure this is what Dr. Eiseley meant when he said that all evil is based on the belief that we are man. Once you see that God has incarnated itself on earth as individual being, you will no longer have "man whose breath is in his nostrils." You will have children of God.

The way of bringing this into practical experience is this: First of all, know the letter of truth that is incorporated in this message. Then, during your longest daily period of meditation when you are most free of outside influences, close your eyes and review several of these principles in your mind—especially with the word *I*. Realize: "In this invisible *I* that I am is embodied my life and everything needful that pertains to that life. I do not have to go anywhere for it, because it is already *embodied* in the *I* that I Am."Review several of the principles that may come to your thought, but the following is the important part: Settle into a listening attitude, "Speak Lord; thy servant heareth."[8] Let the inner ear be open because now you are going to hear with the invisible ears, and you are going to hear the inaudible word of God. Just let that peace be upon you until you feel the period is ended—two minutes, three minutes, five minutes—and then get up and go about your business. You have not asked for anything, nor have you decreed anything. All you have done is at-one-ed your Self with your source, communed with your source. You have made room for the spirit of God to awaken in your consciousness. Then it will do its work in you and for you and through you and before you. Always it will do it. If any human wish or desire enters into that meditation, even the desire for good, you have lost the benefit of it because you have separated yourself from the conviction that only God performs in you and through you and for you that which God ordains.

It is a high form of prayer to realize: "He performeth that which he gives me to do,"[9] because no longer will there be any reliance on the belief that God is going to prosper your will, even when you think it is a good will. Many times parents write me: "Is it not right that my children should go to college?" My answer is this: "If you think God's wisdom is not sufficient to govern your child." We have not had proof as yet that only children who attend college are happy and successful. No! A college education did not seem to be a necessary factor in the lives of Thomas Edison, Henry Ford, and the Wright brothers. Therefore, why outline what God's destiny should be for any individual? It is true that there are now strict rules that a college degree is necessary for the minister of a church, but God has no rules for those in its ministry. Therefore, why feel that you must tell God what it must do for your children? Experience shows me that students are ready to give up all forms of outlined prayers, except those which deal with their children. They are God's children and, if college or marriage or not marriage are part of their destinies, so it will be.

Are you your brother's keeper? No, except to the extent that you are the keeper of the truth about your brother and your neighbor. Humanly each one must work out his salvation, but spiritually you must hold no one in bondage to humanhood. You must maintain the consciousness of everyone as being God-consciousness individually expressing itself. In the healing work this is very important, because there is a temptation to believe that the patient or the patient's family is interfering with his spiritual progress. This is not true. This again is judging by the five physical senses in which you have "made a human being," you have "created a human being." No, you have not! You have accepted the false sense of sense testimony, for it is a universal relationship that "I and my Father are one" and that *one* is God.

EXPERIENCE GOD

April 19, 1964
Between Two Worlds
Honolulu, Hawaii

WE ARE GOING to continue the subject "Between Two Worlds" and so, in your meditation, let thought go into that period between two worlds and see what kind of an unfoldment you can be aware of. The secret of the two worlds is buried within your own consciousness and, regardless of how much I may tell you about it, you still will not know it until you have received confirmation, instruction, or inspiration on it from within your Self.

Please remember this: This Infinite Way message is unique in that it does not teach you to rely on the teaching, the books, or the revelator. The Infinite Way has a teacher and books and teachings only for the purpose of leading you back to the kingdom of God within your Self, so that you may be taught of God. Always remember that the world has lost truth because the followers of religious teachings have begun to let the Buddha or Jesus Christ or Paul carry on for them. Even in modern teachings there has been the acknowledgment that Mrs. Eddy and Mrs. Fillmore and Ernest Holmes were God-inspired, and then their followers took the attitude of sitting at the feet of the Master. To be instructed is right and as it should be, but you must not plan to spend your life there.

The major problem in my personal life is that of trying to avoid any relationship between my students and myself or the students of our teachers, whereby the individual begins to believe that we are God-inspired and so "let us sit and partake of his or her light." That is good up to a certain point, but remember that we in The Infinite Way are not trying to develop a following, nor are we trying to develop fame or fortune. I at least, and some of the teachers who have learned from me, are trying (sometimes even against the pressure of students) to bring to you the awareness that you have just as much access to the kingdom of God as we have. If you want to heal, you can do as much as any of us have done. That is the message of The Infinite Way.

So it is that you are living between two worlds,- the world of material sense and the world of spiritual consciousness. I would like you to understand the fullness of what that means, so I am turning you within for instruction. Catch a glimpse of what I have said about coming to this study, this path, for fulfillment. Even while you are working out specific problems, reserve an area of your consciousness where you re-member that the solving of problems is not really your purpose in spiritual study and meditation, but that the goal actually is fulfillment–to be filled full of God, to be filled full of the spirit–to have God-realization.

For a moment let us ponder the term God-realization. What do I mean by God-realization? Actually, what I mean is this: Contemplate: What is God or what is the kingdom of God? What is the nature of the life which is God? What is the gift of God? The gift of God is not money; it is not matter, not body. The gift of God is not an automobile or a house or property, because the gift of

God is nothing that partakes of the material nature. The gift of God is something of an incorporeal spiritual nature and, when you receive the gift of God, it translates itself out into your experience in a tangible form which may well be automobiles or houses or property.

Come to understand that a composer cannot receive a piece of music and an inventor cannot receive an idea for an automobile or a television set. The composer receives an impulse that takes the form of a melody and then the melody comes out of the voice, the piano or the violin. Likewise, the inventor receives an impulse which takes form as an idea, and he can then take the idea and mold it into a telephone or a wireless or anything else, but God cannot give the inventor a telephone. Therefore, when you go to God you must go for a gift of God, not for a perfect heart, liver or lung. The gift of God is a spiritual impulse which takes form in the mind and then comes forth as a harmonious body. But if you do not receive that impulse, you will never get down to the form.

When Jesus said: "Man shall not live by bread alone,"[1] he knew God could not turn a stone into bread but he knew if he received the spiritual impulse, the bread would appear. God could not give Moses a "cloud by day and a pillar of fire by night."[2] All Moses could do was go within until he received an impulse, an awareness of God's grace, an awareness of God's love, and then his needs were fulfilled. What would you do if you received the gift of multiplying loaves and fishes? You know right well you would be arrested and put in prison if you began to multiply bread or diamonds or gold. Do you not see how foolish it is to go to God for material things? If you pray for the gift of God, the grace of God, the awareness of the presence of God, it comes in the form of something tangible that you can share and give away.

The mistake of the orthodox religious world has been the belief that one can turn to a God of spirit for material things, a belief the church adopted from the ancient pagans, so, except for the metaphysical movements, religion today is where it was three thousand years ago. Their mistake has been in calling God "Mind," and then believing that Mind is an instrument for the individual's use in attaining material good. This is a mistake, and truth will not prosper if it is not truth. Even if a world-wide organization is built, it will crumble if it is not founded on truth.

Our way is to receive an awareness of God's kingdom and gifts. Then, whatever our demonstration is on earth, we carry it with us when we go. Spiritual principles are the treasures we lay up in heaven. Human health or human wealth can disappear but, if you have the spirit of God in you, will it not restore the lost years of the locust? Therefore, what difference does it make if you lose or give away all that you have, as long as you have the spirit of God which is the substance of it? If fruit is removed from a tree, whether the fruit blew off or whether it was picked or stolen, the tree immediately begins to form a new supply. In other words, you judge your barrenness by the state of your pocketbook instead of by your consciousness.

The Infinite Way is fully dedicated to spiritual fulfillment. Understand the nature of the spiritual kingdom and the nature of the spiritual gifts. Understand the source of spiritual health and spiritual wealth. The points that were brought out on this morning's tape must be consciously remembered: "Between Two Worlds—Reconciliation and Fulfillment," 1964 Oahu & Maui Series, Reel V, Side1. Then when you hear someone remark that it is not right to go to God for healing, you can say: "We do not go to God for healing. We go to God for God's grace and health is one of the added things when grace has been attained."

In the presence of life, how can there be death? In the presence of infinity, how can there be a destructive influence? Do you see how that sets The Infinite Way apart from metaphysical practice, and how you cannot find any similarity? The only thing that could be similar would be a teaching that says: "Seek ye first the kingdom of God,"[3] and take no thought for automobiles or yachts or livers or lungs. There are equalities with Buddha and Jesus because that was their goal, the one Self appearing as many. The Master taught: "Turn to me for I am come that ye might have life abundant. Therefore, turn to me," which is the same teaching as The Infinite Way. Buddha taught: "Seek me, abide in me, acknowledge me as the source of all," which is the same teaching as The Infinite Way.

On April 9 Pope Paul VI visited the city prison in Rome and, in talking to the men, explained that he had not come for any romantic reason or for any humanitarian reason, but because he beheld the Christ in them. Pope Paul recognized it when he said to these men in prison, "I see the Christ incarnate in you." But if he saw it in those prisoners, he must have seen it first in Jesus or in Pope John. He had to first witness it in someone before he could see it in itself. Then, because he did not set it apart, because he did not make the mistake of believing that a human being is God or the Christ, he finally saw it in all men. He then must have seen: "'His rain falls on the just and the unjust,'⁴ so I must go over to that prison." He did not tell the prisoners they were the Christ. No! He said: "I see the Christ *incarnate* in you. I see your true identity."

So it is with us. It was not given to any one of us to first behold the Christ of our own identity. That would be ego so intense that we would burn up with it. Most of us perhaps perceived the Christ in Jesus, John, Paul, or Gautama the Buddha. We always behold it in someone and then the light begins to dawn: "God really cannot have just one Son," and that is when the vision begins to enlarge. You start recognizing the divinity of Jesus, John, Paul, Gautama, and you suddenly realize: "They were all men like I was until *realization* dawned, and then the Christ was made evident." That brings the Christ alive in you and you then say: "Ah! I too." As you continue on and on you find that it is incarnated in all, and you begin to realize that the Master was not repelled by the woman taken in adultery. Remember that adultery was punishable by death in those days, but he still recognized the incarnation of the Christ. By this time you reach the point Paul reached, where he knew Christ is incarnated in mankind—not only good mankind but bad mankind. What counts is this: Does something within us lead us to an individual who can awaken it in us, or to a book, or to a teaching? Then, although our sins are scarlet, we are restored. Right identity! Christ incarnate in man!

It may take several generations before the cardinals and the archbishops and the bishops and the priests accept that and look into the eyes of their saints and sinners and say: "I am looking *through* you. I do not care if you are good or bad!" It may take two generations for the Protestant church to say: "Behold the incarnation of Christ in man." Then witness what kind of a race there will be on earth, with everyone in church looking at his neighbor and saying: "Thou art the Christ." The entire nature of the world will be changing in the next two generations. I could not see that it would strike through the Pope and that it is beginning to strike through the Episcopal Church, but it is. And so we have a line that begins with some unknown called Krishna to Gautama the Buddha to Jesus the Christ to The Infinite Way. It is a straight line—one teaching.

In last year's work you have the name of God revealed. Moses would not permit even his priests to voice the name of God. Why? Because it could be misunderstood. When an individual knows the name of God his life changes, and this must be the next step that is revealed through The Infinite Way, through the consciousness of those who are accepted as authority. It was revealed in March through Dr. Eiseley, subtly and hiddenly but, for those who have eyes to see, very clearly. It must now come out through all the avenues that the world can accept as authorities. The world of Buddhism did not accept Gautama; only his followers accepted him. Jesus Christ was less known in his day than I am known in my day, and I am practically unknown. He was so little known that the great historian of his day made just two statements about him: "We hear there is a Hebrew rabbi who is preaching and healing, and he is influencing many. We have just heard he was crucified." That is how little Jesus Christ was known, yet his words were published by those in authority even though they were not accepted when they came from his own lips. They were published and then, in the mysterious way the spirit has, the world accepted them as authority. "Render unto Caesar," because ultimately Caesar has to publish the message!

Through these papers and the tapes of 1963 and 1964, I hope that more Infinite Way students will begin to spiritually perceive the nature of the message instead of perpetuating the false belief that it is another form of materia medica, or of going to God for material good. God is omnipresence and God is the same for all, but the secret of The Infinite Way lies in the word *consciousness.* There is only one God, but no one has God until he experiences it. Any God that has to be prayed to is not God. There is no withholding and there is no giving in God. When you experience God, you find *is*-ness. "Son, thou art ever with me, and all that I have is thine."[5] We have been going to God for what we want, not for what God has to give, and there is no such God. There is no God that gives or withholds or heals. When you are in the presence of God you are in the presence of fulfillment. Attaining the experience of God is the attainment of all the added things, with no asking and no telling.

Through prayer and meditation you have the power of coming into the presence of God, and in this you find you are in the presence of fulfillment, with all things added unto you.

ACCESS TO INFINITY

April 26, 1964
Between Two Worlds
Honolulu, Hawaii

"TO BE POPULAR or not to be popular? That is the question." After a lesson such as we had this morning, it would be very easy to be popular because the message sounded so beautiful as it was coming through. It would be a simple matter to be popular by saying nothing more about it, but actually that lesson can only be of benefit in proportion to what you do with it now that you have it: "Between Two Worlds–Man of Earth, Man In Christ, Life By Grace," 1964 Oahu & Maui Series, Reel V, Side 2.

Let us take the unfoldment about the source, divine consciousness, infinite consciousness being the consciousness of the men and women of the past, present, and future–going back six thousand years and looking ahead to the next six thousand years and to all the men and women who will appear on the surface of the earth. Then remember that the infinite consciousness of all the spiritual lights, inventors, composers, writers, is that same consciousness that has appeared on earth, will appear on earth, and is available to us on earth here and now. Remember that we, through our individual consciousness, have access to the infinite consciousness and that this includes not only spiritual wisdom but all of the wisdom of the ages: commercial, economic, artistic.

If you go back to the wisdom schools of Egypt two thousand years B.C., you will read of the discoveries of mathematics, science, and all of the principles that govern navigation, and you will have to ask yourself, "Whence came this?" You will then discover that these men, living in monasteries with only blank walls and a very limited amount of writing material, brought forth these laws of mathematics through their hours and hours and weeks and months and years of inner searching. They were the very laws that were responsible for the road building, the palaces, temples, and pyramids which now exist in Egypt, India, China, Cambodia, and South America. Thousands of years before our ancestors in the United States were living in tepees and log cabins, these people in foreign lands were living in beautiful palaces and temples, sculptured in a manner that we have not as yet achieved on the American continent. Whence came this wisdom? Out of the consciousness of men who had access to the infinite consciousness. A lesson such as we had this morning means nothing unless it leads you to books or to other experiences that will send your mind all over the world searching out the great discoveries in science, invention, art, music, and make you pause and ponder: "Whence come? Whence come?"

The consciousness of individual man is absolutely infinite, and individually you can sit down, enter your consciousness, and bring forth infinity. You can then look around you and see what you have not acquired, or what you did acquire and then lost, and laugh at it as if it were but a grain of dust in comparison to the infinity to which you have access. And, it is not necessary that you go anywhere, or meet miracle people, or have your fortunes told; all you need do is turn within. Those of you who do this are going to make startling discoveries, and so I caution you: Do not talk it over with anyone. There is no easier way to lose it, because no one can believe it except those who have been there before you.

Because of the almost worldwide spread of The Infinite Way during this short time, we are receiving quite a few requests for the story of my life. Why? Because they think they will discover the secret in it. Yes, I could tell them when and where I was born and where I went to school, but they would then say: "That does not account for the miracle of The Infinite Way." Of course not! Imagine what would happen if I tried to tell it. Why? Because, as many have recognized, The Infinite Way is constituted of the wisdom of the East and West and the Near East. It is all there. Where did I get it, since I had no access to books or schools through which I could discover it? I got it from the original source of the East and the West and Near East.

Behind every individual who has ever received a spiritual truth, or an invention, music, or art, there is one infinite consciousness which is its source. And when you tap that, you tap all of the branches that have gone out from the source. "My conscious oneness with God constitutes my oneness with all spiritual being and idea," and this cannot be limited to time, space, or place. Do you not see that all of this can take place only through introspection, cogitation, contemplation, meditation—anything that takes the attention away from the outside world and draws it back to that center within your Self—to "let the imprisoned splendor escape"?

An activity of grace leads you to this kingdom, this realm of consciousness within you, and then an activity of grace starts the flow. Enter the sanctuary, close the door of the five physical senses, and listen to *Me:*

Seek Me, *infinite divine being, and* I *will make you fishers of men. Jesus will not do it nor will Joel do it, but* I *will, that* I *that is the* I *of your inner being.* I *will make you fishers of men.* I *will lead you in a way.* I *will go before you.* I *will prepare mansions for you.* I *will never leave thee nor forsake thee.*

Do you not see that you are led back to the realm of the *I,* and this *I* is the manna—the bread, the meat, the wine and the water—which flows by the same divine grace that populates the earth with men, animals, vegetables, and minerals, and creates each and every thing unto a purpose?

The way in which this works is a mystery to us and, because it sometimes appears in such natural ways, we do not realize that it was actually prompted by a divine grace. For instance about the time that gasoline engines were invented, oil was discovered in the ground. With this discovery came a process of changing oil into gasoline, and so our automotive life became possible. We were then told that the earth supply of oil was running short and in a certain number of years there would not be enough oil to supply the nation's increasing needs. Almost within that same year a citizen of the United States invented a new gadget whereby the amount of oil coming from the ground was quadrupled, so the country then had four times as much oil as before. This week we learn that another inventor has made a discovery which doubles that! As if that were not enough, it has been discovered that the soil of Canada is filled with oil.

Do you not see that we of ourselves cannot know these things, unless these ideas which become inventions pour into our consciousness? Individuals had to go within themselves to find these secrets. They were not in books; they had to be discovered within themselves. The real consciousness of man is infinite, and the moment you stop limiting it to your education and your environment, infinity can flow. When all of this is revealed it makes an interesting philosophy, but it only becomes a way of life when an individual adopts it into his experience and determines to have specific periods day and night until meditation is an automatic process that continues even while sleeping. Great revelations are given during sleep when the human mind is still.

If you keep this principle secret and sacred among those who hear it or read it, and if you practice it conscientiously, such miracles will take place in your life as you yourself could not believe possible. The reason is this: If you think of it in terms of God's grace, you will see how infinite it can be. You will see that it is not limited to you; it is limited only to God's grace and your receptivity. Then by your example, by your light, the world will seek that light—and it will find it, because this is a universal truth. Therefore, the demonstration of infinity in your experience is measured by the extent to which you practice a principle of this nature—never revealing it, never speaking of it, and never trying to teach it until you are so consciously one with it that it is already flowing.

Yes, one could become very popular teaching this principle to individuals, allowing them to believe through ignorance that it was for their benefit and that it would do great things for them. But that would be misleading, because God's grace cannot be limited to an individual. This passage is therefore given to us: "The vine consumeth not its own grapes." In other words, we are the vine through which this message comes. It blesses us, but its major blessing is that others are led to us and then it becomes a universal truth which blesses the entire universe.

Eventually this causes a disruption in your life when, as a businessman you find less time for your business or when, as a housewife, you find less time for your home and more and more you discover you are being drawn into a universal scheme of things. The Master, and I am not speaking of a man but the spirit of God within you, says: "Come and follow me and I will make you fishers of men,"[1] and it pulls you out of your little fishing job into an activity that enables this grace you have discovered to bless the world. "I will make you fishers of men."

In the moment you prove that the infinite consciousness of this universe is your individual consciousness, and that you have access to the consciousness which is, ever has been and ever shall be, you are called out as a fisher of men to be the light unto the world. Light does not go out looking for places in which to shine. Like the sun which stays fast in the heavens, a light shines and lets the rest of the world come to it.

As we in some measure become the light, we hold what we have received sacredly and secretly until the world starts to come to our doorway for it. We may travel the world, not on a save the world basis, but only because the world has invited us. If we remained in one city, it would cost those who come here thousands and thousands of dollars. But by traveling, we can carry the message to those who seek us, and for only a few dollars. And when we travel, it is only to go where we are drawn by those who have "ears to hear and eyes to see."

The whole secret of the spiritual life is to know that you have access to infinity through your own consciousness and then go within sufficiently often to let the flow appear, to "let the imprisoned splendor escape"—and then be careful never to personalize it and think you have become good or that you have become spiritual. Remember you have become an instrument or a transparency for an infinite, universal grace. You choke it and shut it off immediately if you personalize it, but you can increase the flow by realizing it as an infinite grace flowing universally. Like the tree that is showing forth God's grace, this does not glorify us. It lets us stand still and show forth God's glory. Anything else is catering to the ego, and the ego must die as completely as the tree that cannot say "I" and thinks it is something of itself. And so it is that this reconciles us to God, and thereby fulfills us.

OMNIPRESENCE

May 10, 1964

RELAX AND LET the mental strain fall away, because we wish to be transparencies through which the Spirit can flow. Remember you are not here to get anything. When we have large lecture audiences, it is to be expected that many people come to receive something or to gain something or to learn something. This is legitimate, just as it is legitimate when we first come to a metaphysical teaching to seek something in the outer realm: better health or increased supply or improved relationships. However, in a small group of this nature, you have learned at least in some measure that anything you are going to get is only in proportion to the flow of the spirit. Therefore, your mind should not be on achieving something or on learning something, but rather resting in the assurance that there is a spirit in man.

Let this spirit flow, and the spirit that flows through you will feed you; but it will do something far more than that, because it will feed each one of us. What feeds me will continue to feed you; what feeds you will continue to feed me. What feeds us will feed those in this room and, because the flow of spirit cannot be limited or stopped, it will continue to flow out of this room into the world. Just as the life of the tree not only feeds the tree but produces fruit on the tree, so it is in our spiritual life.

We no longer think in terms of feeding "me and my family," but we let it produce enough fruit to feed the world. Relax and take this as a law to remember: The only tension there is in meditation is when you are trying to get something. The moment you release the desire to get, you will relax.

A little now about our trip. In Portland, Seattle, and Chicago, Mrs. Daisy Shigemura of Hawaii, Mrs. Eileen Bowden of Canada, Miss Lorene McClintock of New York, Mrs. Virginia Stephenson of California, and Miss Lorraine Sinkler of Chicago will be conducting Infinite Way teacher classes on meditation, spiritual healing, and ways and means of studying the monthly Letter. These will be in addition to my own lecture and classwork, so it will be a heavy program, but one that will bring forth a deep and rich consciousness. "I, if I be lifted up, will draw all men unto me."[1] Therefore, as our Infinite Way group is lifted up, the spirit will go beyond the confines of the walls and reach human consciousness.

In Europe, our editor Miss Lorraine Sinkler will join Emma, Daisy Shigemura, and me and, in addition to my lecture and classwork there, Mrs. Shigemura and Miss Sinkler will have programs on meditation, healing work, and specific principles of daily living. Infinite Way teachers from Australia, New Zealand, and South Africa will also join us in England, as will teachers from Germany, Holland, and Switzerland. Furthermore, about thirty students from the United States expect to be a part of our group in Europe, so there is going to be a tremendous uniting on this Infinite Way safari. Most of these are individuals who have dedicated themselves to meditation and to the understanding of God. The Infinite Way is really only a means to that end and, because their main goal is God-realization, this way of life offers them that opportunity.

You can be assured there will be a rich consciousness functioning constantly, and there is no reason why you should not participate. Why? Because consciousness, the consciousness of the *I Am* which you are, is not related to the body. It is not inside of or confined to a body. Actually this consciousness that *I Am* is omnipresent where you are. Spiritual consciousness, enlightened consciousness, Christ-consciousness cannot be confined to a body, therefore you can contact it wherever it is. The consciousness that is manifest in this room at this moment is likewise manifest in Capetown, South Africa, Australia, New York, or London.

This principle is so universally recognized by the illumined that the Order of Elks maintains an activity whereby members unite once a day in silent prayer—whether they are in Hawaii or in Africa or in New York—showing that they recognize the one consciousness. A masonic body meets daily to unite in this one consciousness, and there are religious groups where provision is made for their members to unite in the one consciousness at specific hours throughout the day and night. There are prayer groups operating throughout the world which have been organized by religious and non-religious groups to unite at certain times for special prayer.

In The Infinite Way we go a step further. We recognize this divine consciousness as omnipresence, and therefore we do not set aside a specific time to unite with it. Why? Because it is *always* omnipresence. I am in meditation twenty-four hours a day, even when I am asleep. It is not my personal human consciousness that benefits you, but my personal consciousness which is in oneness with the divine.

As you realize that Infinite Way groups are meeting two or three times a day in Hawaii, New York, Canada, South Africa, New Zealand, Australia, on the European continent, and in the Orient, you will come to see that such groups are meeting almost twenty-four hours a day. Therefore you can close your eyes at any time and realize your oneness with divine consciousness, and eventually you will discover that as you do learn to close your eyes, you will find the practitioner consciousness omnipresent. In that way the entire element of personal healing will gradually be eliminated. "*I* will never leave you nor forsake you,"[2] and it makes no difference whether it was two thousand years ago or today. Therefore, there is no reason why we cannot unite morning, noon, and night in that realized Christ-consciousness wherever we are–and certainly there must be "signs following!"

Let me repeat that prayer in the ordinary sense of the word is an attempt to accomplish the impossible, because it is an attempt to get God or spirit to give us something material and this cannot be successful. The reason for unanswered prayer, as prayer is generally understood, is in the belief that there is a God and a something that God has to give. This denies infinity and omnipresence. If God is infinite, there is nothing besides God, so to think of health, supply or success as being something separate and apart from God is to deny God's allness. Any prayer that looks to God for anything is a form of paganism, because it is a denial of the nature of God, the function of God, and the name of God.

Think! There is no you separate and apart from God, therefore there can be nothing for God to give you.

Since "all things that the Father hath are mine," all that the Father hath is included within you, and to pray for something would be like this tumbler praying for glass. You cannot pray aright without an understanding of the name or nature of God, and you do not have this understanding if you are praying to mental concepts of God. In other words, if you pray to God who is spirit, or if you pray to God as mind or life or Soul, your ignorance of the name and nature of God prevents the success of your prayers.

Ah! But to "know God aright is life eternal," so you might as well decide to leave the Bible alone until you have fulfilled that one passage. Why? Because without an inner awareness of that passage of truth, the rest of the Bible is meaningless. To know God aright does not mean to know another name or another meaning for God. No! It means to know God, to be aware of God, to be conscious of God, and to know God as God is—yes, actually to experience God.

If we are to live the life of a contemplative whereby we live by "every word that proceedeth out of the mouth of God," then contemplation or meditation must be the means of our approach to God. And since we have taken the passage "To know him aright is life eternal," this must be the subject of contemplative meditation until a second passage of Scripture projects itself into consciousness.

If you continue long enough in "knowing God aright," I can tell you what the next passage will be. The voice will say: "Be still, and know that I am God."[3] After this second passage reveals itself to you, what kind of praying you do depends upon how forcibly the passage enters your thought. Think! If *I* am God, this *I* is already closer than breathing; and because we have discovered that its nature is omniscience, the all-knowing, it must already know your needs. Its nature is omnipresence so you need go nowhere to contact it, and because it is omnipotence there is no power to oppose its will. What else is there to do but be still! If your child were ill or in trouble, what greater love could you display than to sit down, be still, and *let* the presence of God do its work, *let* the love of God be made manifest, *let* the power of God flow? Do you not see how egotistical it would be to go further and do something for your child, your patient, or your friend?

As you contemplate and meditate on the nature of prayer, it will not be long before these passages unfold:

In quietness and in confidence shall be your strength[4] . . . Take no thought for your life[5] . . . Acknowledge him in all thy ways[6] . . . My peace I give unto you[7]. . . .Thy grace is my sufficiency.[8]

Think of the depth and the power of your prayer when it becomes a silence based on the understanding that "*I* am God. I in the midst of thee am mighty."[9]

For centuries it has been a complete waste of time to tell God what we want, how much we want, or when we want it, and there is nothing more nonsensical than prayers for peace on earth. There can be no peace on earth until there is peace in my individual consciousness and yours, and there will be no peace in my consciousness or yours unless God is there. Otherwise there is always a conflict between your self or myself or his self or her self. In The Infinite Way it is recognized that *I* is God; only then can there be no discord or strife between us because there is only one consciousness. Peace on earth will only come about with the universal recognition of the Fatherhood of God and the Brotherhood of Man. With that recognition there can be no strife because it then makes no difference what church we go into or what church we stay out of.

The cause of more than one-half of the wars on earth can be attributed to religious conflicts. Always religious struggle has caused war. The other cause of warfare is money, business, or property. You may have read of many causes for World War I, but none of these reports were true. The only reason for World War I was industry—competition between England and the German empire. There was also but one reason for World War II: the allies did not allow the defeated Germans to "get back on their feet." In other words, there was a determination to make a peasant race of the defeated German nation and withhold their industrial Rhine and Ruhr areas from them—which were restored only through war. Materialistic concepts of life, both in religion and industry, are the causes of warfare.

Likewise, if we here were to have personal quarrels, they would be caused by religion or money. Once we come into an agreement that there in only one God, no longer can there be religious strife; and once we have attained a spiritual concept of supply, there can never be a disagreement between us concerning money. How much money or how little money each of us has is of no interest then, and what passes between us is free will. This can be observed in families. When there is no religious disagreement or no economic disagreement, there is no unhappiness, and what measure of tribulations do arise are only little peccadilloes which come up and quickly disappear.

If one were to judge by the newspapers, one might be led to believe that infidelity is the cause of broken homes, but do not believe it. Infidelity is not a cause but an effect, and when there is an agreement to let each other live his or her financial and religious life, there is no reason for infidelity. The same thing applies to alcohol and drugs; these are not causes, but effects of economic or religious disagreement.

Prayer reinstates the original harmony when prayer is a "be still," so let us follow that through. There are about forty or fifty of us gathered together today, and let us now agree that there are forty or fifty different states of consciousness and two sexes. Therefore discords of one name or another could enter this group so let us now see how we would resolve them and how we would maintain harmony thereafter. First let us agree that there is a transcendental something called the Buddha-mind or spiritual consciousness or the mind that was also in Christ Jesus. Let us agree that there is something of a transcendental nature, and that prayer or meditation is the means of bringing it into expression in our midst. We close our eyes and bring to conscious remembrance:

Be still, and know that I *—here in the center of your being—is God. Be still, and know that* I *—in the center of being of every individual here—is God.*

Be still and let the divine will be done on earth as it is in heaven. Let the peace, My peace, descend upon us and be released among us. Let God's grace flow in and through us. Speak, Lord; for thy servant heareth.

We are then completely still and eventually we feel the deep breath, the flow, the spiritual quiet. What happens now to the discord—hate, bigotry, bias, jealousy?

Few students can attain this realization of the presence during their first contemplation or meditation, which is why spiritual principles must be studied and practiced. It may take years before a student is able to settle down in quiet and in confidence, but however long it takes I can assure you it is worthwhile. Why? Because the minute a student brings that peace of God into a situation, in the home or in the business or in the school room, it dissolves opposition.

There are now three major national problems in the United States, namely: (1) Civil Rights, which has to do with race segregation; (2) prayer in the schools, which has to do with religion; and (3) income taxes, which have to do with money. Think what a nation there would be if these were eliminated! Is there a reason for those three problems? None at all! There is a way of attaining success according to the human standard of success, which is to divide and to conquer. In other words keep the country divided racially, and keep the people highly taxed. That has always been the human picture and it cannot be brought to an end by changing the political party from Republican to Democratic or from Democratic to Republican. The only change will come through prayer, the prayer that does not ask for anything or for anyone, the prayer that is "quietness and confidence and stillness" in this realization: There is no power in heaven or on earth greater than *I Am*.

Let the *I* which is omnipresence, omniscience, and omnipotence come through. "Be still, and know that *I* am God." Then, be still! In the presence of this spiritual realization the material existence loses its claim of power. There is a spirit in man, so be still and let it flow. "Be still and know that *I* am God," and beside *Me* there is no other. Rest and relax in the awareness of that power, and let it go before you to establish harmonious relationships between religions and between races.

Did the Civil War settle anything? Of course not. Will another war settle anything? Of course not. Only the prayers of a righteous man will end racial strife. The righteous man is not an individual who thinks he knows what is best for the nation; rather, the righteous man is one who is sure he does not know and is willing to "be still, and know that *I* am God." This is enough to know, and then *let* this knowing do its work. "Ye shall know the truth and the truth shall make you free."[10]

All the marriage counselors and all the psychologists cannot make for a happy household. To be able to engage in righteous prayer, to be able to sit in one's household every day for five or ten minutes and "be still, and know that *I* am God," and let the household be permeated with that divine presence and stillness–this is the only way in which to unite a family. It does not mean there will be no differences of opinion. It is natural that two people with different backgrounds should sometimes disagree, because we are all entitled to our individuality.

The curse of this age is the desire for security. Everyone in the world wants security. If you could imagine what life would be like should you attain it, you would quickly see that life has to be an adventure and a challenge, which includes concern and worry. This is part of our heritage of individuality and progress. It takes a strong Soul to be able to live in the *now,* and then go out into the world and do what one is led to do, even if it means searching for new countries. There are no lands to be explored in the external realm, and this is the first time that man has been led to explore the realm of consciousness—and to think that this realm of consciousness is as uninhabited as the outer world was uninhabited ten thousand years ago! Actually, consciousness is a word we have introduced into the English language—then realize that consciousness is infinite and that we know so little about it.

Think of the new lands to be discovered in consciousness and you will discern that it takes courage. Life will be brand new in that realm, so if you are looking for security there is no assurance that you will find it. When the Master said: "Leave your nets and follow me,"[11] he gave no assurance of security. People who are secure never venture forth or take a chance, and had our ancestors been secure, what would have happened? Thank heaven for insecurity—or for the lack of security!

Remember that even in the midst of your immediate insecurity, whether it is one of sin, disease, or lack, as you attain this inner peace through prayer, contemplation, meditation, you find an actual inner peace that leads to an outer glory. Do not look to man for that glory; do not look to social security checks or investment checks, because they cannot bring you the inner peace that you must have.

"Ten righteous men can save a city."[12] Who are the righteous men? Those who indulge in righteous prayer. What is righteous prayer? That which seeks nothing for oneself, but seeks only the presence of God.

SCRIPTURAL REFERENCES

The author regularly instructed his students to "catch the spirit" of the letter of truth and not to become unduly focused on the words themselves. In many of his talks, he paraphrased and combined Biblical passages to more clearly reveal the truth contained in Scripture. In an effort to keep this work in the style in which it was delivered, some of the scriptural passages referenced in the text may not be a verbatim quotation of the passage cited herein.

January 20, 1963
1. John 19:11
2. John 5:30
3. II Corinthians 3:17
4. I Samuel 3:9

January 27, 1963
1. Matthew 23:9
2. John 9:25
3. Exodus 20:5
4. John 19:11
5. John 10:30

February 3, 1963
1. Galatians 6:7
2. Luke 17:21
3. John 8:32
4. II Corinthians 3:17
5. II Corinthians 12:9
6. John 10:30

February 10, 1963
1. Matthew 3:15
2. Zechariah 4:6

February 10, 1963 (Continued)
3. Matthew 5:39
4. Exodus 3:5
5. Proverbs 3:6

February 17, 1963
1. Psalms 43:5
2. Job 26:7
3. John 9:25
4. John 14:10
5. Isaiah 2:22

February 24, 1963
1. I John 4:4
2. John 14:27
3. Isaiah 55:8
4. Matthew 26:39
5. Isaiah 45:2
6. John 12:32
7. John 16:7
8. Matthew 6:25

March 3, 1963
1. Matthew 7:14
2. Luke 15:31

March 3, 1963 (Continued)
3. John 10:30
4. Psalms 24:1
5. Isaiah 54:17
6. John 12:45
7. Matthew 23:9
8. Isaiah 9:6
9. Matthew 16:23

March 9, 1963
1. Matthew 6:19–21
2. I Corinthians 3:16
3. John 16:15

March 10, 1963
1. Acts 10:34
2. Matthew 6:25
3. Psalms 24:1
4. Luke 15:31
5. II Corinthians 12:9
6. John 10:30
7. John 16:15
8. John 8:32
9. John 16:33
10. John 19:11
11. Matthew 24:35
12. Luke 13:34

March 17, 1963
1. John 14:6
2. John 6:41
3. Matthew 4:4

March 24, 1963
1. John 12:45
2. Galatians 2:20
3. Matthew 4:4
4. Matthew 7:14

March 31, 1963
1. Luke 17:21

March 31, 1963 (Continued)
2. Romans 8:39
3. Matthew 6:1
4. Matthew 6:4
5. Matthew 8:4
6. Matthew 7:12
7. Matthew 19:19
8. Luke 18:17

April 7, 1963
1. Acts 17:23
2. Psalms 91:7
3. I Samuel 3:9
4. Isaiah 11:6
5. Genesis 1:1
6. Matthew 25:40
7. Matthew 18:22
8. Matthew 5:44
9. Luke 23:34
10. John 8:32

April 21, 1963
1. Matthew 6:25
2. John 15:4
3. Isaiah 55:8
4. II Corinthians 6:2
5. Hebrews 13:5

April 28, 1963
1. Luke 12:14
2. John 8:11
3. Matthew 9:2
4. Luke 23:34
5. II Chronicles 32:8
6. Matthew 5:39
7. John 18:11
8. Isaiah 30:15
9. Zechariah 4:6
10. John 19:11

April 28, 1963 (Continued)
11. John 8:46
12. John 14:27
13. John 18:36

May 5, 1963
1. Isaiah 9:6
2. Galatians 3:28
3. John 1:14
4. I Samuel 3:9
5. Matthew 25:5
6. Matthew 18:2
7. Matthew 14:27

May 12, 1963
1. Luke 15:31
2. Psalms 24:1
3. Matthew 10:8

May 18, 1963
1. John 8:58
2. I Corinthians 2:14
3. Matthew 9:22
4. John 5:30

May 19, 1963
1. II Peter 3:8
2. Genesis 18:32
3. Isaiah 54:17
4. Matthew 18:2
5. Matthew 14:27

May 26, 1963
1. Matthew 23:9

June 2, 1963
1. Psalms 16:11
2. I Kings 19:12
3. Psalms 46:10

June 2, 1963 (Continued)
4. Isaiah 30:15
5. Psalms 46:6
6. Proverbs 3:5
7. Proverbs 3:6
8. I Samuel 3:9
9. Psalms 91:7
10. Matthew 16:24
11. John 18:36
12. John 14:27
13. Matthew 5:39
14. John 18:11
15. I Corinthians 2:14
16. Romans 8:7
17. Matthew 6:4
18. II Corinthians 12:9
19. John 4:24

June 9, 1963
1. John 18:36
2. John 10:30
3. Luke 15:31
4. John 10:10
5. I Corinthians 3:16
6. Mark 2:27
7. Genesis 18:32

June 16, 1963
1. II Chronicles 32:8
2. John 5:8
3. Matthew 9:30
4. John 6:41
5. Matthew 28:20
6. John 15:4
7. Acts 3:6
8. John 15:7
9. Luke 12:32
10. Matthew 6:33
11. Psalms 46:6

June 23, 1963
1. Matthew 6:6
2. John 10:30
3. Luke 15:31
4. Luke 24:49
5. Galatians 6:7

July 7, 1963
1. I Corinthians 2:14
2. II Corinthians 5:1
3. Matthew 19:17
4. John 7:16
5. Galatians 6:8
6. John 10:30
7. Luke 15:31

July 14, 1963
1. I Corinthians 2:14
2. John 18:36
3. John 14:27
4. Matthew 6:25
5. John 4:24
6. John 4:21
7. John 12:45
8. Galatians 6:7
9. Luke 17:21
10. John 4:14
11. John 4:32
12. John 12:45
13. John 8:58
14. Matthew 28:20
15. Luke 18:22
16. Proverbs 3:6
17. John 15:4
18. Matthew 19:17

July 27, 1963
1. Luke 12:48
2. John 10:10

July 27, 1963 (Continued)
3. Exodus 3:14
4. John 10:30

July 28, 1963
1. Galatians 6:7
2. John 14:6
3. Matthew 19:17
4. John 4:14
5. John 5:31
6. John 5:30
7. John 7:16
8. Galatians 2:20
9. Psalms 19:1

August 4, 1963
1. John 10:10
2. Romans 8:38
3. I Corinthians 2:14
4. Romans 8:9
5. Romans 8:17
6. II Corinthians 12:2
7. John 3:4
8. John 4:32
9. Matthew 14:27
10. Luke 15:31

August 5, 1963
1. John 10:30
2. Acts 7:33
3. John 14:9
4. Matthew 24:35
5. Exodus 13:21
6. Matthew 18:20

August 11, 1963
1. I Corinthians 15:10
2. Romans 8:7
3. Matthew 8:18

August 11, 1963 (Continued)
4. II Corinthians 12:9
5. Proverbs 3:6
6. Matthew 4:4
7. John 14:9
8. I Samuel 3:9

August 16, 1963
1. Galatians 2:20
2. John 5:30
3. Matthew 6:19,20
4. Psalms 16:11

August 24, 1963
1. I Corinthians 2:14
2. John 15:6
3. Psalms 91:7
4. John 16:7
5. Matthew 26:38

September 2, 1963
1. James 5:16
2. Psalms 37:25
3. Matthew 18:20
4. Genesis 18:32
5. John 15:13
6. Matthew 18:22
7. John 14:27

September 7, 1963
1. Luke 10:4
2. Matthew 25:40
3. John 10:30
4. John 12:45

September 14, 1963
1. Revelation 21:27
2. I Corinthians 2:14
3. John 5:8
4. Luke 17:21

September 21, 1963
1. Luke 10:4

September 28, 1963
1. John 18:36
2. John 5:30
3. I Samuel 3:9
4. II Corinthians 2:9
5. Galatians 2:20
6. Job 23:14
7. Psalms 138:8

September 29, 1963
1. Philippians 2:5
2. John 11:25
3. John 4:14
4. John 8:11
5. John 16:7
6. Genesis 26:24
7. Psalms 91:7
8. John 15:5,6
9. Exodus 3:5
10. Hebrews 13:5
11. Matthew 16:15
12. Matthew 16:16
13. Matthew 16:17
14. John 10:30

September 30, 1963
1. John 8:32

January 1, 1964
1. I Corinthians 2:14
2. Isaiah 30:15
3. Matthew 24:44
4. Psalms 46:10
5. Matthew 6:25

January 1, 1964 (Continued)
6. Psalms 91:7
7. Psalms 91:1
8. John 15:5
9. Matthew 6:25

January 10, 1964
1. Mark 9:9
2. Revelation 3:20
3. I Samuel 3:9
4. Matthew 6:4
5. John 6:41
6. John 11:25
7. John 10:10
8. Luke 15:31
9. John 14:27
10. John 5:30
11. John 14:10
12. Matthew 25:40

January 26, 1964
1. John 18:36
2. II Corinthians 12:9
3. Matthew 6:27

February 2, 1964
1. Matthew 5:39
2. John 18:11
3. Luke 10:7

February 7, 1964
1. Malachi 3:6
2. Matthew 6:25
3. John 4:32
4. John 5:8
5. John 8:11
6. John 4:31
7. John 4:32
8. John 12:45

February 7, 1964 (Continued)
9. John 10:30
10. Galatians 2:20
11. John 10:10
12. Matthew 19:17
13. John 8:58
14. Matthew 28:20

February 9, 1964
1. I Corinthians 3:19
2. John 9:25
3. Psalms 85:8
4. Matthew 7:14
5. Matthew 10:34

February 15, 1964
1. Job 9:12
2. Acts 10:34
3. Hebrews 13:8
4. John 12:32
5. John 4:32
6. John 6:51

February 16, 1964
1. Matthew 7:16
2. I Samuel 3:9
3. Matthew 9:2
4. Luke 23:43
5. Matthew 8:4

March 15, 1964
1. Revelation 3:20
2. Matthew 23:9
3. Galatians 2:20
4. I Corinthians 15:53
5. Ezekiel 18:32
6. Habakkuk 1:13

March 22, 1964
1. Ecclesiastes 11:1

March 22, 1964 (Continued)
2. Matthew 7:14
3. John 18:36

March 29, 1964
1. Matthew 16:17
2. John 19:11
3. Isaiah 54:17

April 5, 1964
1. I Corinthians 2:14
2. Matthew 4:4
3. Romans 8:16
4. Psalms 24:1
5. Luke 23:34

April 12, 1964
1. John 10:34
2. I Corinthians 3:16
3. Genesis 3:11
4. Matthew 28:20
5. Hebrews 13:5
6. John 10:10
7. Matthew 4:4
8. I Samuel 3:9
9. Job 23:14

April 19, 1964
1. Matthew 4:4
2. Exodus 13:21
3. Matthew 6:33
4. Matthew 5:45
5. Luke 15:31

April 26, 1964
1. Matthew 4:19

May 10, 1964
1. John 12:32
2. Hebrews 13:5
3. Psalms 46:10
4. Isaiah 30:15
5. Matthew 6:25
6. Proverbs 3:6
7. John 14:27
8. II Corinthians 12:9
9. Zephaniah 3:17
10. John 8:32
11. Matthew 4:20
12. Genesis 18:32